Best Flag Football Plays

The Playbook for Winning Flag Football Teams

DILLON HESS

To Brett Favre,

*the Best Flag Football Player
there ever would have been*

Table of Contents

Introduction	1
Plays	
4-Wide Formation	5
3-Wide Formation	63
Trips Formation	121
Stacks Formation	179
Bunch Formation	237
Advanced Strategies	295
Index	
Routes	301
Distance	317
About the Author	323

Introduction

Who is this book for?

The Best Flag Football Playbook is the best way to transform your team and develop the strategy needed to become a winning flag football team. First and foremost, however, this book is not just for Football games played with Flags. Let me repeat that:

This Book is Not Limited to Football Games Played with Flags!!!

This book contains a plethora of passing concepts and strategies that can directly be implemented into any form of football competition. While this book was originally created in response to the increasing popularity of Intramural and Recreational Flag Football leagues, the same principles and strategies can be applied to any type of Football. This can range anywhere from touch football games in the back yard, to Pop Warner youth football games, to 7-on-7 High school tournaments, to intramural and recreational leagues, to Division I College football games played on ESPN. These plays and strategies can be leveraged across any level of modern football to help you score touchdowns and win games.

Number of Players

In the same way that this book is not limited to certain types of football, it is also true that this book is not limited to a certain number of players on the field. Traditional Flag Football is played in a 7-on-7 fashion with seven players on each side of the ball. Regardless of the number of players, however, each of these plays and route concepts can be executed no matter how many players are on each side of the ball. It can be 4-on-4, 5-on-5, 6-on-6, or 11-on-11.

These plays and strategies don't break down depending on a certain number of players on the field. The assumption of this book is that you will be playing 7-on-7, however, you will be able to make the proper adjustments of altering the number of Lineman or Wide Receivers in accordance with the rules and regulations of your league.

Formations and Alignment

Five of the most successful formation in football are portrayed in this book to place your team in the best position for success. The alignment of the Wide Receivers should be tailored to your league appropriately. For the purpose of this book, many of the formations have been standardized to place all the Wide Receivers directly on the line of scrimmage.

Different leagues will have different rules and regulations for proper alignment. For example, a standard 7 on 7 league will typically require at least 3 players to be on the line of scrimmage, and up to 4 players can be behind that line of Scrimmage. For the sake of simplicity, this book has standardized the formations with most players located directly on the line of scrimmage. However, the plays and routes will remain the same regardless of if rules force certain players to be on the line of scrimmage or one step off of the line of scrimmage. (See page 296 in the Advanced Strategies section for an in-depth discussion on formations and alignment)

Lineman

Additionally, the success of the plays found in this book is not dependent on the number or positioning of the lineman. This book is made under the assumption that you can utilize lineman as blockers, and therefore, all the formations contain seven players on the field with 1 or 2 lineman plus a center. Some leagues may not even permit lineman, so depending on the rules of your league, you can disregard the lineman entirely. The focus of this book is on the passing game concepts of the Wide Receivers routes and the reads for the Quarterback. (For an advanced assessment on lineman and blocking strategies for Flag Football, see page 297 in the Advanced Strategies section.)

Routes

This book contains the basic routes and terminologies that are generally understood by the football community. Some plays, however, contain advanced routes utilizing additional features. Most football players will be familiar with a majority of the routes found in this book, however, there is an entire section (starting on page 301) that thoroughly describes the terminology and intricacies of all the routes contained within. The Routes section in the index (page 301) will not only provide an illustration and description of the route, but it will reference every play in the book that contains a version of that route.

Final Words

After years of compiling the best strategies and passing concepts for a successful football team, it is the author's intent that the strategies found in this book can transform any football team into a strategic force to be reckoned with. By learning how to recognize the defense's response to certain route concepts and plays found in this book, the Quarterback will be better equipped to make reads and determine where to throw the football. By learning the nuances of certain routes, the Wide Receivers will become better route runners and find themselves open downfield due to the techniques in this book.

Touchdowns are waiting to be thrown.

The Goal Line is waiting to be crossed.

The End Zone is waiting for your team to celebrate.

Find out how to get there through the plays found in the next 300+ pages

Plays
4-Wide Formation

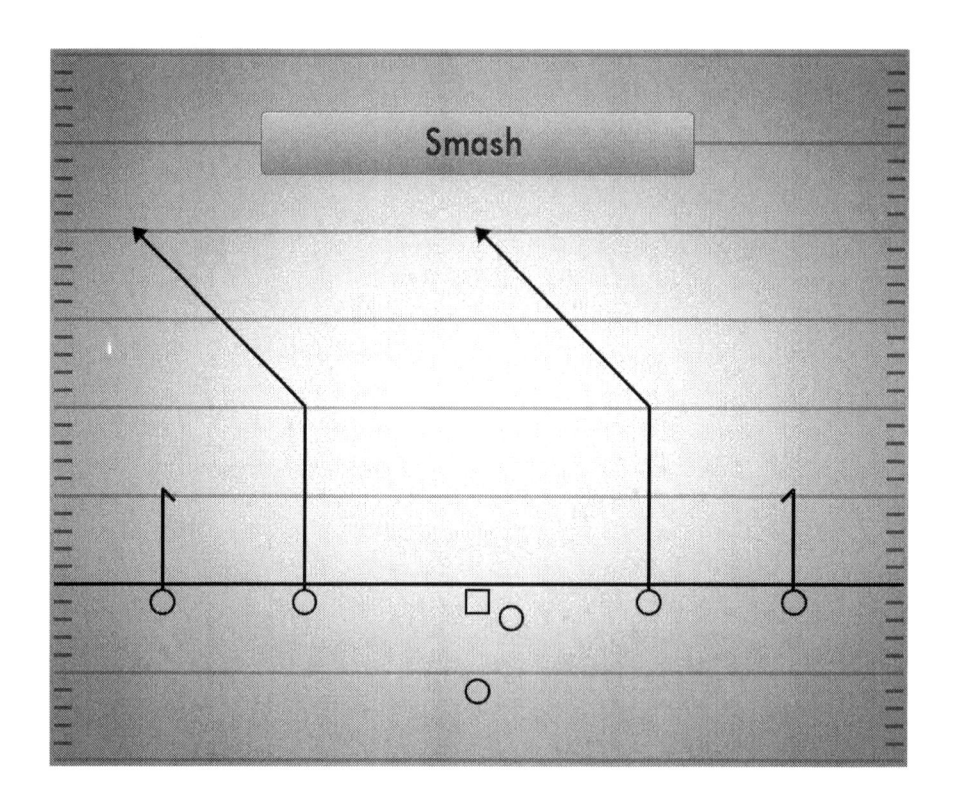

Smash

Utilizing the popular corner/stop route concept, the Smash play will attack many different zones in the defensive secondary. The first read that the Quarterback should make is to watch how the Cornerback plays the routes. If he stays low on the Stop route, then throw it over his head to the Corner route. If he stays high on the corner route, then throw it low to the Wide Receiver running the Stop route, who will be wide open in the flats. No outside linebacker will be able to run out there quick enough if the corner is dropping deep, and the Quarterback makes a quick read.

FORMATION: **4-WIDE FORMATION**

DISTANCE: **SHORT YARDAGE, MEDIUM YARDAGE**

ROUTES IN THIS PLAY: **CORNER, POST, STOP**

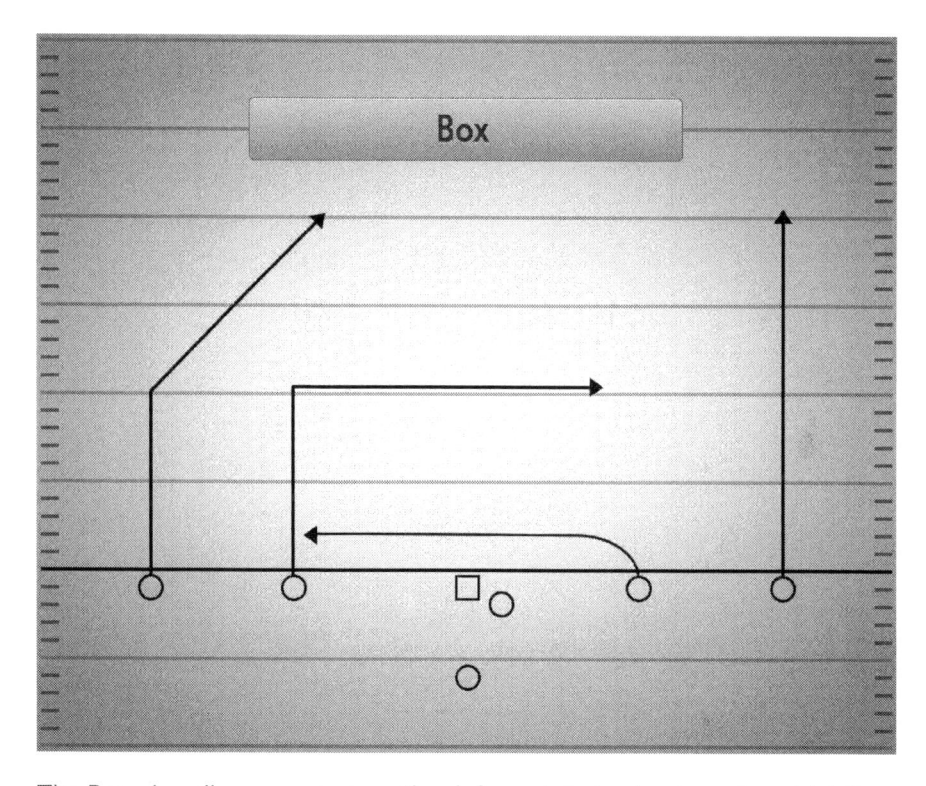

Box

The Box play allows you to trap the defense into having to make a high/low decision. In fact, there are two different high/low areas on the defense that this play attacks.

By singling out the safety, the Quarterback can make a "high/low" read based upon the combination of the Post route and the 10 yard In route. If the safety drops high to guard the Post, then throw it low to the In route. If the safety stays low on the In, then throw it high to the Post.

Additionally, another high/low read takes place at the level of the outside linebacker. The linebacker will have to make the decision to go high and guard the In route, or stay low and guard the Shallow Cross. The Quarterback's read progression should start by reading the Safety on the Post, and then moving down to the In route, and finally hitting the lowest shallow cross underneath, if everything higher is guarded.

FORMATION: **4-WIDE FORMATION**

DISTANCE: **SHORT YARDAGE, LONG YARDAGE, MEDIUM YARDAGE**

ROUTES IN THIS PLAY: **POST, IN, SHALLOW CROSS, STREAK**

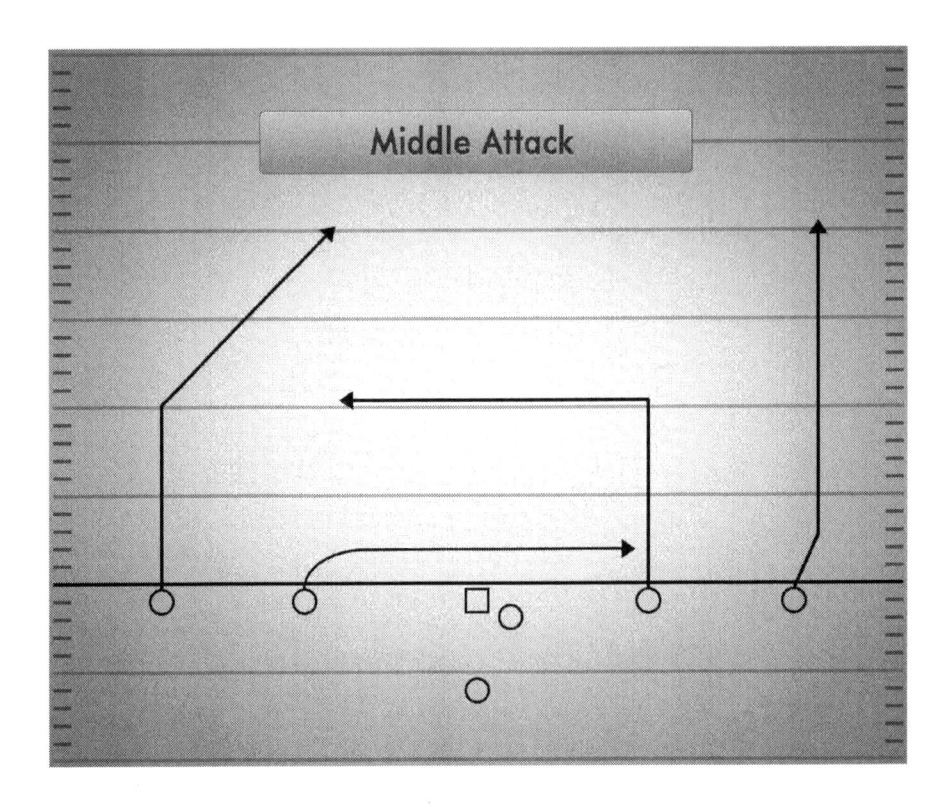

Middle Attack

The Middle Attack play attacks the middle of the defense with three different routes attacking three different levels in the defensive secondary. This allows the Quarterback to read the vertical flow of the defense in order to determine which of the three levels will be the open one. If the defense begins to crowd the middle of the field, then the outside receiver needs to get a wide release to run down the sideline on the fade route to stretch out the secondary.

Middle Attack is a variation of the Box play, but with a reversal of roles for the slot receivers.

FORMATION: **4-WIDE FORMATION**

DISTANCE: **SHORT YARDAGE, LONG YARDAGE, MEDIUM YARDAGE**

ROUTES IN THIS PLAY: **POST, IN, SHALLOW CROSS, FADE**

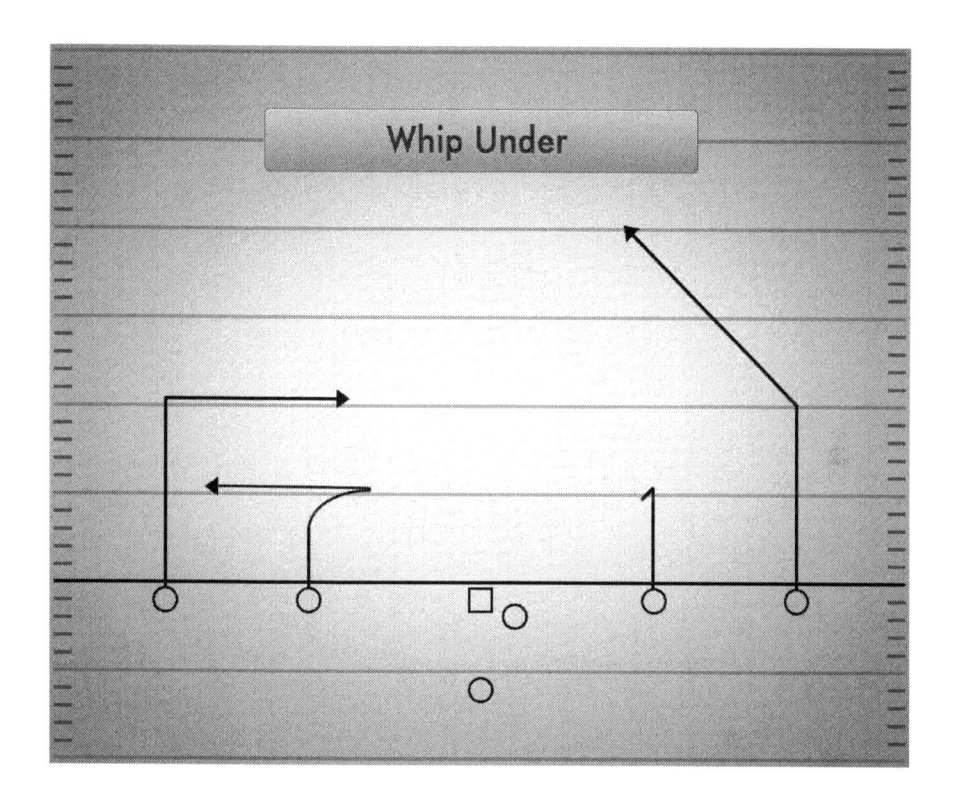

Whip Under

The Whip play is all about misdirection. The hard inside move gets the defense flowing inside, but the quick pivot outside is even more important for a quick move outside. If the inside receiver flowing underneath is covered up, then the outside receiver will be open coming inside over the top.

The Whip is best run in the second half of the game after setting up the defense with a sequence of successful slant plays. The defender will be ready to jump forward on the slant, but the wide out will plant hard and turn fast outside where he will be wide open running away from the defender.

FORMATION: **4-WIDE FORMATION**

DISTANCE: **SHORT YARDAGE, MEDIUM YARDAGE**

ROUTES IN THIS PLAY: **POST, IN, WHIP, STOP**

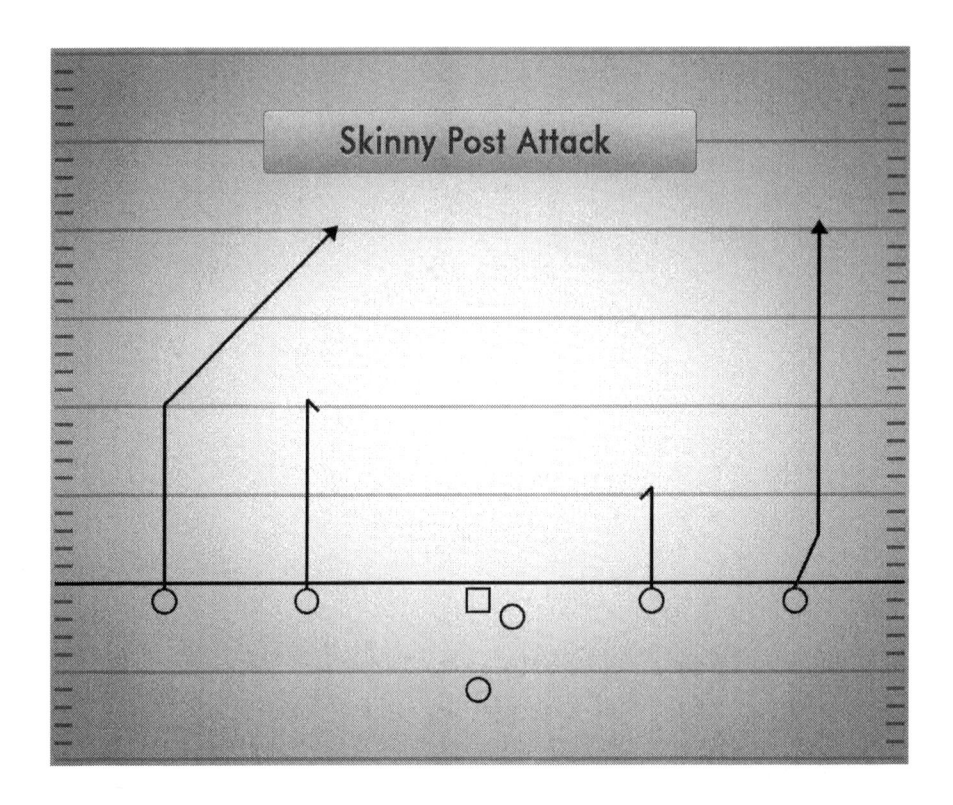

Skinny Post Attack

The Skinny Post Attack play requires special attention to detail. The main point of this play is to put the Safety in a tough situation by attacking his zone with two routes. The most critical route running in this play is the 10-yard Curl route, because it has to be run in a way that attracts the Safety's attention. If the slot receiver successfully gets the Safety to stay down and guard the curl, then the Post route will be wide open over the top.

If the Safety stays deep, however, then the Curl route needs to make sure that he is deep enough over the linebackers in order to be open 10-12 yards downfield. All in all, this play consists of a high/low read on the Safety by placing on route in the front of the Safety's zone, and the other over the top of the Safety's zone.

FORMATION: **4-WIDE FORMATION**

DISTANCE: **LONG YARDAGE, MEDIUM YARDAGE**

ROUTES IN THIS PLAY: **POST, FADE, STOP, CURL**

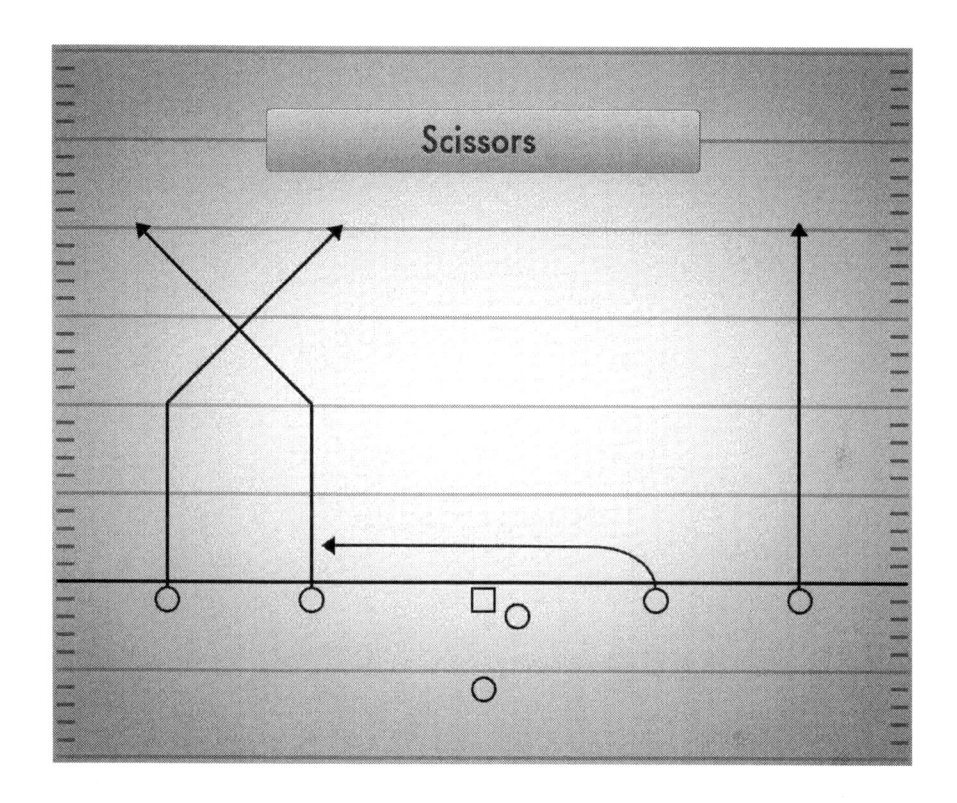

Scissors

Scissors is a great play to cut through the defensive secondary by converging two receivers across each other on one half of the field. The Post route goes over the top of the Corner route. The Post is the first read coming across the top, followed up by the Corner cutting through below.

The most important aspect of the play is that both routes run quickly up field at the same time and cut across each other simultaneously to wreak havoc on the downfield defenders.

FORMATION: **4-WIDE FORMATION**

DISTANCE: **LONG YARDAGE**

ROUTES IN THIS PLAY: **CORNER, POST, SHALLOW CROSS, STREAK**

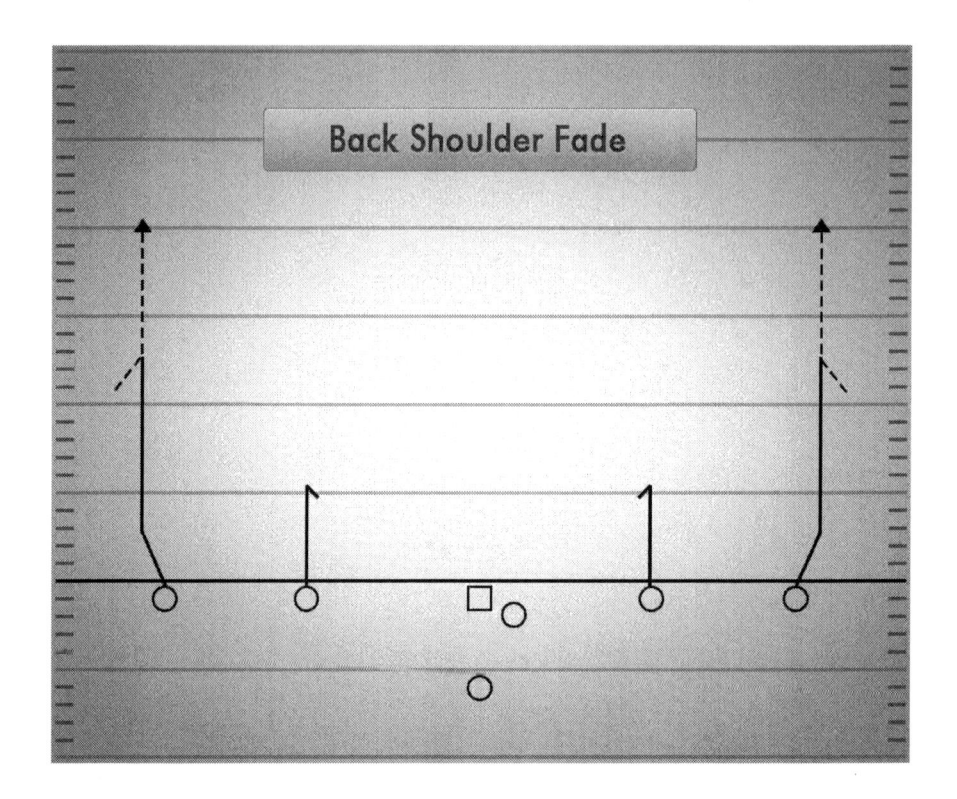

Back Shoulder Fade

The Back Shoulder fade is a go-to play for goal line situations. It gives the Receiver two options to choose from based upon how the defender guards him. If the Cornerback is guarding deep, then the Quarterback can throw the ball short, but if the Cornerback is play up close, then the Quarterback can throw the ball over the top.

Communication and chemistry between the Quarterback and the Receiver is of the utmost importance. Both the thrower and the route runner need to be on the same page to execute this play properly. Great chemistry will lead to great results on the Back Shoulder fade.

FORMATION: **4-WIDE FORMATION**

DISTANCE: **SHORT YARDAGE**

ROUTES IN THIS PLAY: **FADE, STOP**

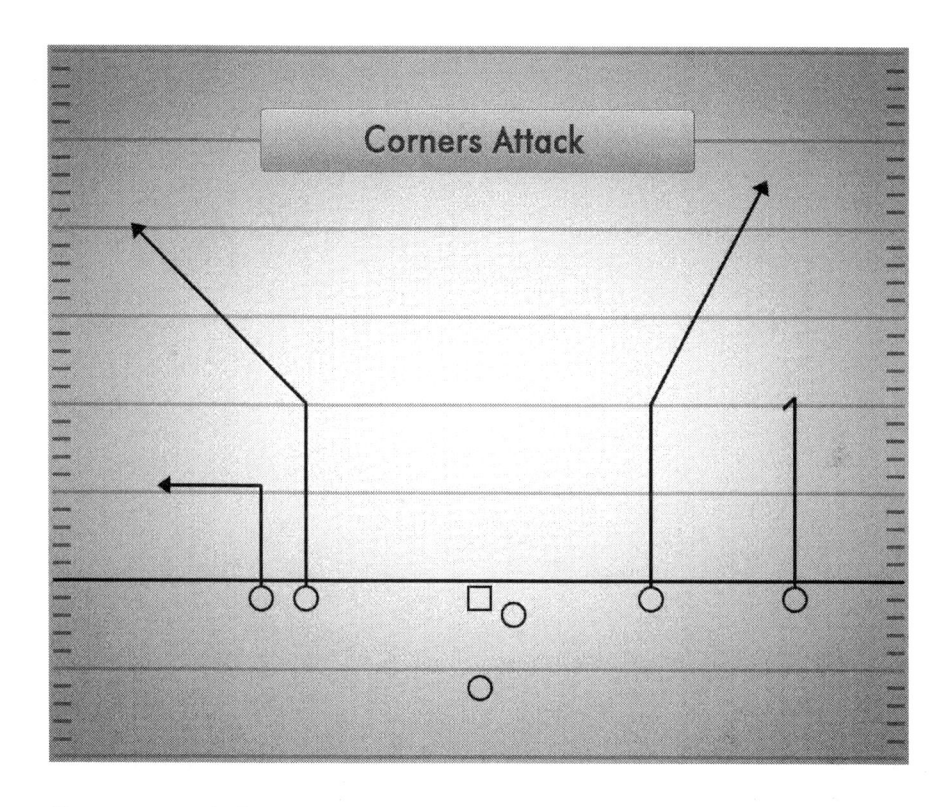

Corners Attack

Corners attack does just what its name says it does: Attack the Corners. The corner routes get depth into the corner of the defensive secondary, while the underneath routes wreak havoc in the flats. The slot receiver who runs the corner in combination with the 10-yard curl, has to make sure that he gets depth so that he is properly spaced over the top of the Curl route.

The Quarterback has to make a pre-snap decision on to select what side he wants to go to. Once that decision is made, read the Cornerback to see if he is staying on the deep corner, or cheating on the flat.

FORMATION: **4-WIDE FORMATION**

DISTANCE: **LONG YARDAGE**

ROUTES IN THIS PLAY: **CORNER, CURL, OUT**

Ridge Force

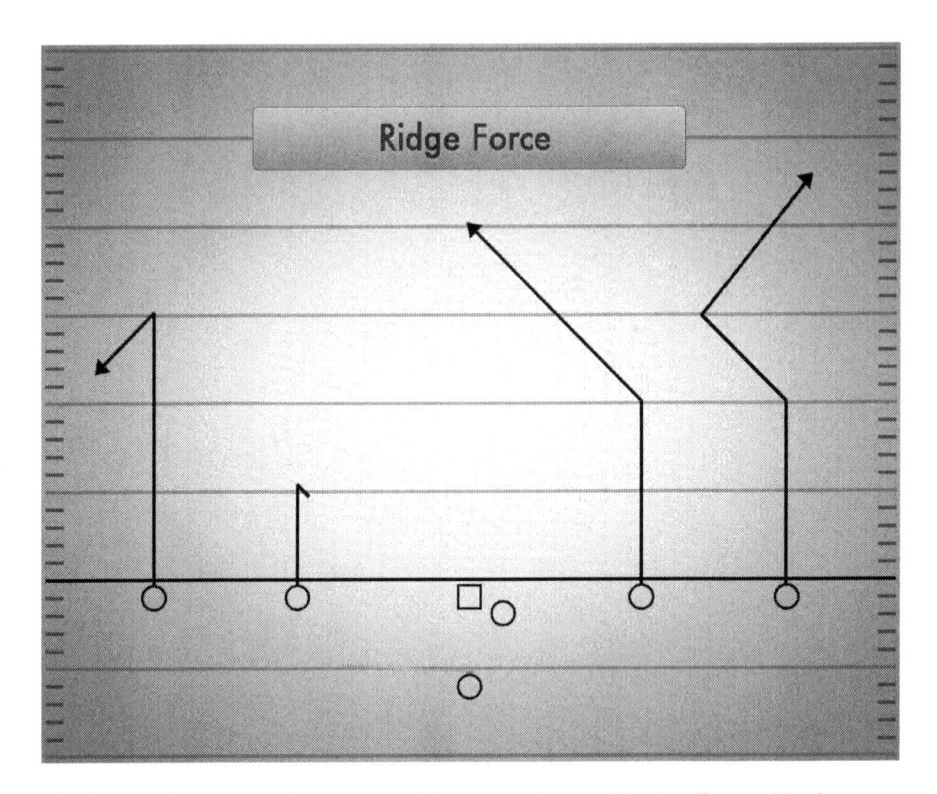

The Ridge Force play forces the defense to flow with the flow with the combination of the two post routes coming across the top ridge of the defensive secondary. Once the defenders start flowing with the combination of those routes, the outside receivers breaks hard to the outside on the Post Corner route.

The double move by the outside receiver will force the Safety into a hard decision if he is playing in a cover 2 zone, because he will be sitting right in the middle of two deep routes into his territory, but he can only choose to guard on of them.

If the defense is in a three deep formation and/or playing in a Cover three, then the QB will most likely want to drop down and hit the Comeback route on the other side of the field.

FORMATION: **4-WIDE FORMATION**

DISTANCE: **LONG YARDAGE**

ROUTES IN THIS PLAY: **POST, STOP, POST CORNER, COMEBACK**

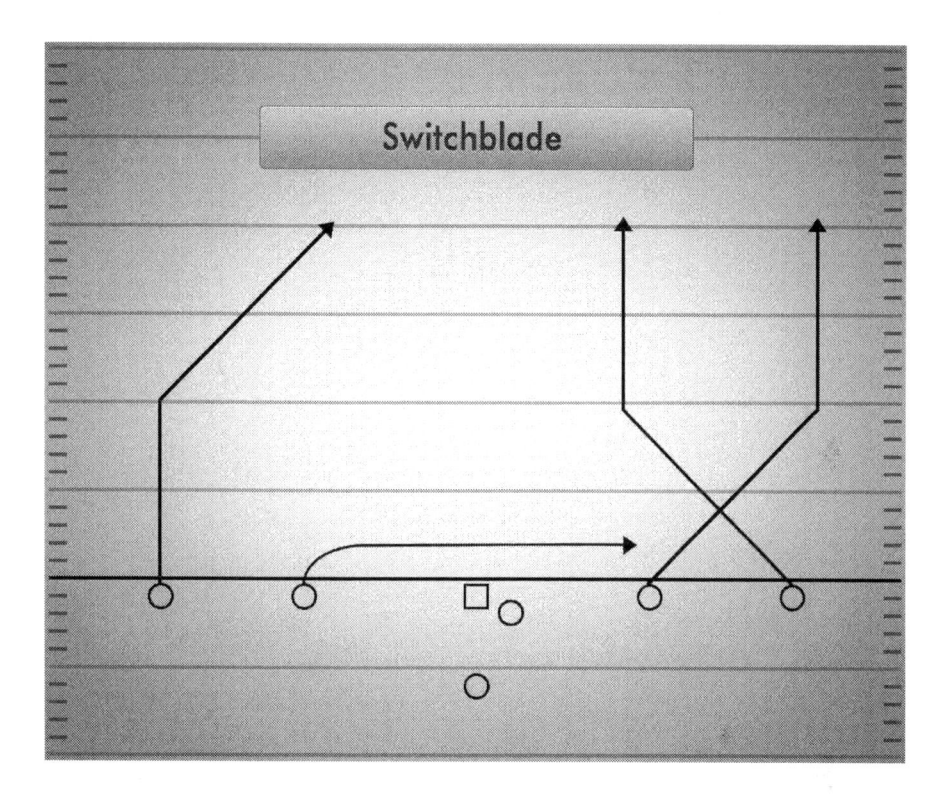

Switchblade

The Switchblade is a deadly combination route that cuts right through the defense by switching two receivers as they run their routes up field. A man-to-man defense will have trouble keeping up with both of the downfield receivers, and a zone defense will be thrown for a loop as the routes cut right through the zone.

The Quarterback has the option of cutting his losses if the deep routes aren't open, by checking down to the shallow cross underneath the switch route combination.

FORMATION: 4-WIDE FORMATION

DISTANCE: LONG YARDAGE

ROUTES IN THIS PLAY: POST, SHALLOW CROSS

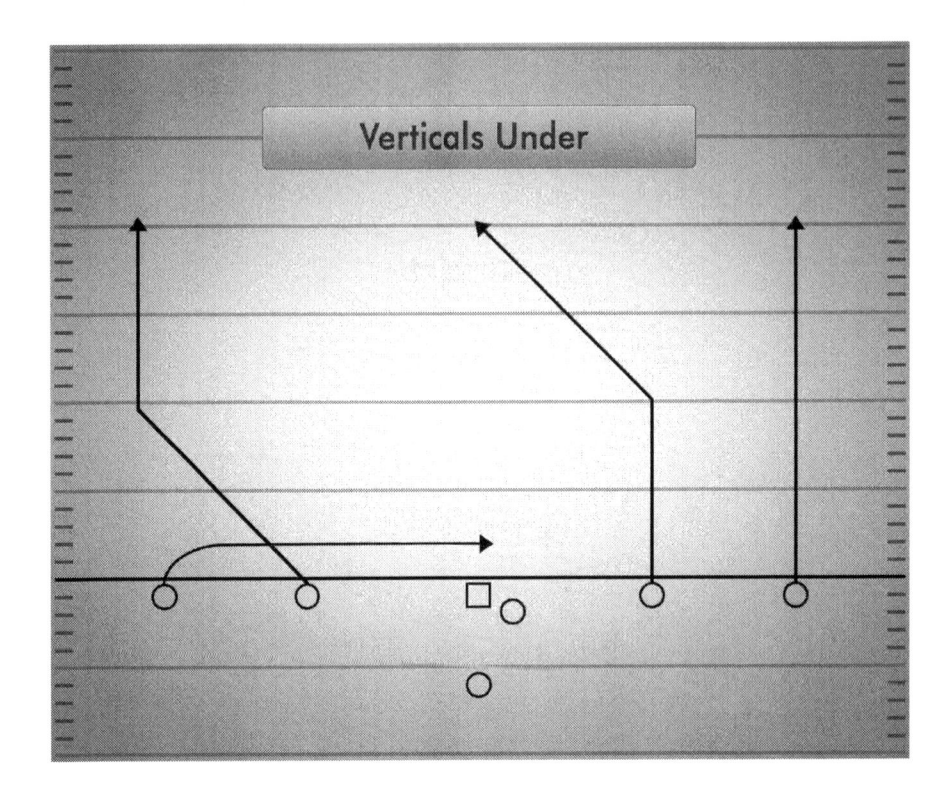

Verticals Under

The Verticals Under play sends the wide receivers up field in a shifted pattern that replaces the territory of the Receiver who is cutting underneath the Verticals.

By pushing the Vertical routes up field hard, it will distract the defense from the Shallow Cross coming underneath. Sometimes, however, the defense will lose track of the receiver taking the place of the underneath route, and he will be open down the sideline for a big gain.

FORMATION: **4-WIDE FORMATION**

DISTANCE: **SHORT YARDAGE, LONG YARDAGE**

ROUTES IN THIS PLAY: **SHALLOW CROSS, STREAK**

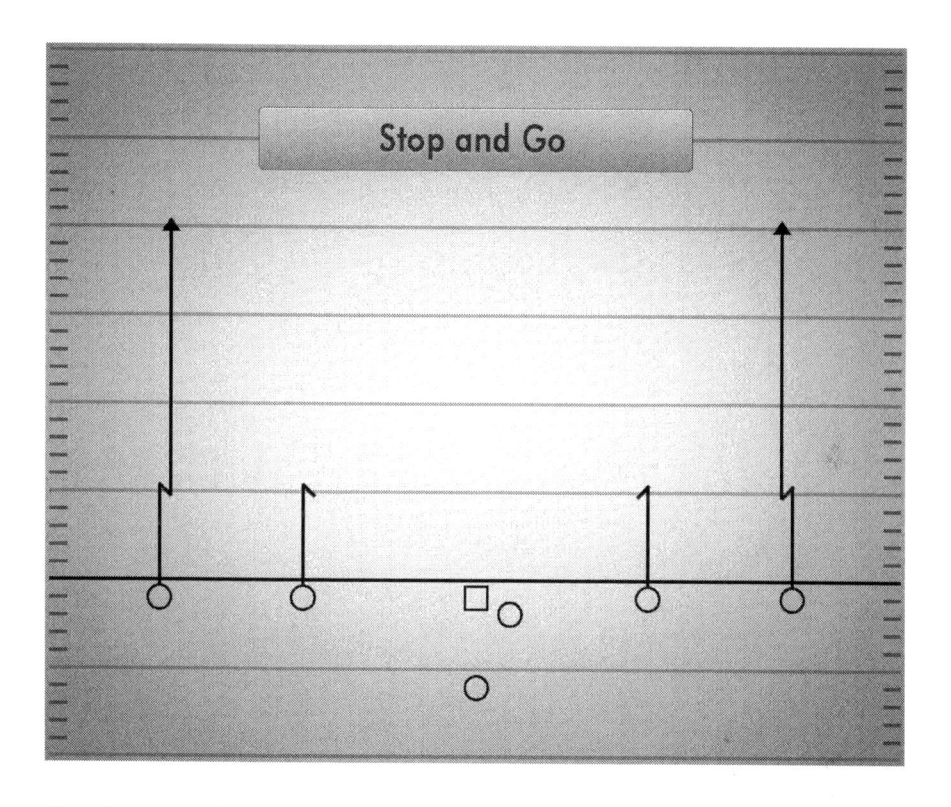

Stop and Go

The Stop and Go route is the most famous double move in all of football. The outside receiver will fake like he is running a 5 yard stop, but will twist and turn quickly up field.

It is imperative that the QB makes a good pump fake to sucker the defense in to jumping up on the short route. Once the pump fake is successfully completed, the QB must regather himself and get ready to throw the ball over the top of the defense to the receiver who is sprinting up field.

FORMATION: **4-WIDE FORMATION**

DISTANCE: **SHORT YARDAGE, LONG YARDAGE**

ROUTES IN THIS PLAY: **STOP**

Comebacks

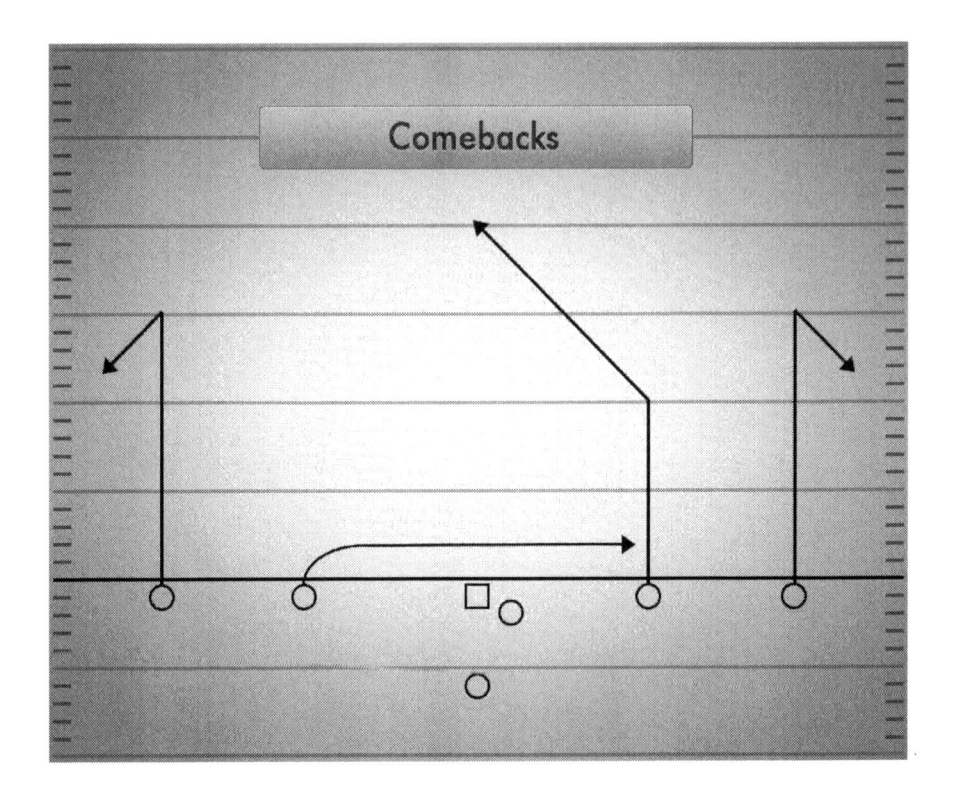

The Comeback route is a great route to run on a defense that is scared of getting beat deep. The way in which the Wide Receivers run the Comeback route is the most important part of the play. The WR will need to push up field hard as if he is running a Fade route or a Streak downfield. Once the defender is turned and running backwards, the WR needs to quickly turn around to the outside, as the QB plays a ball behind on the sideline.

After you scare the defense with the deep ball, the Comeback route is a great route to throw at them in order to pick up a chunk of yards.

FORMATION: **4-WIDE FORMATION**

DISTANCE: **MEDIUM YARDAGE**

ROUTES IN THIS PLAY: **POST, SHALLOW CROSS, COMEBACK**

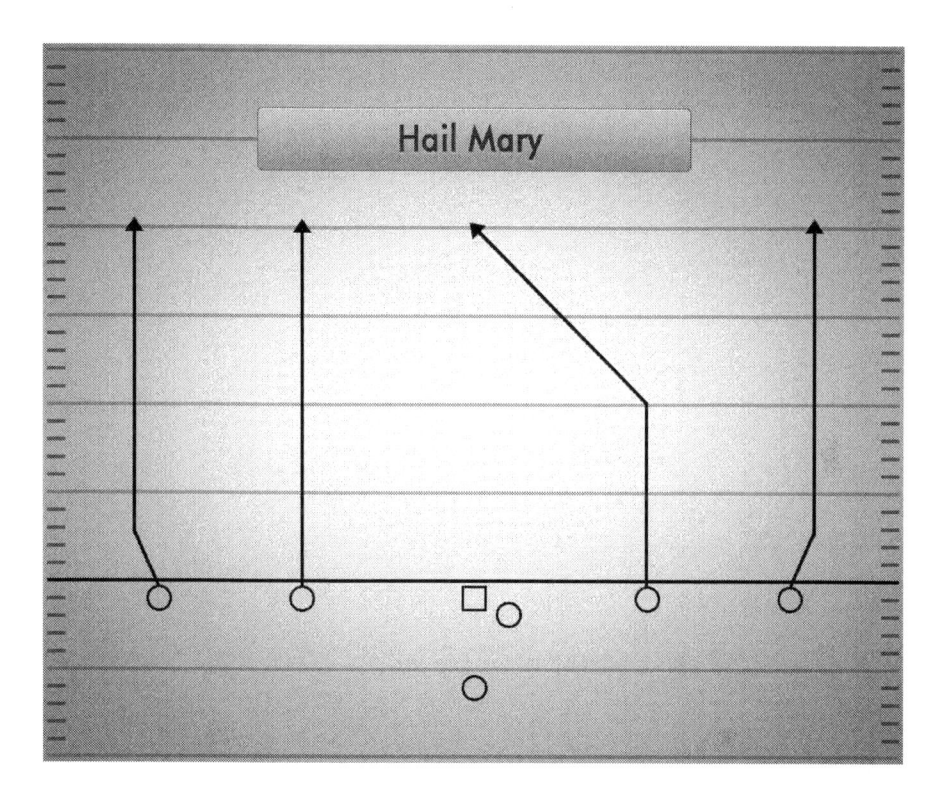

Hail Mary

Hail Mary time! You only need to pull out this play when you need a whole lot of yards all at once.

This version of the Hail Mary play is made to spread out the defense as much as possible, and potentially isolate a defender from the rest of his team. The Quarterback needs to find the WR who is able to get into a one-on-one match up and throw the ball up for a jump ball.

FORMATION: **4-WIDE FORMATION**

DISTANCE: **LONG YARDAGE**

ROUTES IN THIS PLAY: **POST, STREAK, FADE**

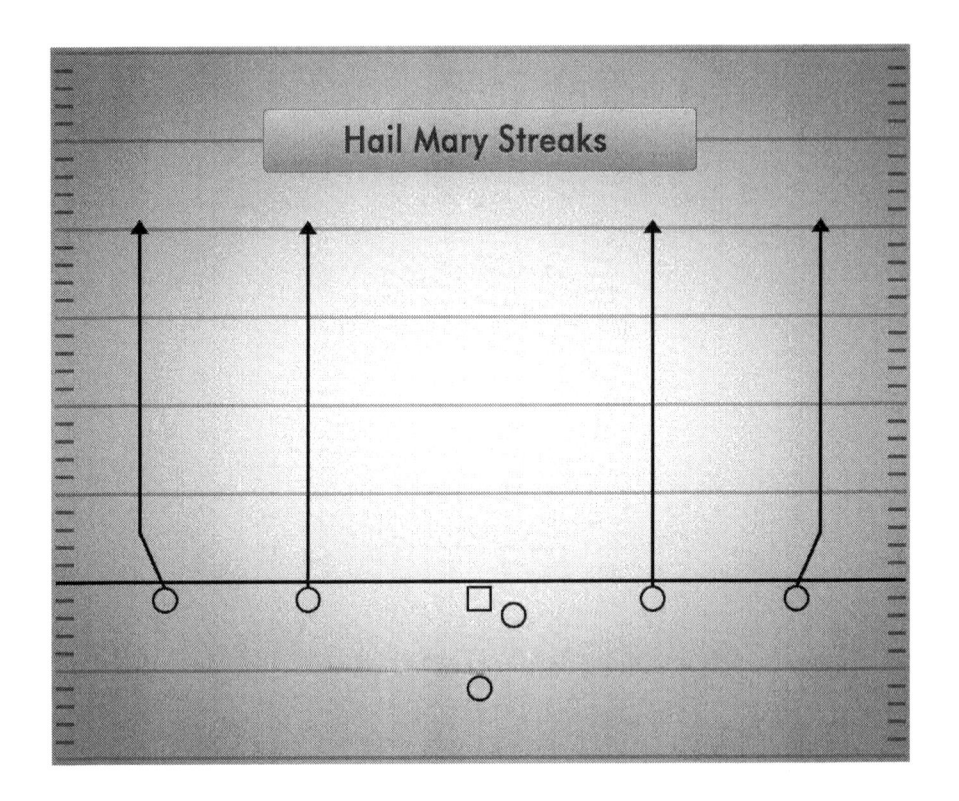

Hail Mary Streaks

Hail Mary time! You only need to pull out this play when you need a whole lot of yards all at once.

This version of the Hail Mary play simply send all the receivers downfield in a straight line in order to get as deep as possible, as fast as possible. Throw the ball up deep and hope for the best.

FORMATION: **4-WIDE FORMATION**

DISTANCE: **LONG YARDAGE**

ROUTES IN THIS PLAY: **STREAK**

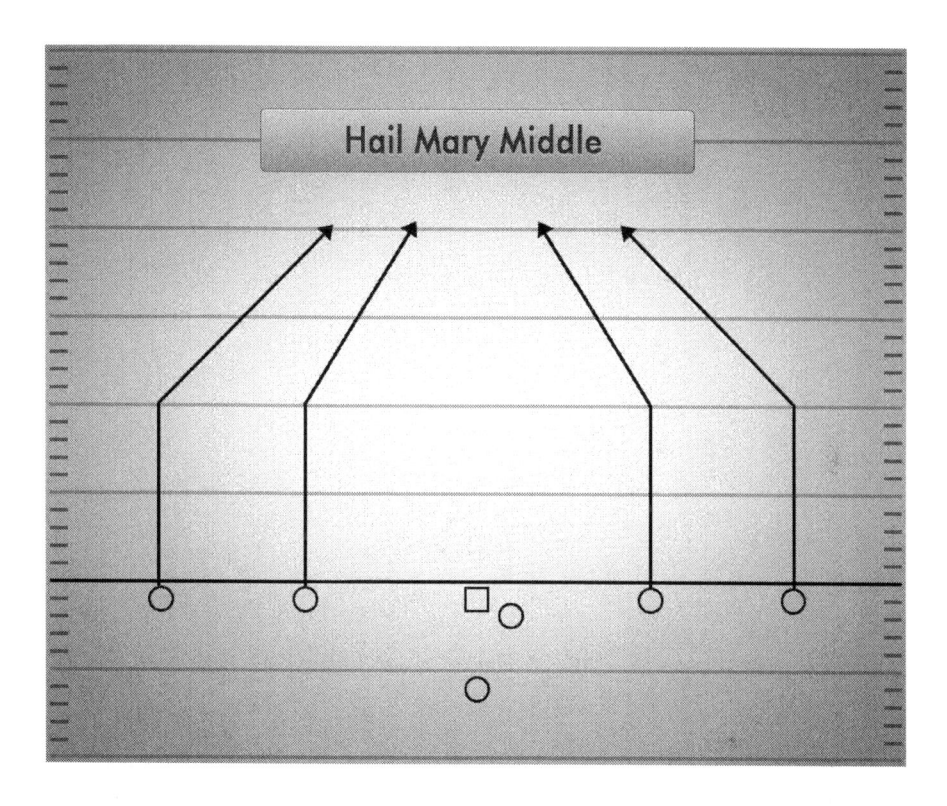

Hail Mary Middle

Hail Mary time! You only need to pull out this play when you need a whole lot of yards all at once.

This version of the Hail Mary play puts all your eggs in one basket by sending every Receiver to the middle of the field. Once all the Receivers are in position, the only thing left for the Quarterback to do is throw the ball as high as he can right into the middle of the field and hope that one of his own players comes down with it.

FORMATION: **4-WIDE FORMATION**

DISTANCE: **LONG YARDAGE**

ROUTES IN THIS PLAY: **POST**

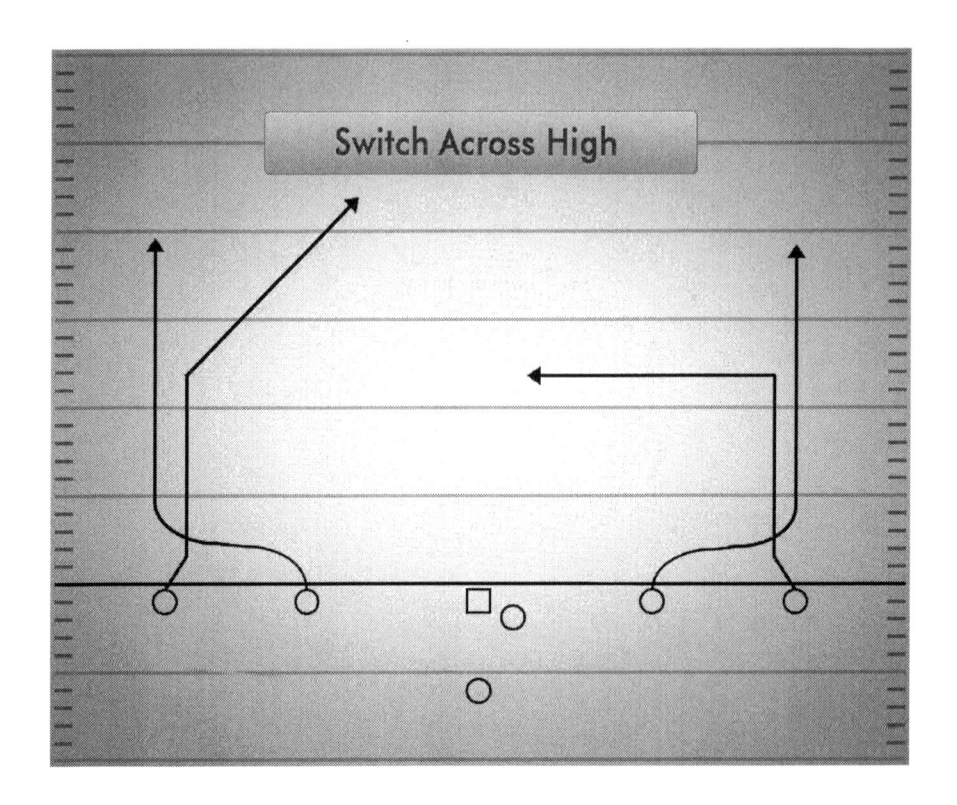

Switch Across High

This is the deeper variation of the Switch Across Low play. The key to this play is creating confusion for the defense at the very start of the play by having the receivers switch across each other on the way to their destination. This switch makes it hard for a zone defense to keep track of all the routes, and makes it very difficult for a man-to-man defense to keep up with the receiver amongst all the chaos going on.

FORMATION: **4-WIDE FORMATION**

DISTANCE: **LONG YARDAGE**

ROUTES IN THIS PLAY: **POST, IN, WHEEL**

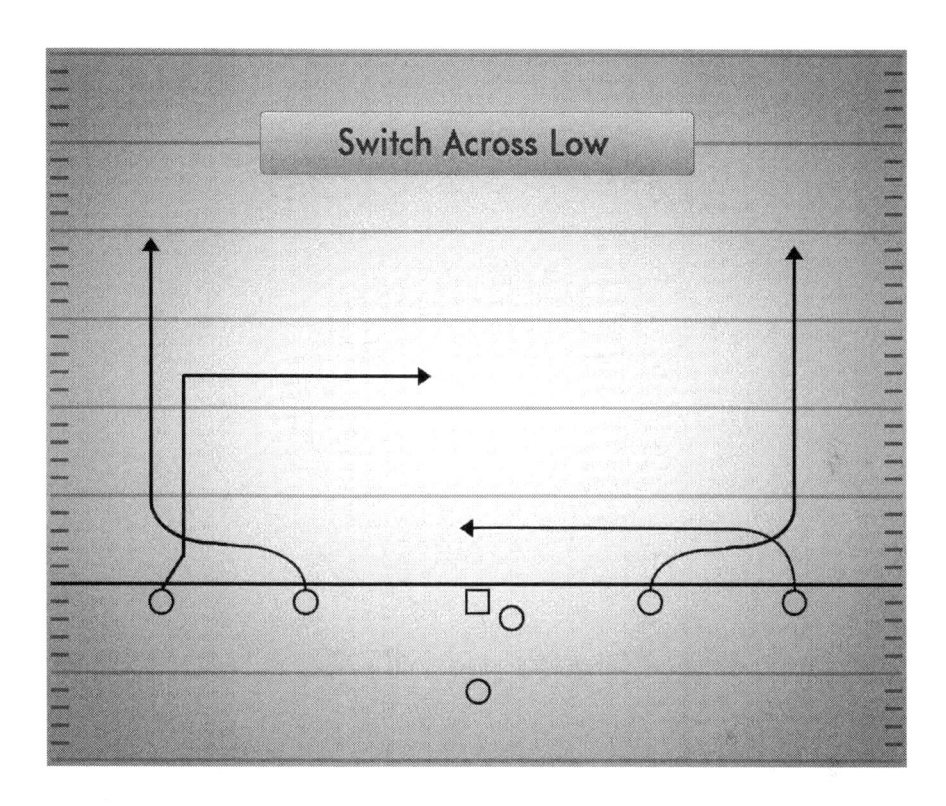

Switch Across Low

This is the shorter variation of the Switch Across High play. The key to this play is creating confusion for the defense at the very start of the play by having the receivers switch across each other on the way to their destination. This switch makes it hard for a zone defense to keep track of all the routes, and makes it very difficult for a man-to-man defense to keep up with the receiver amongst all the chaos going on.

FORMATION: **4-WIDE FORMATION**

DISTANCE: **SHORT YARDAGE, MEDIUM YARDAGE**

ROUTES IN THIS PLAY: **IN, SHALLOW CROSS, WHEEL**

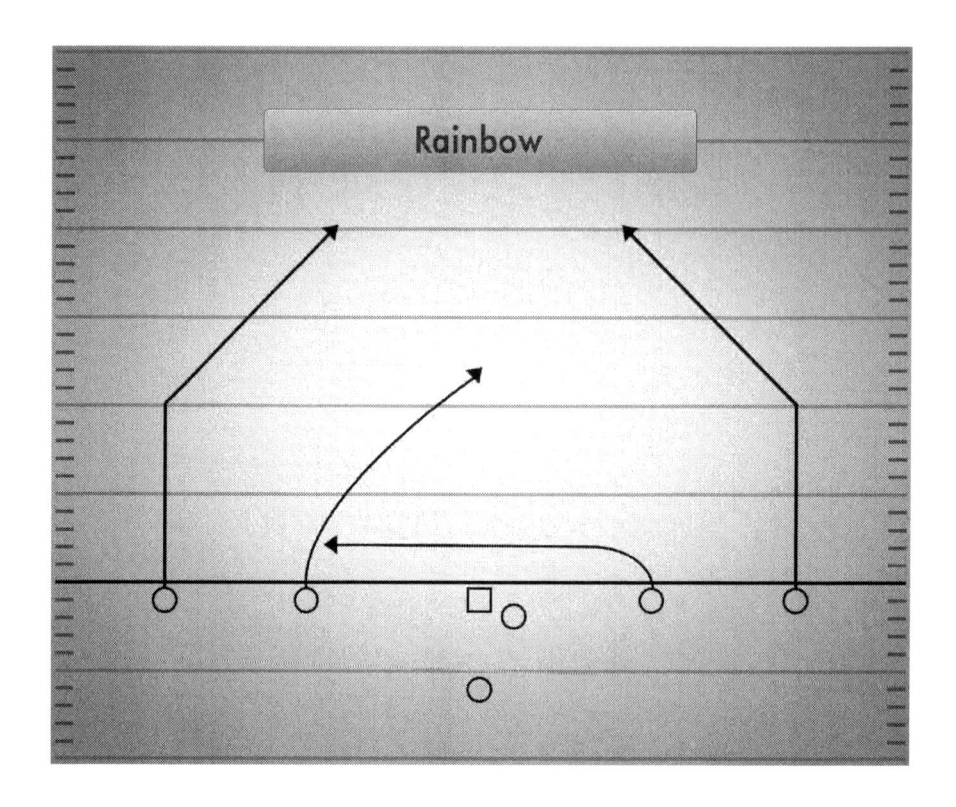

Rainbow

The Rainbow play allows the Wide Receivers to attack the defense by running arcs all across the middle of the field. Each arc is run at a different level of the defense, therefore, combining to create a Rainbow of manly intensity.

The Quarterback can choose to either read the arcs from low to high, or progress from high to low. Finding at least one open man in the Rainbow should be easy with so many routes hitting different levels in the middle of the field.

FORMATION: **4-WIDE FORMATION**

DISTANCE: **SHORT YARDAGE, LONG YARDAGE, MEDIUM YARDAGE**

ROUTES IN THIS PLAY: **POST, SHALLOW CROSS**

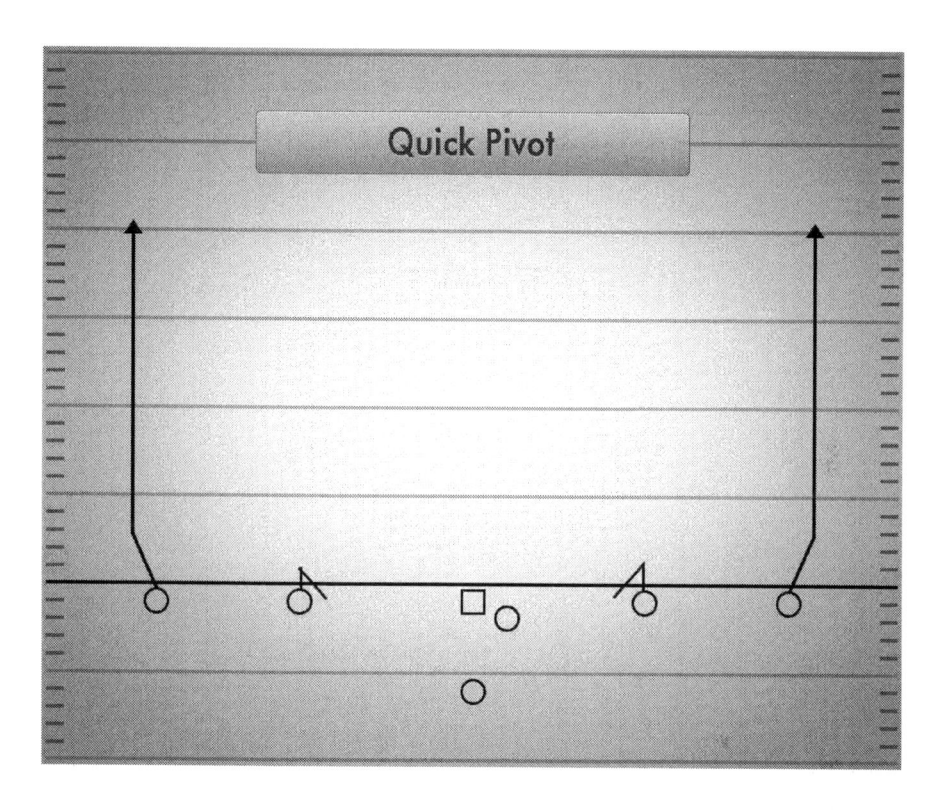

Quick Pivot

The Quick Pivot play is meant to be used as a play against a defense that is backing up off the line of scrimmage. If they are giving too much space to the Wide Receivers, then hit them with this quick pass to catch them off guard. If the Quarterback makes a quick throw to the Receiver, it will give the Receiver a chance to run with the ball in the open field and try to make a defender miss.

It is important that the Receivers push hard off the line of scrimmage for the first few steps, so that the defenders aren't immediately keyed into the fact that it is going to be a quick pass right at the line of scrimmage.

FORMATION: **4-WIDE FORMATION**

DISTANCE: **SHORT YARDAGE**

ROUTES IN THIS PLAY: **FADE**

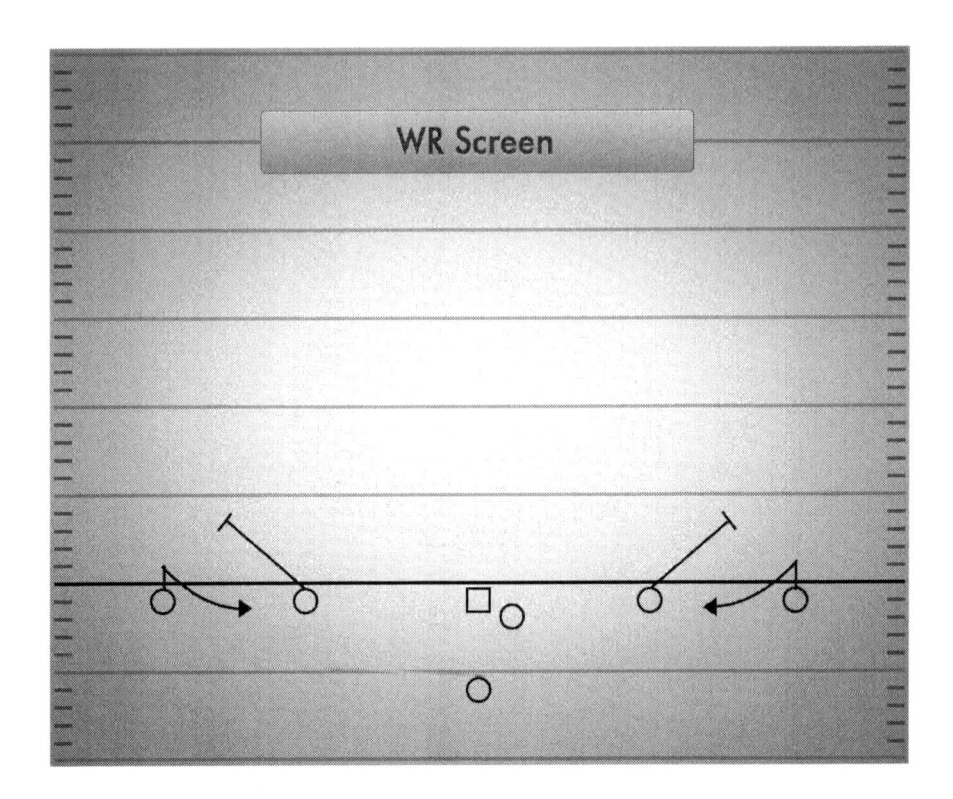

WR Screen

The WR Screen is a play that utilizes blocking by the inside Receivers to enable a running lane for the outside Receiver. The Wide Receiver running the screen route needs to push up field hard for two steps, and the quickly turn around for the ball. Timing is critical on the throw.

The inside Receiver needs to explode of the line of scrimmage directly at the guy who is guarding the outside Receiver. Once that defender turns around, quickly get in his way for the block, and the Receiver catching the screen will be off to the races.

FORMATION: **4-WIDE FORMATION**

DISTANCE: **SHORT YARDAGE**

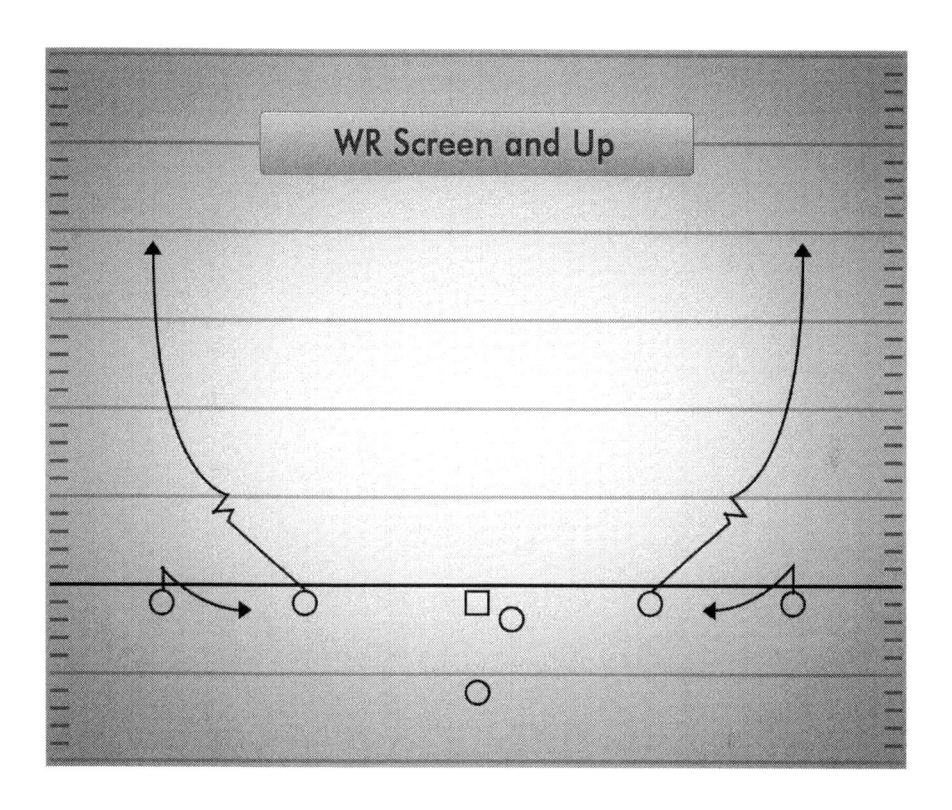

WR Screen and Up

The WR Screen and Up play is a great trick play that takes some time to set up. You have to run the WR Screen play beforehand, and run it successfully. If you begin to hurt them with the Screen, then the defense will start to sneak up forward, and that is when you hit them with the Screen and Up.

The most important aspect of performing this play is the way in which the Wide Receiver fakes his block. He has to run out to the Cornerback as if he is going to block him, and as soon as the Cornerback makes a move to avoid the block, the Receiver then turns on the jets and runs up the sideline. The defense won't even know what hit them until the ball is flying over all their heads.

FORMATION: **4-WIDE FORMATION**

DISTANCE: **LONG YARDAGE**

Slot Choice

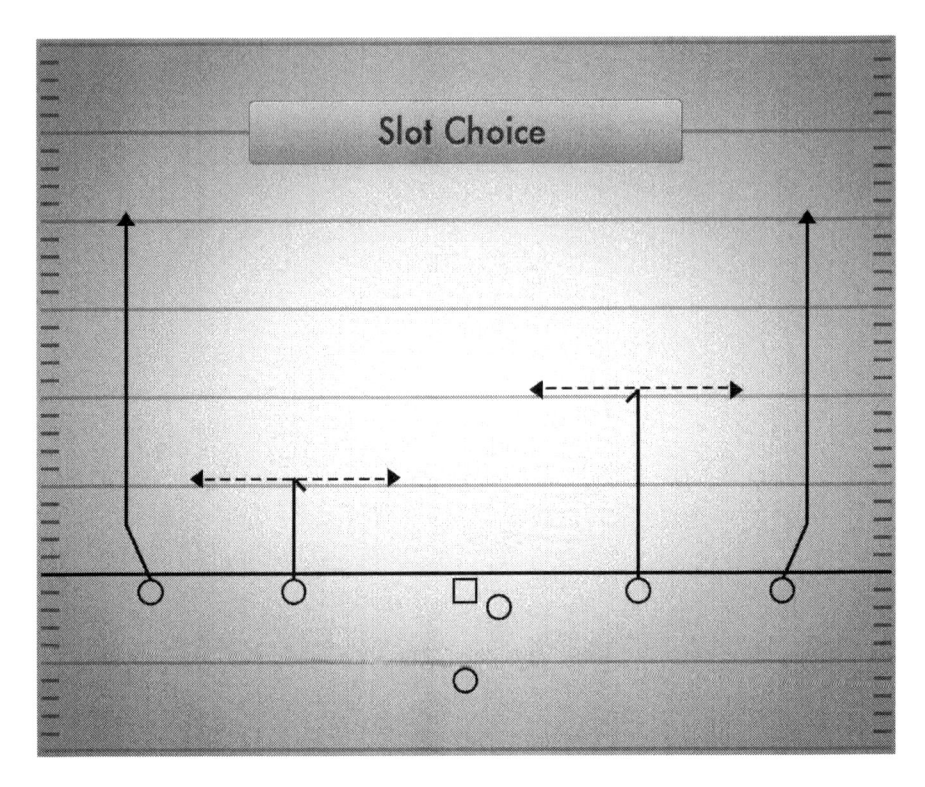

The Slot Choice is meant to be a play that lets the Slot WR get open, no matter what the defense does. The Choice route will either get to its mark and turn around for a stop in place, or it will jet out to the outside, or cut in to the inside.

If the defender is playing inside, then the WR should jet to the outside. If the defender is playing outside, then the WR should jet to the inside. If the defense is playing in a zone, and is giving the WR some space, then the WR should just settle down and wait for the ball.

The Quarterback needs to have great chemistry with the WR so that they are on the same wavelength and can be expecting each other to make the same read.

FORMATION: **4-WIDE FORMATION**

DISTANCE: **SHORT YARDAGE, MEDIUM YARDAGE**

ROUTES IN THIS PLAY: **IN, STREAK, STOP, OUT**

WR Choice

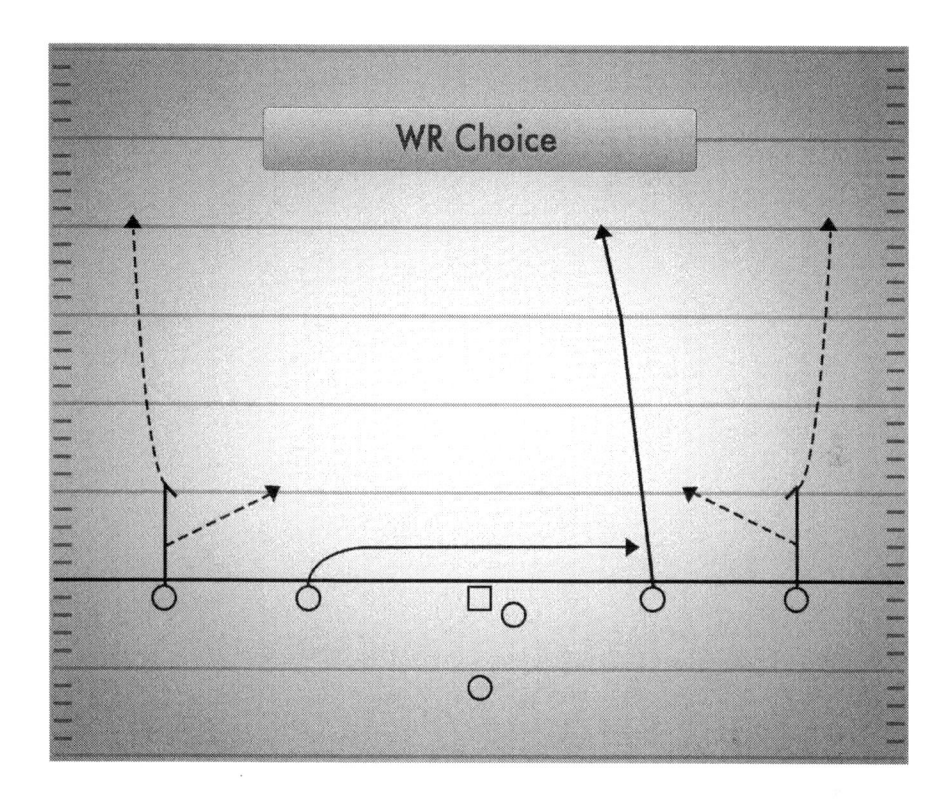

The WR Choice is meant to be a play that lets the Outside WR get open, no matter what the defense does. If the defender is playing inside, then the WR should run up the sideline on a fade. If the defender is playing outside, then the WR should jet to the inside on a slant. If the defense is giving the WR some space, then the WR should just settle down and wait for the ball on a stop route.

The Quarterback needs to have great chemistry with the WR so that they are on the same wavelength and can be expecting each other to make the same read.

FORMATION: 4-WIDE FORMATION

DISTANCE: SHORT YARDAGE, LONG YARDAGE, MEDIUM YARDAGE

ROUTES IN THIS PLAY: SHALLOW CROSS, FADE, STOP, SLANT, SEAM

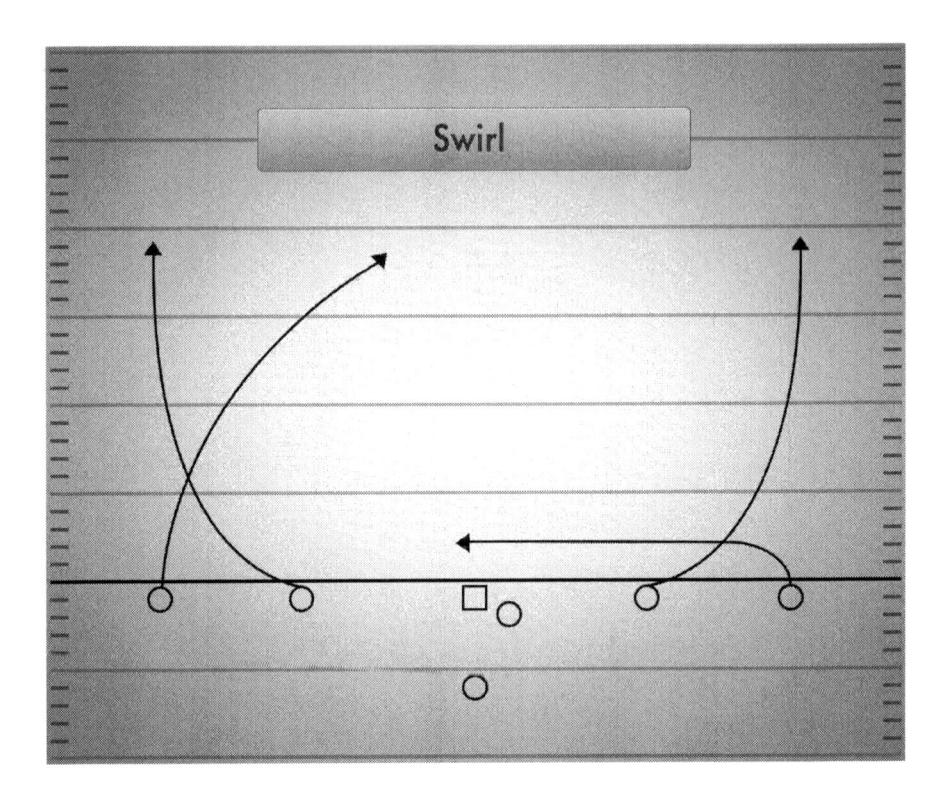

Swirl

The Swirl plays send the defense in a whirlwind by swirling the routes all around across the field. Unlike most plays, there are hardly no straight lines in the route patterns, as all the Wide Receivers are swirling their routes to get to their destination.

The switching and swirling pattern will make it hard for a man defense to keep up, and difficult for a zone defense to keep track.

FORMATION: **4-WIDE FORMATION**

DISTANCE: **SHORT YARDAGE, LONG YARDAGE**

ROUTES IN THIS PLAY: **POST, SHALLOW CROSS, WHEEL**

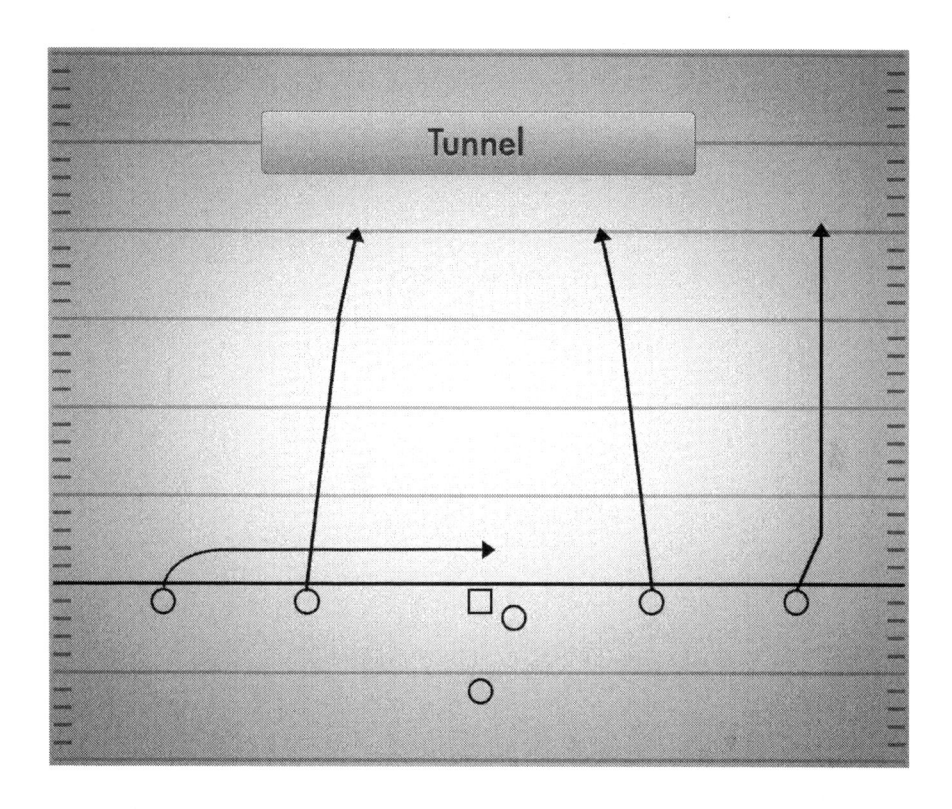

The Tunnel play might look like a deep play when drawn up, but it is really meant to be a play thrown to the Shallow Cross route that is "tunneling" underneath.

The other receivers are used primarily to run off the defense and take all the defenders deep downfield with them. After the defense has backed off, the shallow cross route should be open and have tons of room to run after the catch.

FORMATION: **4-WIDE FORMATION**

DISTANCE: **SHORT YARDAGE**

ROUTES IN THIS PLAY: **SHALLOW CROSS, FADE, SEAM**

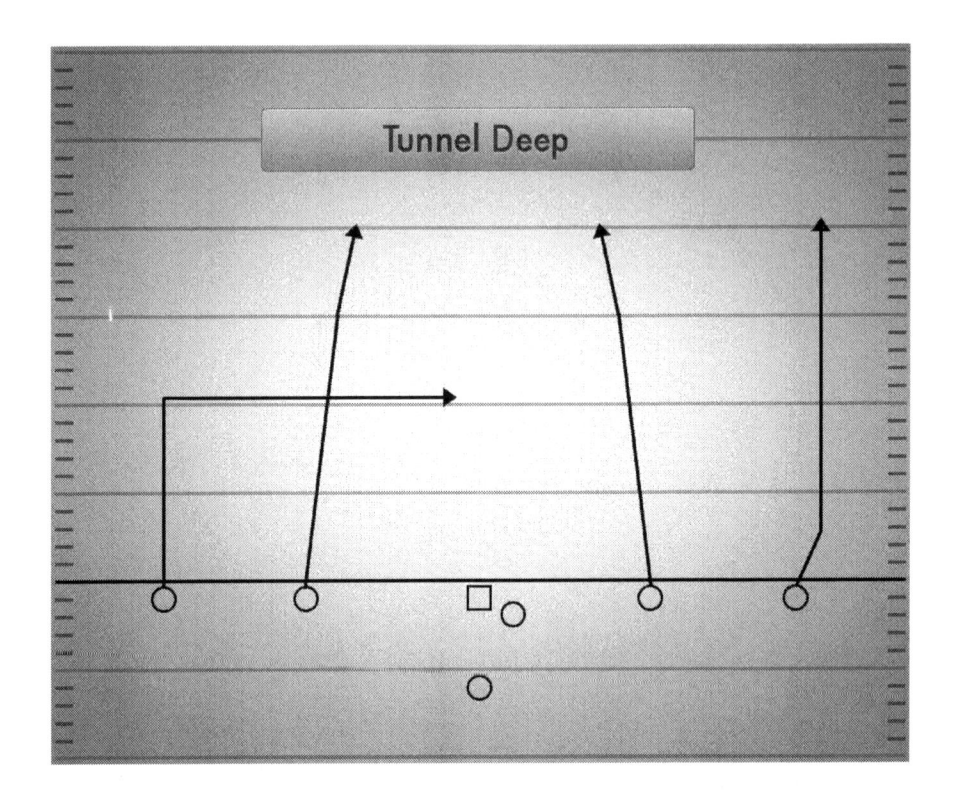

Tunnel Deep

The primary focus of the Tunnel Deep play is to make the defense think that everybody is going deep, and then break off the outside receiver, and hit him coming across the field underneath the deep routes.

The other receivers are used primarily to run off the defense and take all the defenders deep downfield with them. After the defense has backed off, the In route should be open and have tons of room to run after the catch.

FORMATION: **4-WIDE FORMATION**

DISTANCE: **LONG YARDAGE**

ROUTES IN THIS PLAY: **IN, FADE, SEAM**

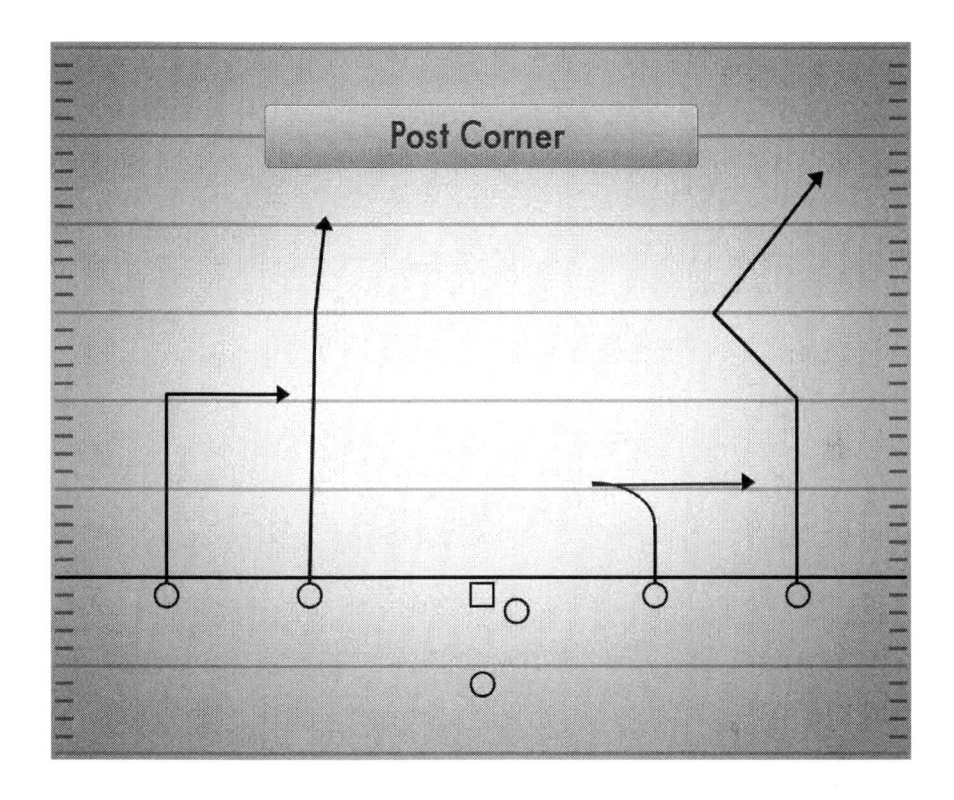

Post Corner

This play is all about setting up the Post-Corner route on the outside. The Receiver running the route has to make it look as if he is running the post, and as soon as he suckers the defense inside, he breaks to the outside and the Quarterback will hit him deep along the sideline.

The Whip route underneath, is used to keep the Cornerback from drifting back towards the Post-Corner. If the Cornerback does carry back deep and get in the way of the Post-Corner, then the Whip route should be open in the flats underneath.

FORMATION: **4-WIDE FORMATION**

DISTANCE: **LONG YARDAGE, MEDIUM YARDAGE**

ROUTES IN THIS PLAY: **IN, WHIP, POST CORNER, SEAM**

Bubble

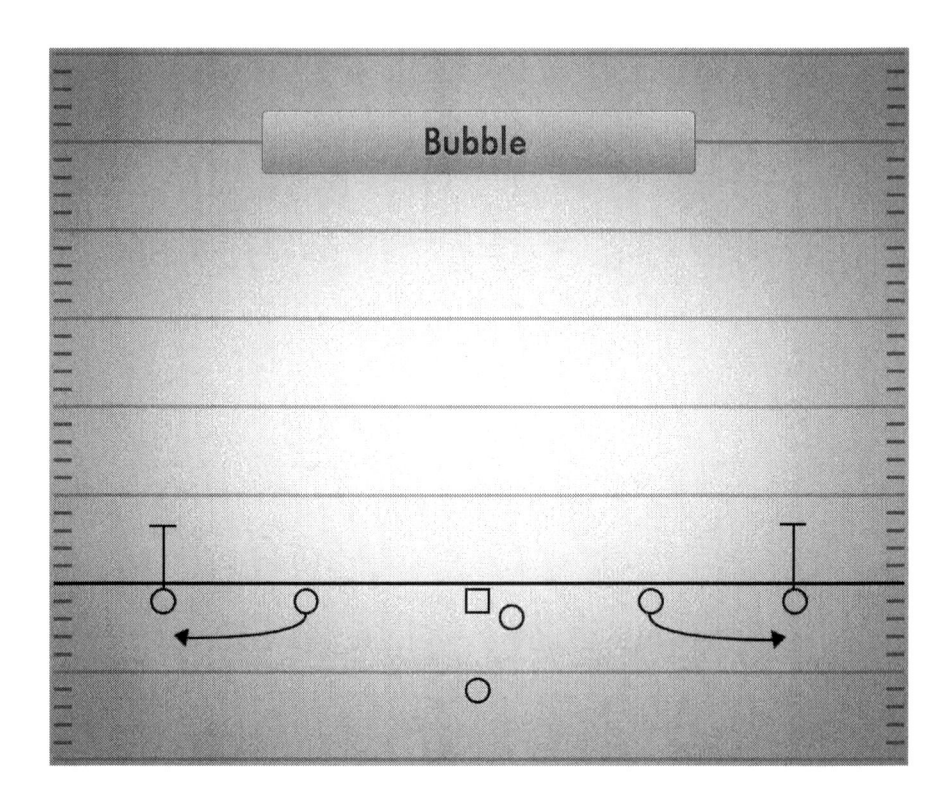

The Bubble play is a simple screen play. The Slot WR will bubble backwards with one step and proceed to drift towards the sideline. The block by the outside WR is critical to the success of the play.

Once the Quarterback delivers the ball the WR will read the block of the outside WR and sprint up the sideline.

FORMATION: **4-WIDE FORMATION**

DISTANCE: **SHORT YARDAGE**

Bubble WR Pass

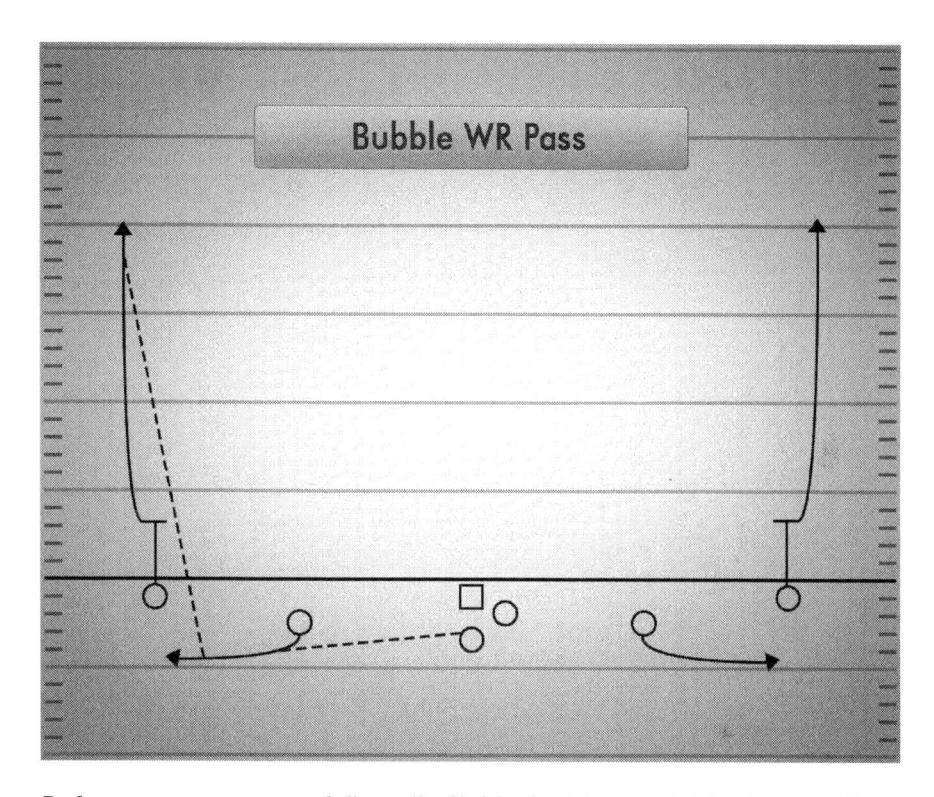

Before you can successfully pull off this double pass trick play, you first need to set it up with the normal Bubble play. After the defense is begins to cheat forward to guard the bubble, that's when you hit them with this Bubble WR Pass play.

The outside WR has to act as if he is going to block the defender like he normally does on the Bubble play, but as soon as he approaches, he needs to sidestep away and start jetting up the sideline. The inside WR needs to make a clean catch and quickly throw it over the defense to the WR who will be open downfield.

One key aspect of this play is that you have to remember that the first throw from the Quarterback has to be backwards, or else the second throw will be illegal. Therefore, the QB should scoot up a bit more than usual, and the WR should line up a little further back than usual, but both have to be done without making it obvious.

FORMATION: 4-WIDE FORMATION

DISTANCE: LONG YARDAGE

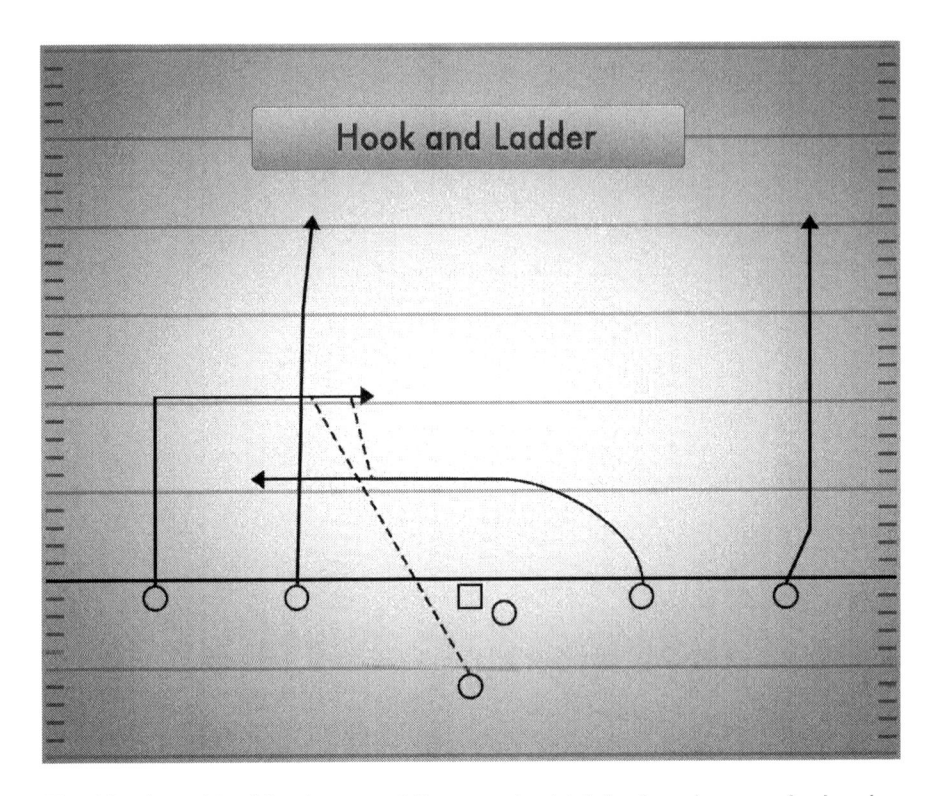

Hook and Ladder

The Hook and Ladder is one of the greatest trick plays in any playbook. It involves incredible timing and perfectly performed maneuvers by multiple individuals, but can be a phenomenally successful play when all the moving parts come together correctly.

The QB must deliver the throw to the In route before he gets too far across the field. The WR running the Shallow Cross must time his crossing route so that he is running underneath the In route immediately after he catches the ball. Once caught, the In route has to quickly secure the ball, and then pitch it backwards to the shallow crosser. The defense will have been moving inwards towards the original receiver, and will be caught off guard when the shallow crosser receives the pitch and is sprinting outward towards the sideline.

FORMATION: **4-WIDE FORMATION**

DISTANCE: **LONG YARDAGE**

ROUTES IN THIS PLAY: **IN, SHALLOW CROSS, FADE, SEAM**

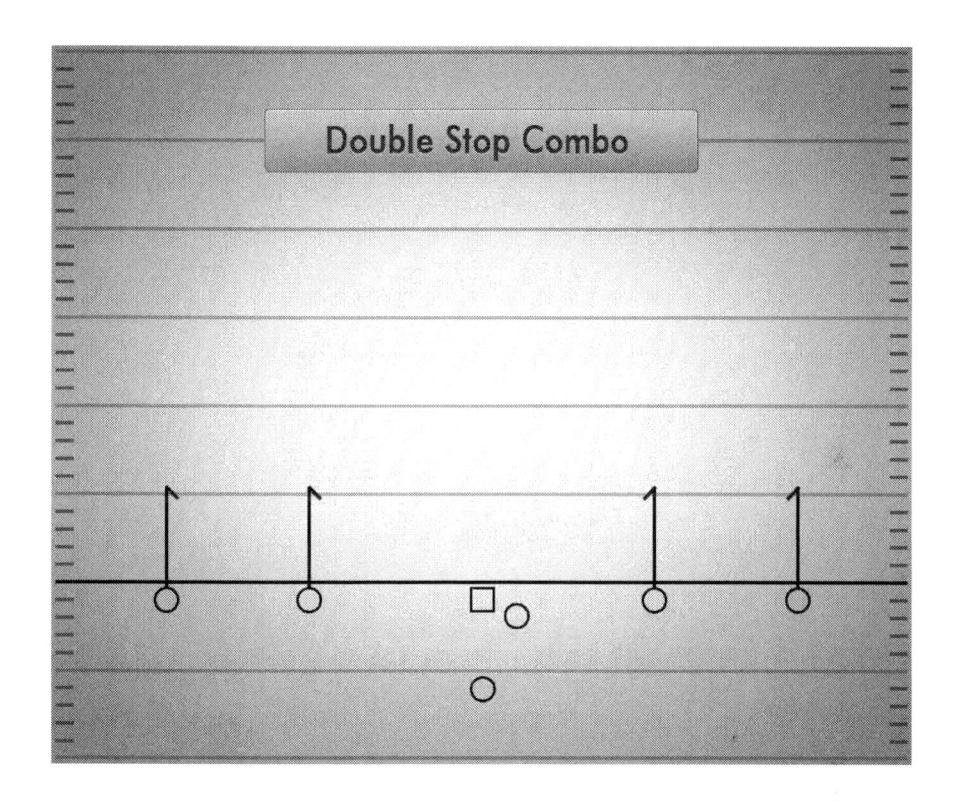

Double Stop Combo

The Double Stop Combo is one of the most fundamental plays of any spread offense passing tree. A simple route concept that quickly presents all the Wide Receivers on a quick 5-yard stop route.

This play can be called early in the game in order to help the QB get settled in, or it can be called in response to a defense that is playing far off the line of scrimmage.

FORMATION: **4-WIDE FORMATION**

DISTANCE: **SHORT YARDAGE**

ROUTES IN THIS PLAY: **STOP**

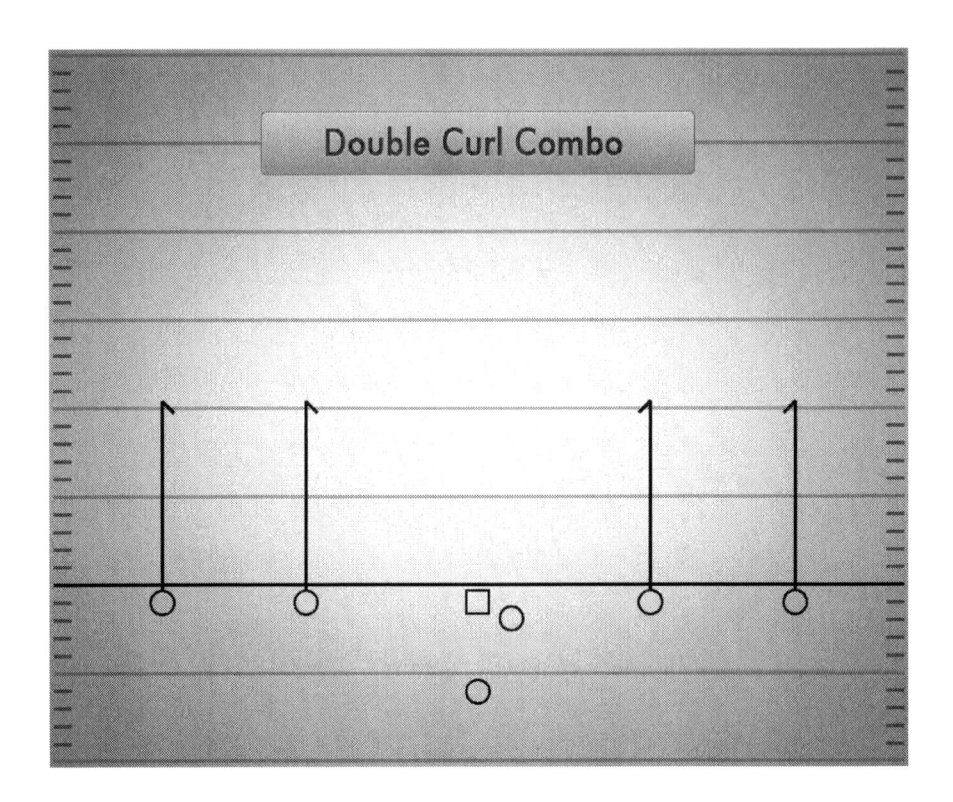

Double Curl Combo

The Double Curl Combo is an extended version of the Double Stop Combo play. It is a simple play for Medium Yardage.

Each Wide Receiver presses hard upfield for ten yards and quickly turns around, orienting their bodies toward the Quarterback who then takes his pick at the open man.

FORMATION: **4-WIDE FORMATION**

DISTANCE: **MEDIUM YARDAGE**

ROUTES IN THIS PLAY: **CURL**

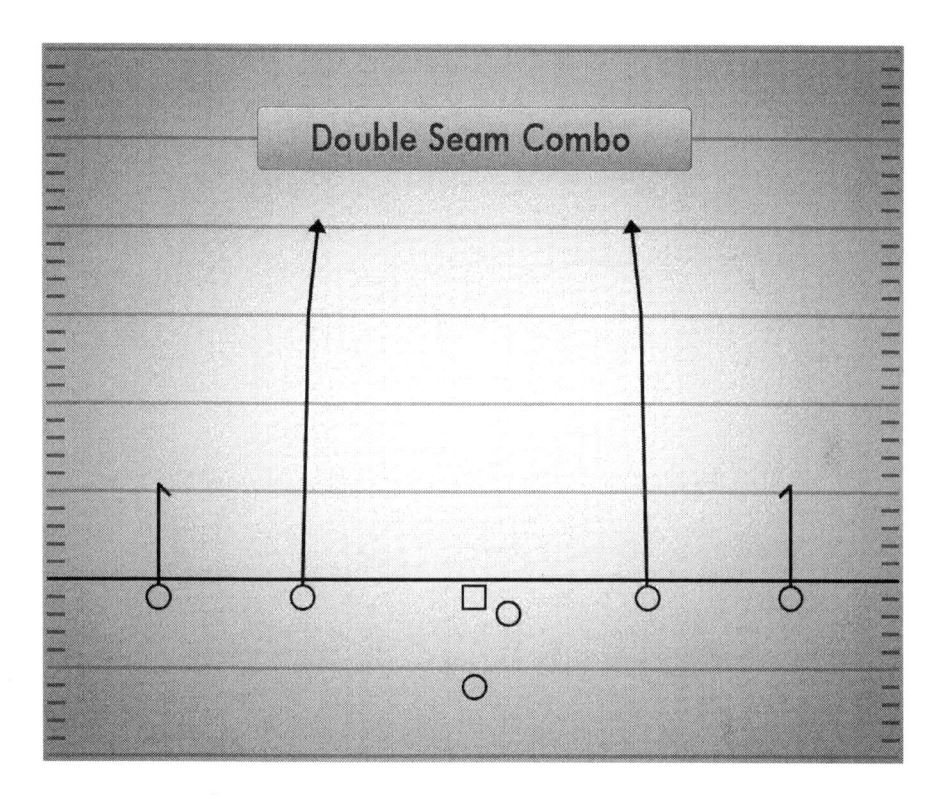

Double Seam Combo

Double Seam Combo is a play that places leverage on the defense up the seams. If the defense drops back to guard the seams, then the Quarterback should through the ball short to the 5-yard stop routes in the flats.

If it is a man-to-man defense, then consider throwing the seams over the top like a fade route, but run from an inside release. Safeties are not accustomed to guarding the fade route, and will therefore put your WR in better position to make the play.

FORMATION: **4-WIDE FORMATION**

DISTANCE: **SHORT YARDAGE, LONG YARDAGE**

ROUTES IN THIS PLAY: **STOP, SEAM**

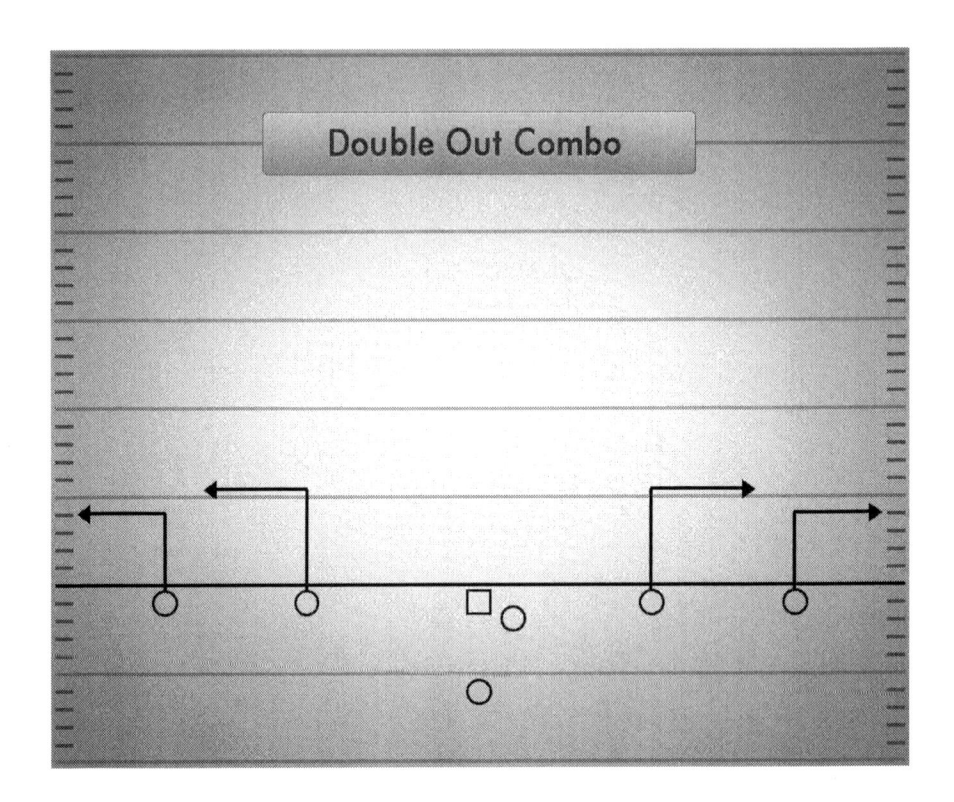

Double Out Combo

The Double Out Combo play places leverage on the outside of the defensive secondary. By attacking the flats with two players, the defender who is guarding the outside zone will be unable to guard both routes.

Versus a man to man defense, the QB must simply make a read based upon which WR makes a better move to the outside against the defender that is guarding him.

FORMATION: **4-WIDE FORMATION**

DISTANCE: **SHORT YARDAGE**

ROUTES IN THIS PLAY: **OUT**

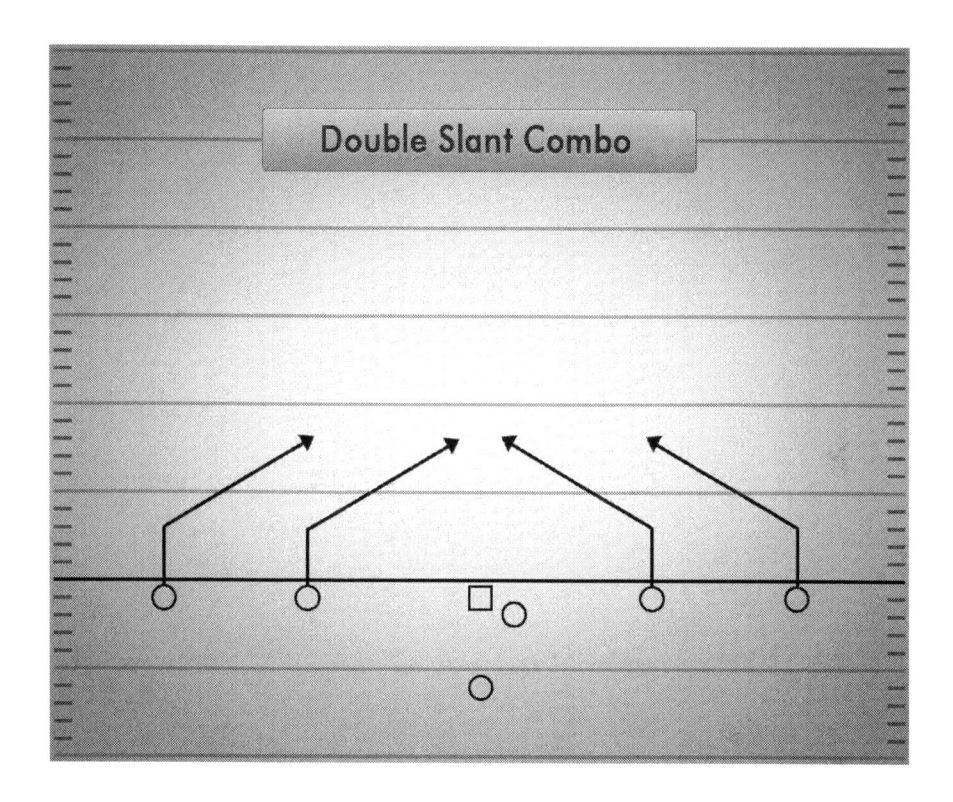

Double Slant Combo

The Double Slant Combo play is a great play to run in a short yardage situation if you have Wide Receivers who can run crisp routes. By making a clean cut to the inside, there will be a window of opportunity for the Quarterback to deliver the ball into the chest of the WR.

This play can also be used as a quick hitting play in the beginning of the game if the defense is playing far off the line of scrimmage. If the defense starts creeping up to guard against the short slant route, then hit them over the top by calling the Slant-and-Up Combo play.

FORMATION: **4-WIDE FORMATION**

DISTANCE: **SHORT YARDAGE**

ROUTES IN THIS PLAY: **SLANT**

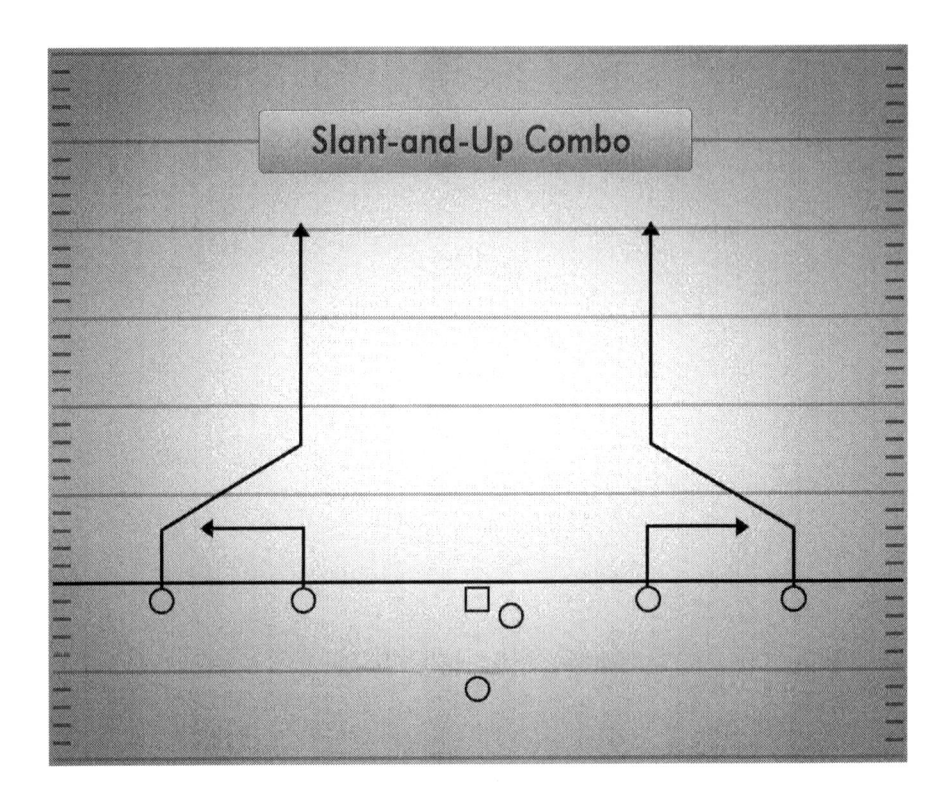

Slant-and-Up Combo

Slant-and-Up Combo is a companion play to the Out-Slant Combo play. By getting the defense used to seeing the Out-Slant combination routes, they will tend to cheat down. That is when you hit them over the top with this play.

As the defense makes a move to jump in front of the slant route, that is right when the WR turns it up field where the QB will throw it over the top for a long gain or a Touchdown.

FORMATION: **4-WIDE FORMATION**

DISTANCE: **LONG YARDAGE**

ROUTES IN THIS PLAY: **OUT, SLANT**

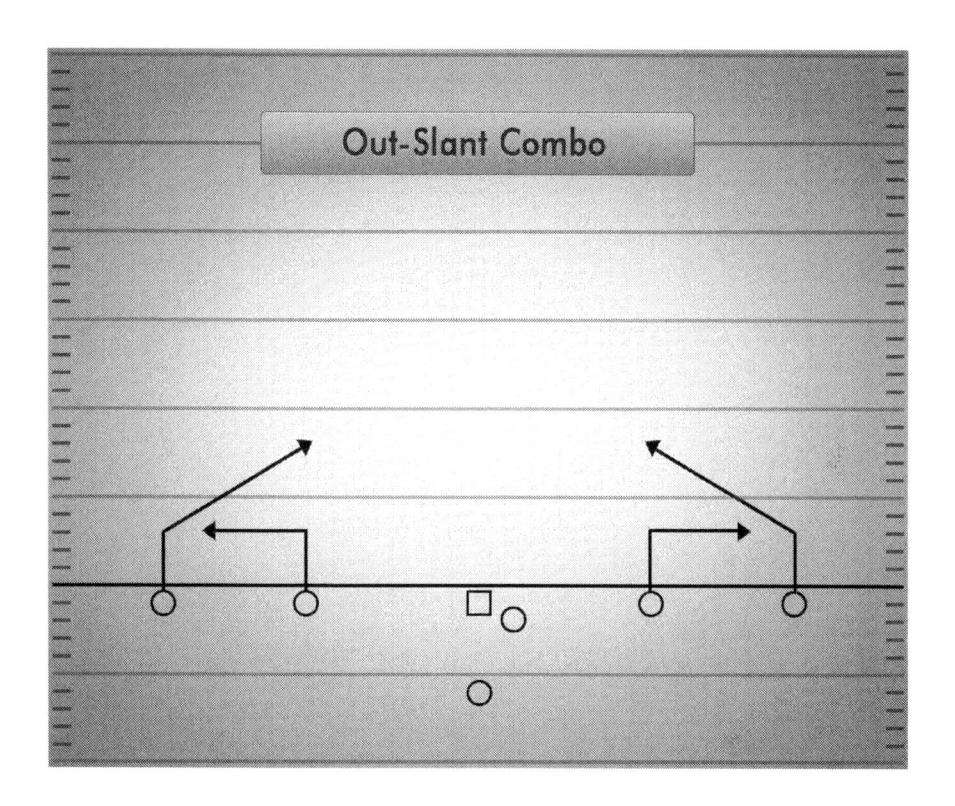

Out-Slant Combo

The Out-Slant Combo twists the defense around regardless of if they are playing man-to-man or zone. If they are playing zone, then the defense won't be able to keep track of the crossing patterns, and the man-to-man defense won't be able to keep up with the quick crossing cuts.

After the defense has gotten used to seeing this out-slant crossing pattern, mix things up by hitting them over the top with either the Slant-and-Up Combo play or the Out-and-Up Combo play.

FORMATION: **4-WIDE FORMATION**

DISTANCE: **SHORT YARDAGE**

ROUTES IN THIS PLAY: **OUT, SLANT**

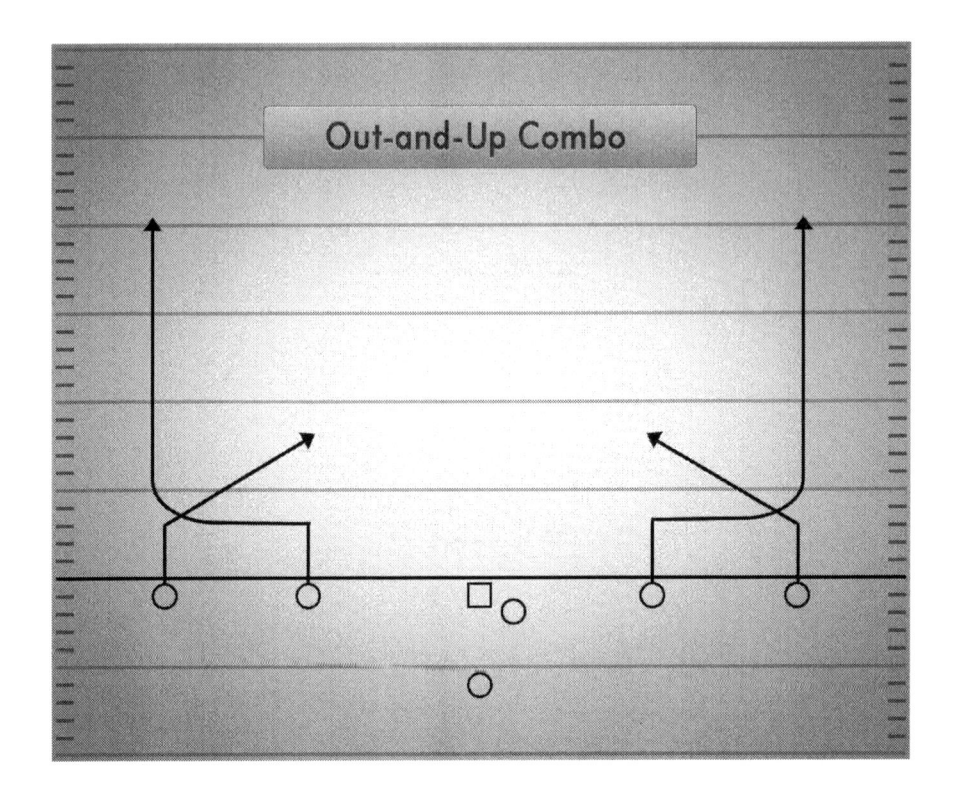

Out-and-Up Combo

The Out-and Up Combo is a companion play to the Out-Slant Combo play. After you have gotten the defense used to the shorter out route, hit them over the top with the Out-and-Up.

The part that makes this play extremely dangerous is against a man to man defense where the defender on the Out-and-Up route will have to run underneath the slant route, and will therefore be in a bad position to keep up with the inside WR who is now sprinting wide open up the sideline.

FORMATION: **4-WIDE FORMATION**

DISTANCE: **LONG YARDAGE**

ROUTES IN THIS PLAY: **OUT, SLANT**

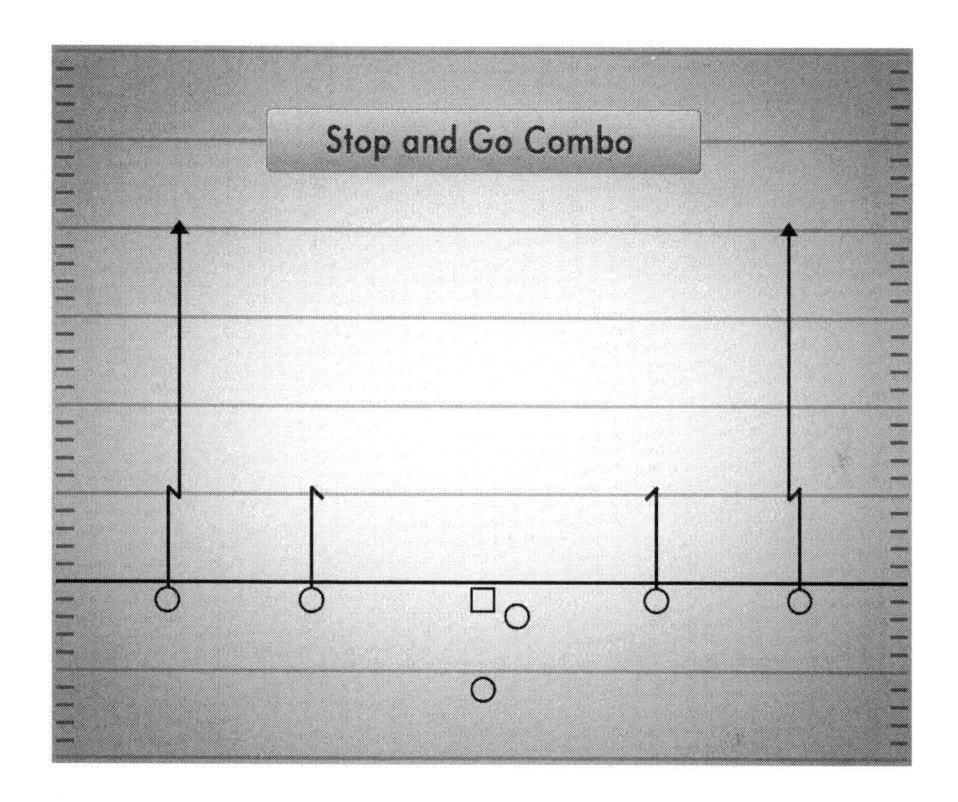

Stop and Go Combo

The Stop and Go route is one of the most famous double moves in all of football. After you have set up this play by repeatedly running the Double Stop Combo play, then surprise them with the Stop and Go and they won't know what hit them.

It is important that the Wide Receiver makes has break up the sideline after he stops. That way he is able to get passed the Cornerback easier.

FORMATION: **4-WIDE FORMATION**

DISTANCE: **LONG YARDAGE**

ROUTES IN THIS PLAY: **STOP**

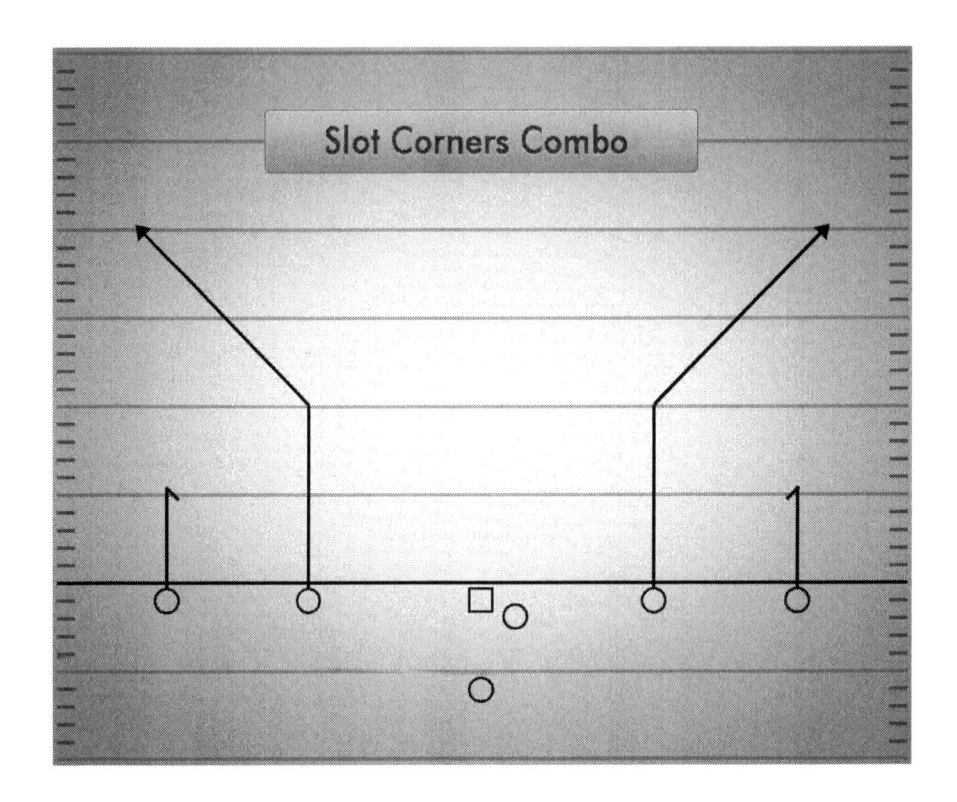

Slot Corners Combo

The Slot Corners play is a great play to use in order to isolate the Cornerback. The only thing that the Quarterback needs to read is how the Cornerback is positioning himself.

If the CB drops back underneath the Corner Route, then throw the ball to the stop on the outside. If the CB stay shallow in the flats, then throw over his head to the slot WR running the Corner route, making a break to the sideline.

FORMATION: **4-WIDE FORMATION**

DISTANCE: **SHORT YARDAGE, MEDIUM YARDAGE**

ROUTES IN THIS PLAY: **CORNER, STOP**

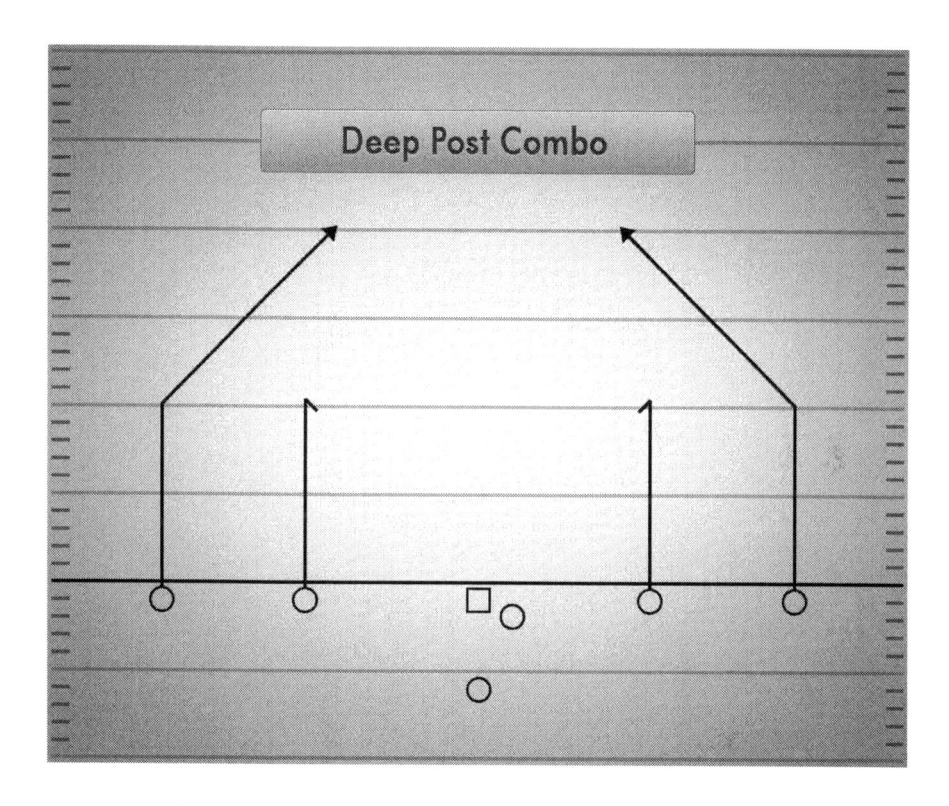

Deep Post Combo

The Deep Post Combo is a great way to attack downfield. The Post Route needs to be a skinny post with a trajectory that doesn't cross the middle of the field. The Slot Receiver needs to run his Curl Route in a way that grabs the attention of the Safety.

The Quarterback's read should be focused on the Safety. If the Safety stays high and guards the Post Route, then drop down and throw it to the Curl Route. If, however, the Safety is drawn down to the Slot Receiver running the Curl, then throw over his head to the Post running downfield.

FORMATION: **4-WIDE FORMATION**

DISTANCE: **LONG YARDAGE, MEDIUM YARDAGE**

ROUTES IN THIS PLAY: **POST, CURL**

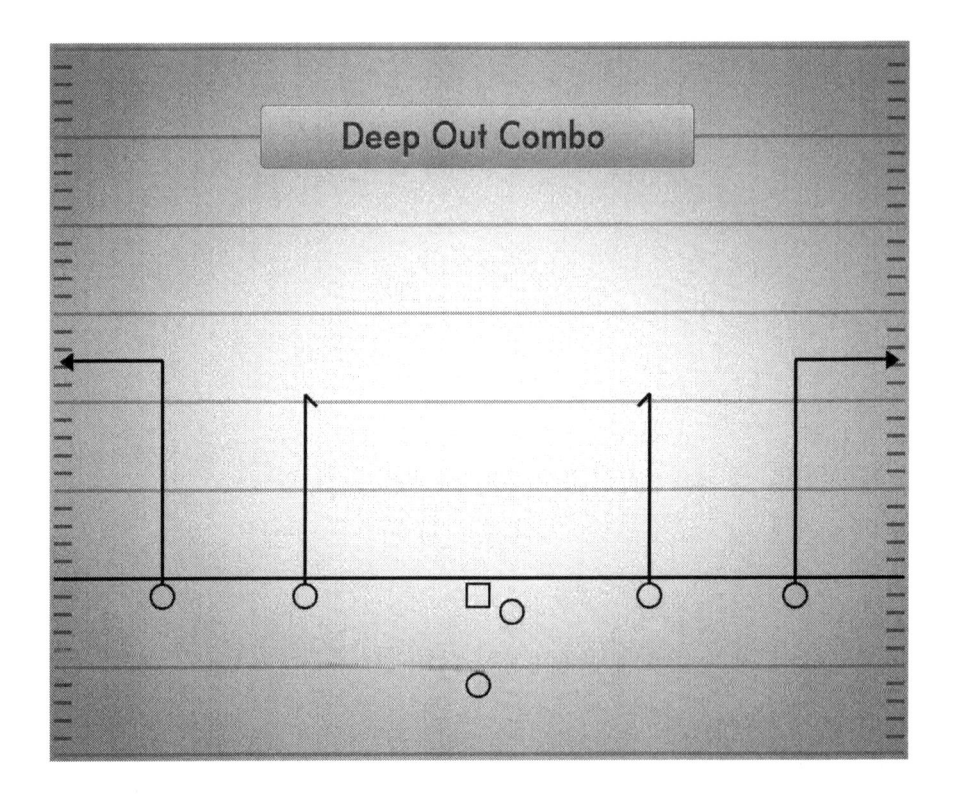

Deep Out Combo

The Deep Out Combo is similar to the Double Curl Combo play with a variation that send the outside WRs towards the sideline on a Deep Out Route.

The QB should make a pre-snap read to determine what side he is going to throw to. Once the side has been determined, then disregard the other half of the field and the read is locked into being between the Deep Out or the Curl Route.

FORMATION: **4-WIDE FORMATION**

DISTANCE: **MEDIUM YARDAGE**

ROUTES IN THIS PLAY: **CURL, OUT**

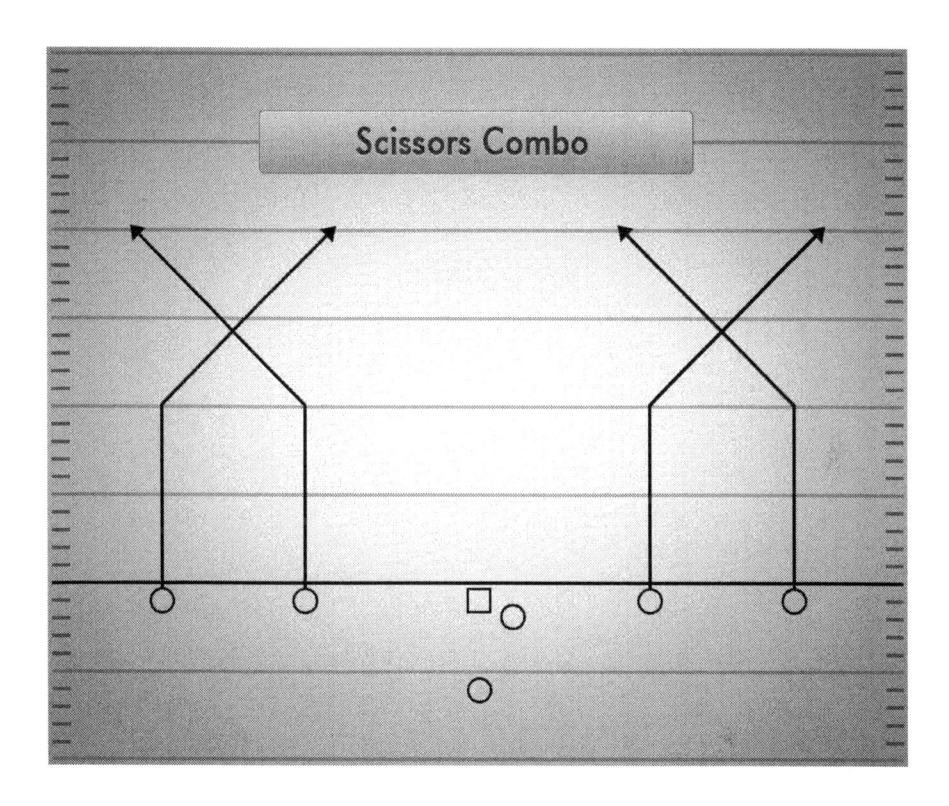

Scissors Combo

The Scissors Combo play is a mirrored play with the same route concept of a Post Route and a Corner Route on both sides.

The Wide Receivers need to cleanly run their routes by converging across each other at the point of the downfield cuts in order to disorient the defense and break free into the open field.

FORMATION: **4-WIDE FORMATION**

DISTANCE: **LONG YARDAGE**

ROUTES IN THIS PLAY: **CORNER, POST**

Switchblade Combo

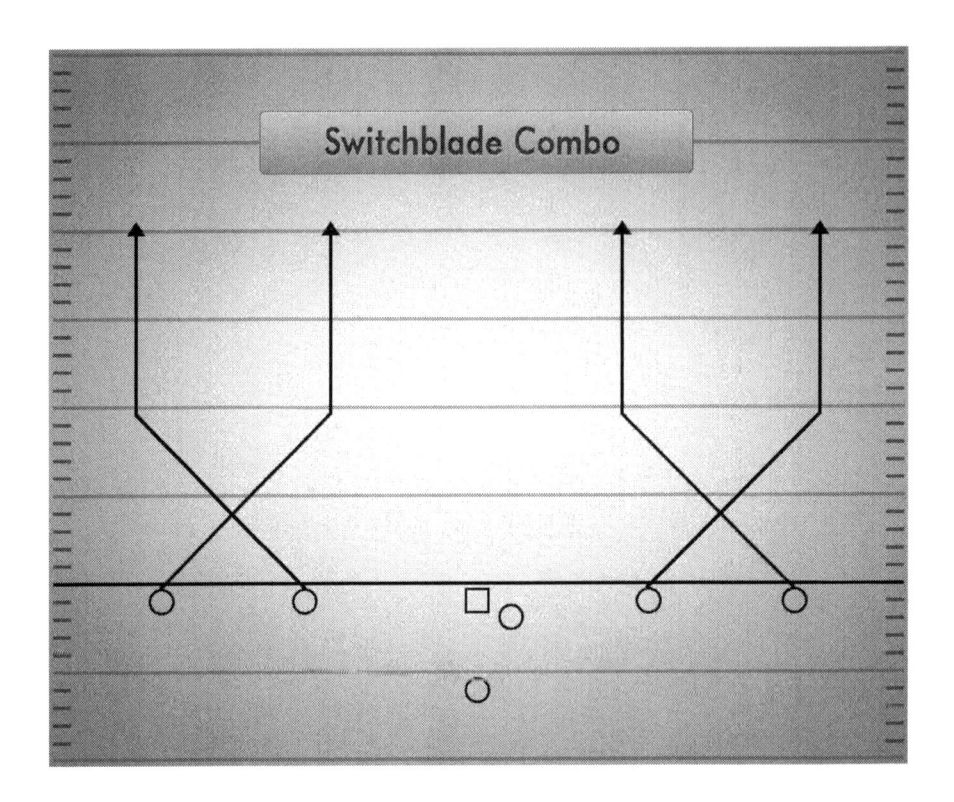

The Switchblade Combo play is intended to create a rub between the two combination receivers in order to break free from their defenders.

This play will work best against a man-to-man defense, because it is easy to lose the defenders when the Receivers cross and then break free going upfield.

FORMATION: 4-WIDE FORMATION

DISTANCE: LONG YARDAGE

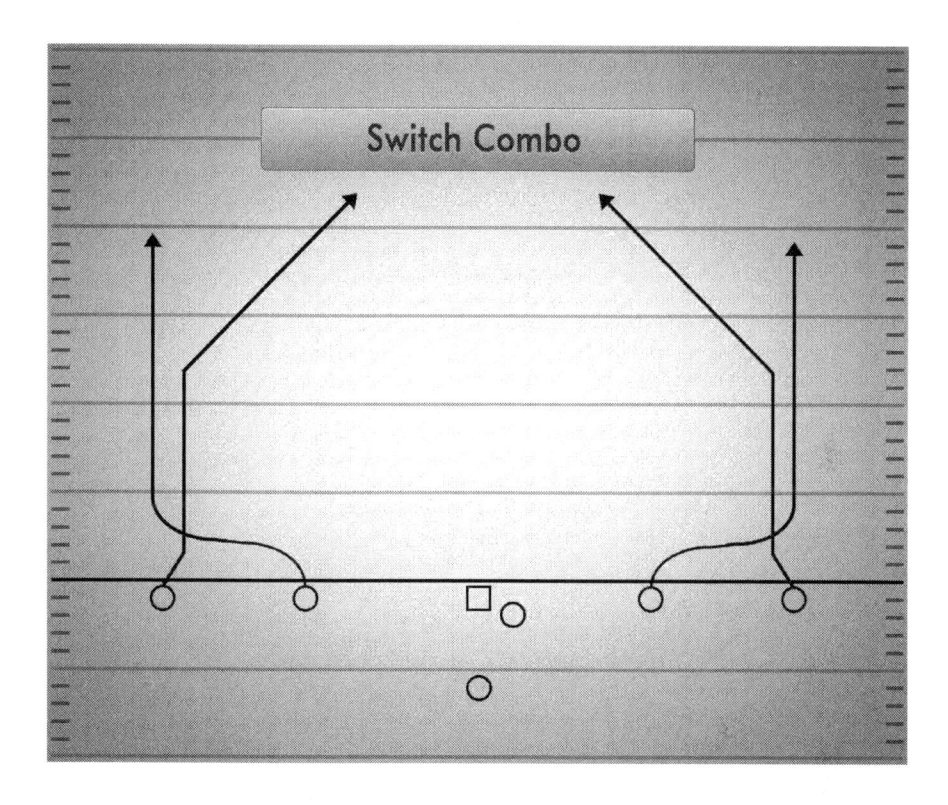

Switch Combo

Switch Combo is the classic switch play where the receivers use their routes to "switch" their positions on the field. The Outside Receiver gets upfield fast and runs a Post Route. The Slot Receiver goes underneath the Outside Receiver and then jets up the sideline.

The Quarterback should read the deep safeties. This play uses four players to attack zones that usually only have two, or maybe 3, defenders responsible for guarding them. Use your eyes to influence the defensive backs' movement, and then find the open WR running downfield.

FORMATION: **4-WIDE FORMATION**

DISTANCE: **LONG YARDAGE**

ROUTES IN THIS PLAY: **POST**

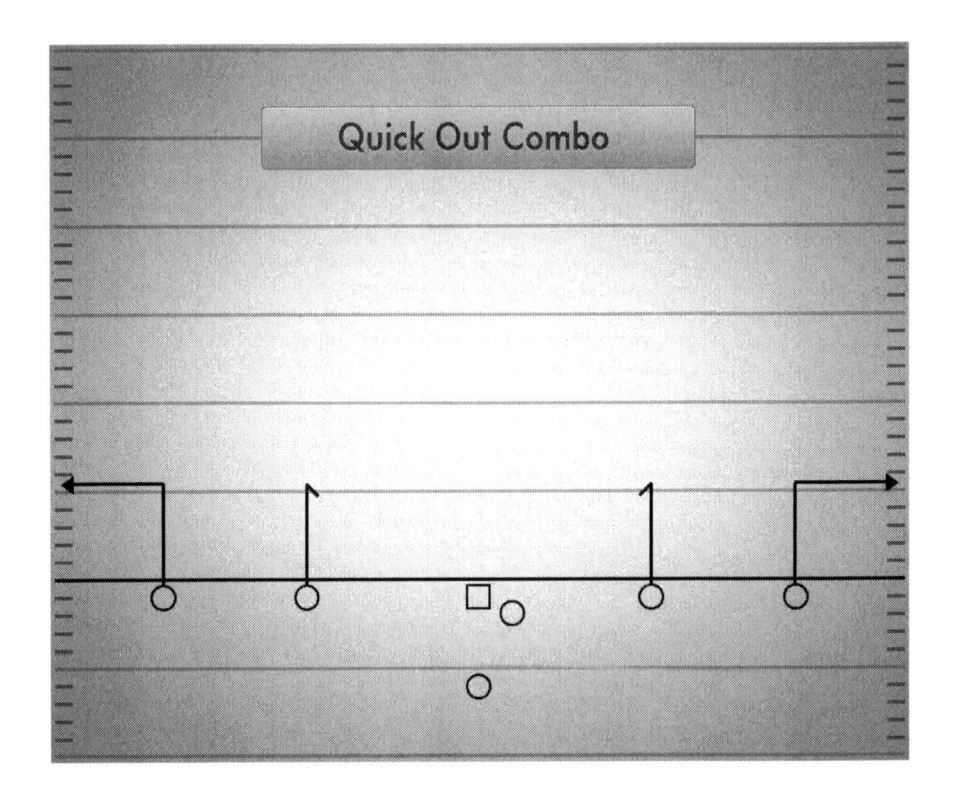

Quick Out Combo

Quick Cut Combo is a variation of the standard Double Stop Combo play, and a shorter version of the Deep Out Combo play.

The Quarterback should select one side of the field on the pre-snap read, and then as the play begins, determine which of the Wide Receivers gets in better position against the defense on his route.

FORMATION: **4-WIDE FORMATION**

DISTANCE: **SHORT YARDAGE**

ROUTES IN THIS PLAY: **STOP, OUT**

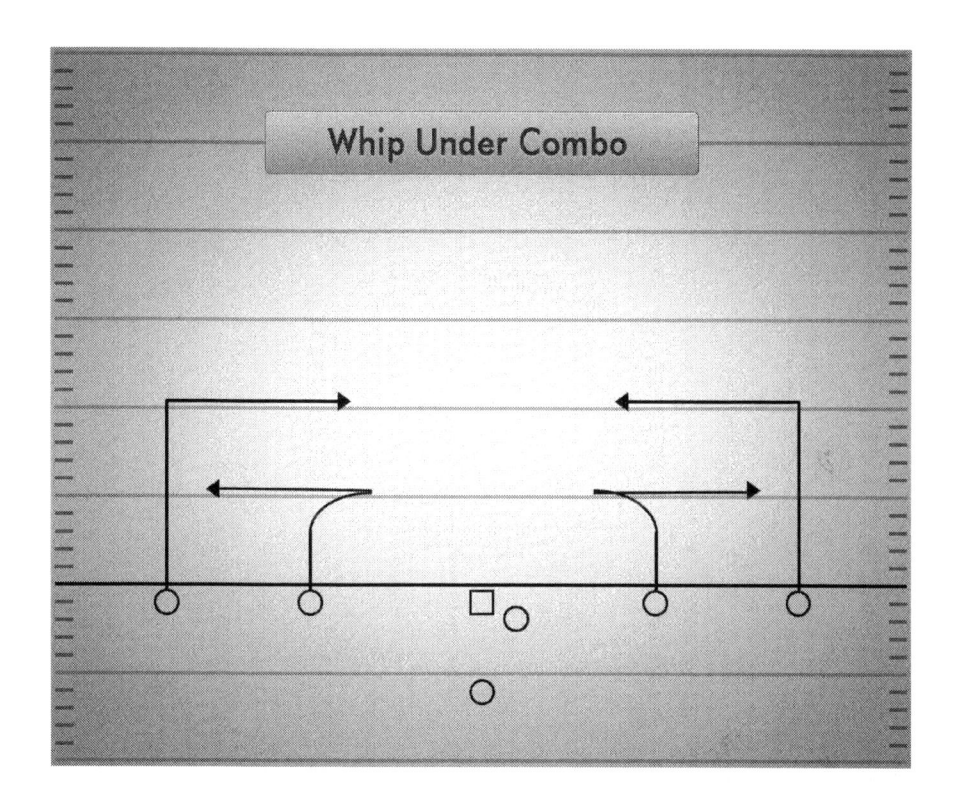

Whip Under Combo

The Whip Under Combo play is a great play to get some horizontal flow in your route concepts going. The crucial aspect of the play is the way in which the Whip Route is run by the Slot Receiver. The route must start of looking like an inside movement, but then the WR must plant his foot and spin (face toward the QB) and jet hard to the sideline.

If the Slot Receiver is not able to get open with the Whip Route, then the horizontal movement underneath should clear out to reveal the outside Receiver open on the In Route.

FORMATION: **4-WIDE FORMATION**

DISTANCE: **SHORT YARDAGE, MEDIUM YARDAGE**

ROUTES IN THIS PLAY: **IN, OUT**

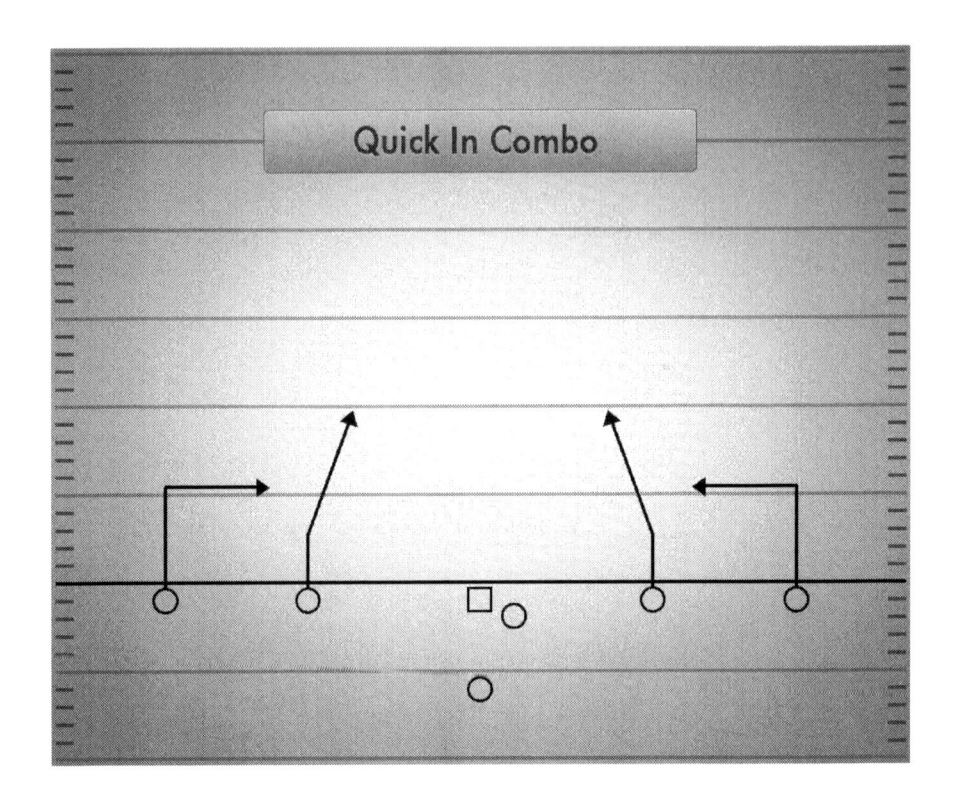

Quick In Combo

The Quick In Combo play is built to be a quick hitter. The Slot Receiver presses off the line of scrimmage in order to create space underneath for the Outside Receiver to be open for the In route.

The QB must make a pre-snap read to determine which side of the field is giving up the most position in the inside zone based upon formation alignment.

FORMATION: **4-WIDE FORMATION**

DISTANCE: **SHORT YARDAGE**

ROUTES IN THIS PLAY: **IN, SEAM**

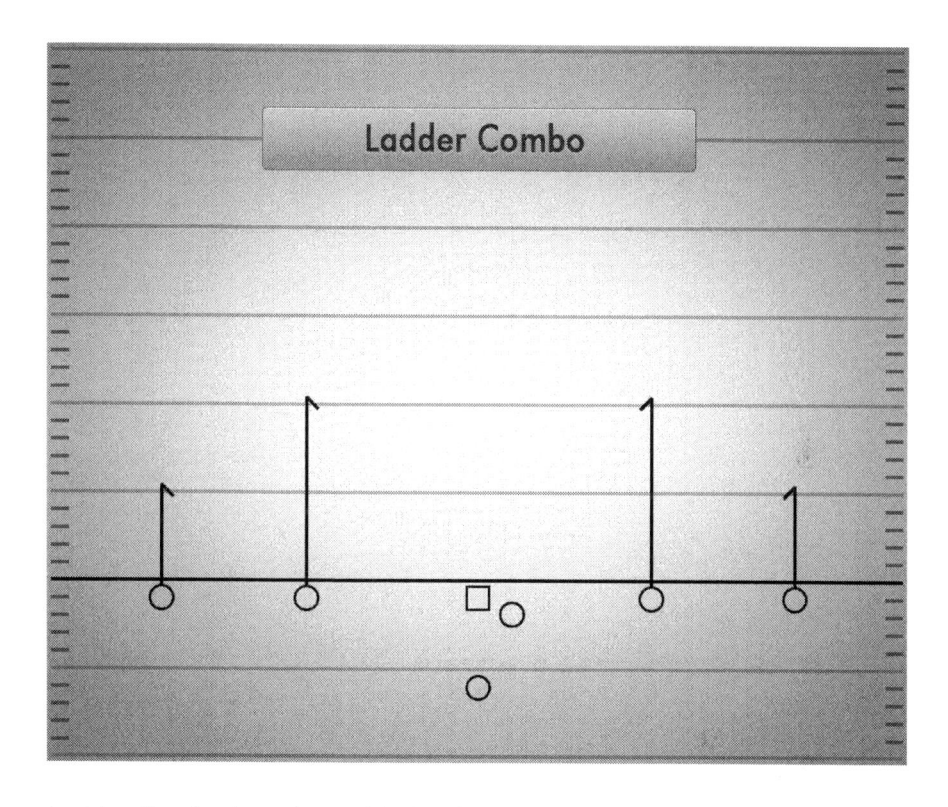

Ladder Combo

Ladder Combo is a play to hit the defense at varying vertical positions. All receivers run a stop and curl routes, but the lengths of the routes vary based upon their alignment.

The Quarterback should make his read just as if he is climbing up a "ladder." First look at the 5-Yard stop, and then work your way up to the 10-yard curl.

FORMATION: **4-WIDE FORMATION**

DISTANCE: **SHORT YARDAGE, MEDIUM YARDAGE**

ROUTES IN THIS PLAY: **STOP, CURL**

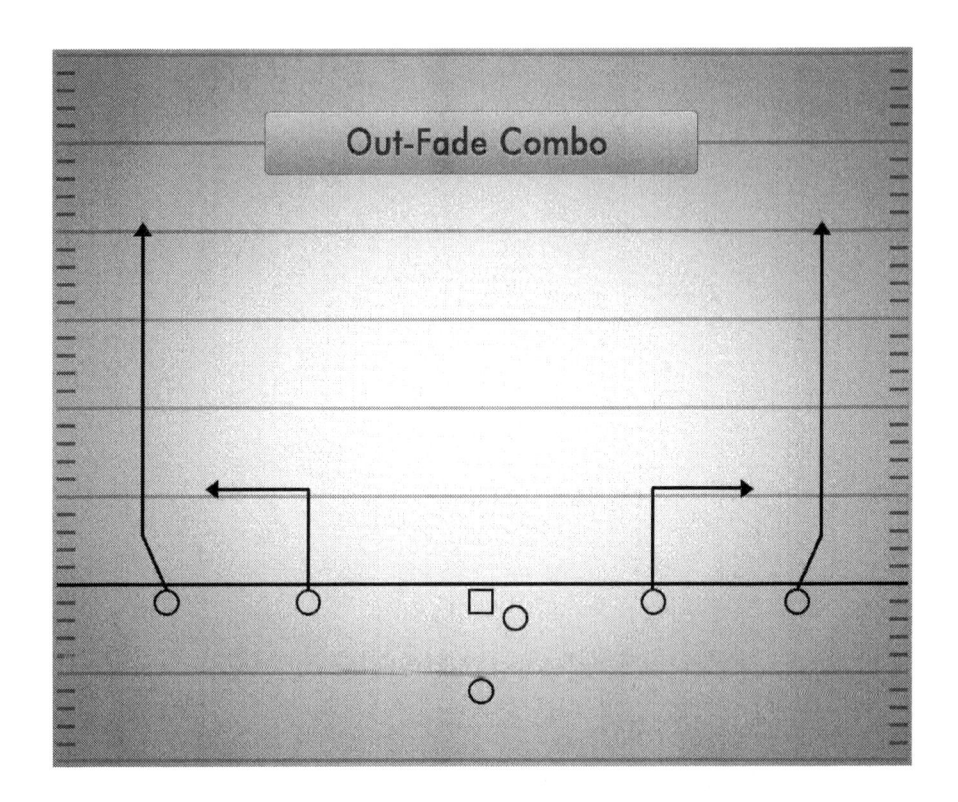

Out-Fade Combo

The Out-Fade route combination is one of the most popular route concepts in any football team's playbook. A Fade Route up the sideline on the outside combined with an Out Route from the Slot Receiver from the inside.

The Quarterback's read should be locked in on the defensive Cornerback. If the Cornerback drifts deep with the Fade, then throw the ball to the Out Route in the flats. If the Cornerback stays in the flats to jump on the Out, then throw it over the top to the Fade.

FORMATION: **4-WIDE FORMATION**

DISTANCE: **SHORT YARDAGE, MEDIUM YARDAGE**

ROUTES IN THIS PLAY: **FADE, OUT**

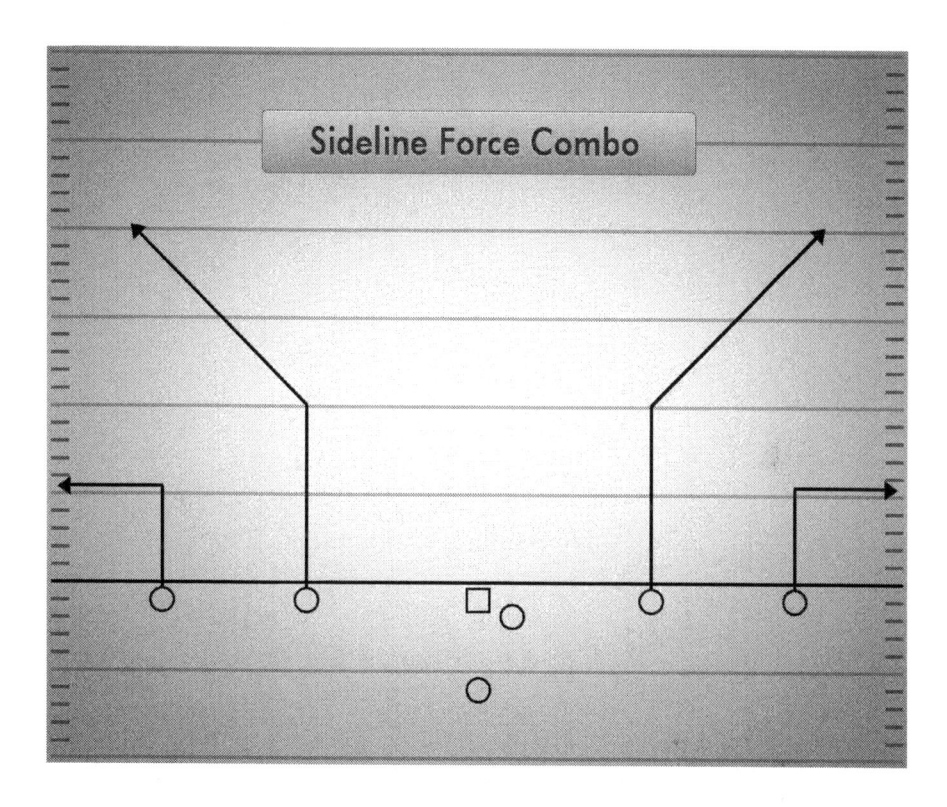

Sideline Force Combo

The Sideline Force Combo play is a shorter version of the Sideline Force Deep Combo play. The main goal of this play is to force the routes to the sideline.

This play is very effective when you need to manage the time on the clock because it allows the Receivers to quickly get out of bounds after the catch the ball.

FORMATION: **4-WIDE FORMATION**

DISTANCE: **SHORT YARDAGE, MEDIUM YARDAGE**

ROUTES IN THIS PLAY: **CORNER, OUT**

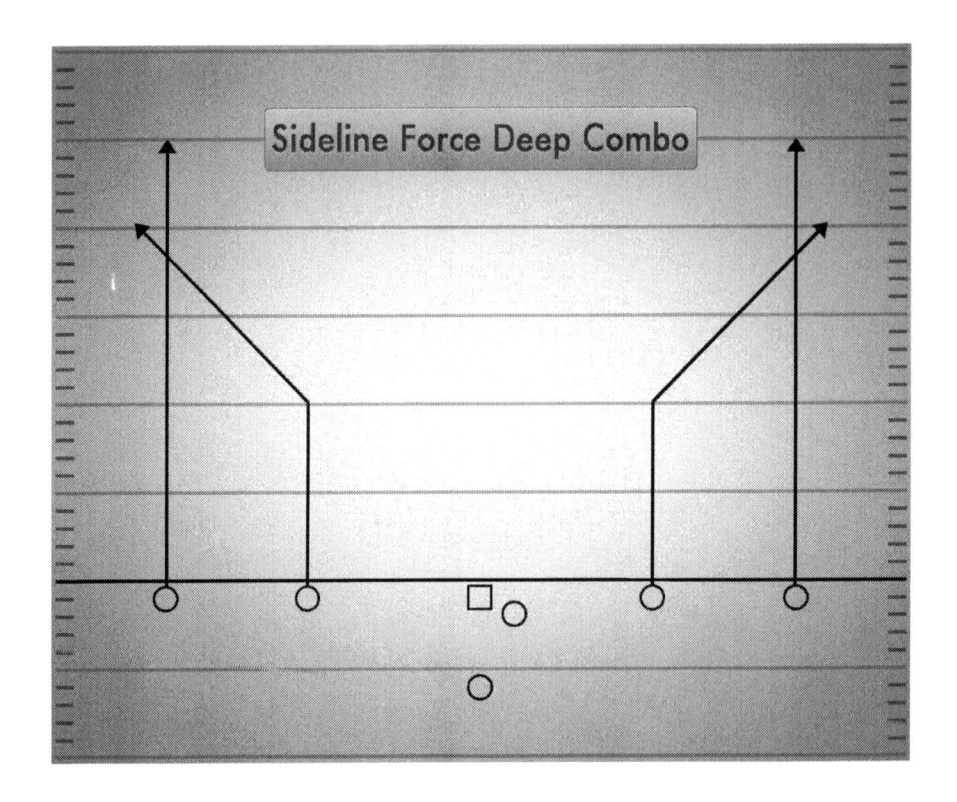

Sideline Force Deep Combo

The Sideline Force Deep Combo play is the deep version of the Sideline Force Combo play. The purpose of this play is to get the Wide Receivers in close proximity to the sideline while running deep downfield.

This play is very effective when you need to manage the time on the clock because it allows the Receivers to quickly get out of bounds after the catch the ball.

FORMATION: **4-WIDE FORMATION**

DISTANCE: **LONG YARDAGE**

ROUTES IN THIS PLAY: **CORNER, STREAK**

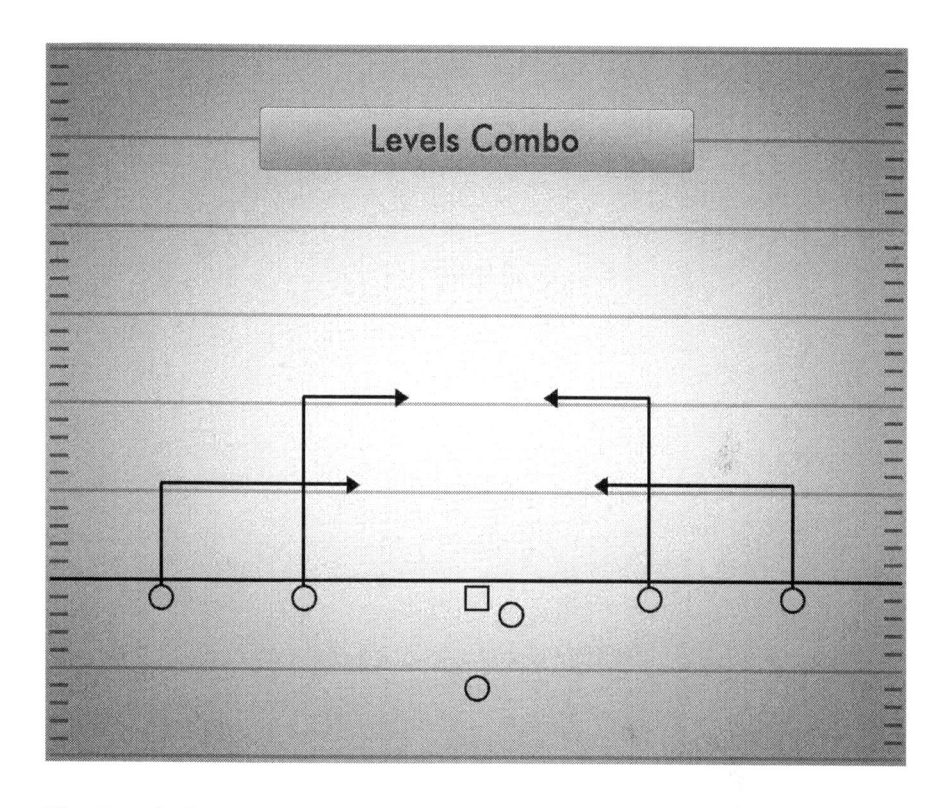

Levels Combo

The Levels Combo play is a great way to attack different vertical portions of the defensive secondary. The Wide Receivers run In Routes at varying distances down the field.

The horizontal movement should create a space for the Quarterback to find an opening to throw into, especially combined with the alternating vertical positioning of the routes.

FORMATION: **4-WIDE FORMATION**

DISTANCE: **SHORT YARDAGE, MEDIUM YARDAGE**

ROUTES IN THIS PLAY: **IN**

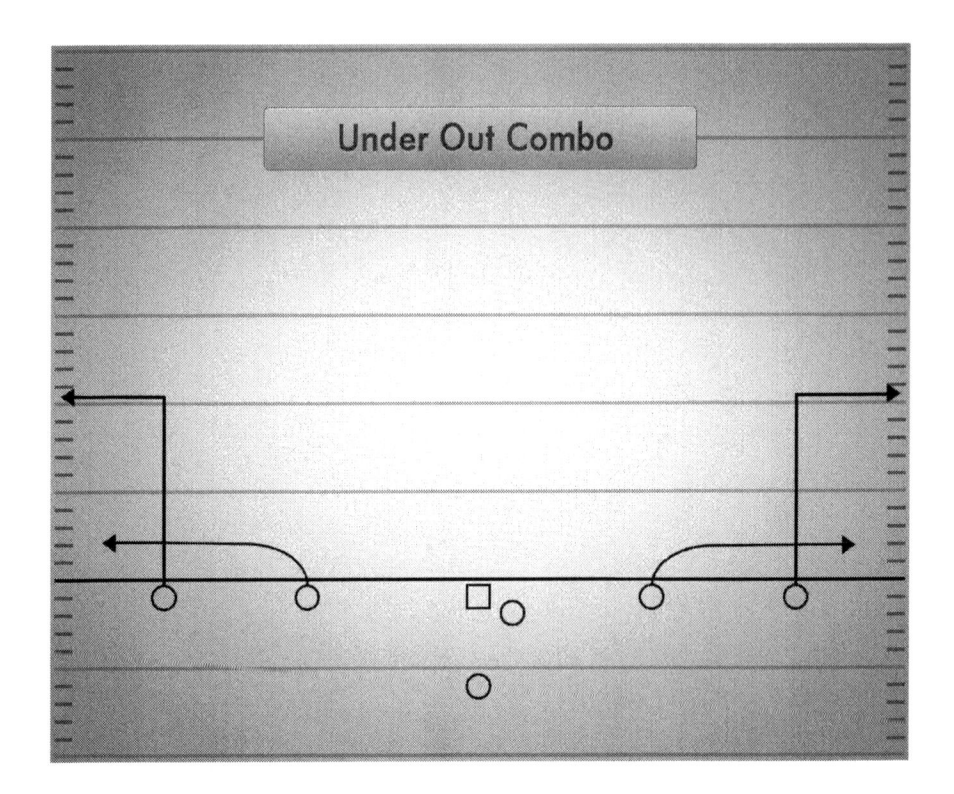

Under Out Combo

The Under Out Combo play positions the inside WR on a quick out underneath the deeper out. This places pressure on the flats of the defensive secondary by placing two WR on each side of the zone.

By splitting the responsibilities of the Cornerback, the Quarterback will have to see which one the Cornerback decides to guard, and then deliver the ball to the appropriate WR.

FORMATION: **4-WIDE FORMATION**

DISTANCE: **SHORT YARDAGE, MEDIUM YARDAGE**

ROUTES IN THIS PLAY: **OUT**

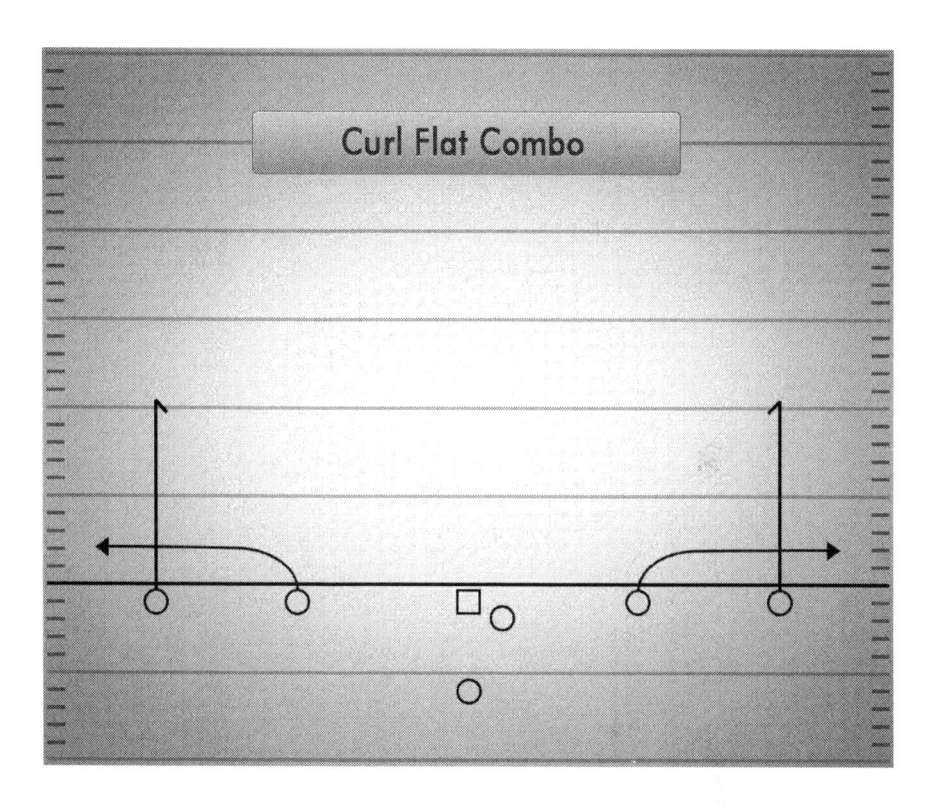

Curl Flat Combo

The Curl Flat Combo play attacks the defensive flat zone on the outside with a quick Out Route and a Curl Route over the top.

The Quarterback will want to look first at the quick out, and if the defense flowed fast to guard the out, then that means the curl route should be curling around in the open space right behind them.

FORMATION: **4-WIDE FORMATION**

DISTANCE: **SHORT YARDAGE, MEDIUM YARDAGE**

ROUTES IN THIS PLAY: **CURL, OUT**

Plays

3-Wide Formation

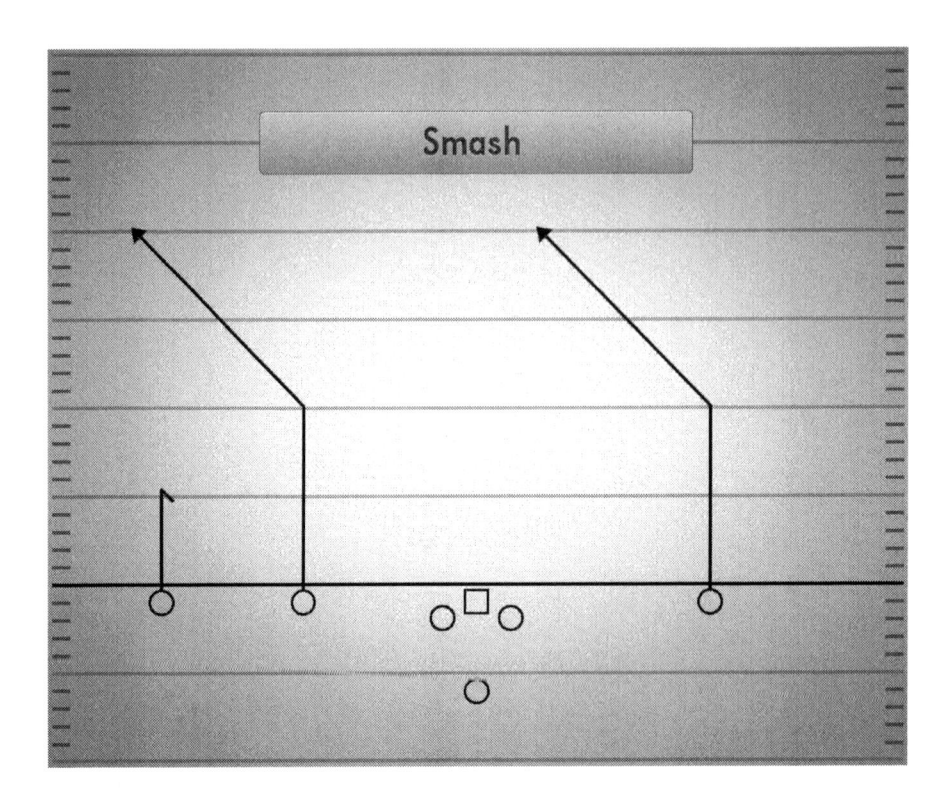

Smash

Utilizing the popular corner/stop route concept, the Smash play will attack many different zones in the defensive secondary. The first read that the Quarterback should make is to watch how the Cornerback plays the routes. If he stays low on the Stop route, then throw it over his head to the Corner route. If he stays high on the corner route, then throw it low to the Wide Receiver running the Stop route, who will be wide open in the flats. No outside linebacker will be able to run out there quick enough if the corner is dropping deep, and the Quarterback makes a quick read.

FORMATION: **3-WIDE FORMATION**

DISTANCE: **SHORT YARDAGE, MEDIUM YARDAGE**

ROUTES IN THIS PLAY: **CORNER, POST, STOP**

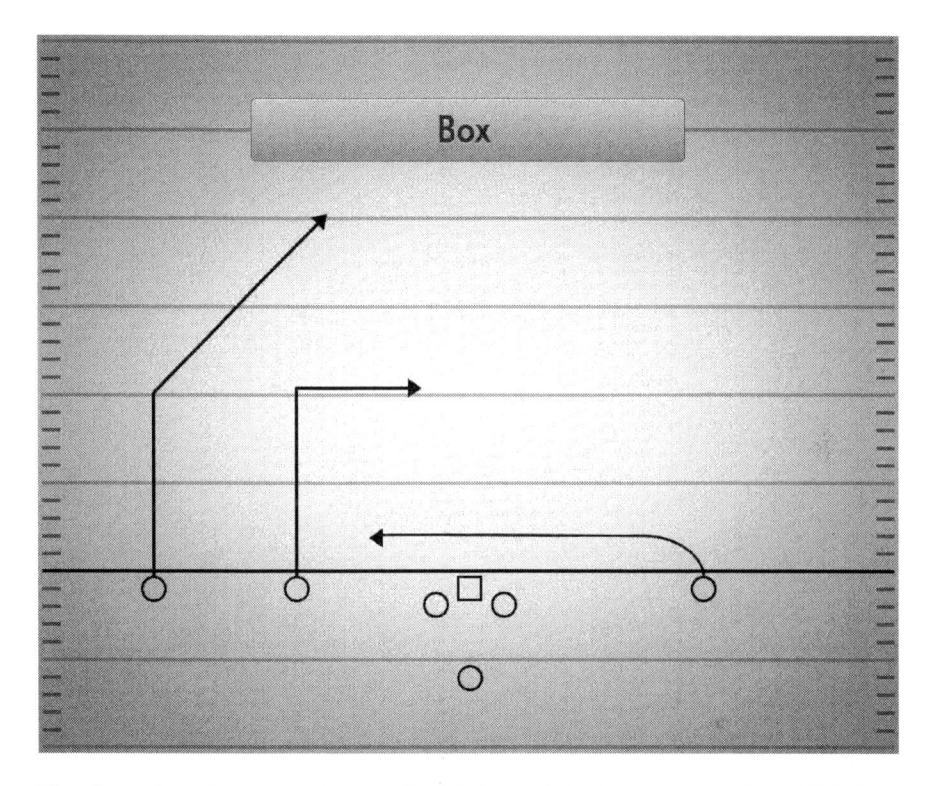

The Box play allows you to trap the defense into having to make a high/low decision. In fact, there are two different high/low areas on the defense that this play attacks.

By singling out the safety, the Quarterback can make a "high/low" read based upon the combination of the Post route and the 10 yard In route. If the safety drops high to guard the Post, then throw it low to the In route. If the safety stays low on the In, then throw it high to the Post.

Additionally, another high/low read takes place at the level of the outside linebacker. The linebacker will have to make the decision to go high and guard the In route, or stay low and guard the Shallow Cross. The Quarterback's read progression should start by reading the Safety on the Post, and then moving down to the In route, and finally hitting the lowest shallow cross underneath, if everything higher is guarded.

FORMATION: 3-WIDE FORMATION

DISTANCE: SHORT YARDAGE, LONG YARDAGE, MEDIUM YARDAGE

ROUTES IN THIS PLAY: POST, IN, SHALLOW CROSS, STREAK

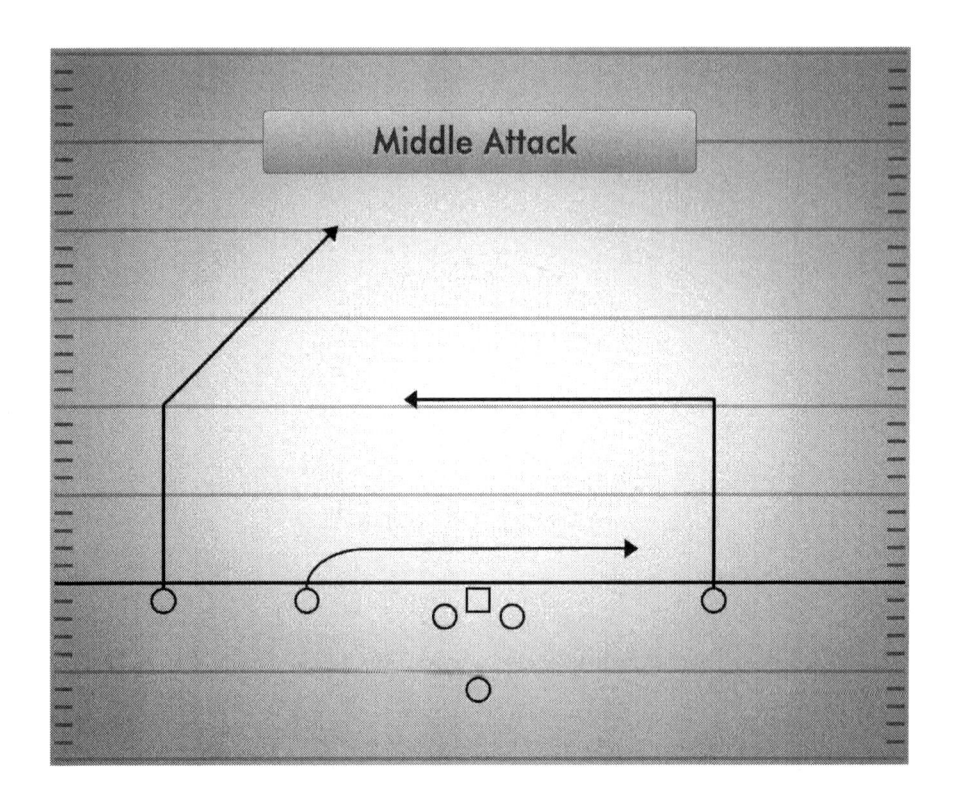

Middle Attack

The Middle Attack play attacks the middle of the defense with three different routes attacking three different levels in the defensive secondary. This allows the Quarterback to read the vertical flow of the defense in order to determine which of the three levels will be the open one. If the defense begins to crowd the middle of the field, then the outside receiver needs to get a wide release to run down the sideline on the fade route to stretch out the secondary.

Middle Attack is a variation of the Box play, but with a reversal of roles for the slot receivers.

FORMATION: **3-WIDE FORMATION**

DISTANCE: **SHORT YARDAGE, LONG YARDAGE, MEDIUM YARDAGE**

ROUTES IN THIS PLAY: **POST, IN, SHALLOW CROSS, FADE**

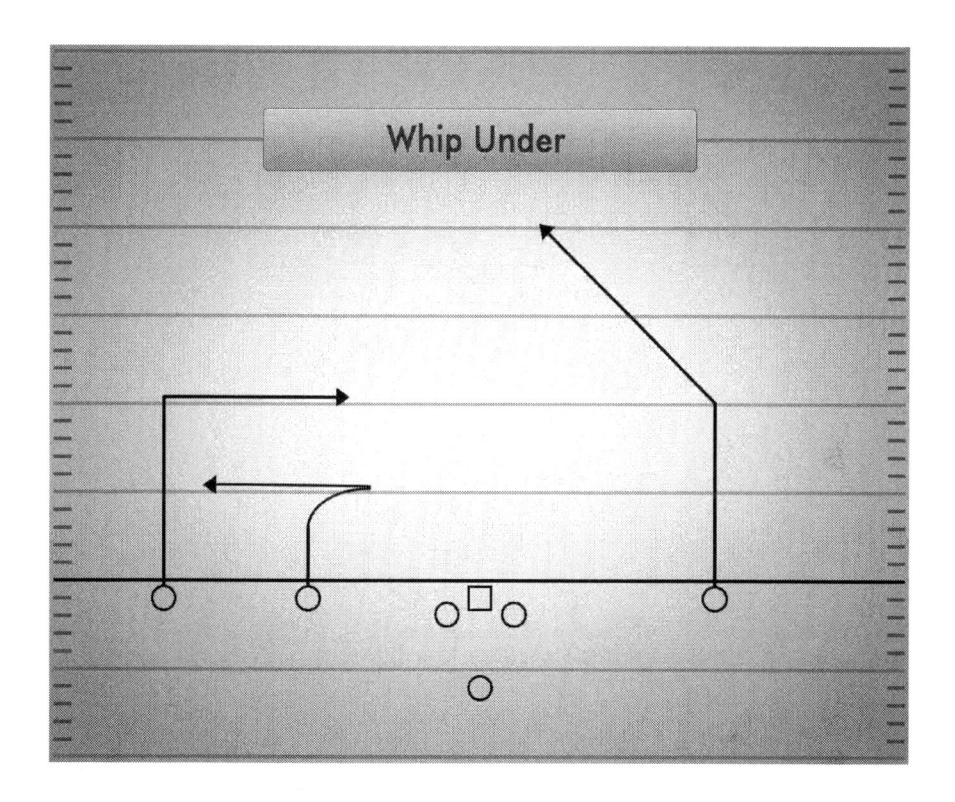

Whip Under

The Whip play is all about misdirection. The hard inside move gets the defense flowing inside, but the quick pivot outside is even more important for a quick move outside. If the inside receiver flowing underneath is covered up, then the outside receiver will be open coming inside over the top.

The Whip is best run in the second half of the game after setting up the defense with a sequence of successful slant plays. The defender will be ready to jump forward on the slant, but the wide out will plant hard and turn fast outside where he will be wide open running away from the defender.

FORMATION: **3-WIDE FORMATION**

DISTANCE: **SHORT YARDAGE, MEDIUM YARDAGE**

ROUTES IN THIS PLAY: **POST, IN, WHIP**

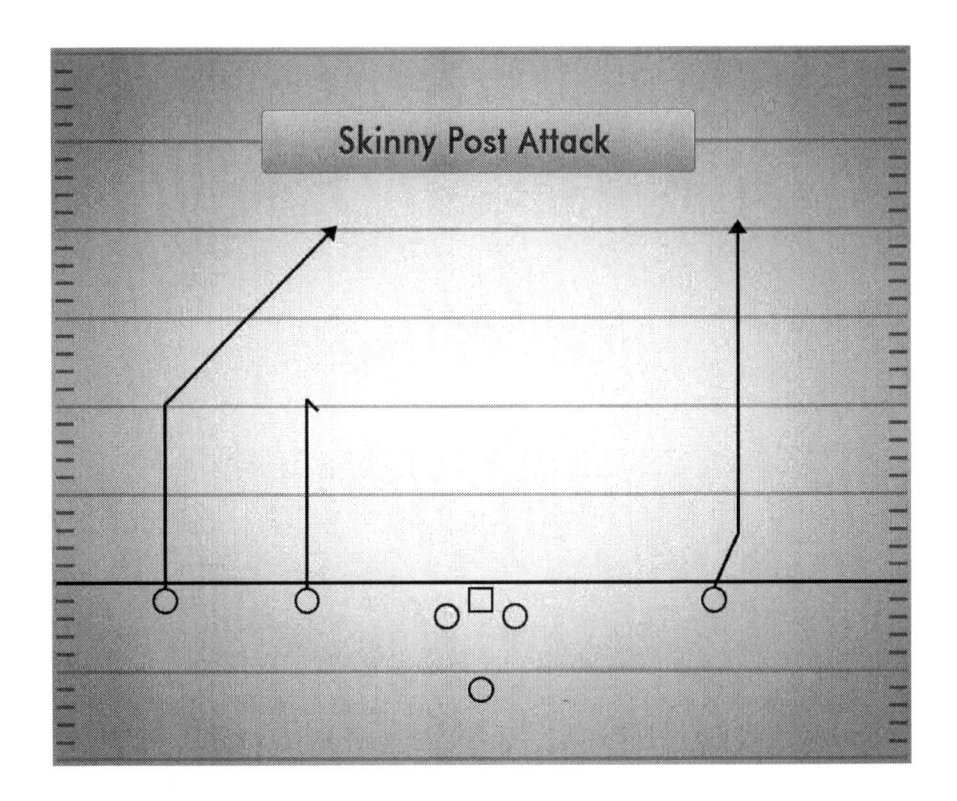

Skinny Post Attack

The Skinny Post Attack play requires special attention to detail. The main point of this play is to put the Safety in a tough situation by attacking his zone with two routes. The most critical route running in this play is the 10-yard Curl route, because it has to be run in a way that attracts the Safety's attention. If the slot receiver successfully gets the Safety to stay down and guard the curl, then the Post route will be wide open over the top.

If the Safety stays deep, however, then the Curl route needs to make sure that he is deep enough over the linebackers in order to be open 10-12 yards downfield. All in all, this play consists of a high/low read on the Safety by placing on route in the front of the Safety's zone, and the other over the top of the Safety's zone.

FORMATION: 3-WIDE FORMATION

DISTANCE: LONG YARDAGE, MEDIUM YARDAGE

ROUTES IN THIS PLAY: POST, FADE, STOP, CURL

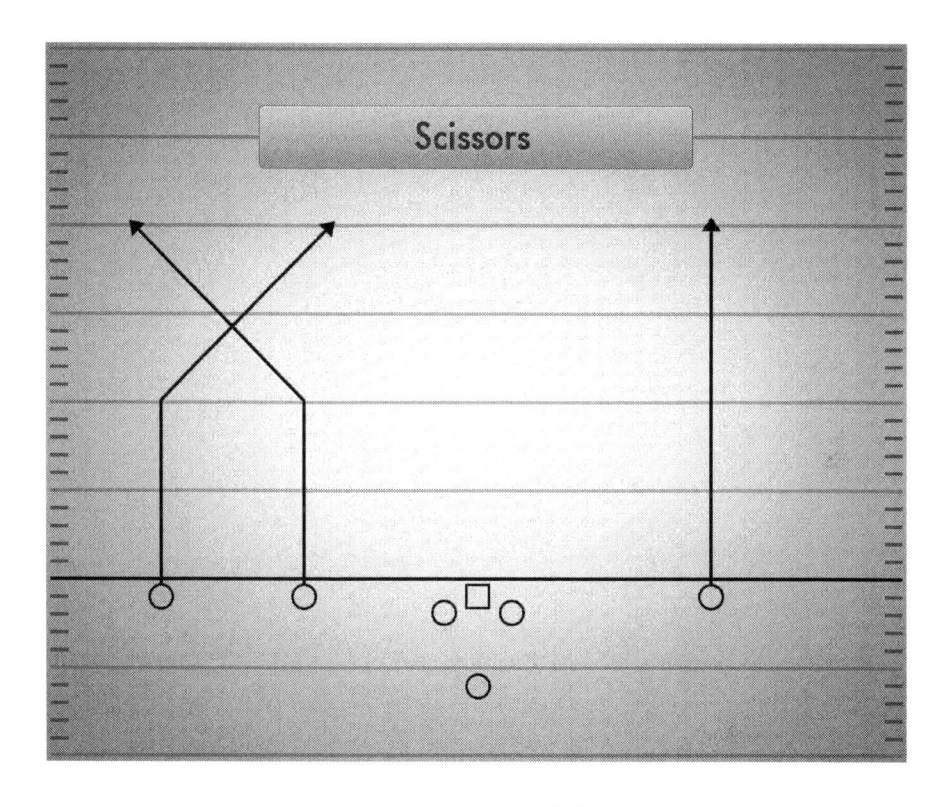

Scissors

Scissors is a great play to cut through the defensive secondary by converging two receivers across each other on one half of the field. The Post route goes over the top of the Corner route. The Post is the first read coming across the top, followed up by the Corner cutting through below.

The most important aspect of the play is that both routes run quickly up field at the same time and cut across each other simultaneously to wreak havoc on the downfield defenders.

FORMATION: **3-WIDE FORMATION**

DISTANCE: **LONG YARDAGE**

ROUTES IN THIS PLAY: **CORNER, POST, SHALLOW CROSS, STREAK**

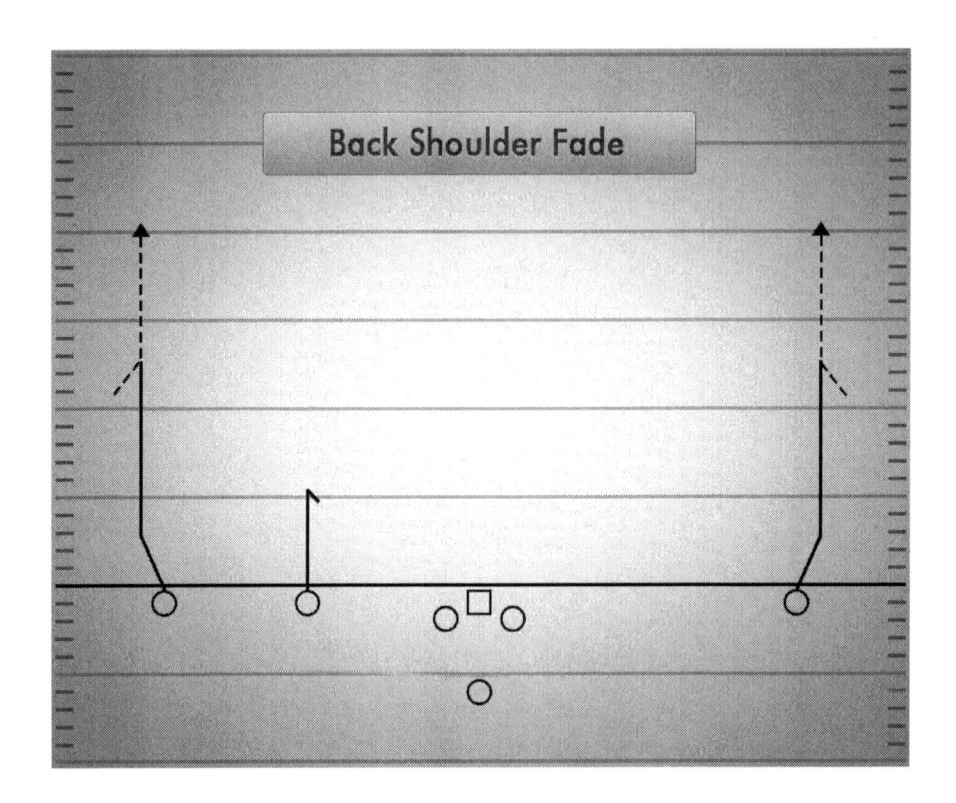

Back Shoulder Fade

The Back Shoulder fade is a go-to play for goal line situations. It gives the Receiver two options to choose from based upon how the defender guards him. If the Cornerback is guarding deep, then the Quarterback can throw the ball short, but if the Cornerback is play up close, then the Quarterback can throw the ball over the top.

Communication and chemistry between the Quarterback and the Receiver is of the utmost importance. Both the thrower and the route runner need to be on the same page to execute this play properly. Great chemistry will lead to great results on the Back Shoulder fade.

FORMATION: **3-WIDE FORMATION**

DISTANCE: **SHORT YARDAGE**

ROUTES IN THIS PLAY: **FADE, STOP**

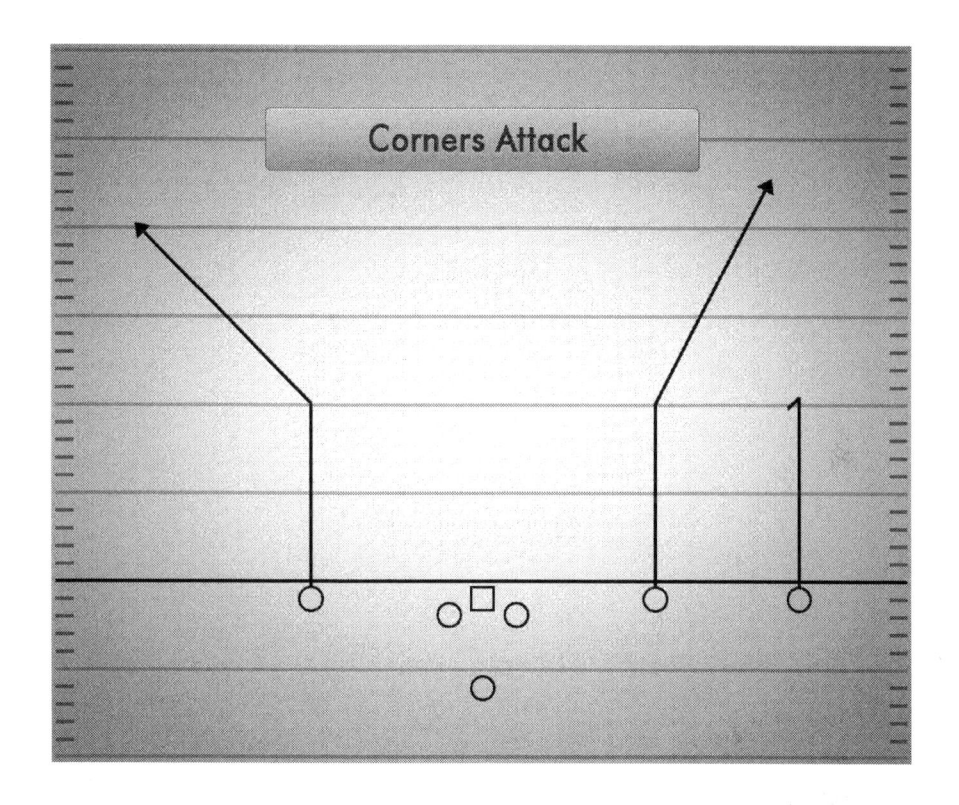

Corners Attack

Corners attack does just what its name says it does: Attack the Corners. The corner routes get depth into the corner of the defensive secondary, while the underneath routes wreak havoc in the flats. The slot receiver who runs the corner in combination with the 10-yard curl, has to make sure that he gets depth so that he is properly spaced over the top of the Curl route.

The Quarterback has to make a pre-snap decision on to select what side he wants to go to. Once that decision is made, read the Cornerback to see if he is staying on the deep corner, or cheating on the flat.

FORMATION: 3-WIDE FORMATION

DISTANCE: LONG YARDAGE

ROUTES IN THIS PLAY: CORNER, CURL, OUT

Ridge Force

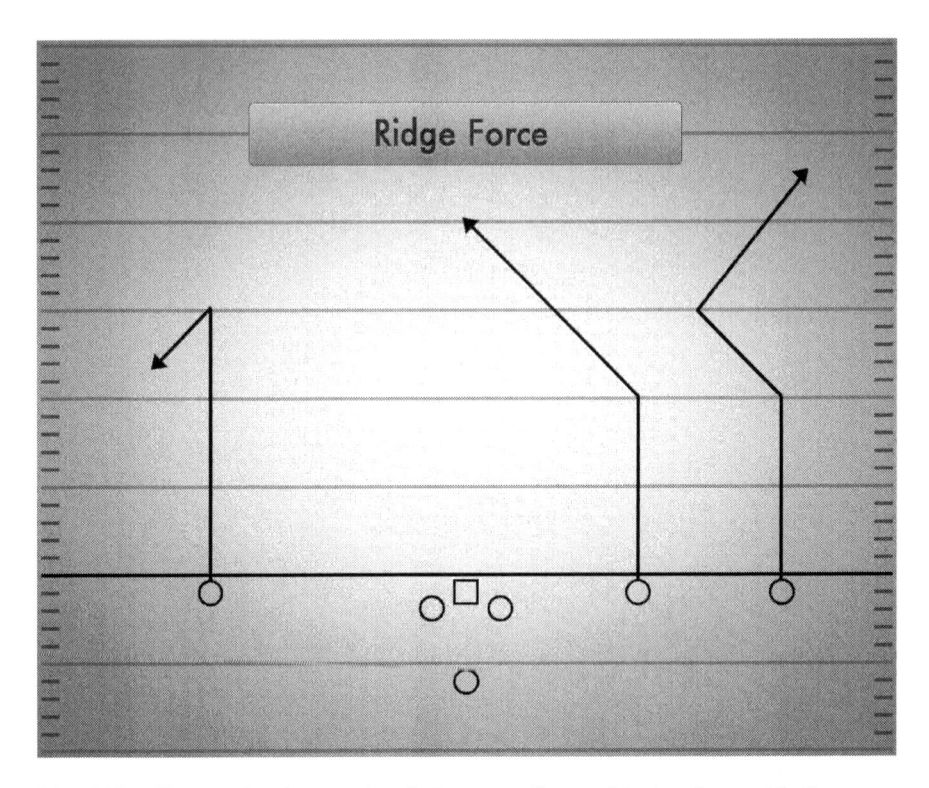

The Ridge Force play forces the defense to flow with the flow with the combination of the two post routes coming across the top ridge of the defensive secondary. Once the defenders start flowing with the combination of those routes, the outside receivers breaks hard to the outside on the Post Corner route.

The double move by the outside receiver will force the Safety into a hard decision if he is playing in a cover 2 zone, because he will be sitting right in the middle of two deep routes into his territory, but he can only choose to guard on of them.

If the defense is in a three deep formation and/or playing in a Cover three, then the QB will most likely want to drop down and hit the Comeback route on the other side of the field.

FORMATION: **3-WIDE FORMATION**

DISTANCE: **LONG YARDAGE**

ROUTES IN THIS PLAY: **POST, STOP, POST CORNER, COMEBACK**

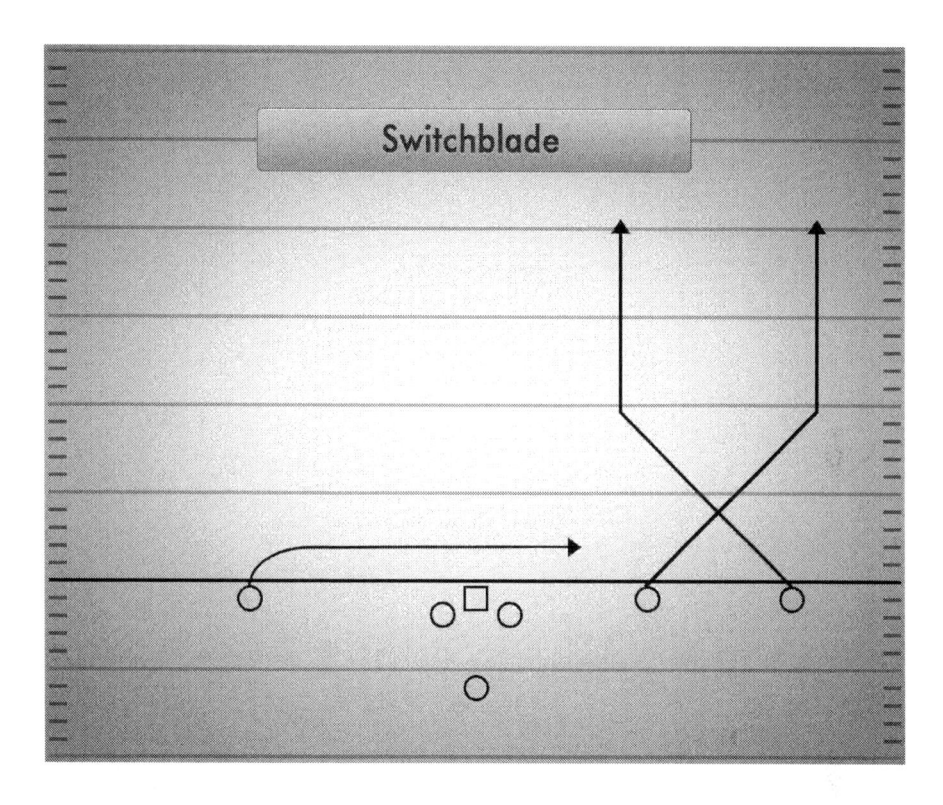

Switchblade

The Switchblade is a deadly combination route that cuts right through the defense by switching two receivers as they run their routes up field. A man-to-man defense will have trouble keeping up with both of the downfield receivers, and a zone defense will be thrown for a loop as the routes cut right through the zone.

The Quarterback has the option of cutting his losses if the deep routes aren't open, by checking down to the shallow cross underneath the switch route combination.

FORMATION: **3-WIDE FORMATION**

DISTANCE: **LONG YARDAGE**

ROUTES IN THIS PLAY: **POST, SHALLOW CROSS**

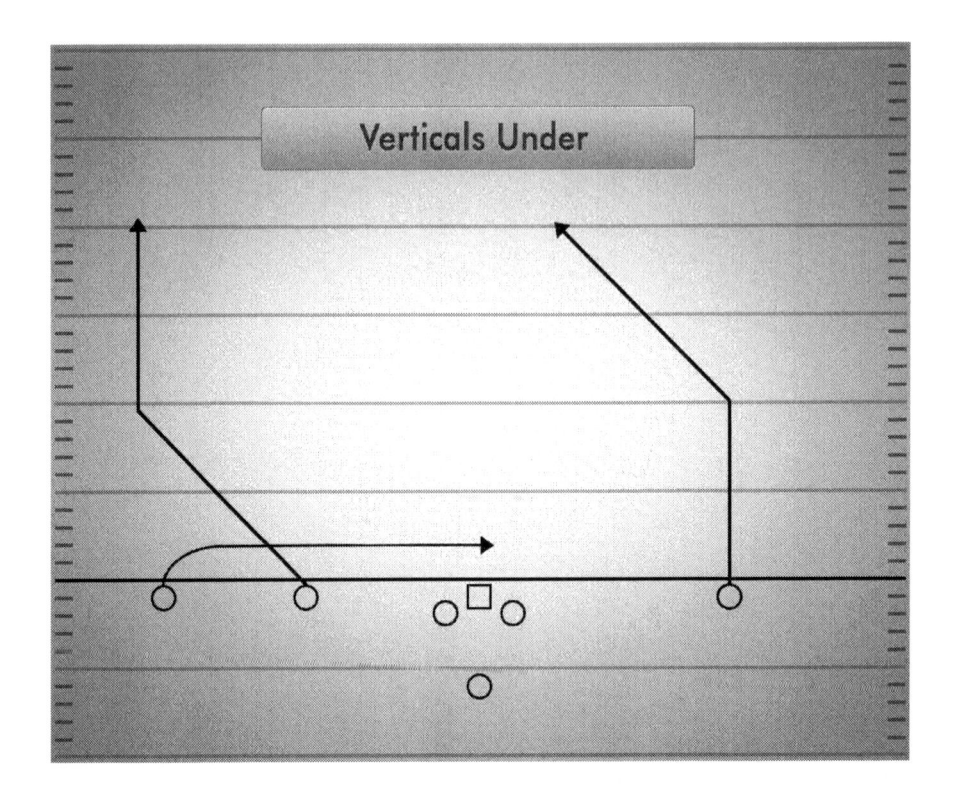

Verticals Under

The Verticals Under play sends the wide receivers up field in a shifted pattern that replaces the territory of the Receiver who is cutting underneath the Verticals.

By pushing the Vertical routes up field hard, it will distract the defense from the Shallow Cross coming underneath. Sometimes, however, the defense will lose track of the receiver taking the place of the underneath route, and he will be open down the sideline for a big gain.

FORMATION: **3-WIDE FORMATION**

DISTANCE: **SHORT YARDAGE, LONG YARDAGE**

ROUTES IN THIS PLAY: **SHALLOW CROSS, STREAK**

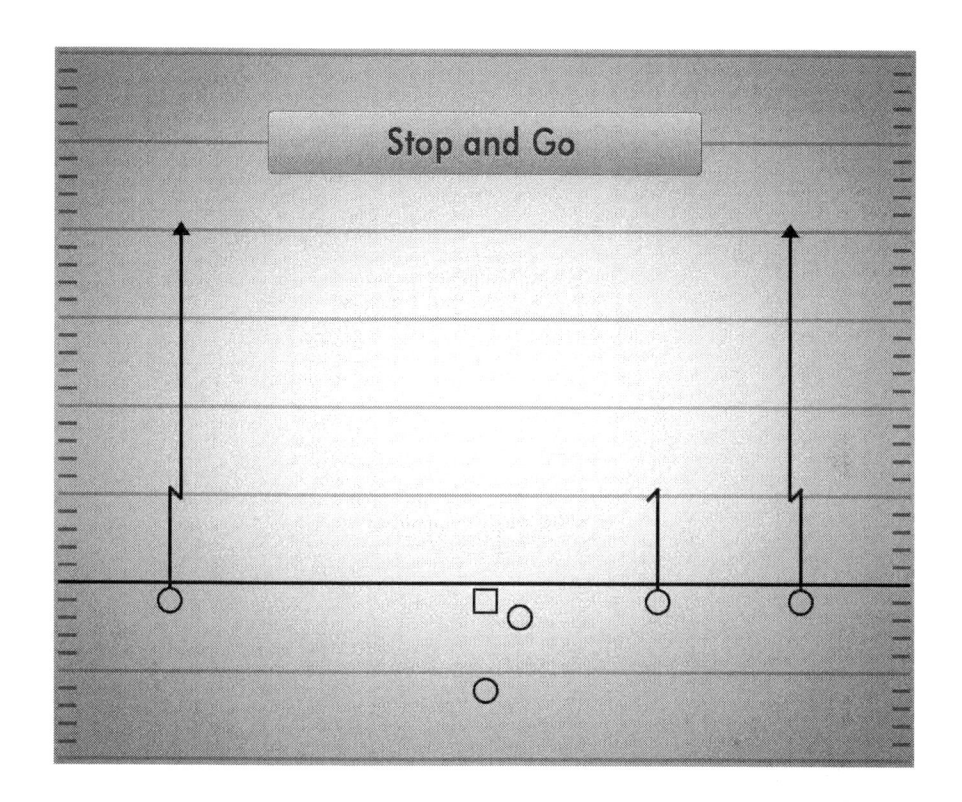

Stop and Go

The Stop and Go route is the most famous double move in all of football. The outside receiver will fake like he is running a 5 yard stop, but will twist and turn quickly up field.

It is imperative that the QB makes a good pump fake to sucker the defense in to jumping up on the short route. Once the pump fake is successfully completed, the QB must regather himself and get ready to throw the ball over the top of the defense to the receiver who is sprinting up field.

FORMATION: 3-WIDE FORMATION

DISTANCE: SHORT YARDAGE, LONG YARDAGE

ROUTES IN THIS PLAY: STOP

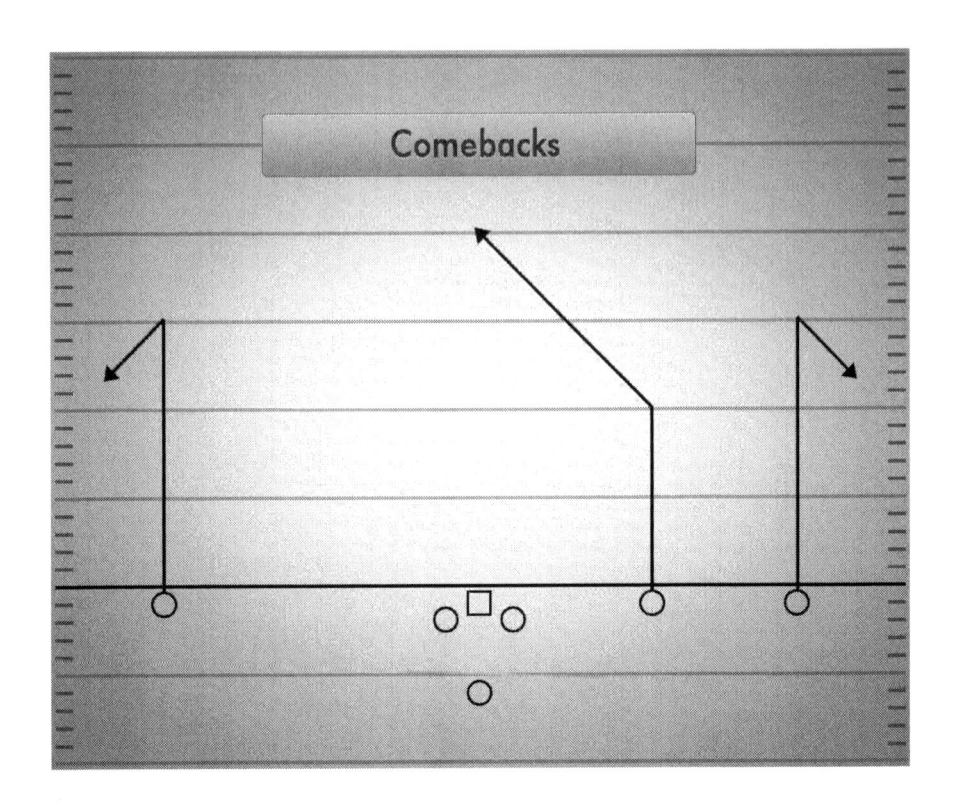

Comebacks

The Comeback route is a great route to run on a defense that is scared of getting beat deep. The way in which the Wide Receivers run the Comeback route is the most important part of the play. The WR will need to push up field hard as if he is running a Fade route or a Streak downfield. Once the defender is turned and running backwards, the WR needs to quickly turn around to the outside, as the QB plays a ball behind on the sideline.

After you scare the defense with the deep ball, the Comeback route is a great route to throw at them in order to pick up a chunk of yards.

FORMATION: **3-WIDE FORMATION**

DISTANCE: **MEDIUM YARDAGE**

ROUTES IN THIS PLAY: **POST, COMEBACK**

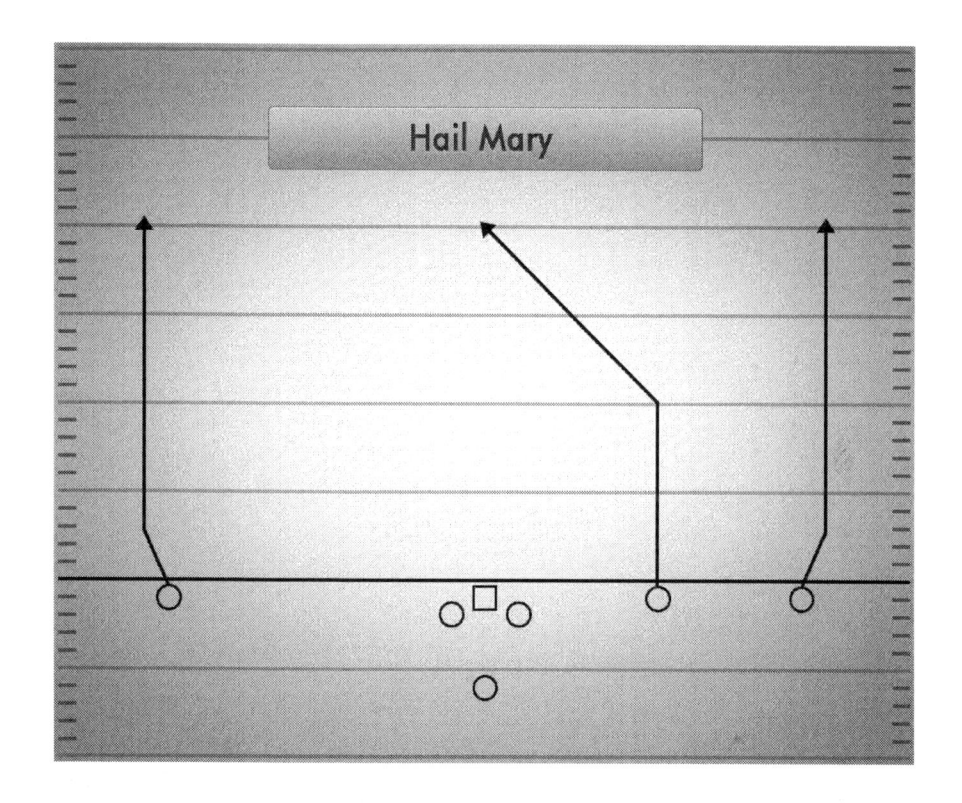

Hail Mary

Hail Mary time! You only need to pull out this play when you need a whole lot of yards all at once.

This version of the Hail Mary play is made to spread out the defense as much as possible, and potentially isolate a defender from the rest of his team. The Quarterback needs to find the WR who is able to get into a one-on-one match up and throw the ball up for a jump ball.

FORMATION: **3-WIDE FORMATION**

DISTANCE: **LONG YARDAGE**

ROUTES IN THIS PLAY: **POST, FADE**

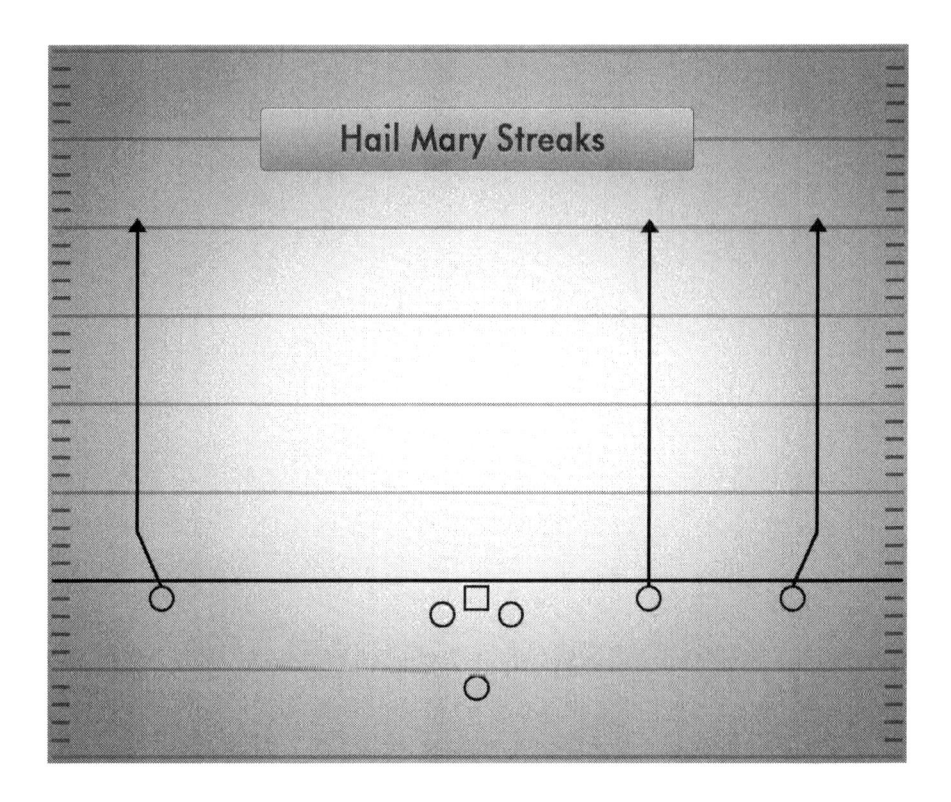

Hail Mary Streaks

Hail Mary time! You only need to pull out this play when you need a whole lot of yards all at once.

This version of the Hail Mary play simply send all the receivers downfield in a straight line in order to get as deep as possible, as fast as possible. Throw the ball up deep and hope for the best.

FORMATION: **3-WIDE FORMATION**

DISTANCE: **LONG YARDAGE**

ROUTES IN THIS PLAY: **STREAK**

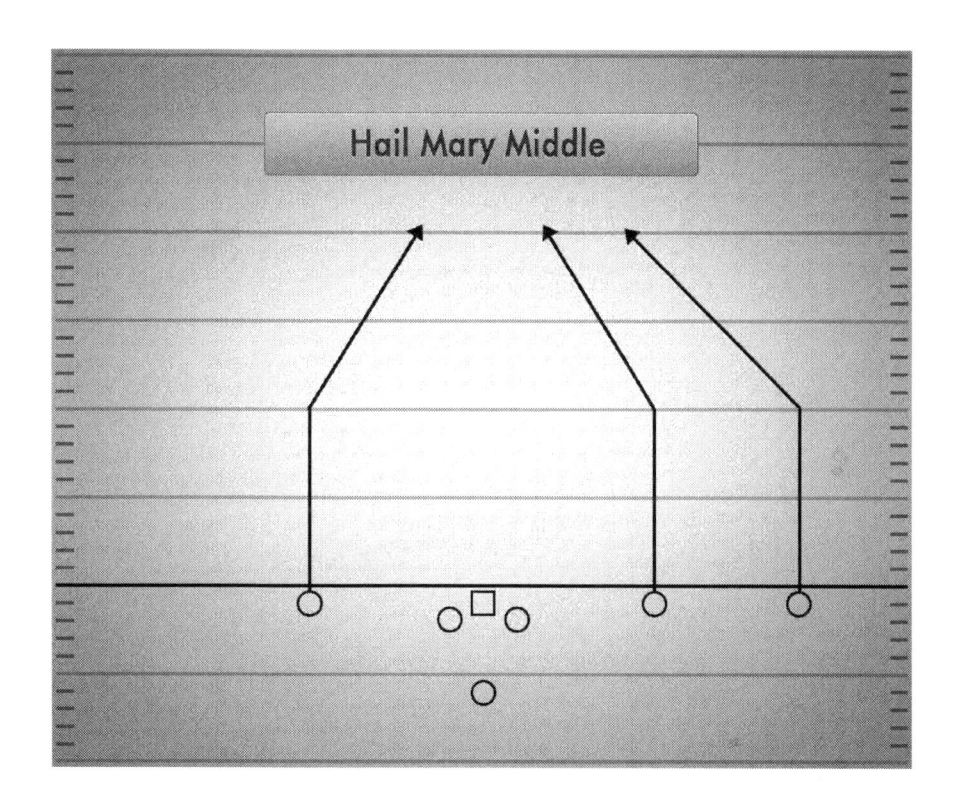

Hail Mary Middle

Hail Mary time! You only need to pull out this play when you need a whole lot of yards all at once.

This version of the Hail Mary play puts all your eggs in one basket by sending every Receiver to the middle of the field. Once all the Receivers are in position, the only thing left for the Quarterback to do is throw the ball as high as he can right into the middle of the field and hope that one of his own players comes down with it.

FORMATION: **3-WIDE FORMATION**

DISTANCE: **LONG YARDAGE**

ROUTES IN THIS PLAY: **POST**

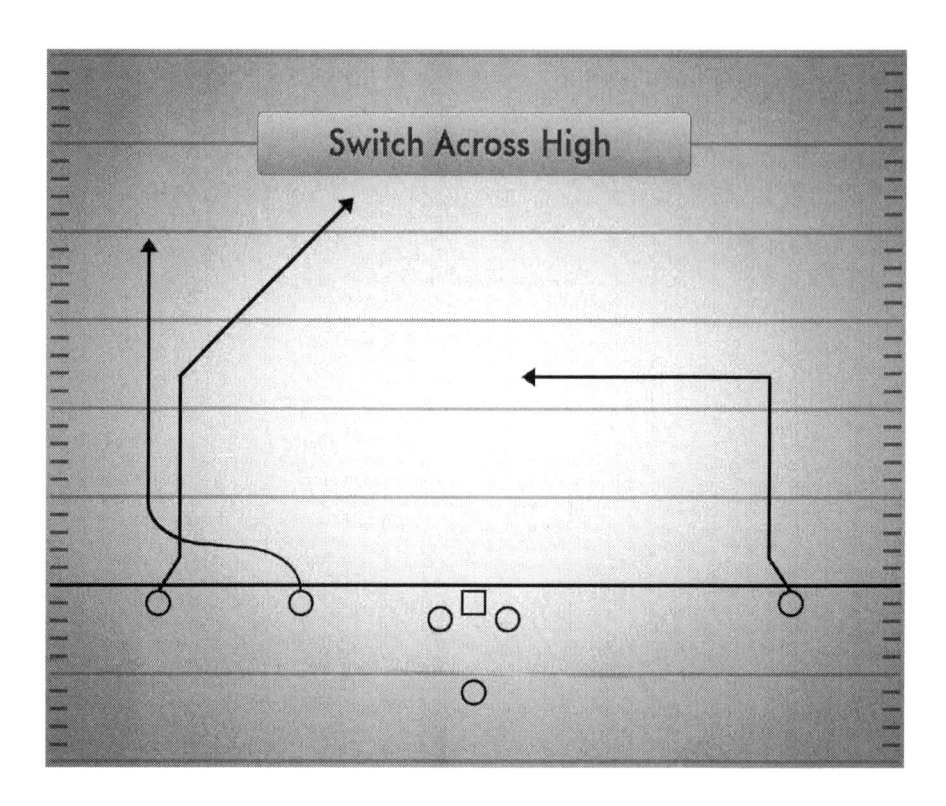

Switch Across High

This is the deeper variation of the Switch Across Low play. The key to this play is creating confusion for the defense at the very start of the play by having the receivers switch across each other on the way to their destination. This switch makes it hard for a zone defense to keep track of all the routes, and makes it very difficult for a man-to-man defense to keep up with the receiver amongst all the chaos going on.

FORMATION: **3-WIDE FORMATION**

DISTANCE: **LONG YARDAGE**

ROUTES IN THIS PLAY: **POST, IN, WHEEL**

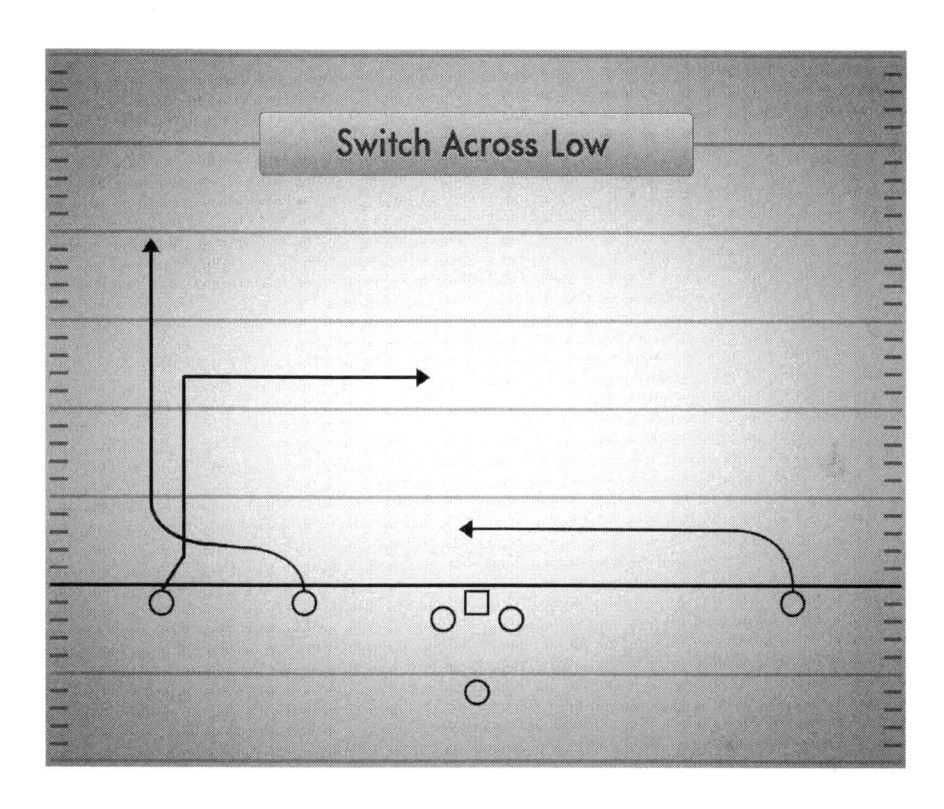

Switch Across Low

This is the shorter variation of the Switch Across High play. The key to this play is creating confusion for the defense at the very start of the play by having the receivers switch across each other on the way to their destination. This switch makes it hard for a zone defense to keep track of all the routes, and makes it very difficult for a man-to-man defense to keep up with the receiver amongst all the chaos going on.

FORMATION: **3-WIDE FORMATION**

DISTANCE: **SHORT YARDAGE, MEDIUM YARDAGE**

ROUTES IN THIS PLAY: **IN, SHALLOW CROSS, WHEEL**

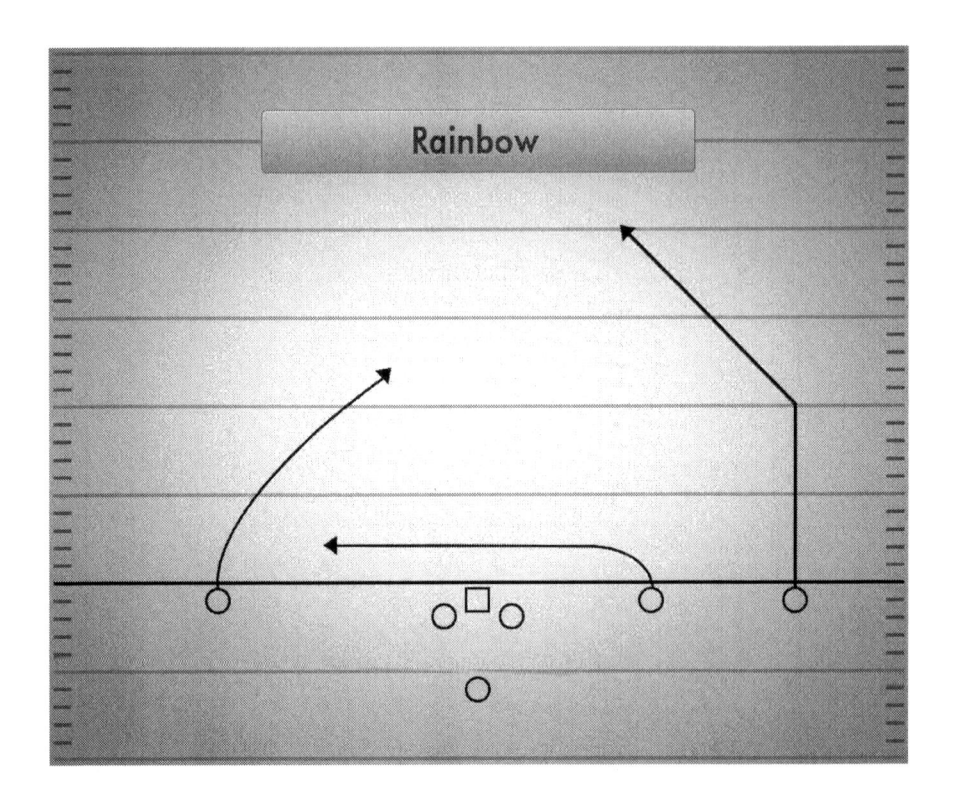

Rainbow

The Rainbow play allows the Wide Receivers to attack the defense by running arcs all across the middle of the field. Each arc is run at a different level of the defense, therefore, combining to create a Rainbow of manly intensity.

The Quarterback can choose to either read the arcs from low to high, or progress from high to low. Finding at least one open man in the Rainbow should be easy with so many routes hitting different levels in the middle of the field.

FORMATION: **3-WIDE FORMATION**

DISTANCE: **SHORT YARDAGE, LONG YARDAGE, MEDIUM YARDAGE**

ROUTES IN THIS PLAY: **POST, SHALLOW CROSS**

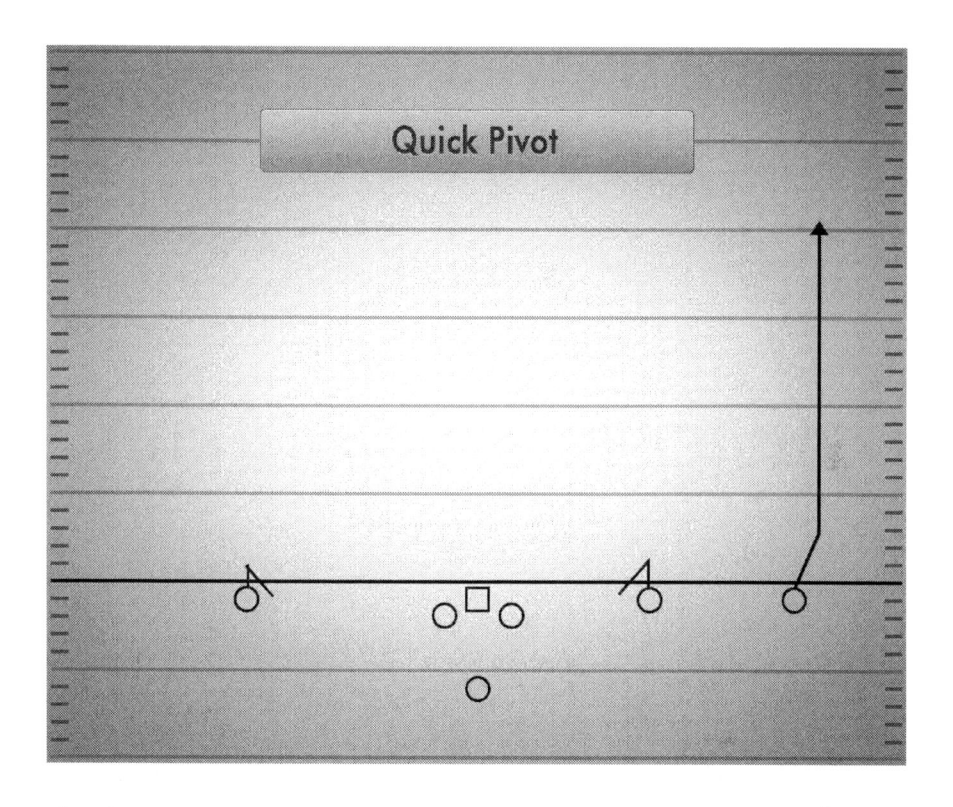

Quick Pivot

The Quick Pivot play is meant to be used as a play against a defense that is backing up off the line of scrimmage. If they are giving too much space to the Wide Receivers, then hit them with this quick pass to catch them off guard. If the Quarterback makes a quick throw to the Receiver, it will give the Receiver a chance to run with the ball in the open field and try to make a defender miss.

It is important that the Receivers push hard off the line of scrimmage for the first few steps, so that the defenders aren't immediately keyed into the fact that it is going to be a quick pass right at the line of scrimmage.

FORMATION: **3-WIDE FORMATION**

DISTANCE: **SHORT YARDAGE**

ROUTES IN THIS PLAY: **FADE**

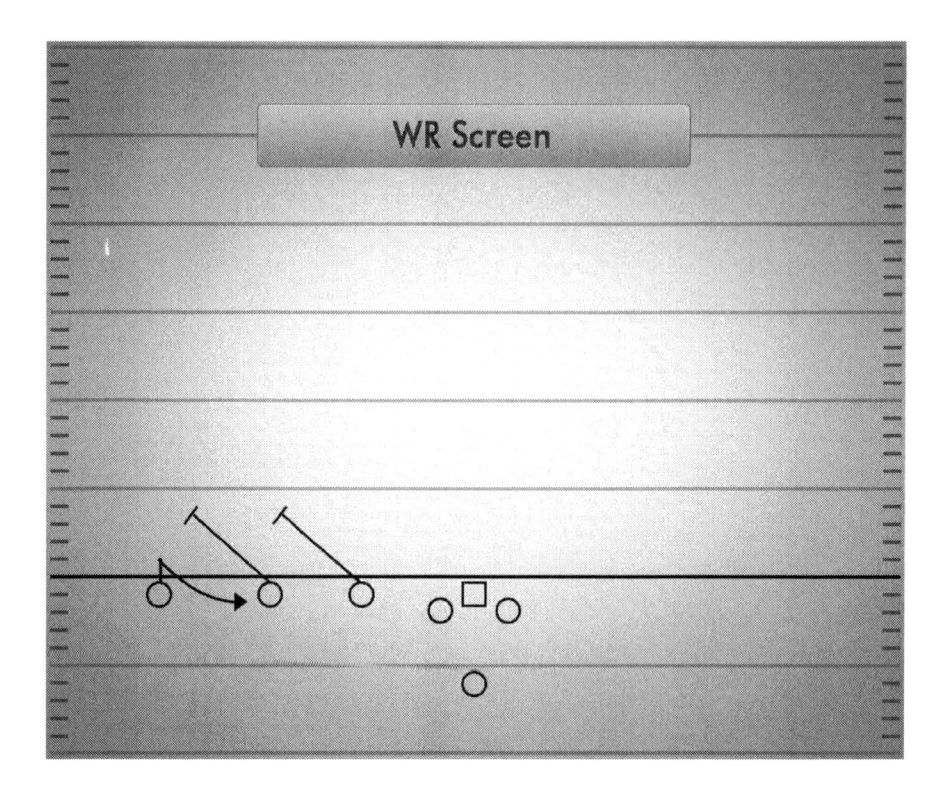

WR Screen

The WR Screen is a play that utilizes blocking by the inside Receivers to enable a running lane for the outside Receiver. The Wide Receiver running the screen route needs to push up field hard for two steps, and the quickly turn around for the ball. Timing is critical on the throw.

The inside Receiver needs to explode of the line of scrimmage directly at the guy who is guarding the outside Receiver. Once that defender turns around, quickly get in his way for the block, and the Receiver catching the screen will be off to the races.

FORMATION: **3-WIDE FORMATION**

DISTANCE: **SHORT YARDAGE**

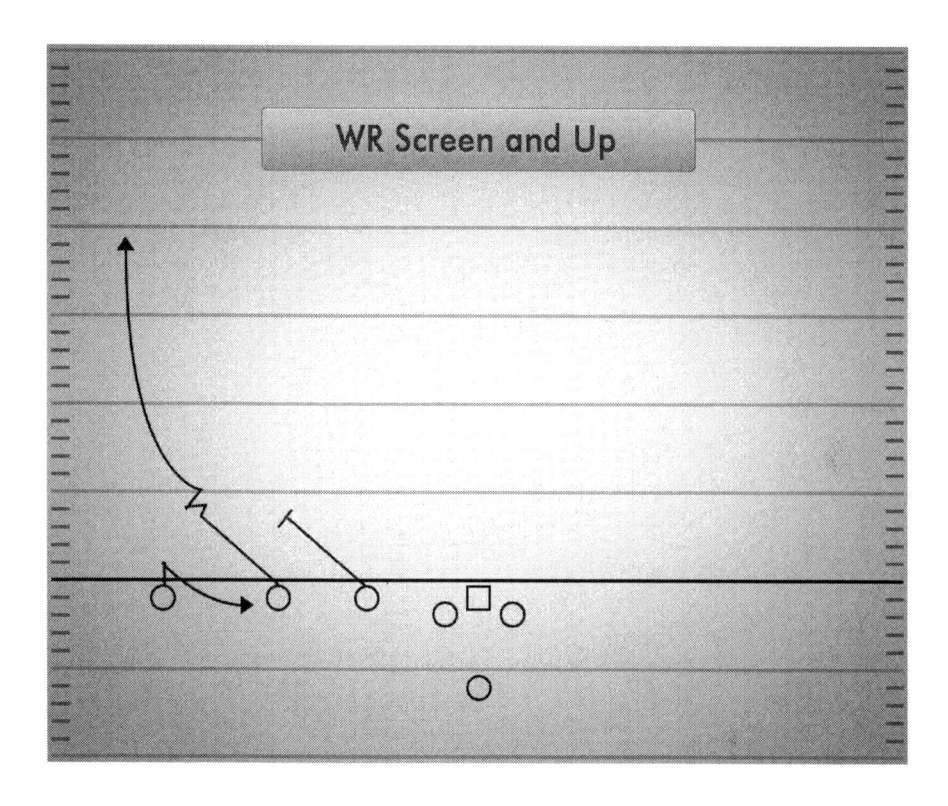

WR Screen and Up

The WR Screen and Up play is a great trick play that takes some time to set up. You have to run the WR Screen play beforehand, and run it successfully. If you begin to hurt them with the Screen, then the defense will start to sneak up forward, and that is when you hit them with the Screen and Up.

The most important aspect of performing this play is the way in which the Wide Receiver fakes his block. He has to run out to the Cornerback as if he is going to block him, and as soon as the Cornerback makes a move to avoid the block, the Receiver then turns on the jets and runs up the sideline. The defense won't even know what hit them until the ball is flying over all their heads.

FORMATION: **3-WIDE FORMATION**

DISTANCE: **LONG YARDAGE**

Slot Choice

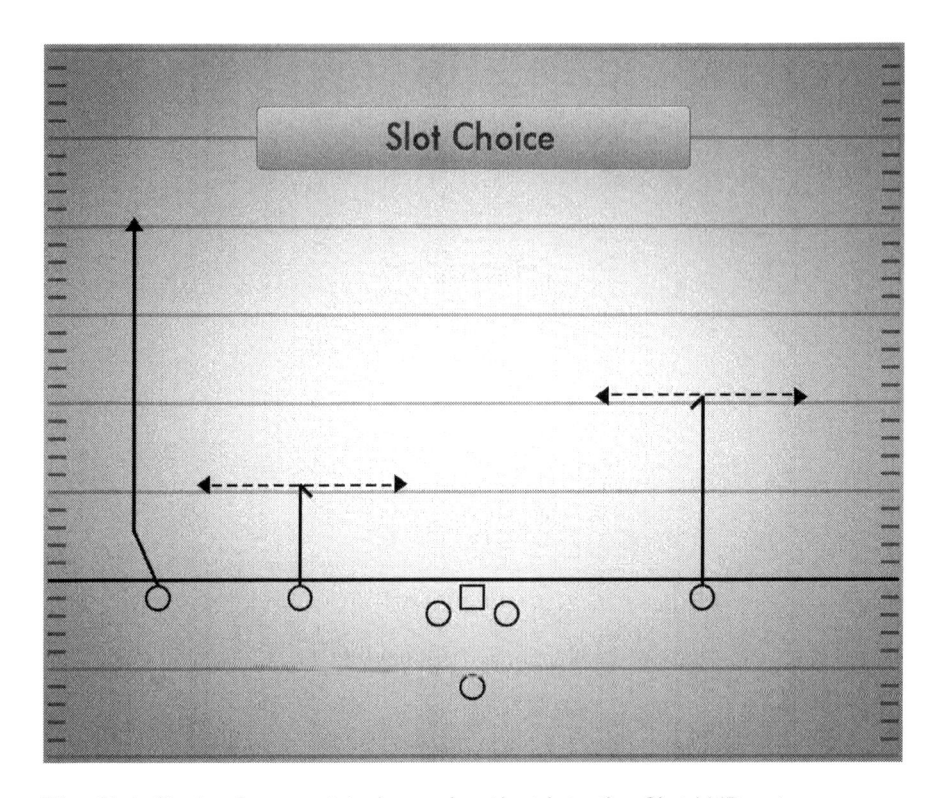

The Slot Choice is meant to be a play that lets the Slot WR get open, no matter what the defense does. The Choice route will either get to its mark and turn around for a stop in place, or it will jet out to the outside, or cut in to the inside.

If the defender is playing inside, then the WR should jet to the outside. If the defender is playing outside, then the WR should jet to the inside. If the defense is playing in a zone, and is giving the WR some space, then the WR should just settle down and wait for the ball.

The Quarterback needs to have great chemistry with the WR so that they are on the same wavelength and can be expecting each other to make the same read.

FORMATION: **3-WIDE FORMATION**

DISTANCE: **SHORT YARDAGE, MEDIUM YARDAGE**

ROUTES IN THIS PLAY: **IN, STREAK, STOP, OUT**

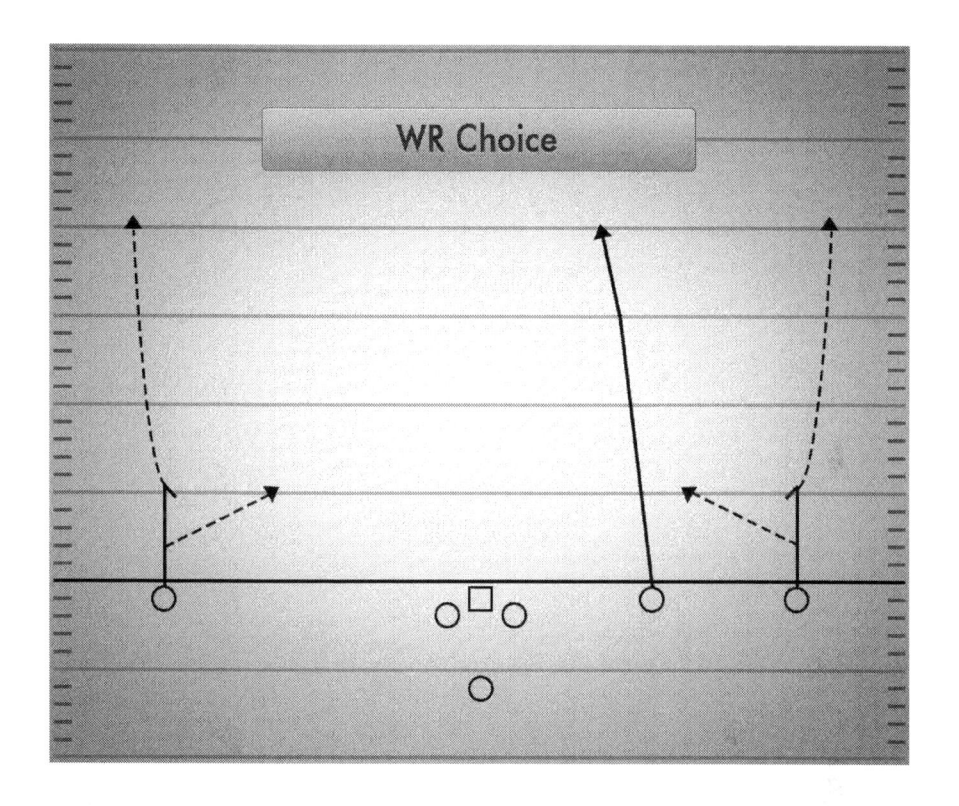

WR Choice

The WR Choice is meant to be a play that lets the Outside WR get open, no matter what the defense does. If the defender is playing inside, then the WR should run up the sideline on a fade. If the defender is playing outside, then the WR should jet to the inside on a slant. If the defense is giving the WR some space, then the WR should just settle down and wait for the ball on a stop route.

The Quarterback needs to have great chemistry with the WR so that they are on the same wavelength and can be expecting each other to make the same read.

FORMATION: 3-WIDE FORMATION

DISTANCE: SHORT YARDAGE, LONG YARDAGE, MEDIUM YARDAGE

ROUTES IN THIS PLAY: FADE, STOP, SLANT, SEAM

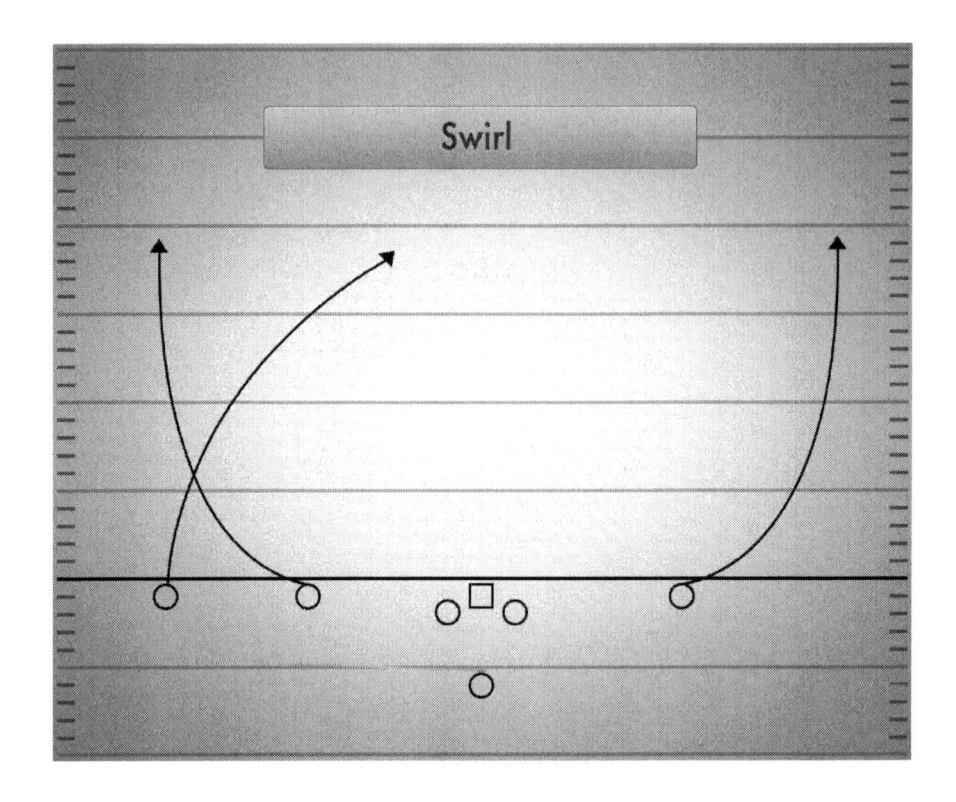

Swirl

The Swirl plays send the defense in a whirlwind by swirling the routes all around across the field. Unlike most plays, there are hardly no straight lines in the route patterns, as all the Wide Receivers are swirling their routes to get to their destination.

The switching and swirling pattern will make it hard for a man defense to keep up, and difficult for a zone defense to keep track.

FORMATION: **3-WIDE FORMATION**

DISTANCE: **LONG YARDAGE**

ROUTES IN THIS PLAY: **POST, WHEEL**

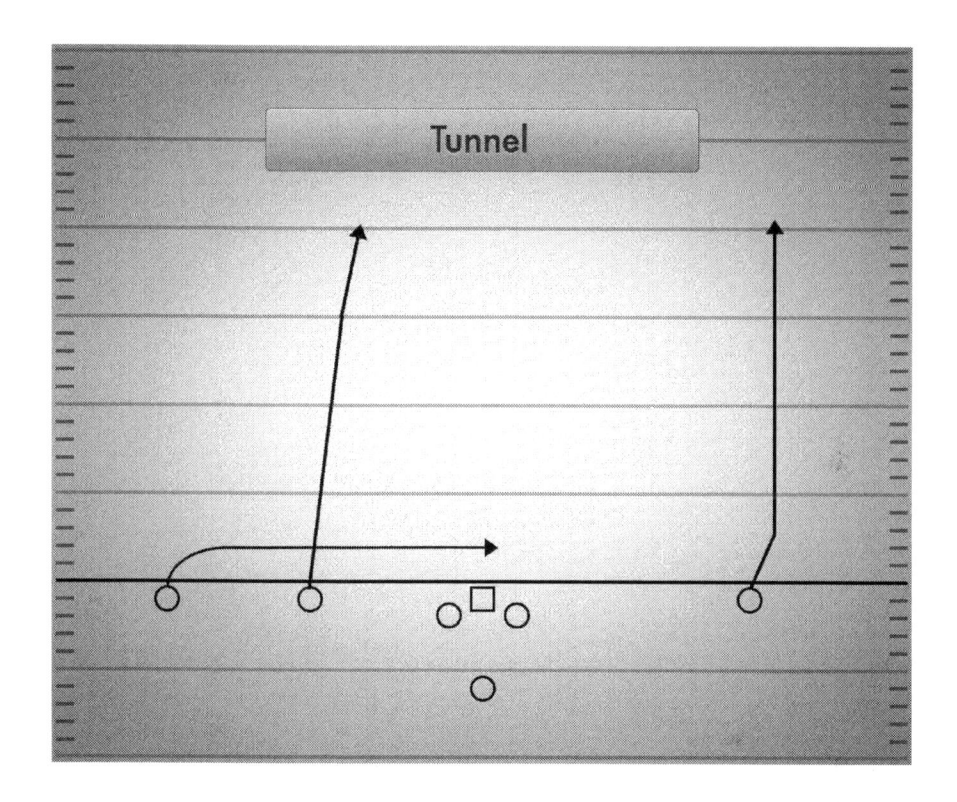

The Tunnel play might look like a deep play when drawn up, but it is really meant to be a play thrown to the Shallow Cross route that is "tunneling" underneath.

The other receivers are used primarily to run off the defense and take all the defenders deep downfield with them. After the defense has backed off, the shallow cross route should be open and have tons of room to run after the catch.

FORMATION: **3-WIDE FORMATION**

DISTANCE: **SHORT YARDAGE**

ROUTES IN THIS PLAY: **SHALLOW CROSS, FADE, SEAM**

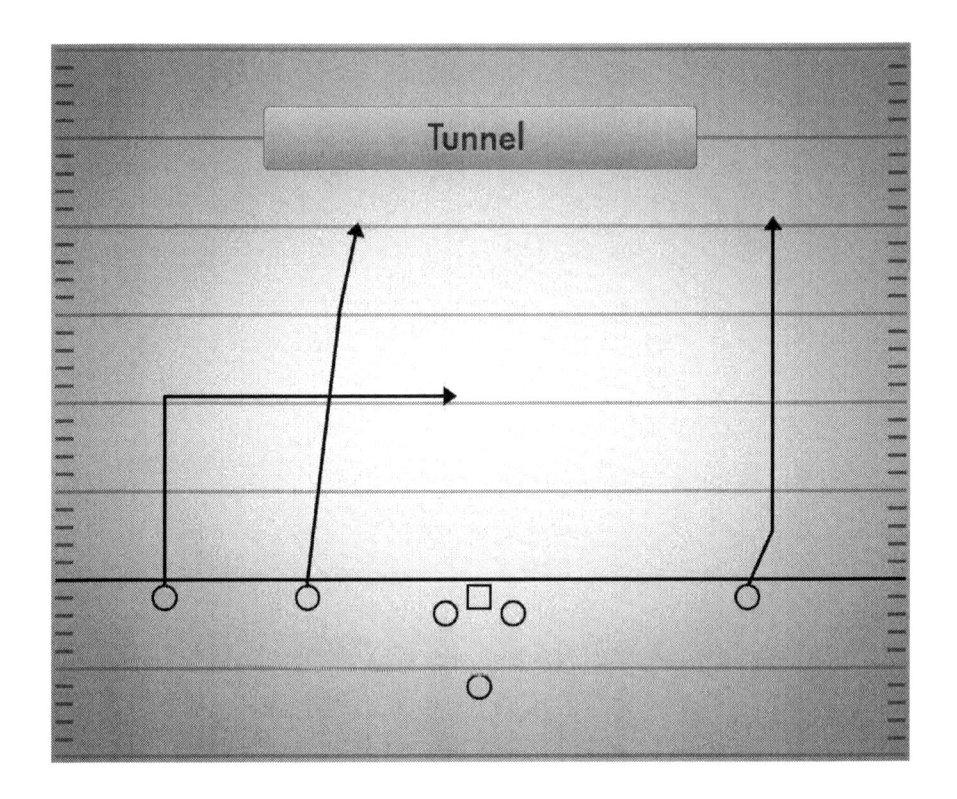

Tunnel

The primary focus of the Tunnel Deep play is to make the defense think that everybody is going deep, and then break off the outside receiver, and hit him coming across the field underneath the deep routes.

The other receivers are used primarily to run off the defense and take all the defenders deep downfield with them. After the defense has backed off, the In route should be open and have tons of room to run after the catch.

FORMATION: **3-WIDE FORMATION**

DISTANCE: **LONG YARDAGE**

ROUTES IN THIS PLAY: **IN, FADE, SEAM**

Post Corner

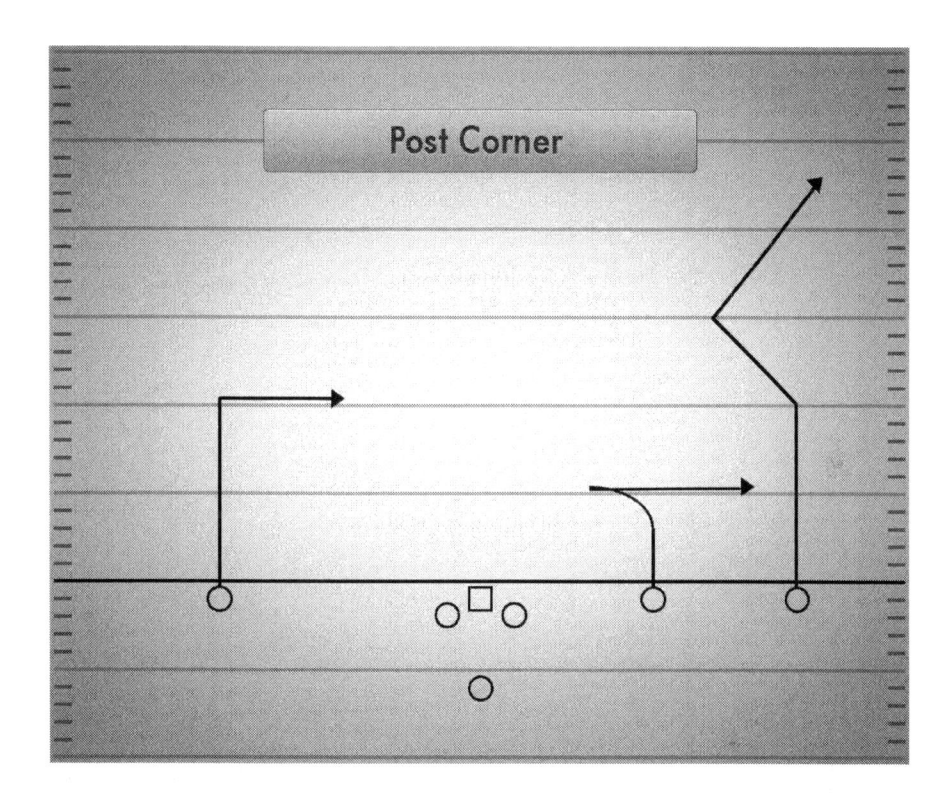

This play is all about setting up the Post-Corner route on the outside. The Receiver running the route has to make it look as if he is running the post, and as soon as he suckers the defense inside, he breaks to the outside and the Quarterback will hit him deep along the sideline.

The Whip route underneath, is used to keep the Cornerback from drifting back towards the Post-Corner. If the Cornerback does carry back deep and get in the way of the Post-Corner, then the Whip route should be open in the flats underneath.

FORMATION: **3-WIDE FORMATION**

DISTANCE: **LONG YARDAGE, MEDIUM YARDAGE**

ROUTES IN THIS PLAY: **IN, WHIP, POST CORNER**

Bubble

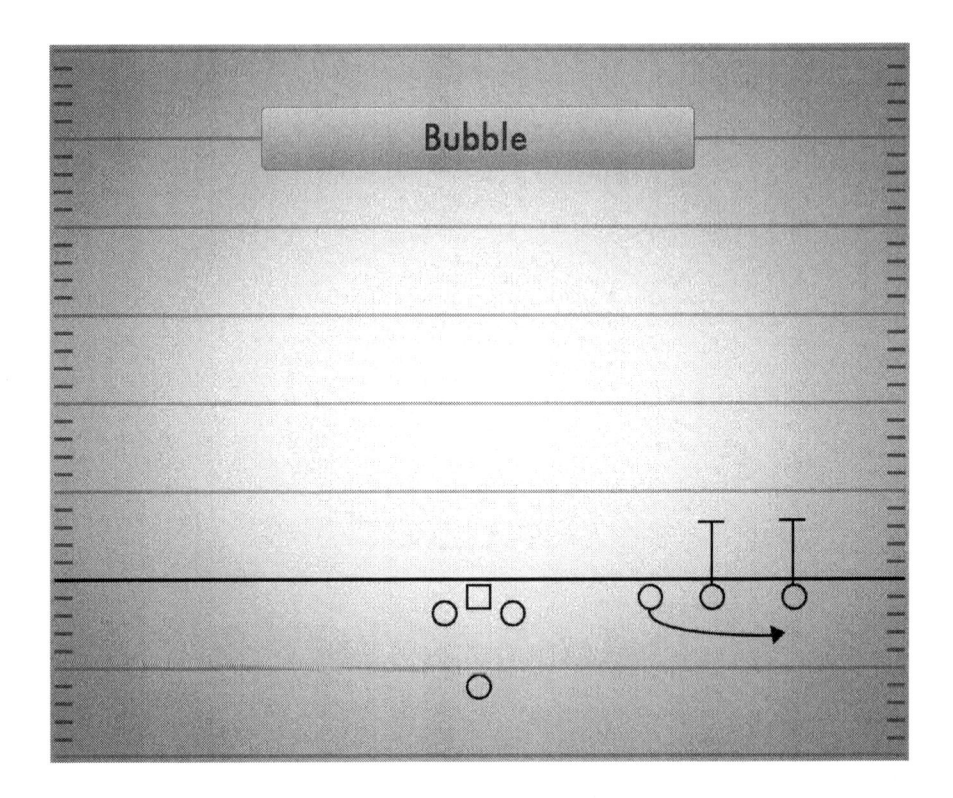

The Bubble play is a simple screen play. The Slot WR will bubble backwards with one step and proceed to drift towards the sideline. The block by the outside WR is critical to the success of the play.

Once the Quarterback delivers the ball the WR will read the block of the outside WR and sprint up the sideline.

FORMATION: **3-WIDE FORMATION**

DISTANCE: **SHORT YARDAGE**

Bubble WR Pass

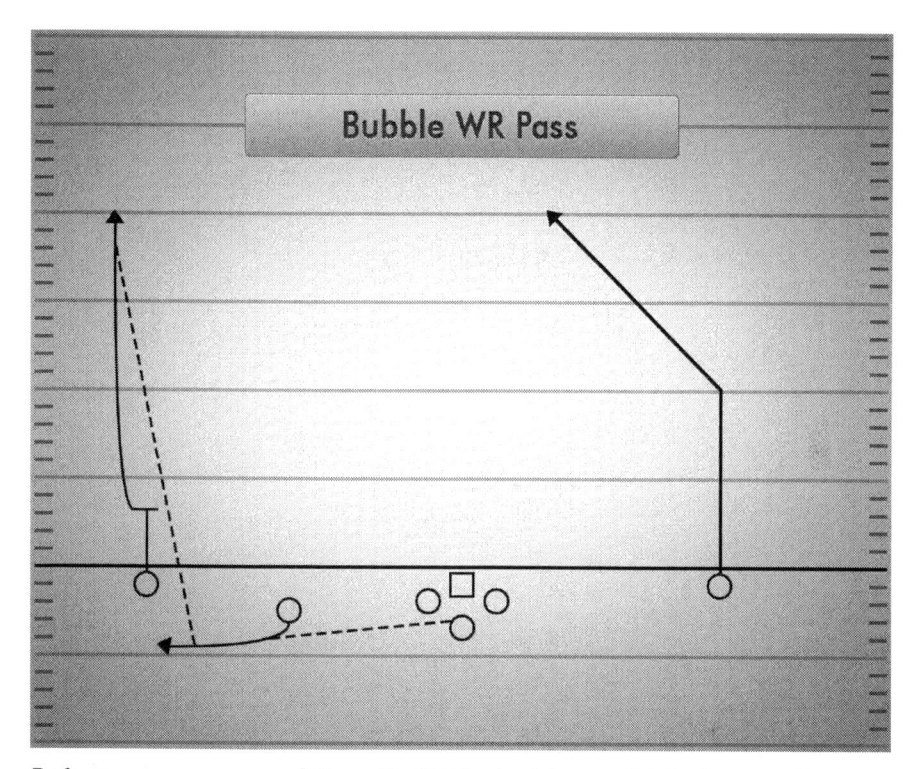

Before you can successfully pull off this double pass trick play, you first need to set it up with the normal Bubble play. After the defense is begins to cheat forward to guard the bubble, that's when you hit them with this Bubble WR Pass play.

The outside WR has to act as if he is going to block the defender like he normally does on the Bubble play, but as soon as he approaches, he needs to sidestep away and start jetting up the sideline. The inside WR needs to make a clean catch and quickly throw it over the defense to the WR who will be open downfield.

One key aspect of this play is that you have to remember that the first throw from the Quarterback has to be backwards, or else the second throw will be illegal. Therefore, the QB should scoot up a bit more than usual, and the WR should line up a little further back than usual, but both have to be done without making it obvious.

FORMATION: **3-WIDE FORMATION**

DISTANCE: **LONG YARDAGE**

ROUTES IN THIS PLAY: **POST**

Hook and Ladder

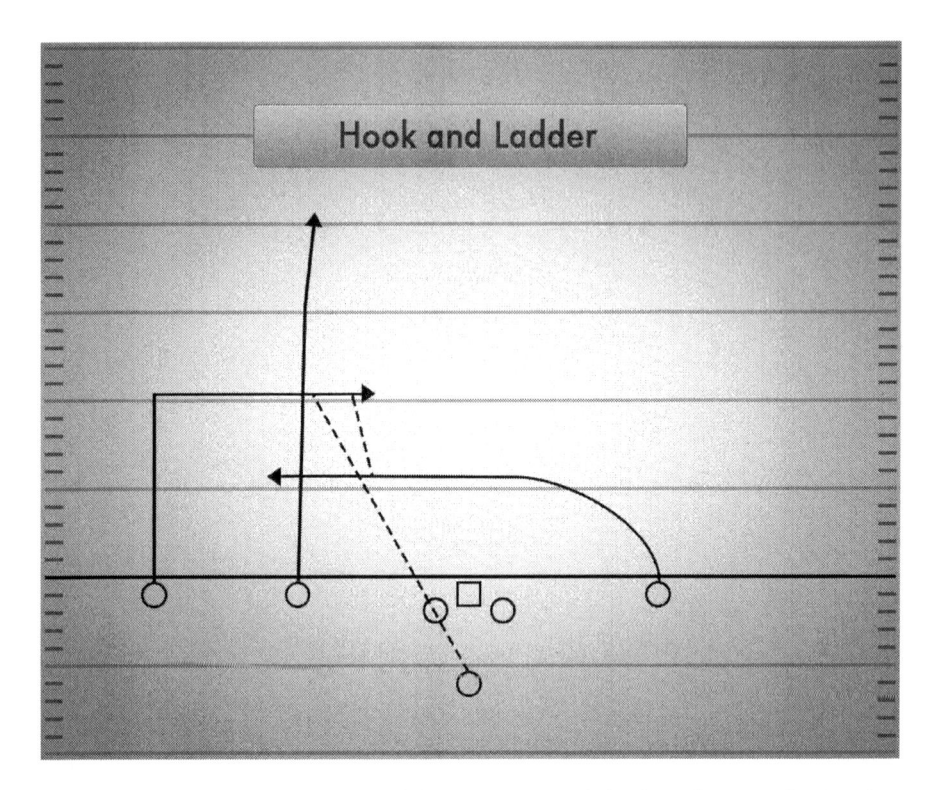

The Hook and Ladder is one of the greatest trick plays in any playbook. It involves incredible timing and perfectly performed maneuvers by multiple individuals, but can be a phenomenally successful play when all the moving parts come together correctly.

The QB must deliver the throw to the In route before he gets too far across the field. The WR running the Shallow Cross must time his crossing route so that he is running underneath the In route immediately after he catches the ball. Once caught, the In route has to quickly secure the ball, and then pitch it backwards to the shallow crosser. The defense will have been moving inwards towards the original receiver, and will be caught off guard when the shallow crosser receives the pitch and is sprinting outward towards the sideline.

FORMATION: **3-WIDE FORMATION**

DISTANCE: **LONG YARDAGE**

ROUTES IN THIS PLAY: **IN, SHALLOW CROSS, SEAM**

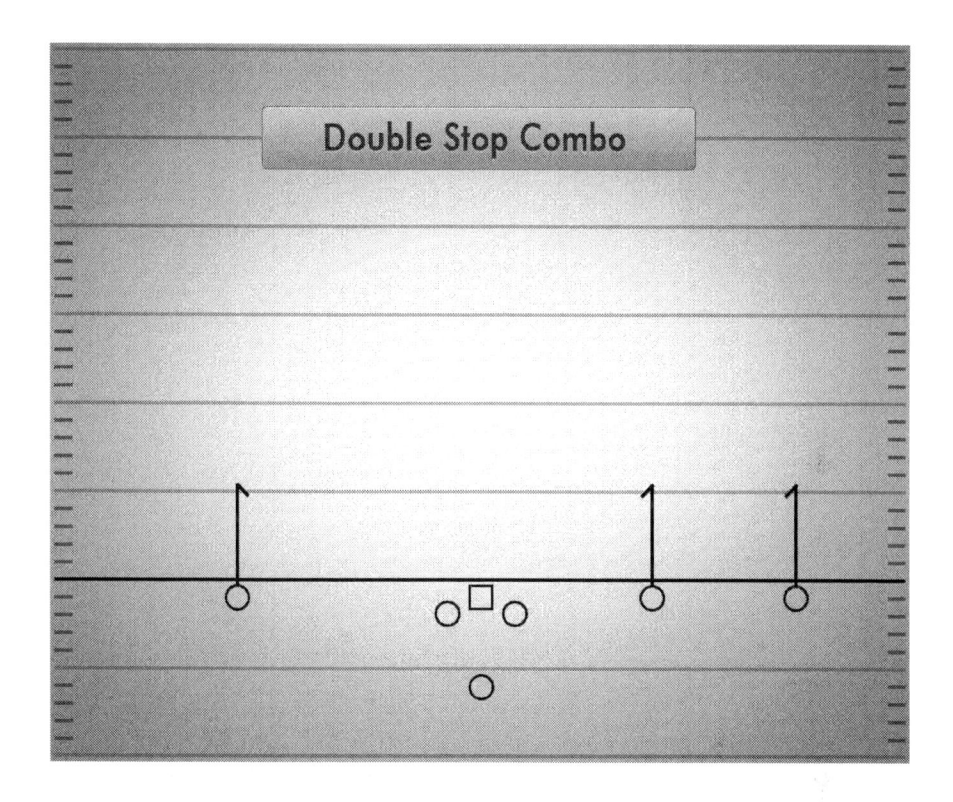

Double Stop Combo

The Double Stop Combo is one of the most fundamental plays of any spread offense passing tree. A simple route concept that quickly presents all the Wide Receivers on a quick 5-yard stop route.

This play can be called early in the game in order to help the QB get settled in, or it can be called in response to a defense that is playing far off the line of scrimmage.

FORMATION: **3-WIDE FORMATION**

DISTANCE: **SHORT YARDAGE**

ROUTES IN THIS PLAY: **STOP**

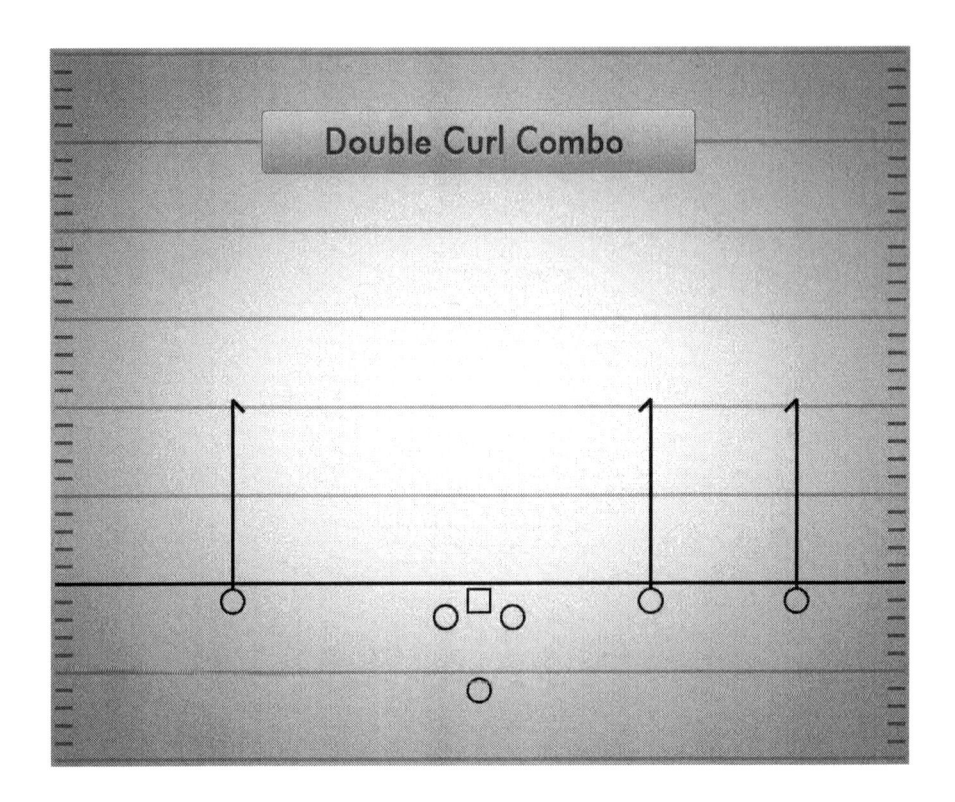

Double Curl Combo

The Double Curl Combo is an extended version of the Double Stop Combo play. It is a simple play for Medium Yardage.

Each Wide Receiver presses hard upfield for ten yards and quickly turns around, orienting their bodies toward the Quarterback who then takes his pick at the open man.

FORMATION: **3-WIDE FORMATION**

DISTANCE: **MEDIUM YARDAGE**

ROUTES IN THIS PLAY: **CURL**

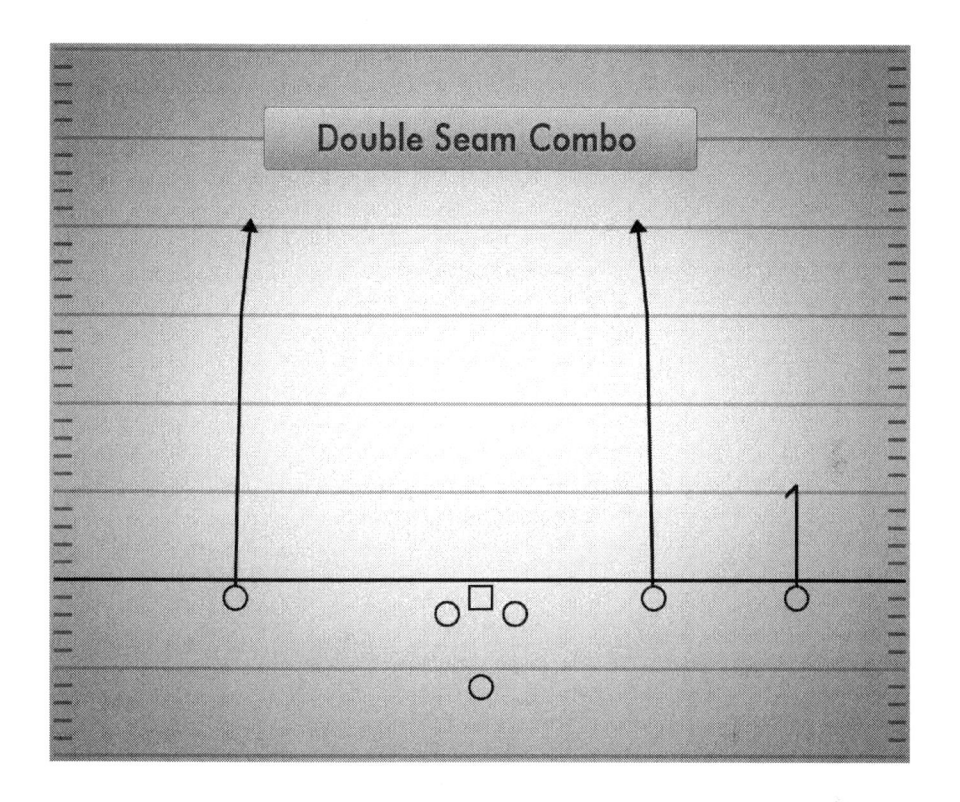

Double Seam Combo

Double Seam Combo is a play that places leverage on the defense up the seams. If the defense drops back to guard the seams, then the Quarterback should through the ball short to the 5-yard stop routes in the flats.

If it is a man-to-man defense, then consider throwing the seams over the top like a fade route, but run from an inside release. Safeties are not accustomed to guarding the fade route, and will therefore put your WR in better position to make the play.

FORMATION: 3-WIDE FORMATION

DISTANCE: SHORT YARDAGE, LONG YARDAGE

ROUTES IN THIS PLAY: STOP, SEAM

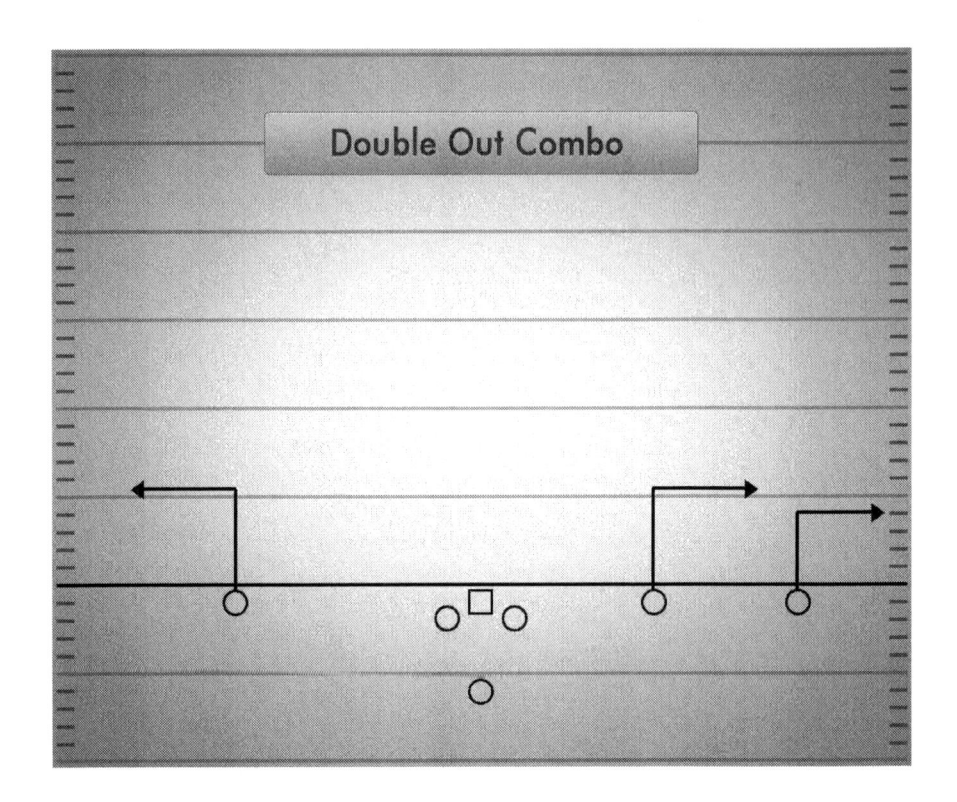

Double Out Combo

The Double Out Combo play places leverage on the outside of the defensive secondary. By attacking the flats with two players, the defender who is guarding the outside zone will be unable to guard both routes.

Versus a man to man defense, the QB must simply make a read based upon which WR makes a better move to the outside against the defender that is guarding him.

FORMATION: **3-WIDE FORMATION**

DISTANCE: **SHORT YARDAGE**

ROUTES IN THIS PLAY: **OUT**

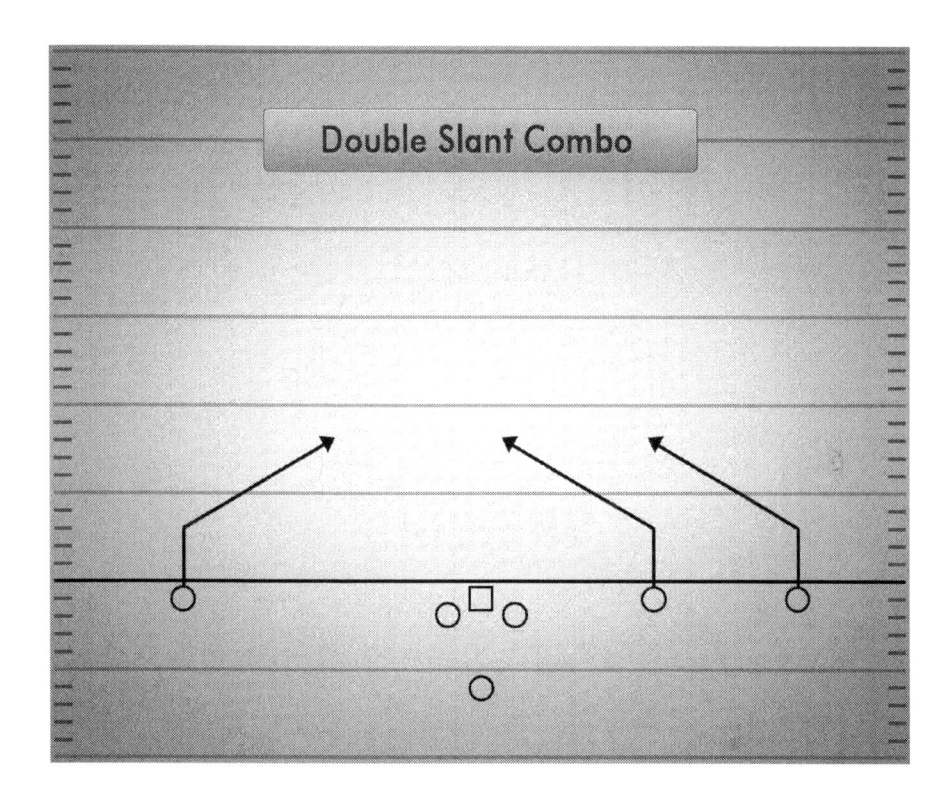

Double Slant Combo

The Double Slant Combo play is a great play to run in a short yardage situation if you have Wide Receivers who can run crisp routes. By making a clean cut to the inside, there will be a window of opportunity for the Quarterback to deliver the ball into the chest of the WR.

This play can also be used as a quick hitting play in the beginning of the game if the defense is playing far off the line of scrimmage. If the defense starts creeping up to guard against the short slant route, then hit them over the top by calling the Slant-and-Up Combo play.

FORMATION: **3-WIDE FORMATION**

DISTANCE: **SHORT YARDAGE**

ROUTES IN THIS PLAY: **SLANT**

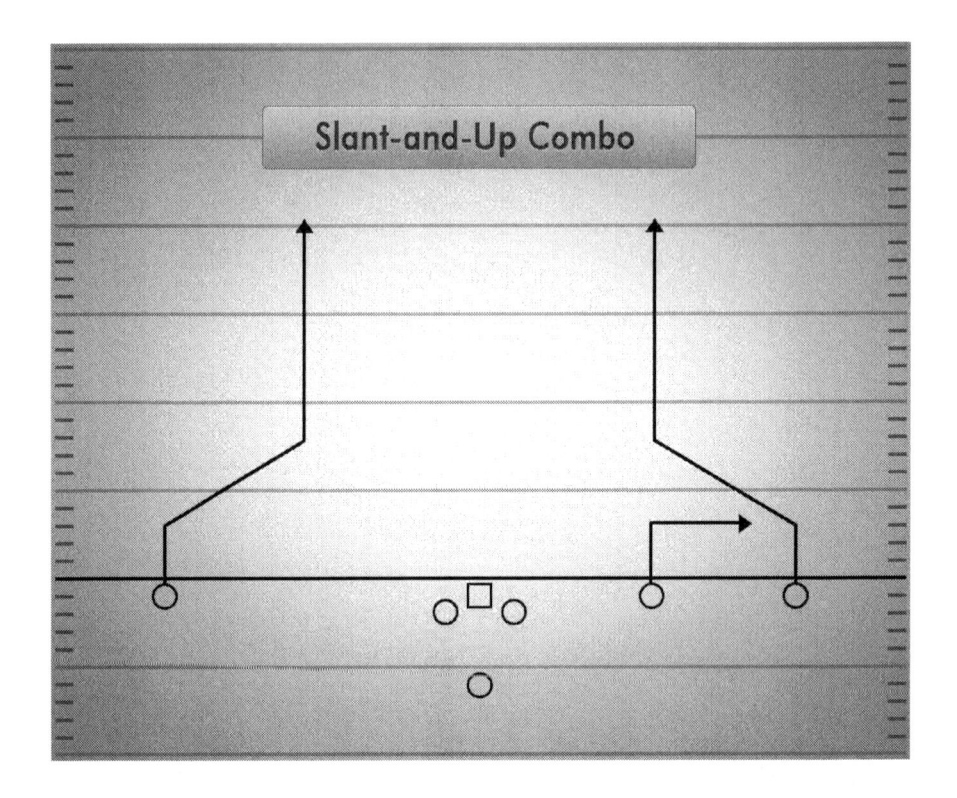

Slant-and-Up Combo

Slant-and-Up Combo is a companion play to the Out-Slant Combo play. By getting the defense used to seeing the Out-Slant combination routes, they will tend to cheat down. That is when you hit them over the top with this play.

As the defense makes a move to jump in front of the slant route, that is right when the WR turns it up field where the QB will throw it over the top for a long gain or a Touchdown.

FORMATION: **3-WIDE FORMATION**

DISTANCE: **LONG YARDAGE**

ROUTES IN THIS PLAY: **OUT, SLANT**

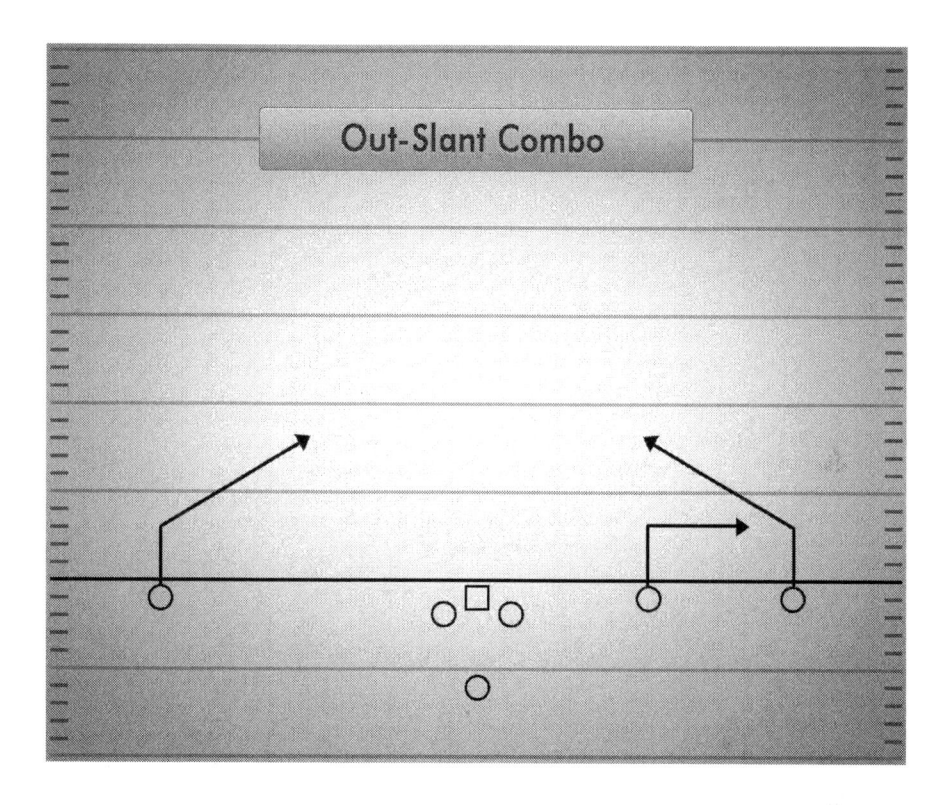

Out-Slant Combo

The Out-Slant Combo twists the defense around regardless of if they are playing man-to-man or zone. If they are playing zone, then the defense won't be able to keep track of the crossing patterns, and the man-to-man defense won't be able to keep up with the quick crossing cuts.

After the defense has gotten used to seeing this out-slant crossing pattern, mix things up by hitting them over the top with either the Slant-and-Up Combo play or the Out-and-Up Combo play.

FORMATION: **3-WIDE FORMATION**

DISTANCE: **SHORT YARDAGE**

ROUTES IN THIS PLAY: **OUT, SLANT**

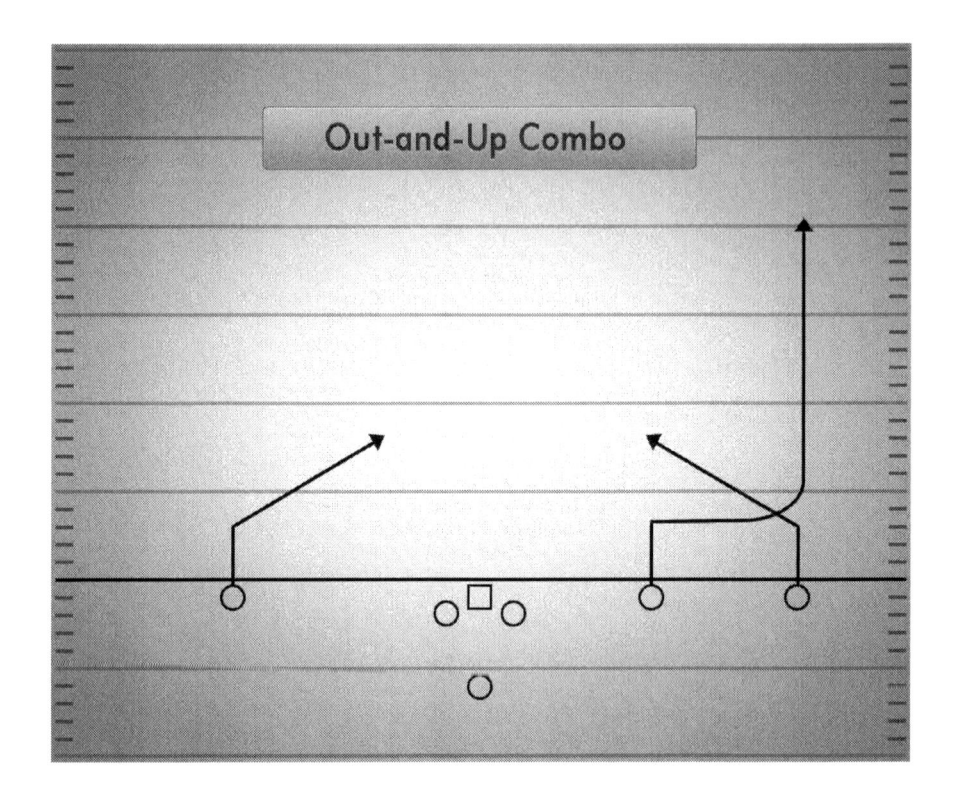

Out-and-Up Combo

The Out-and Up Combo is a companion play to the Out-Slant Combo play. After you have gotten the defense used to the shorter out route, hit them over the top with the Out-and-Up.

The part that makes this play extremely dangerous is against a man to man defense where the defender on the Out-and-Up route will have to run underneath the slant route, and will therefore be in a bad position to keep up with the inside WR who is now sprinting wide open up the sideline.

FORMATION: **3-WIDE FORMATION**

DISTANCE: **LONG YARDAGE**

ROUTES IN THIS PLAY: **OUT, SLANT**

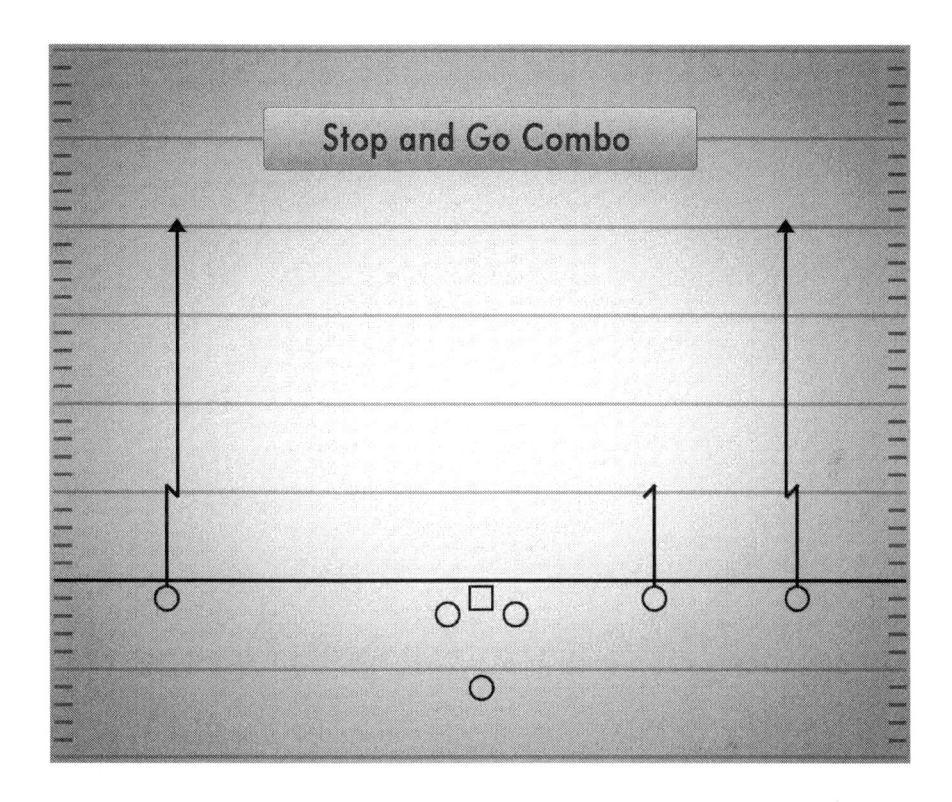

Stop and Go Combo

The Stop and Go route is one of the most famous double moves in all of football. After you have set up this play by repeatedly running the Double Stop Combo play, then surprise them with the Stop and Go and they won't know what hit them.

It is important that the Wide Receiver makes has break up the sideline after he stops. That way he is able to get passed the Cornerback easier.

FORMATION: **3-WIDE FORMATION**

DISTANCE: **LONG YARDAGE**

ROUTES IN THIS PLAY: **STOP**

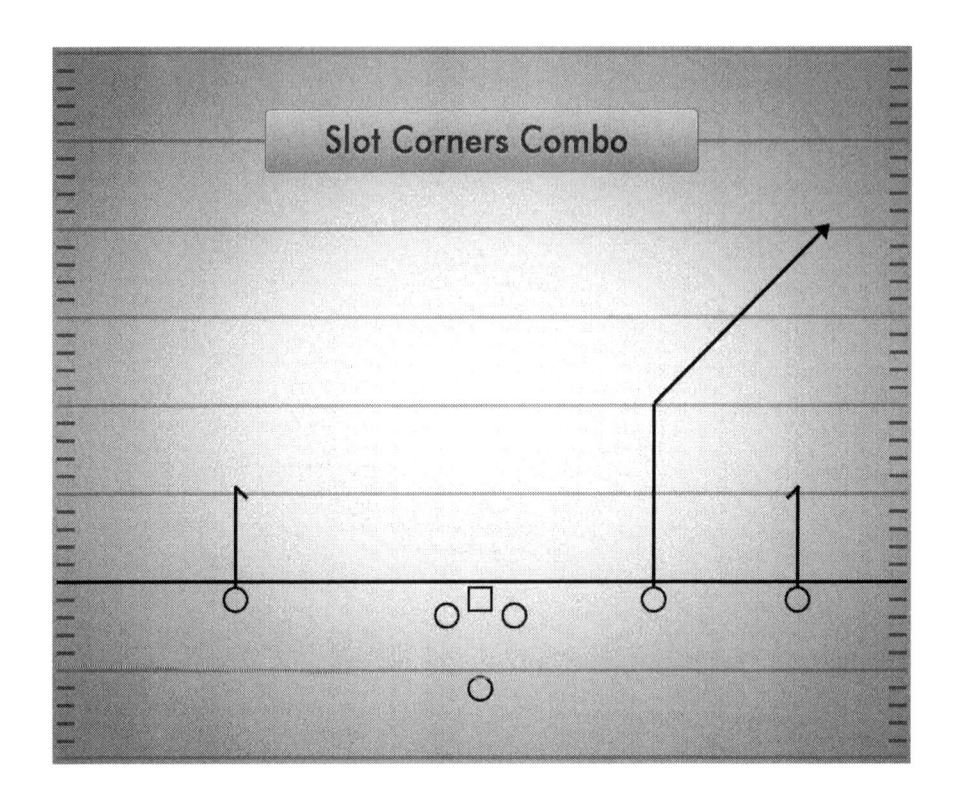

Slot Corners Combo

The Slot Corners play is a great play to use in order to isolate the Cornerback. The only thing that the Quarterback needs to read is how the Cornerback is positioning himself.

If the CB drops back underneath the Corner Route, then throw the ball to the stop on the outside. If the CB stay shallow in the flats, then throw over his head to the slot WR running the Corner route, making a break to the sideline.

FORMATION: **3-WIDE FORMATION**

DISTANCE: **SHORT YARDAGE, MEDIUM YARDAGE**

ROUTES IN THIS PLAY: **CORNER, STOP**

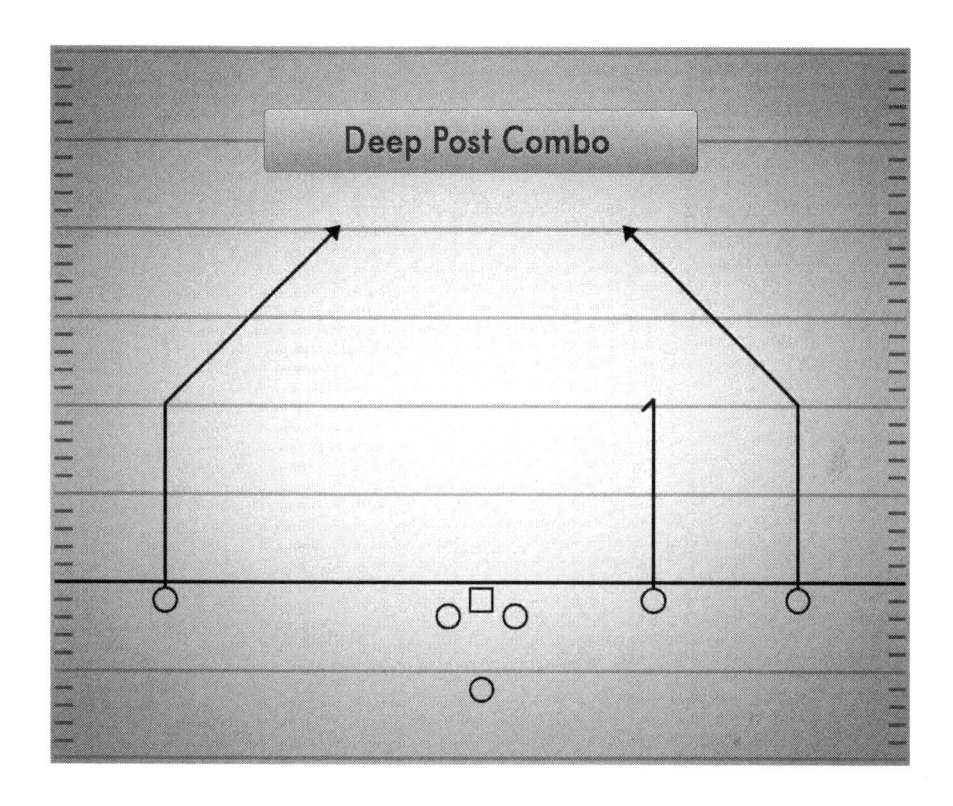

Deep Post Combo

The Deep Post Combo is a great way to attack downfield. The Post Route needs to be a skinny post with a trajectory that doesn't cross the middle of the field. The Slot Receiver needs to run his Curl Route in a way that grabs the attention of the Safety.

The Quarterback's read should be focused on the Safety. If the Safety stays high and guards the Post Route, then drop down and throw it to the Curl Route. If, however, the Safety is drawn down to the Slot Receiver running the Curl, then throw over his head to the Post running downfield.

FORMATION: **3-WIDE FORMATION**

DISTANCE: **LONG YARDAGE, MEDIUM YARDAGE**

ROUTES IN THIS PLAY: **POST, CURL**

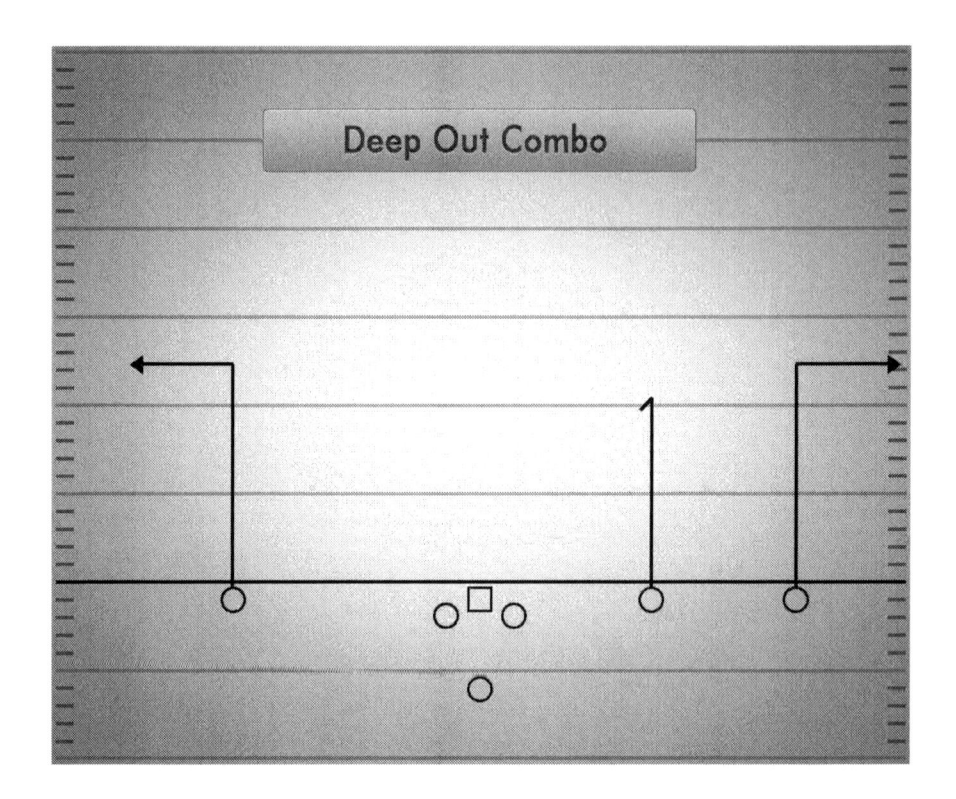

Deep Out Combo

The Deep Out Combo is similar to the Double Curl Combo play with a variation that send the outside WRs towards the sideline on a Deep Out Route.

The QB should make a pre-snap read to determine what side he is going to throw to. Once the side has been determined, then disregard the other half of the field and the read is locked into being between the Deep Out or the Curl Route.

FORMATION: **3-WIDE FORMATION**

DISTANCE: **MEDIUM YARDAGE**

ROUTES IN THIS PLAY: **CURL, OUT**

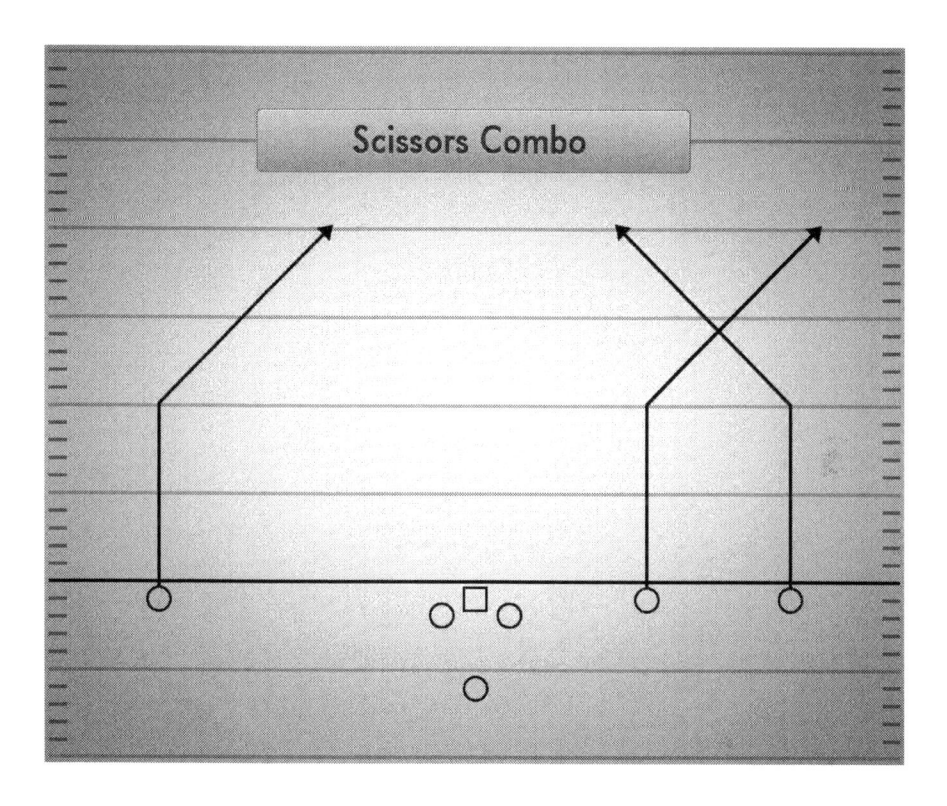

Scissors Combo

The Scissors Combo play is a mirrored play with the same route concept of a Post Route and a Corner Route on both sides.

The Wide Receivers need to cleanly run their routes by converging across each other at the point of the downfield cuts in order to disorient the defense and break free into the open field.

FORMATION: **3-WIDE FORMATION**

DISTANCE: **LONG YARDAGE**

ROUTES IN THIS PLAY: **CORNER, POST**

Switchblade Combo

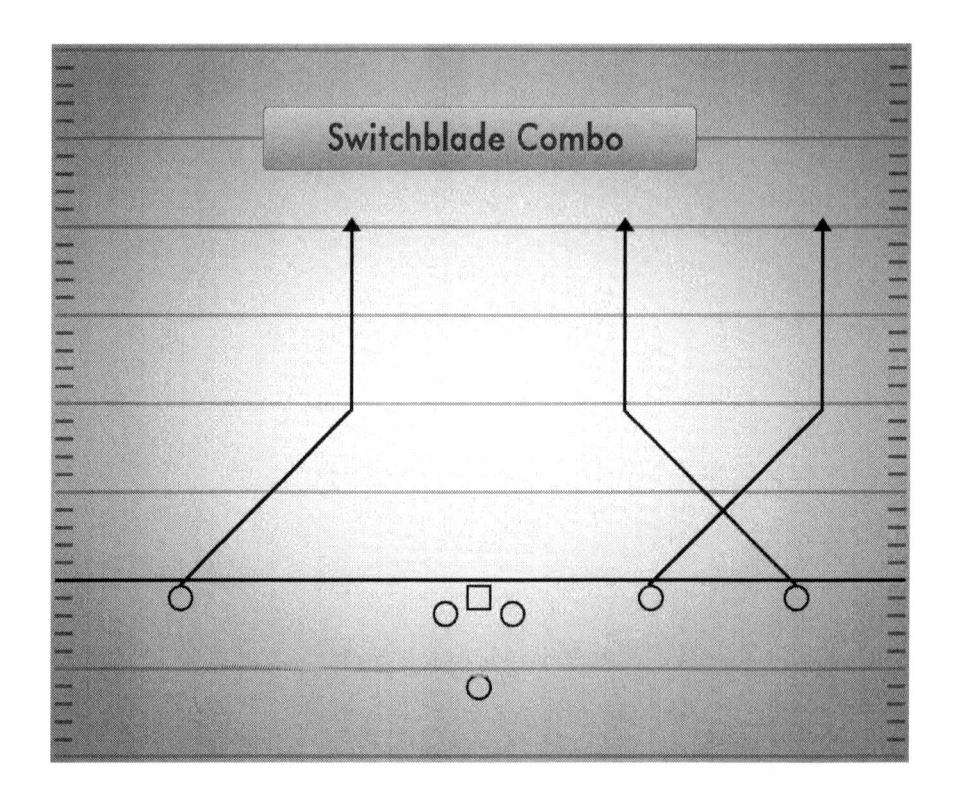

The Switchblade Combo play is intended to create a rub between the two combination receivers in order to break free from their defenders.

This play will work best against a man-to-man defense, because it is easy to lose the defenders when the Receivers cross and then break free going upfield.

FORMATION: **3-WIDE FORMATION**

DISTANCE: **LONG YARDAGE**

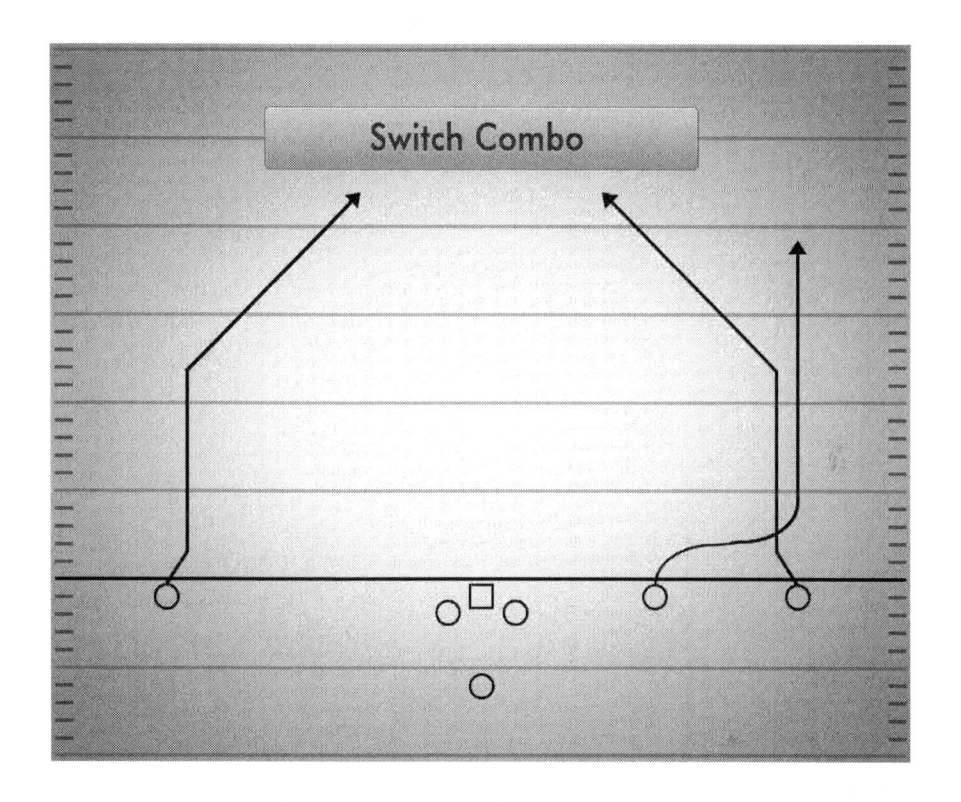

Switch Combo

Switch Combo is the classic switch play where the receivers use their routes to "switch" their positions on the field. The Outside Receiver gets upfield fast and runs a Post Route. The Slot Receiver goes underneath the Outside Receiver and then jets up the sideline.

The Quarterback should read the deep safeties. This play uses four players to attack zones that usually only have two, or maybe 3, defenders responsible for guarding them. Use your eyes to influence the defensive backs' movement, and then find the open WR running downfield.

FORMATION: **3-WIDE FORMATION**

DISTANCE: **LONG YARDAGE**

ROUTES IN THIS PLAY: **POST**

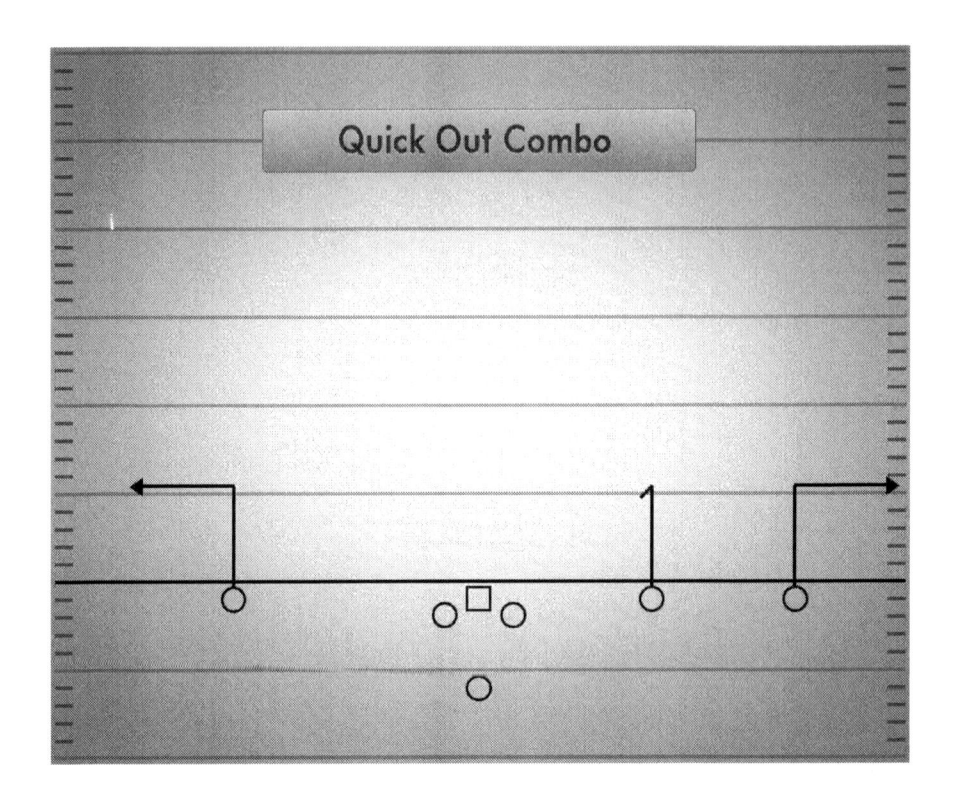

Quick Out Combo

Quick Cut Combo is a variation of the standard Double Stop Combo play, and a shorter version of the Deep Out Combo play.

The Quarterback should select one side of the field on the pre-snap read, and then as the play begins, determine which of the Wide Receivers gets in better position against the defense on his route.

FORMATION: **3-WIDE FORMATION**

DISTANCE: **SHORT YARDAGE**

ROUTES IN THIS PLAY: **STOP, OUT**

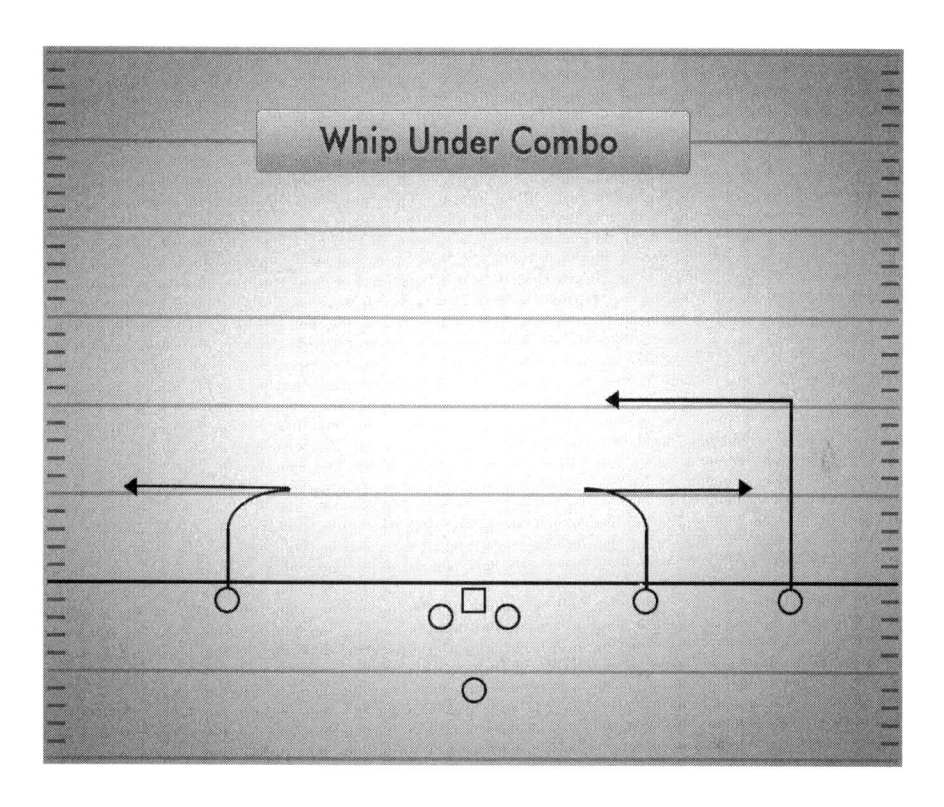

Whip Under Combo

The Whip Under Combo play is a great play to get some horizontal flow in your route concepts going. The crucial aspect of the play is the way in which the Whip Route is run by the Slot Receiver. The route must start of looking like an inside movement, but then the WR must plant his foot and spin (face toward the QB) and jet hard to the sideline.

If the Slot Receiver is not able to get open with the Whip Route, then the horizontal movement underneath should clear out to reveal the outside Receiver open on the In Route.

FORMATION: **3-WIDE FORMATION**

DISTANCE: **SHORT YARDAGE, MEDIUM YARDAGE**

ROUTES IN THIS PLAY: **IN, OUT**

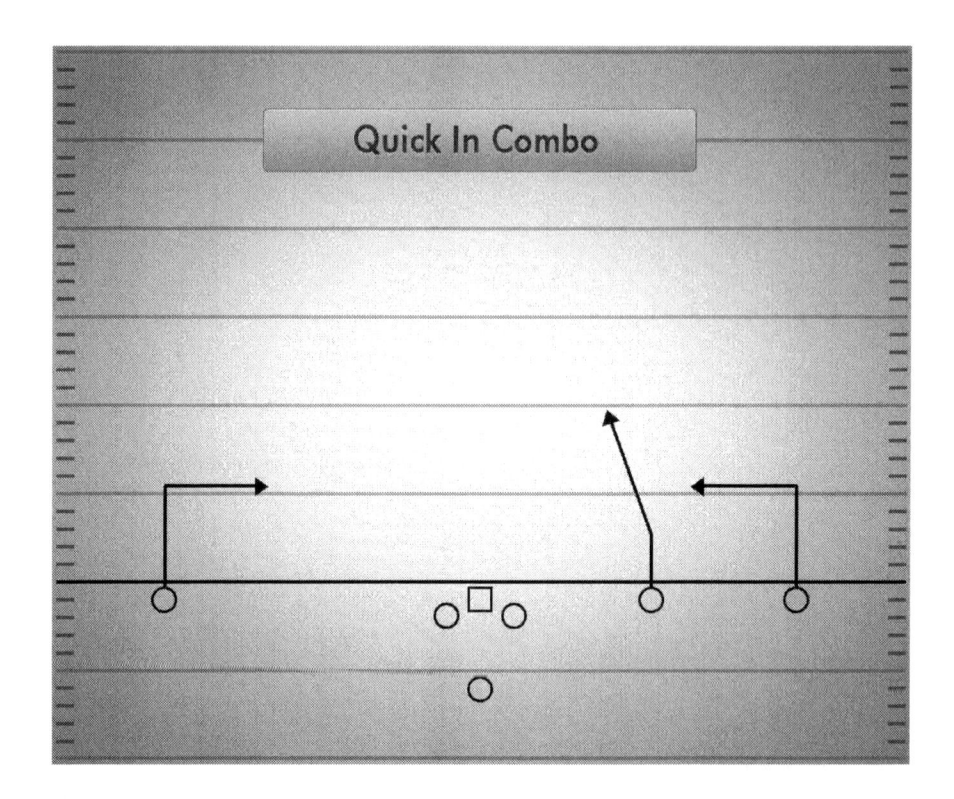

Quick In Combo

The Quick In Combo play is built to be a quick hitter. The Slot Receiver presses off the line of scrimmage in order to create space underneath for the Outside Receiver to be open for the In route.

The QB must make a pre-snap read to determine which side of the field is giving up the most position in the inside zone based upon formation alignment.

FORMATION: **3-WIDE FORMATION**

DISTANCE: **SHORT YARDAGE**

ROUTES IN THIS PLAY: **IN, SEAM**

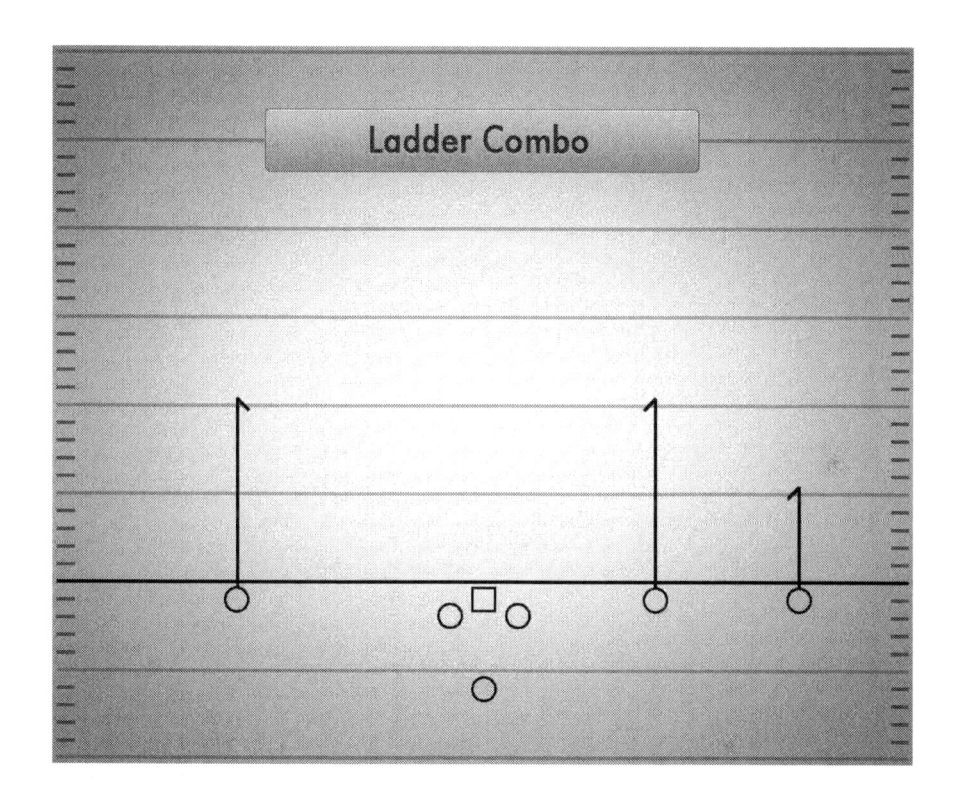

Ladder Combo

Ladder Combo is a play to hit the defense at varying vertical positions. All receivers run a stop and curl routes, but the lengths of the routes vary based upon their alignment.

The Quarterback should make his read just as if he is climbing up a "ladder." First look at the 5-Yard stop, and then work your way up to the 10-yard curl.

FORMATION: **3-WIDE FORMATION**

DISTANCE: **SHORT YARDAGE, MEDIUM YARDAGE**

ROUTES IN THIS PLAY: **STOP, CURL**

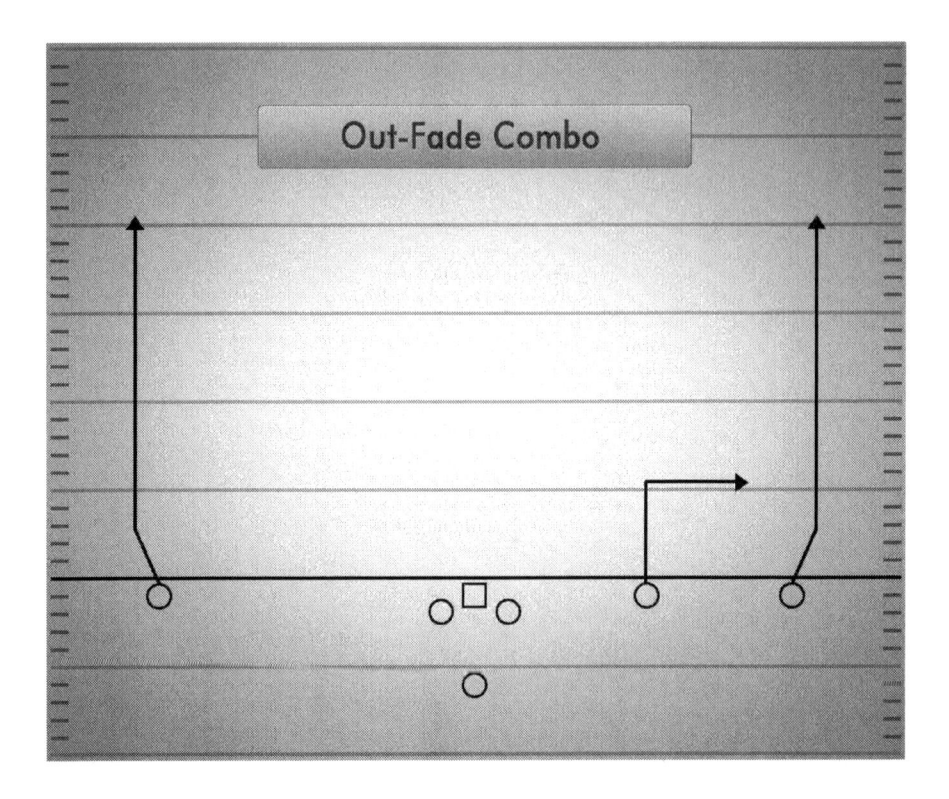

Out-Fade Combo

The Out-Fade route combination is one of the most popular route concepts in any football team's playbook. A Fade Route up the sideline on the outside combined with an Out Route from the Slot Receiver from the inside.

The Quarterback's read should be locked in on the defensive Cornerback. If the Cornerback drifts deep with the Fade, then throw the ball to the Out Route in the flats. If the Cornerback stays in the flats to jump on the Out, then throw it over the top to the Fade.

FORMATION: **3-WIDE FORMATION**

DISTANCE: **SHORT YARDAGE, MEDIUM YARDAGE**

ROUTES IN THIS PLAY: **FADE, OUT**

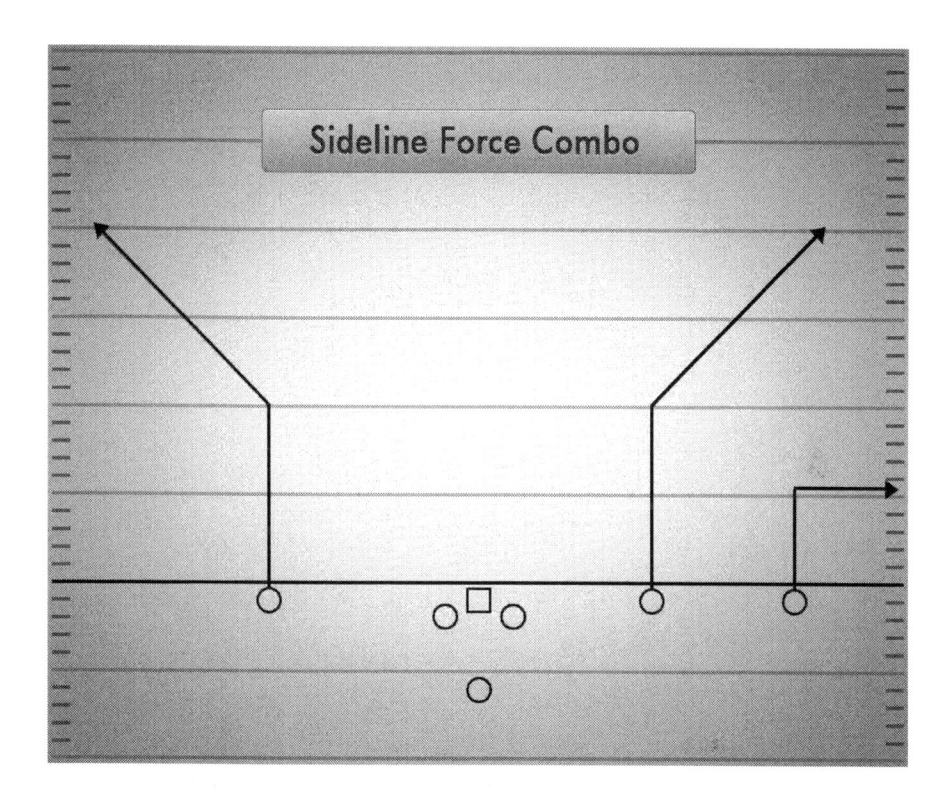

Sideline Force Combo

The Sideline Force Combo play is a shorter version of the Sideline Force Deep Combo play. The main goal of this play is to force the routes to the sideline.

This play is very effective when you need to manage the time on the clock because it allows the Receivers to quickly get out of bounds after the catch the ball.

FORMATION: 3-WIDE FORMATION

DISTANCE: SHORT YARDAGE, MEDIUM YARDAGE

ROUTES IN THIS PLAY: CORNER, OUT

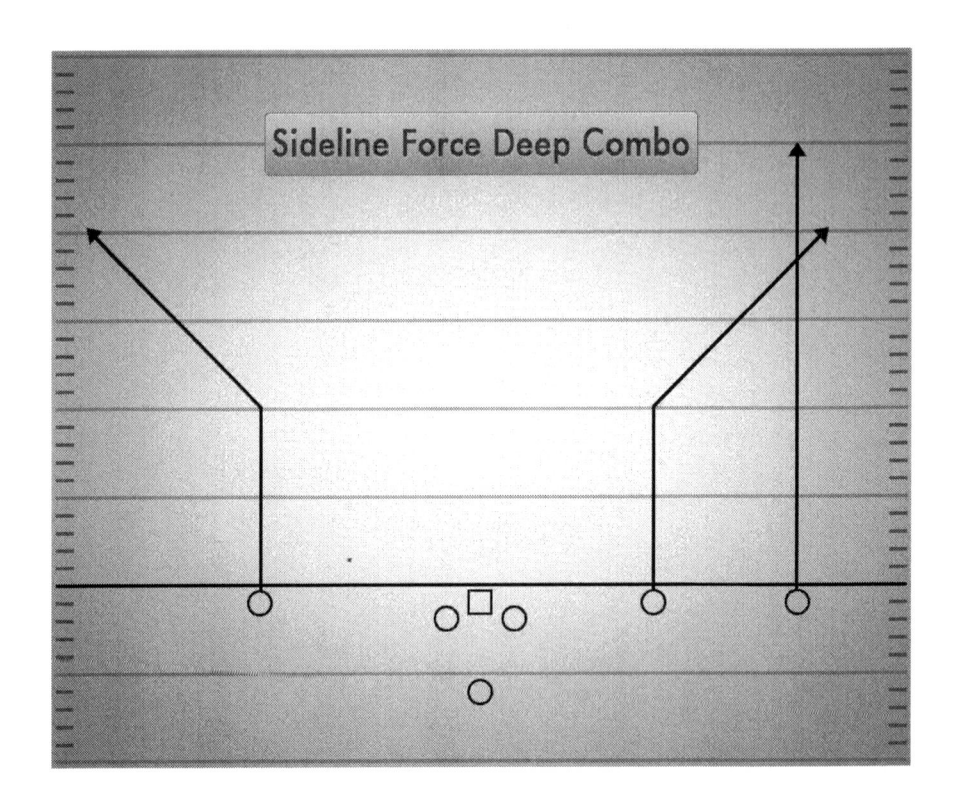

Sideline Force Deep Combo

The Sideline Force Deep Combo play is the deep version of the Sideline Force Combo play. The purpose of this play is to get the Wide Receivers in close proximity to the sideline while running deep downfield.

This play is very effective when you need to manage the time on the clock because it allows the Receivers to quickly get out of bounds after the catch the ball.

FORMATION: **3-WIDE FORMATION**

DISTANCE: **LONG YARDAGE**

ROUTES IN THIS PLAY: **CORNER, STREAK**

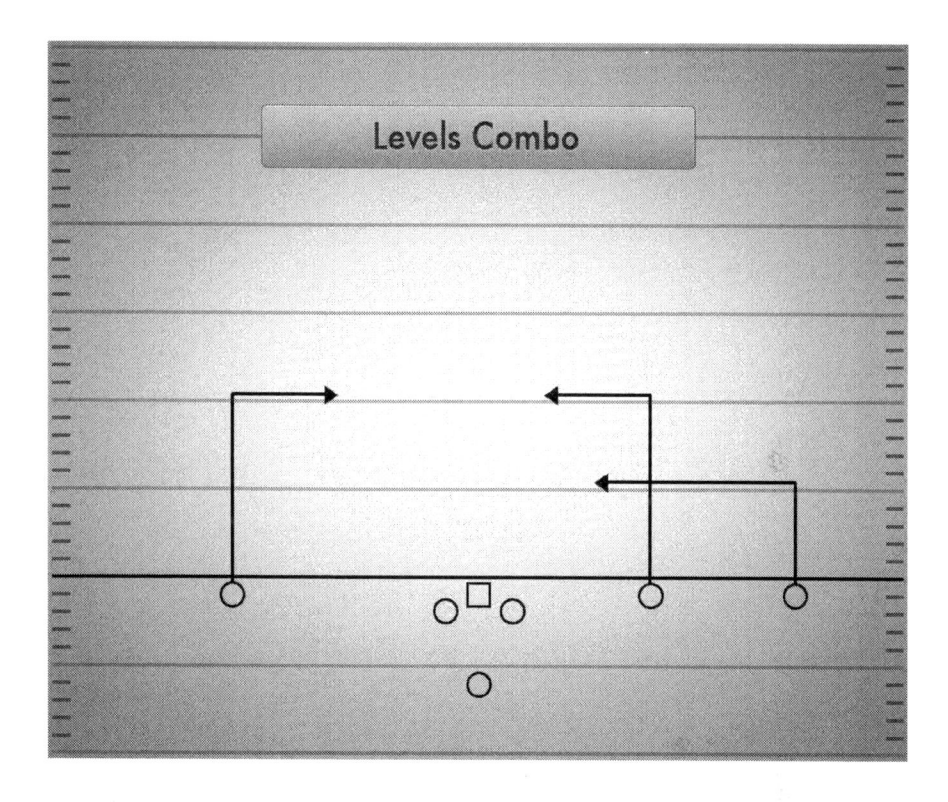

Levels Combo

The Levels Combo play is a great way to attack different vertical portions of the defensive secondary. The Wide Receivers run In Routes at varying distances down the field.

The horizontal movement should create a space for the Quarterback to find an opening to throw into, especially combined with the alternating vertical positioning of the routes.

FORMATION: 3-WIDE FORMATION

DISTANCE: SHORT YARDAGE, MEDIUM YARDAGE

ROUTES IN THIS PLAY: IN

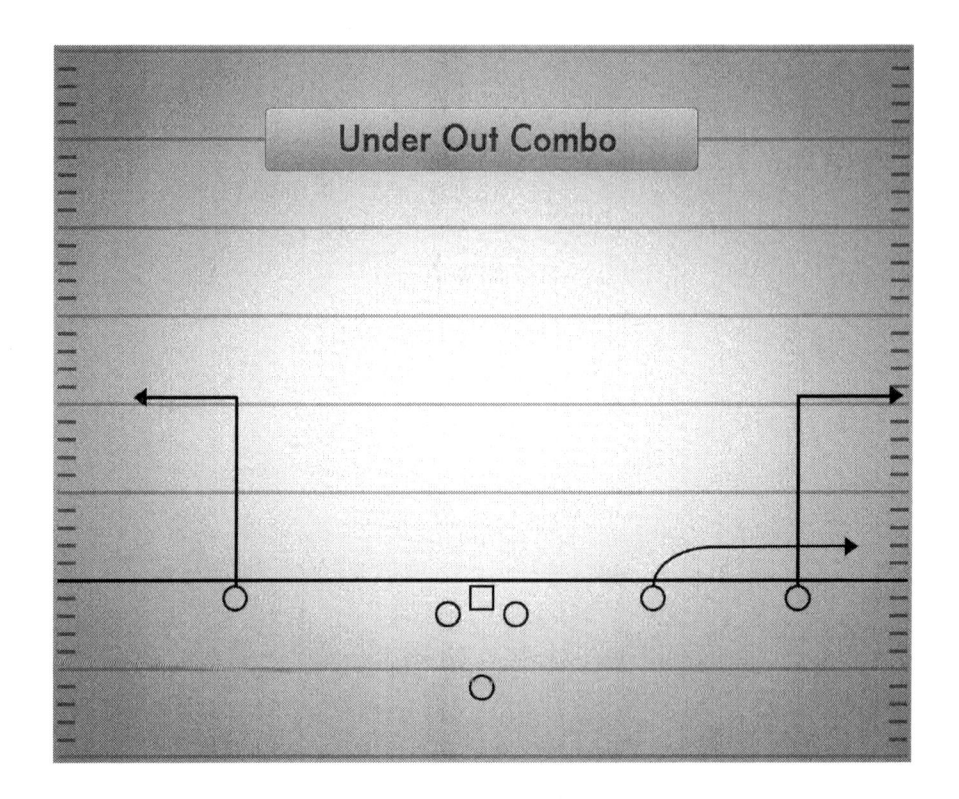

Under Out Combo

The Under Out Combo play positions the inside WR on a quick out underneath the deeper out. This places pressure on the flats of the defensive secondary by placing two WR on each side of the zone.

By splitting the responsibilities of the Cornerback, the Quarterback will have to see which one the Cornerback decides to guard, and then deliver the ball to the appropriate WR.

FORMATION: 3-WIDE FORMATION

DISTANCE: SHORT YARDAGE, MEDIUM YARDAGE

ROUTES IN THIS PLAY: OUT

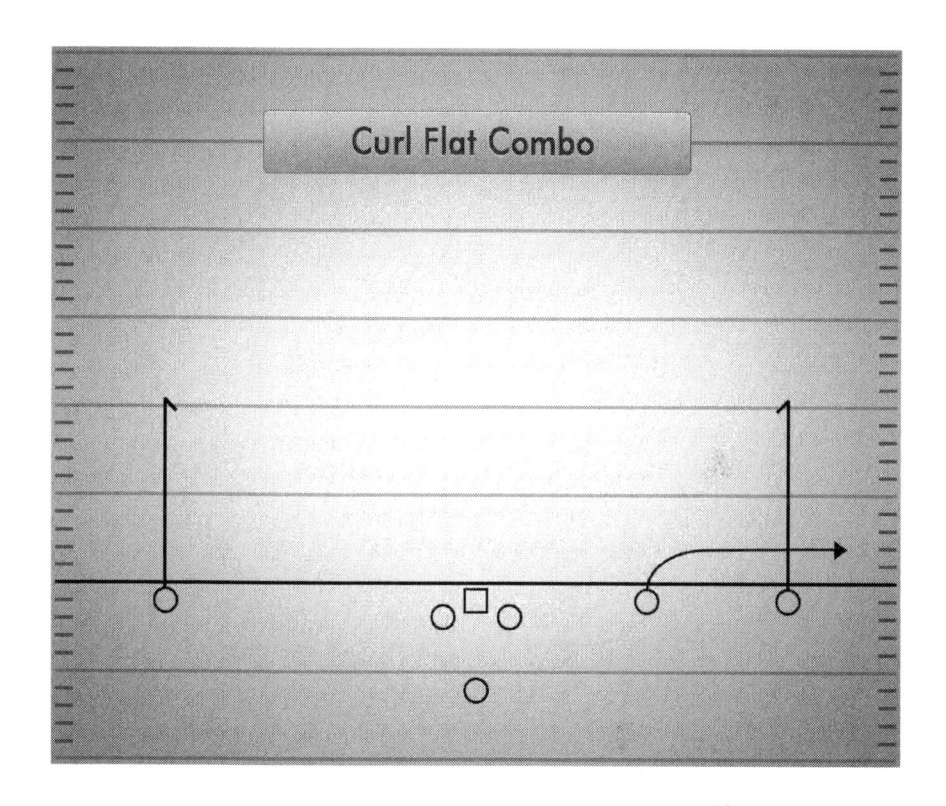

Curl Flat Combo

The Curl Flat Combo play attacks the defensive flat zone on the outside with a quick Out Route and a Curl Route over the top.

The Quarterback will want to look first at the quick out, and if the defense flowed fast to guard the out, then that means the curl route should be curling around in the open space right behind them.

FORMATION: **3-WIDE FORMATION**

DISTANCE: **SHORT YARDAGE, MEDIUM YARDAGE**

ROUTES IN THIS PLAY: **CURL, OUT**

Plays
Trips Formation

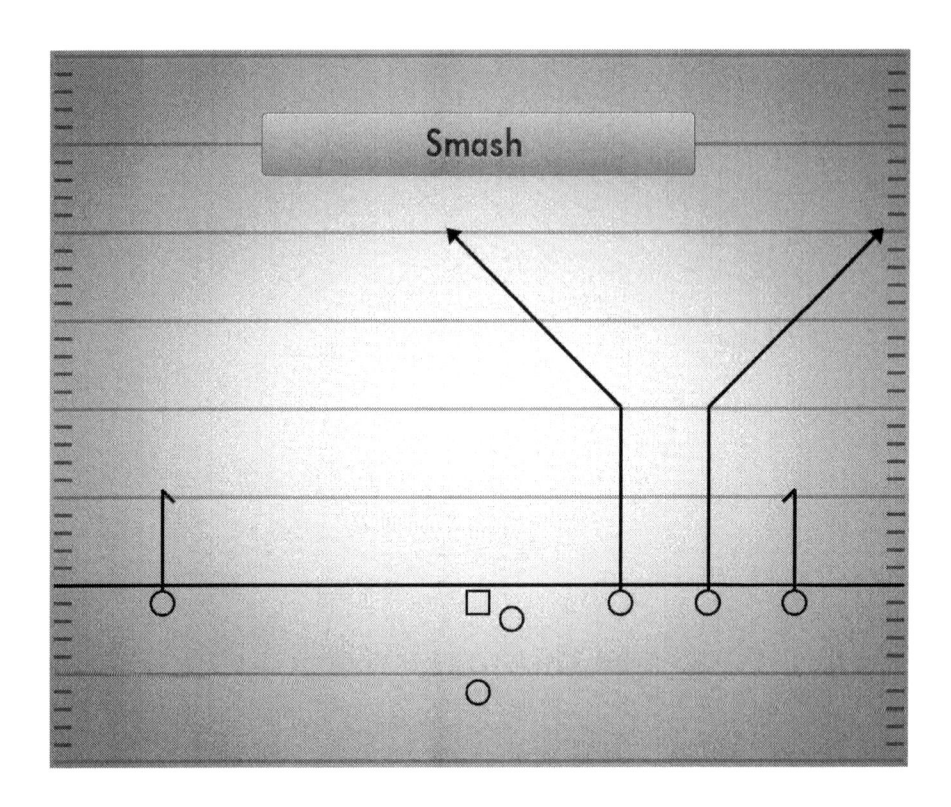

Smash

Utilizing the popular corner/stop route concept, the Smash play will attack many different zones in the defensive secondary. The first read that the Quarterback should make is to watch how the Cornerback plays the routes. If he stays low on the Stop route, then throw it over his head to the Corner route. If he stays high on the corner route, then throw it low to the Wide Receiver running the Stop route, who will be wide open in the flats. No outside linebacker will be able to run out there quick enough if the corner is dropping deep, and the Quarterback makes a quick read.

FORMATION: **TRIPS FORMATION**

DISTANCE: **SHORT YARDAGE, MEDIUM YARDAGE**

ROUTES IN THIS PLAY: **CORNER, POST, STOP**

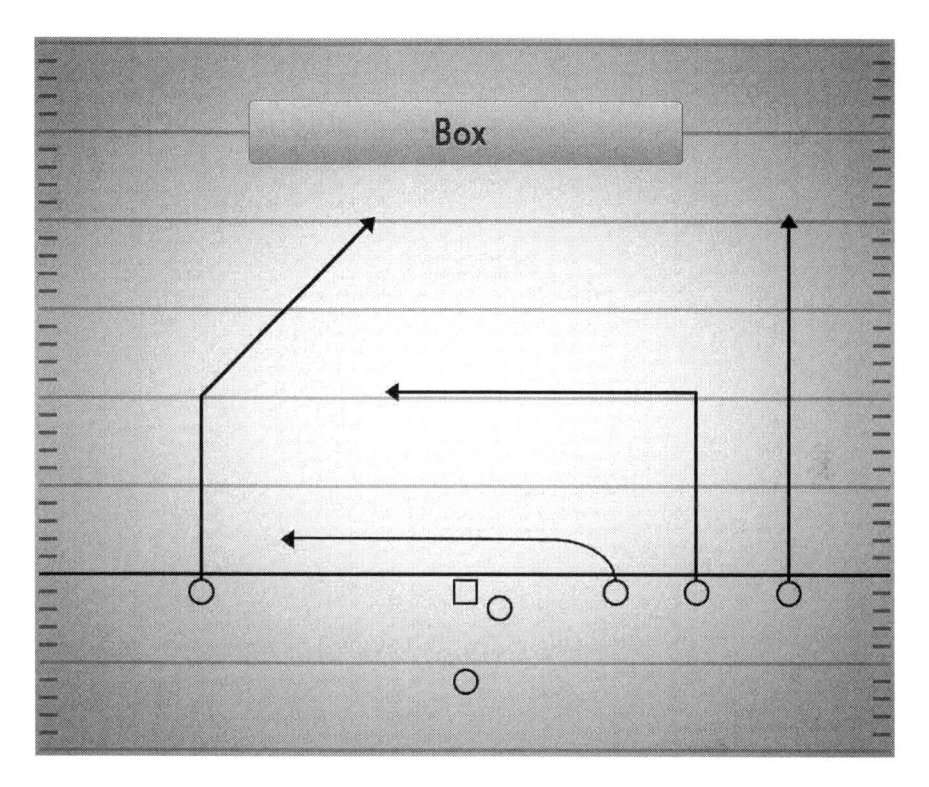

Box

The Box play allows you to trap the defense into having to make a high/low decision. In fact, there are two different high/low areas on the defense that this play attacks.

By singling out the safety, the Quarterback can make a "high/low" read based upon the combination of the Post route and the 10 yard In route. If the safety drops high to guard the Post, then throw it low to the In route. If the safety stays low on the In, then throw it high to the Post.

Additionally, another high/low read takes place at the level of the outside linebacker. The linebacker will have to make the decision to go high and guard the In route, or stay low and guard the Shallow Cross. The Quarterback's read progression should start by reading the Safety on the Post, and then moving down to the In route, and finally hitting the lowest shallow cross underneath, if everything higher is guarded.

FORMATION: **TRIPS FORMATION**

DISTANCE: **SHORT YARDAGE, LONG YARDAGE, MEDIUM YARDAGE**

ROUTES IN THIS PLAY: **POST, IN, SHALLOW CROSS, STREAK**

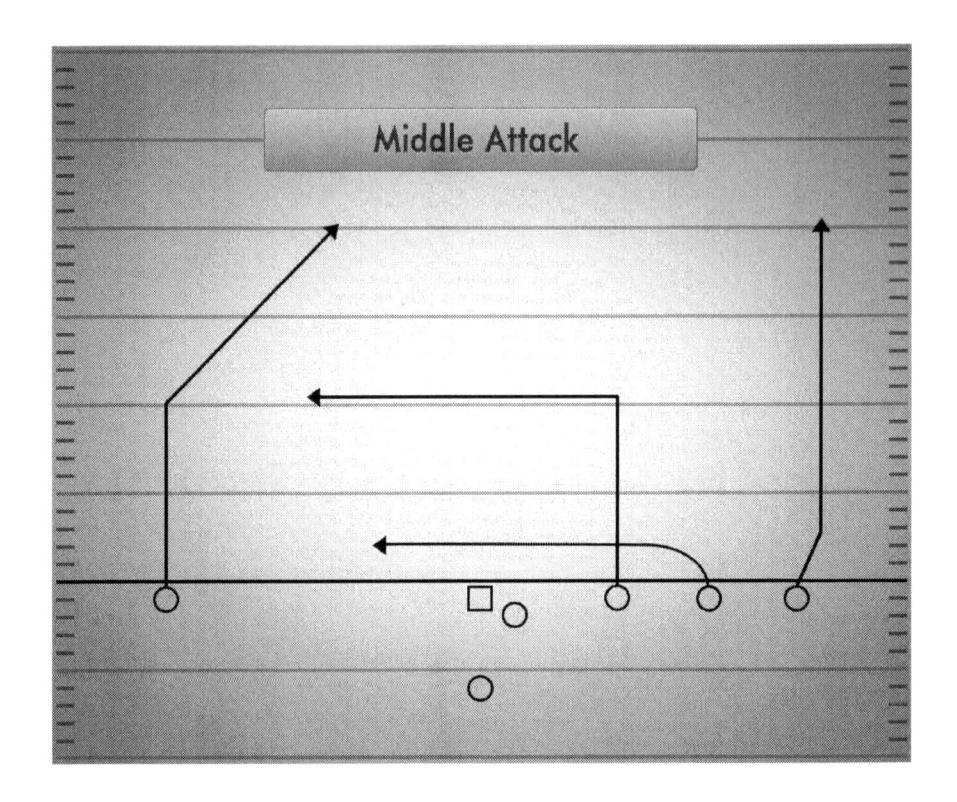

Middle Attack

The Middle Attack play attacks the middle of the defense with three different routes attacking three different levels in the defensive secondary. This allows the Quarterback to read the vertical flow of the defense in order to determine which of the three levels will be the open one. If the defense begins to crowd the middle of the field, then the outside receiver needs to get a wide release to run down the sideline on the fade route to stretch out the secondary.

Middle Attack is a variation of the Box play, but with a reversal of roles for the slot receivers.

FORMATION: **TRIPS FORMATION**

DISTANCE: **SHORT YARDAGE, LONG YARDAGE, MEDIUM YARDAGE**

ROUTES IN THIS PLAY: **POST, IN, SHALLOW CROSS, FADE**

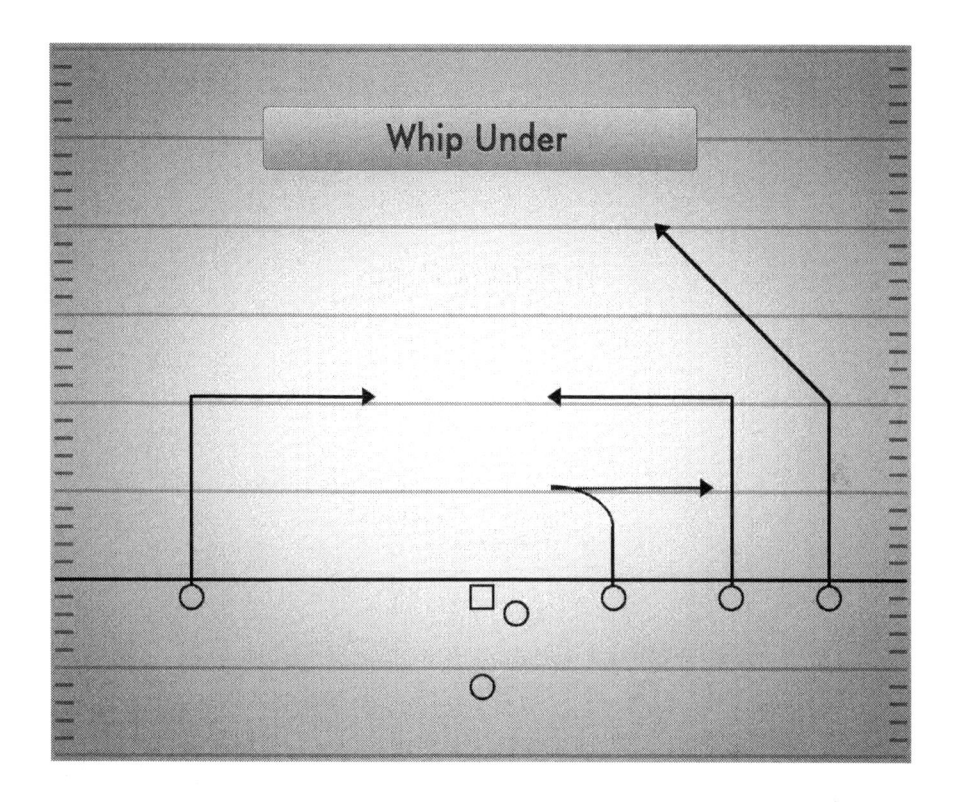

Whip Under

The Whip play is all about misdirection. The hard inside move gets the defense flowing inside, but the quick pivot outside is even more important for a quick move outside. If the inside receiver flowing underneath is covered up, then the outside receiver will be open coming inside over the top.

The Whip is best run in the second half of the game after setting up the defense with a sequence of successful slant plays. The defender will be ready to jump forward on the slant, but the wide out will plant hard and turn fast outside where he will be wide open running away from the defender.

FORMATION: **TRIPS FORMATION**

DISTANCE: **SHORT YARDAGE, MEDIUM YARDAGE**

ROUTES IN THIS PLAY: **POST, IN, WHIP, STOP**

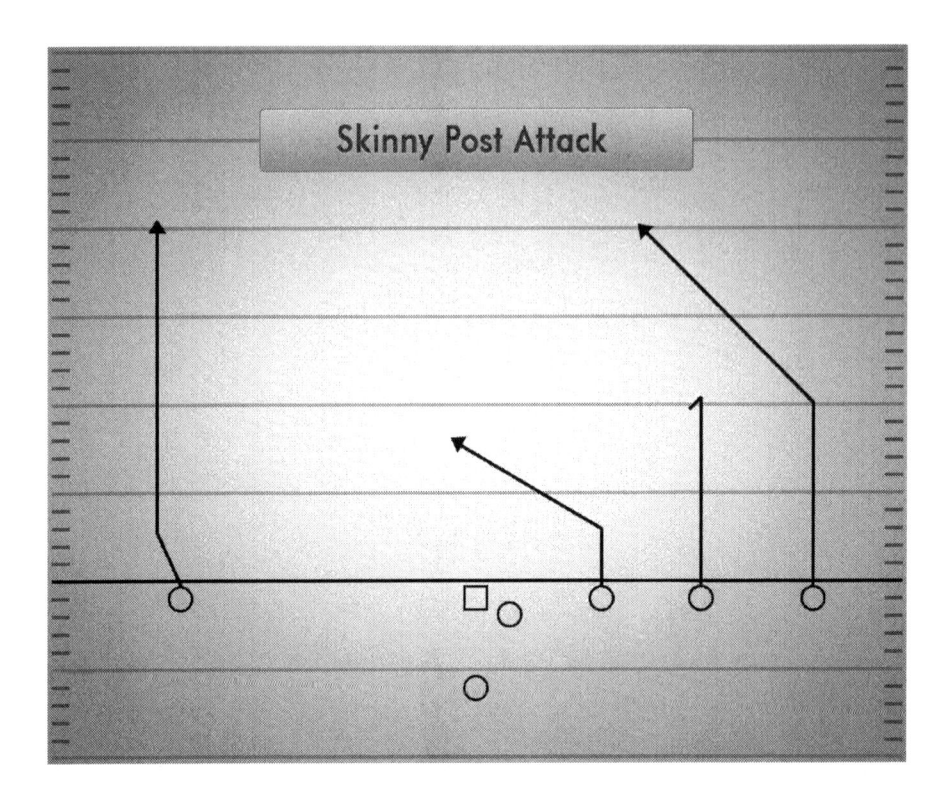

Skinny Post Attack

The Skinny Post Attack play requires special attention to detail. The main point of this play is to put the Safety in a tough situation by attacking his zone with two routes. The most critical route running in this play is the 10-yard Curl route, because it has to be run in a way that attracts the Safety's attention. If the slot receiver successfully gets the Safety to stay down and guard the curl, then the Post route will be wide open over the top.

If the Safety stays deep, however, then the Curl route needs to make sure that he is deep enough over the linebackers in order to be open 10-12 yards downfield. All in all, this play consists of a high/low read on the Safety by placing on route in the front of the Safety's zone, and the other over the top of the Safety's zone.

FORMATION: **TRIPS FORMATION**

DISTANCE: **LONG YARDAGE, MEDIUM YARDAGE**

ROUTES IN THIS PLAY: **POST, FADE, STOP, CURL**

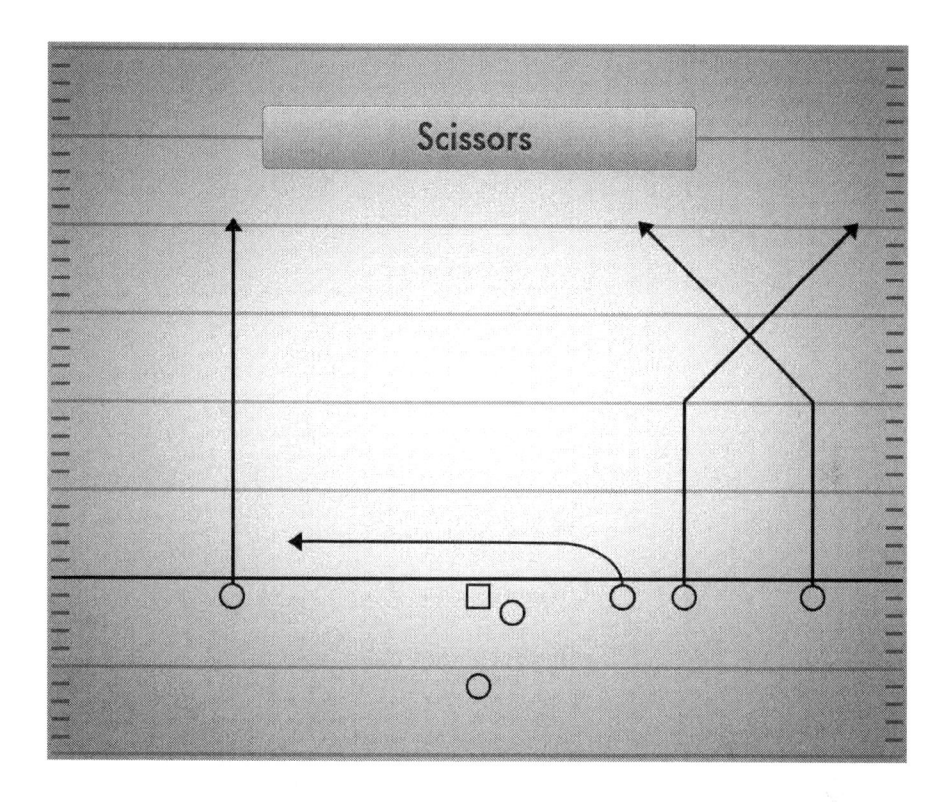

Scissors

Scissors is a great play to cut through the defensive secondary by converging two receivers across each other on one half of the field. The Post route goes over the top of the Corner route. The Post is the first read coming across the top, followed up by the Corner cutting through below.

The most important aspect of the play is that both routes run quickly up field at the same time and cut across each other simultaneously to wreak havoc on the downfield defenders.

FORMATION: TRIPS FORMATION

DISTANCE: LONG YARDAGE

ROUTES IN THIS PLAY: CORNER, POST, SHALLOW CROSS, STREAK

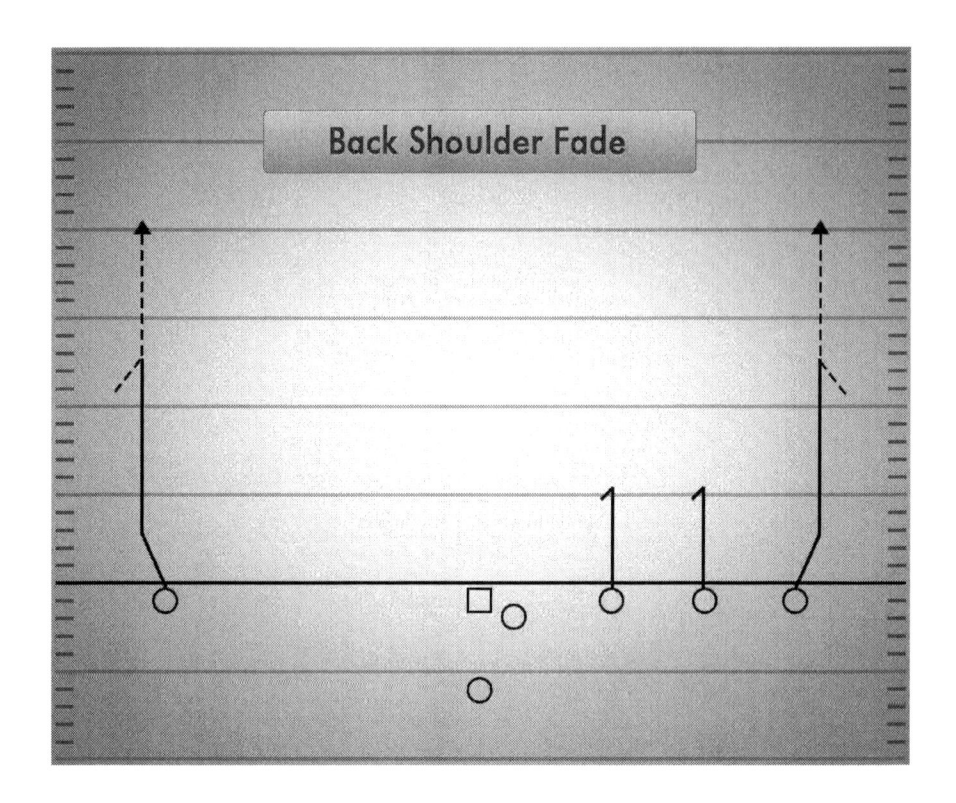

Back Shoulder Fade

The Back Shoulder fade is a go-to play for goal line situations. It gives the Receiver two options to choose from based upon how the defender guards him. If the Cornerback is guarding deep, then the Quarterback can throw the ball short, but if the Cornerback is play up close, then the Quarterback can throw the ball over the top.

Communication and chemistry between the Quarterback and the Receiver is of the utmost importance. Both the thrower and the route runner need to be on the same page to execute this play properly. Great chemistry will lead to great results on the Back Shoulder fade.

FORMATION: **TRIPS FORMATION**

DISTANCE: **SHORT YARDAGE**

ROUTES IN THIS PLAY: **FADE, STOP**

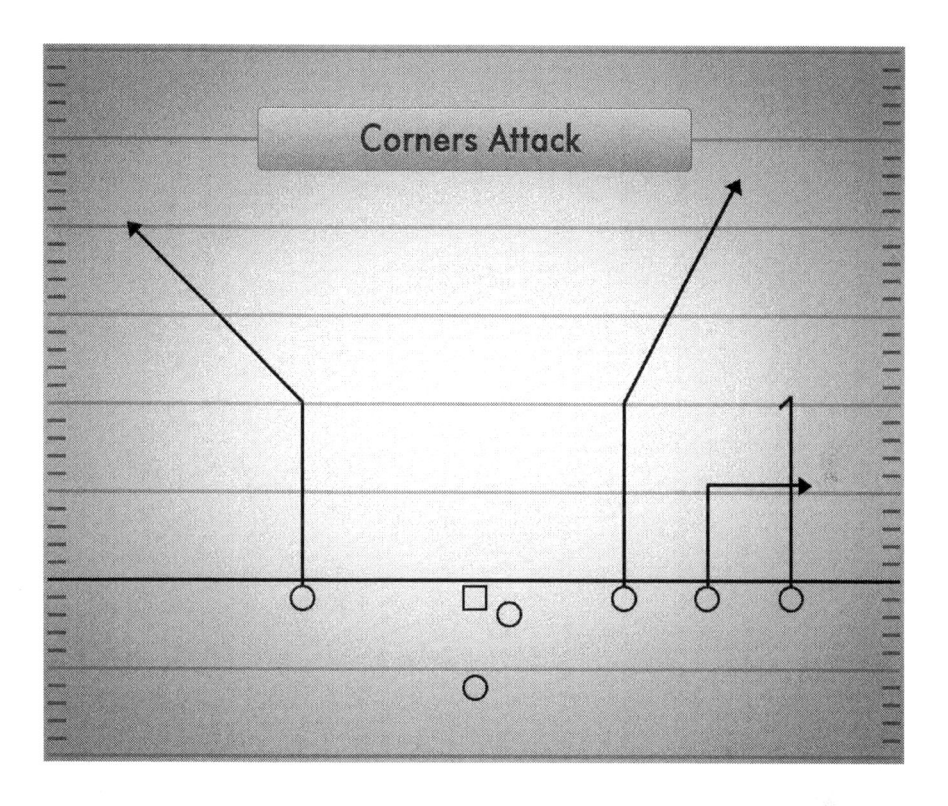

Corners Attack

Corners attack does just what its name says it does: Attack the Corners. The corner routes get depth into the corner of the defensive secondary, while the underneath routes wreak havoc in the flats. The slot receiver who runs the corner in combination with the 10-yard curl, has to make sure that he gets depth so that he is properly spaced over the top of the Curl route.

The Quarterback has to make a pre-snap decision on to select what side he wants to go to. Once that decision is made, read the Cornerback to see if he is staying on the deep corner, or cheating on the flat.

FORMATION: **TRIPS FORMATION**

DISTANCE: **LONG YARDAGE**

ROUTES IN THIS PLAY: **CORNER, CURL, OUT**

Ridge Force

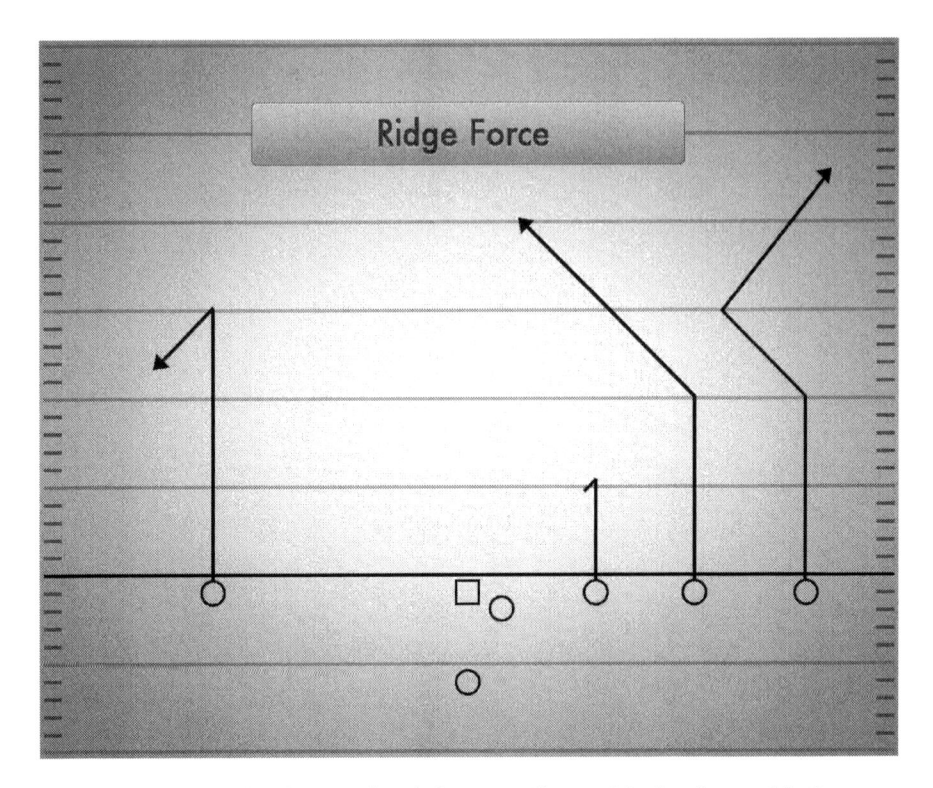

The Ridge Force play forces the defense to flow with the flow with the combination of the two post routes coming across the top ridge of the defensive secondary. Once the defenders start flowing with the combination of those routes, the outside receivers breaks hard to the outside on the Post Corner route.

The double move by the outside receiver will force the Safety into a hard decision if he is playing in a cover 2 zone, because he will be sitting right in the middle of two deep routes into his territory, but he can only choose to guard on of them.

If the defense is in a three deep formation and/or playing in a Cover three, then the QB will most likely want to drop down and hit the Comeback route on the other side of the field.

FORMATION: **TRIPS FORMATION**

DISTANCE: **LONG YARDAGE**

ROUTES IN THIS PLAY: **POST, STOP, POST CORNER, COMEBACK**

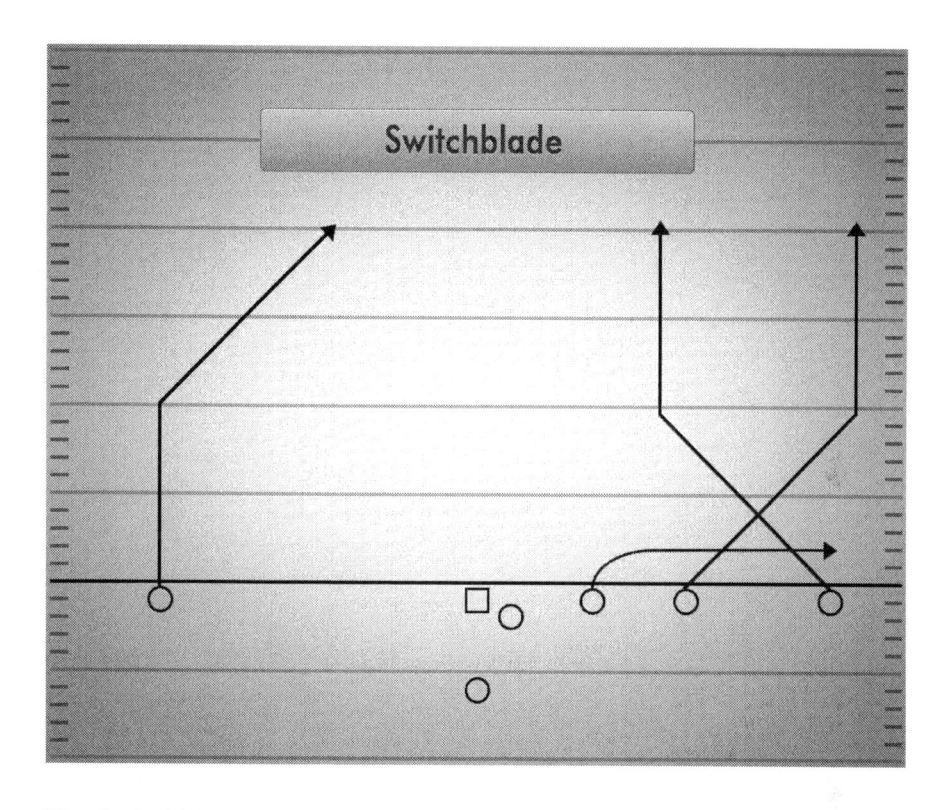

Switchblade

The Switchblade is a deadly combination route that cuts right through the defense by switching two receivers as they run their routes up field. A man-to-man defense will have trouble keeping up with both of the downfield receivers, and a zone defense will be thrown for a loop as the routes cut right through the zone.

The Quarterback has the option of cutting his losses if the deep routes aren't open, by checking down to the shallow cross underneath the switch route combination.

FORMATION: **TRIPS FORMATION**

DISTANCE: **LONG YARDAGE**

ROUTES IN THIS PLAY: **POST, SHALLOW CROSS**

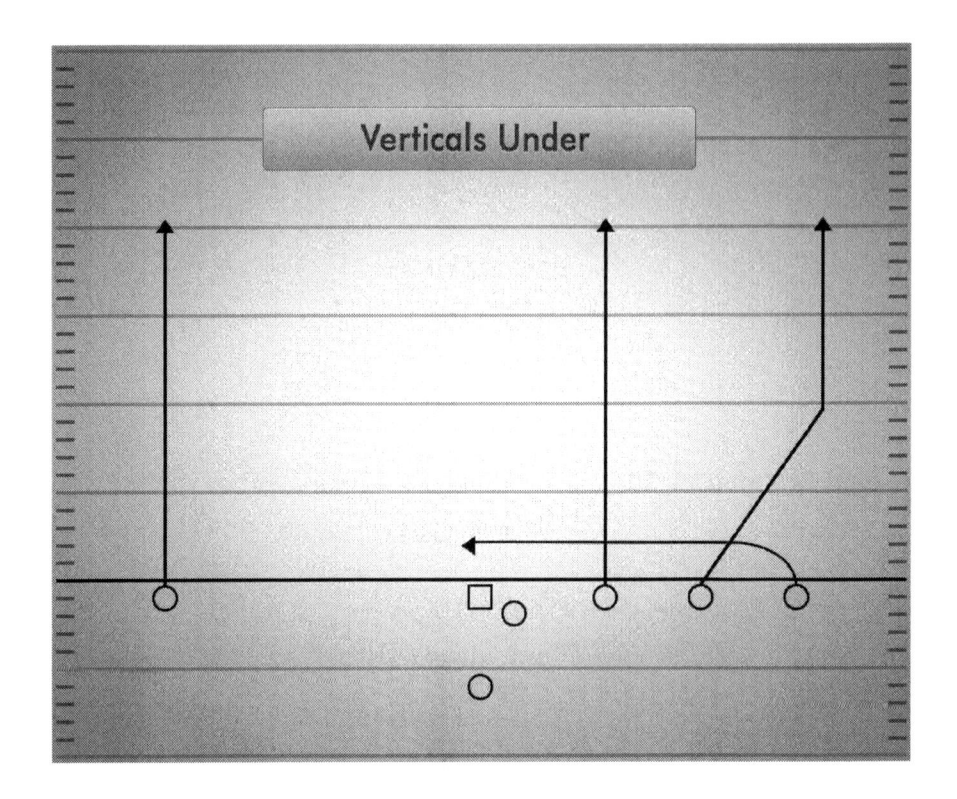

Verticals Under

The Verticals Under play sends the wide receivers up field in a shifted pattern that replaces the territory of the Receiver who is cutting underneath the Verticals.

By pushing the Vertical routes up field hard, it will distract the defense from the Shallow Cross coming underneath. Sometimes, however, the defense will lose track of the receiver taking the place of the underneath route, and he will be open down the sideline for a big gain.

FORMATION: **TRIPS FORMATION**

DISTANCE: **SHORT YARDAGE, LONG YARDAGE**

ROUTES IN THIS PLAY: **SHALLOW CROSS, STREAK**

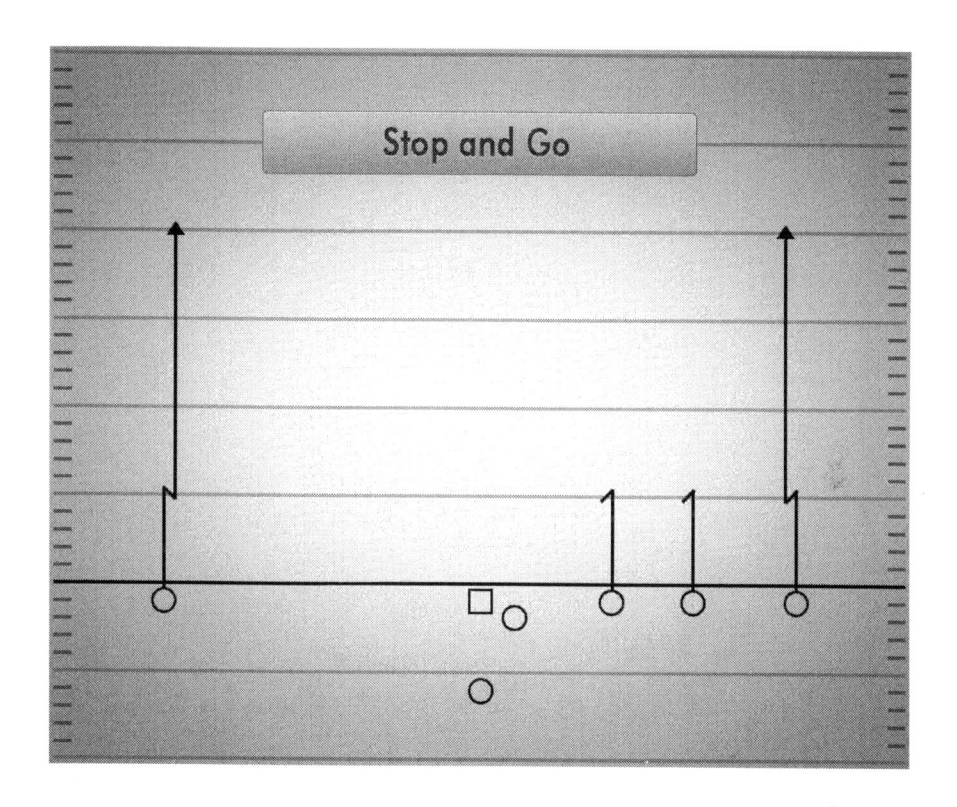

Stop and Go

The Stop and Go route is the most famous double move in all of football. The outside receiver will fake like he is running a 5 yard stop, but will twist and turn quickly up field.

It is imperative that the QB makes a good pump fake to sucker the defense in to jumping up on the short route. Once the pump fake is successfully completed, the QB must regather himself and get ready to throw the ball over the top of the defense to the receiver who is sprinting up field.

FORMATION: **TRIPS FORMATION**

DISTANCE: **SHORT YARDAGE, LONG YARDAGE**

ROUTES IN THIS PLAY: **STOP**

Comebacks

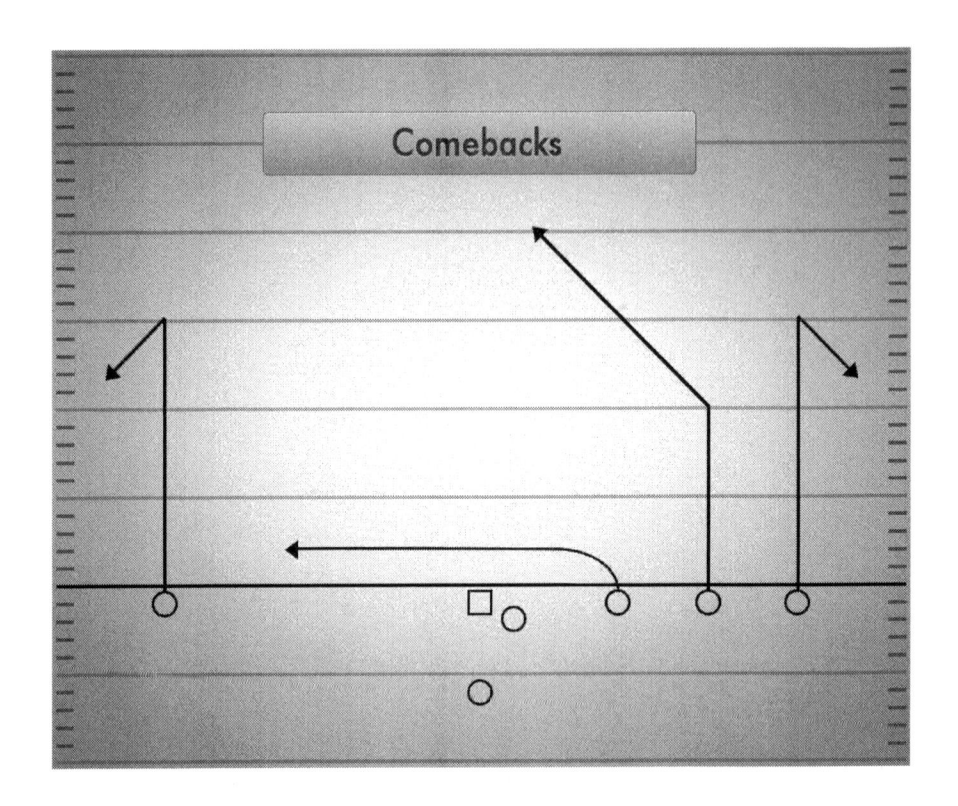

The Comeback route is a great route to run on a defense that is scared of getting beat deep. The way in which the Wide Receivers run the Comeback route is the most important part of the play. The WR will need to push up field hard as if he is running a Fade route or a Streak downfield. Once the defender is turned and running backwards, the WR needs to quickly turn around to the outside, as the QB plays a ball behind on the sideline.

After you scare the defense with the deep ball, the Comeback route is a great route to throw at them in order to pick up a chunk of yards.

FORMATION: **TRIPS FORMATION**

DISTANCE: **MEDIUM YARDAGE**

ROUTES IN THIS PLAY: **POST, SHALLOW CROSS, COMEBACK**

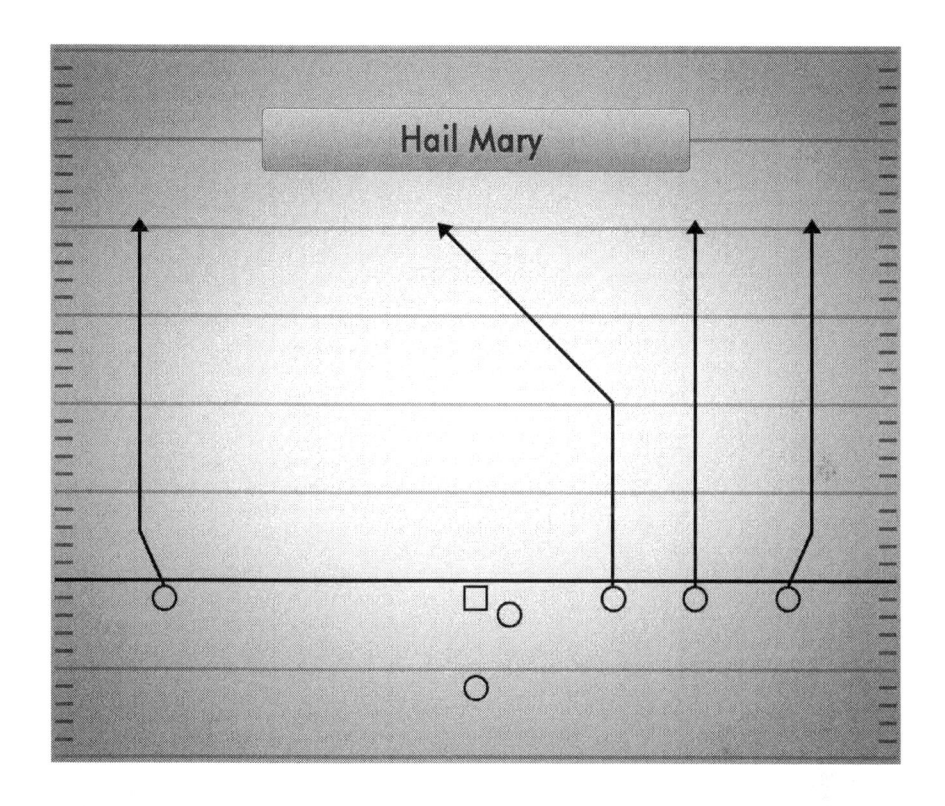

Hail Mary

Hail Mary time! You only need to pull out this play when you need a whole lot of yards all at once.

This version of the Hail Mary play is made to spread out the defense as much as possible, and potentially isolate a defender from the rest of his team. The Quarterback needs to find the WR who is able to get into a one-on-one match up and throw the ball up for a jump ball.

FORMATION: TRIPS FORMATION

DISTANCE: LONG YARDAGE

ROUTES IN THIS PLAY: POST, STREAK, FADE

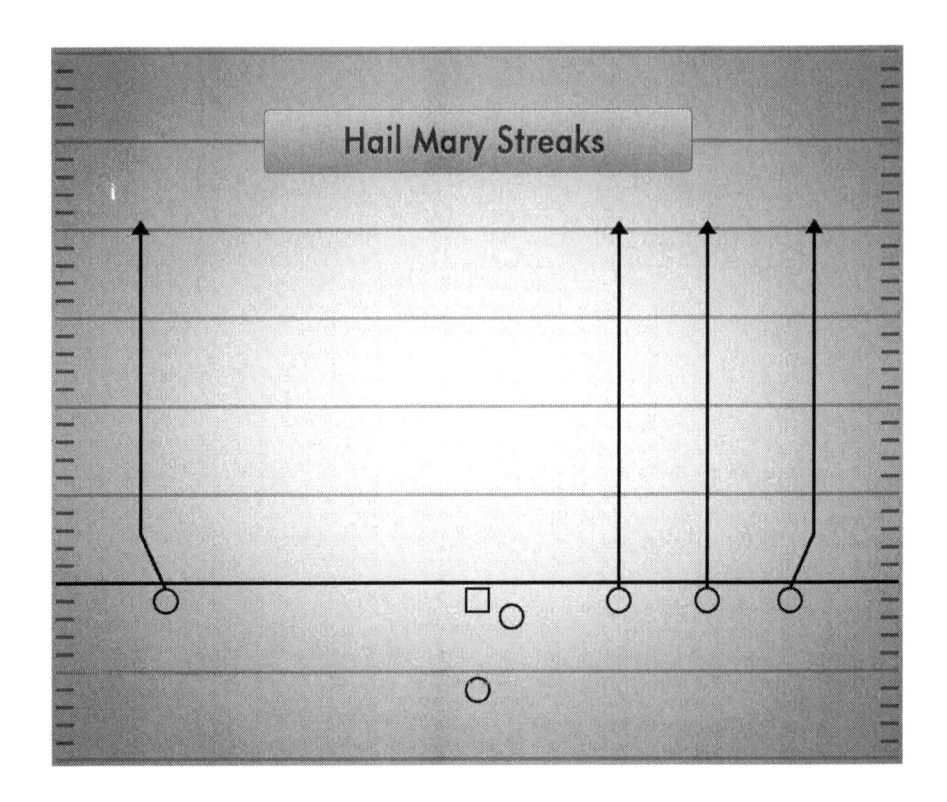

Hail Mary Streaks

Hail Mary time! You only need to pull out this play when you need a whole lot of yards all at once.

This version of the Hail Mary play simply send all the receivers downfield in a straight line in order to get as deep as possible, as fast as possible. Throw the ball up deep and hope for the best.

FORMATION: **TRIPS FORMATION**

DISTANCE: **LONG YARDAGE**

ROUTES IN THIS PLAY: **STREAK**

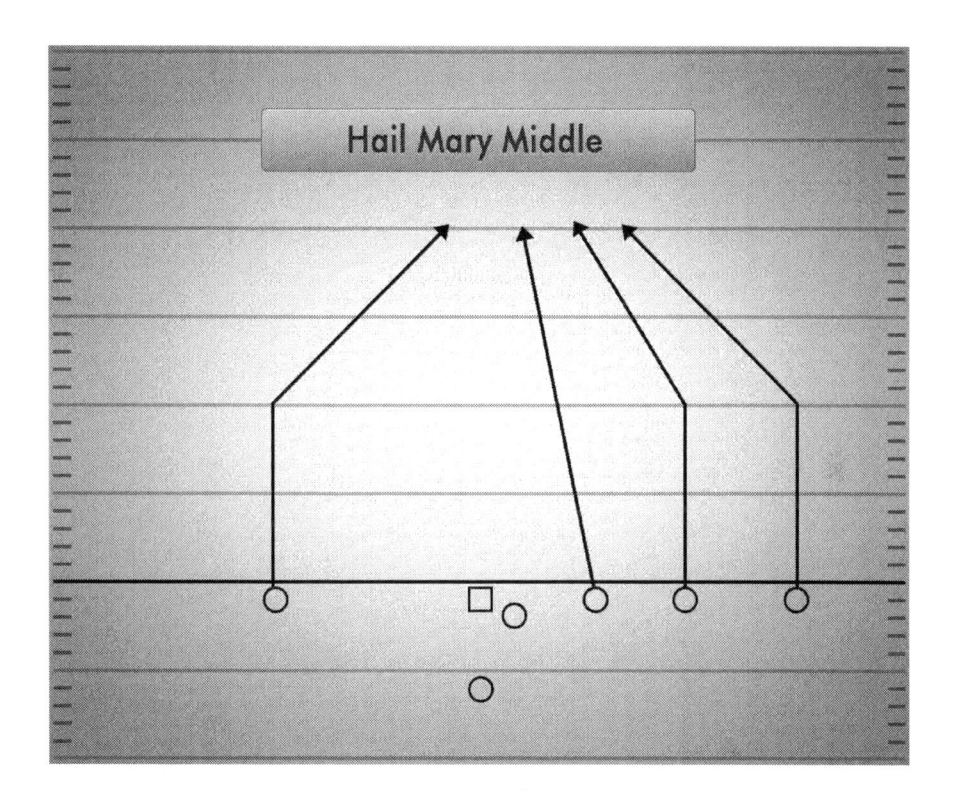

Hail Mary Middle

Hail Mary time! You only need to pull out this play when you need a whole lot of yards all at once.

This version of the Hail Mary play puts all your eggs in one basket by sending every Receiver to the middle of the field. Once all the Receivers are in position, the only thing left for the Quarterback to do is throw the ball as high as he can right into the middle of the field and hope that one of his own players comes down with it.

FORMATION: **TRIPS FORMATION**

DISTANCE: **LONG YARDAGE**

ROUTES IN THIS PLAY: **POST**

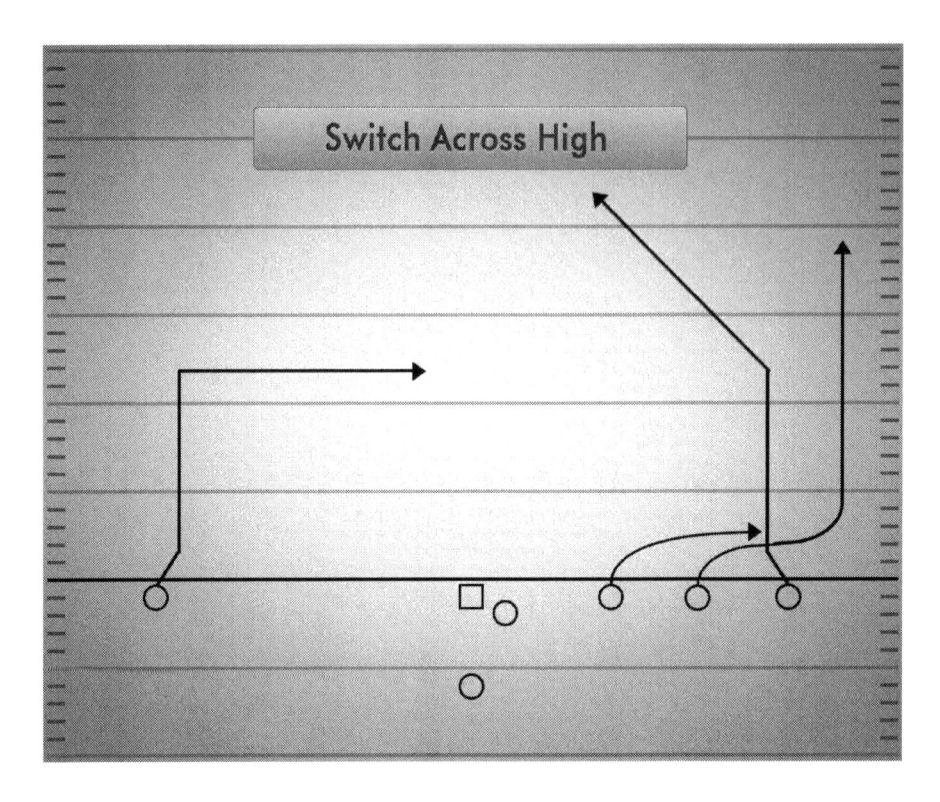

Switch Across High

This is the deeper variation of the Switch Across Low play. The key to this play is creating confusion for the defense at the very start of the play by having the receivers switch across each other on the way to their destination. This switch makes it hard for a zone defense to keep track of all the routes, and makes it very difficult for a man-to-man defense to keep up with the receiver amongst all the chaos going on.

FORMATION: **TRIPS FORMATION**

DISTANCE: **LONG YARDAGE**

ROUTES IN THIS PLAY: **POST, IN, WHEEL**

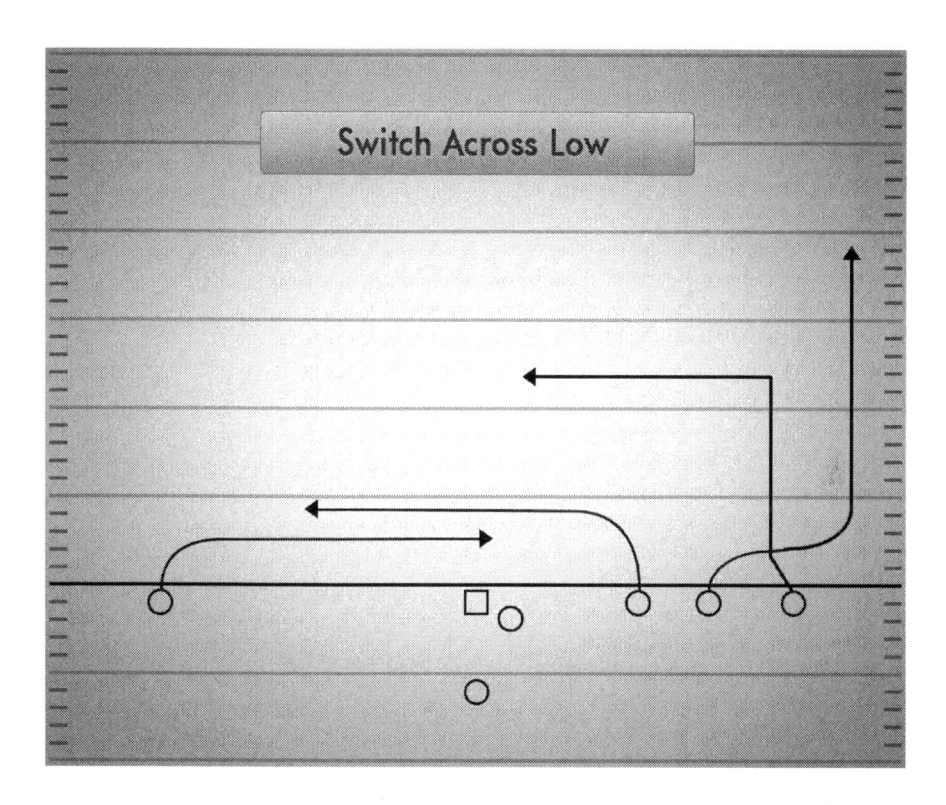

Switch Across Low

This is the shorter variation of the Switch Across High play. The key to this play is creating confusion for the defense at the very start of the play by having the receivers switch across each other on the way to their destination. This switch makes it hard for a zone defense to keep track of all the routes, and makes it very difficult for a man-to-man defense to keep up with the receiver amongst all the chaos going on.

FORMATION: **TRIPS FORMATION**

DISTANCE: **SHORT YARDAGE, MEDIUM YARDAGE**

ROUTES IN THIS PLAY: **IN, SHALLOW CROSS, WHEEL**

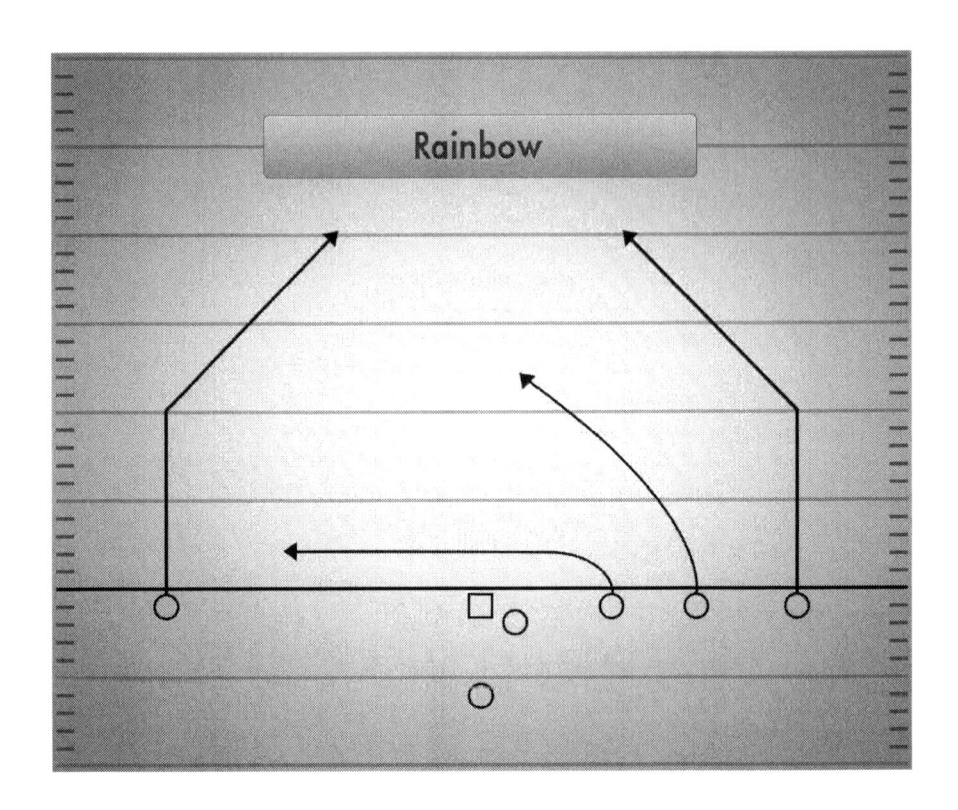

Rainbow

The Rainbow play allows the Wide Receivers to attack the defense by running arcs all across the middle of the field. Each arc is run at a different level of the defense, therefore, combining to create a Rainbow of manly intensity.

The Quarterback can choose to either read the arcs from low to high, or progress from high to low. Finding at least one open man in the Rainbow should be easy with so many routes hitting different levels in the middle of the field.

FORMATION: **TRIPS FORMATION**

DISTANCE: **SHORT YARDAGE, LONG YARDAGE, MEDIUM YARDAGE**

ROUTES IN THIS PLAY: **POST, SHALLOW CROSS**

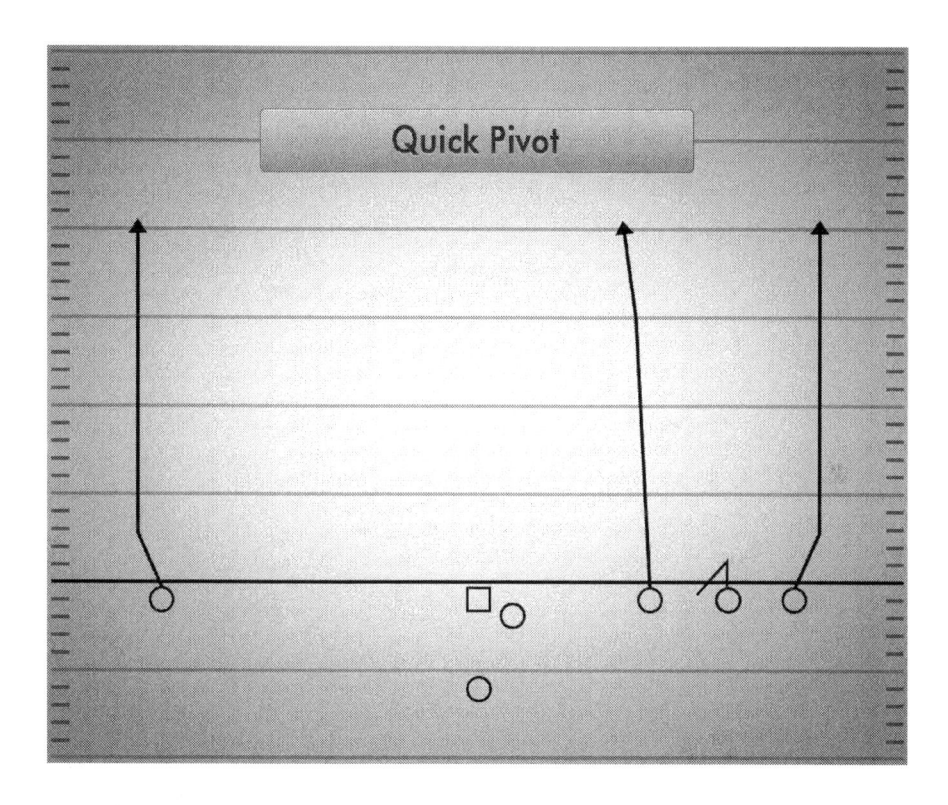

Quick Pivot

The Quick Pivot play is meant to be used as a play against a defense that is backing up off the line of scrimmage. If they are giving too much space to the Wide Receivers, then hit them with this quick pass to catch them off guard. If the Quarterback makes a quick throw to the Receiver, it will give the Receiver a chance to run with the ball in the open field and try to make a defender miss.

It is important that the Receivers push hard off the line of scrimmage for the first few steps, so that the defenders aren't immediately keyed into the fact that it is going to be a quick pass right at the line of scrimmage.

FORMATION: **TRIPS FORMATION**

DISTANCE: **SHORT YARDAGE**

ROUTES IN THIS PLAY: **FADE**

WR Screen

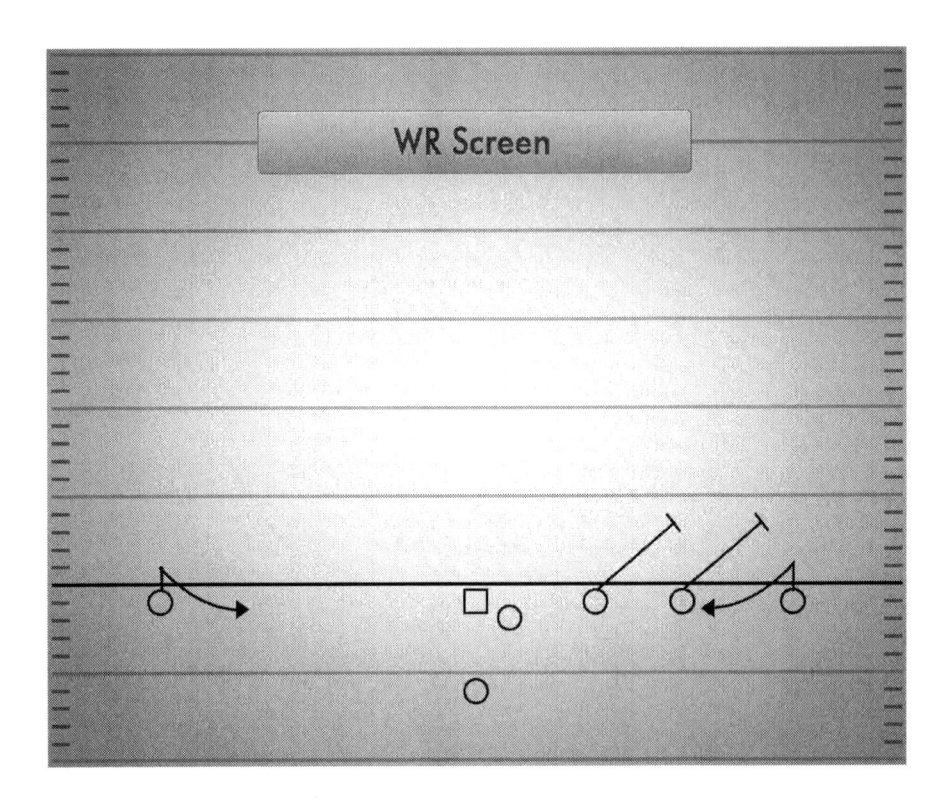

The WR Screen is a play that utilizes blocking by the inside Receivers to enable a running lane for the outside Receiver. The Wide Receiver running the screen route needs to push up field hard for two steps, and the quickly turn around for the ball. Timing is critical on the throw.

The inside Receiver needs to explode of the line of scrimmage directly at the guy who is guarding the outside Receiver. Once that defender turns around, quickly get in his way for the block, and the Receiver catching the screen will be off to the races.

FORMATION: **TRIPS FORMATION**

DISTANCE: **SHORT YARDAGE**

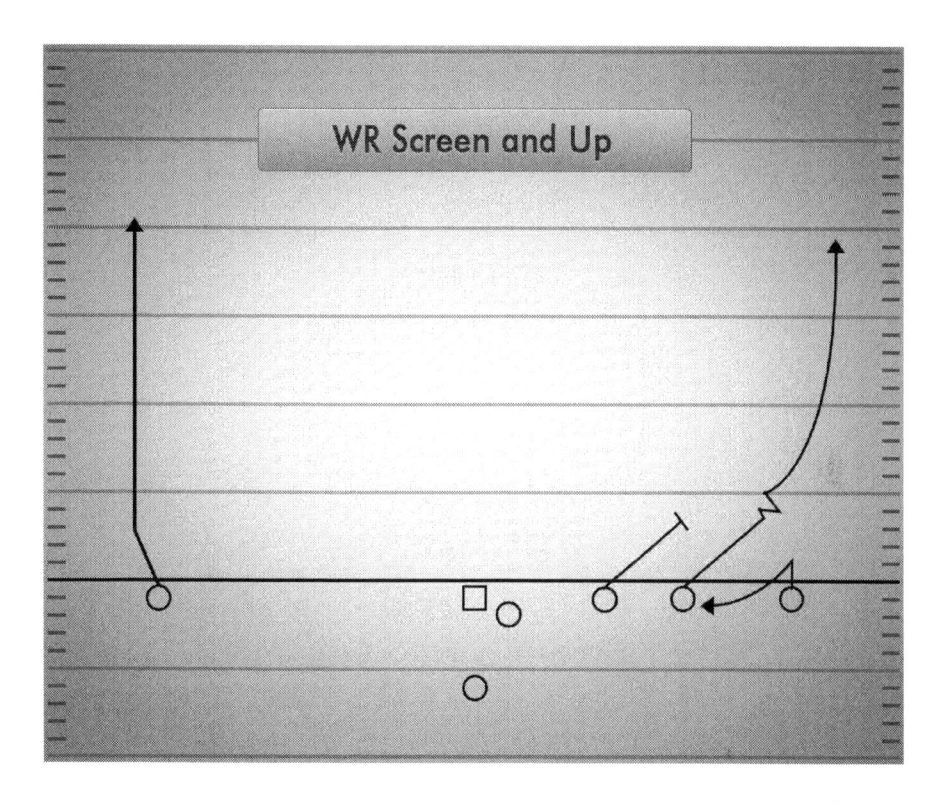

WR Screen and Up

The WR Screen and Up play is a great trick play that takes some time to set up. You have to run the WR Screen play beforehand, and run it successfully. If you begin to hurt them with the Screen, then the defense will start to sneak up forward, and that is when you hit them with the Screen and Up.

The most important aspect of performing this play is the way in which the Wide Receiver fakes his block. He has to run out to the Cornerback as if he is going to block him, and as soon as the Cornerback makes a move to avoid the block, the Receiver then turns on the jets and runs up the sideline. The defense won't even know what hit them until the ball is flying over all their heads.

FORMATION: **TRIPS FORMATION**

DISTANCE: **LONG YARDAGE**

Slot Choice

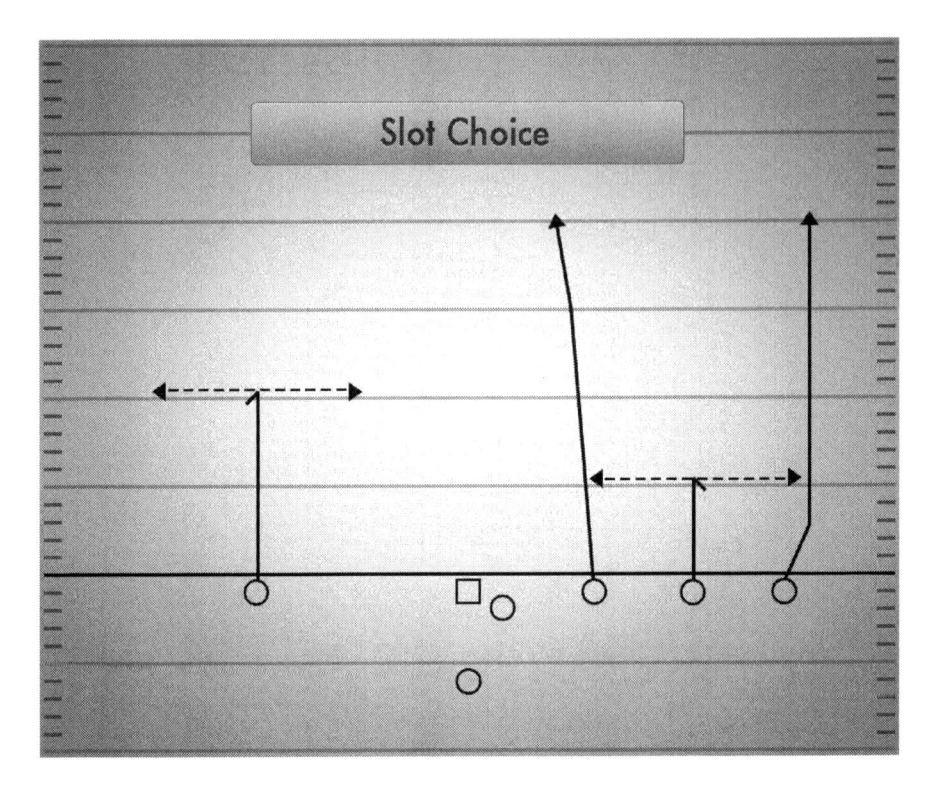

The Slot Choice is meant to be a play that lets the Slot WR get open, no matter what the defense does. The Choice route will either get to its mark and turn around for a stop in place, or it will jet out to the outside, or cut in to the inside.

If the defender is playing inside, then the WR should jet to the outside. If the defender is playing outside, then the WR should jet to the inside. If the defense is playing in a zone, and is giving the WR some space, then the WR should just settle down and wait for the ball.

The Quarterback needs to have great chemistry with the WR so that they are on the same wavelength and can be expecting each other to make the same read.

FORMATION: **TRIPS FORMATION**

DISTANCE: **SHORT YARDAGE, MEDIUM YARDAGE**

ROUTES IN THIS PLAY: **IN, STREAK, STOP, OUT**

WR Choice

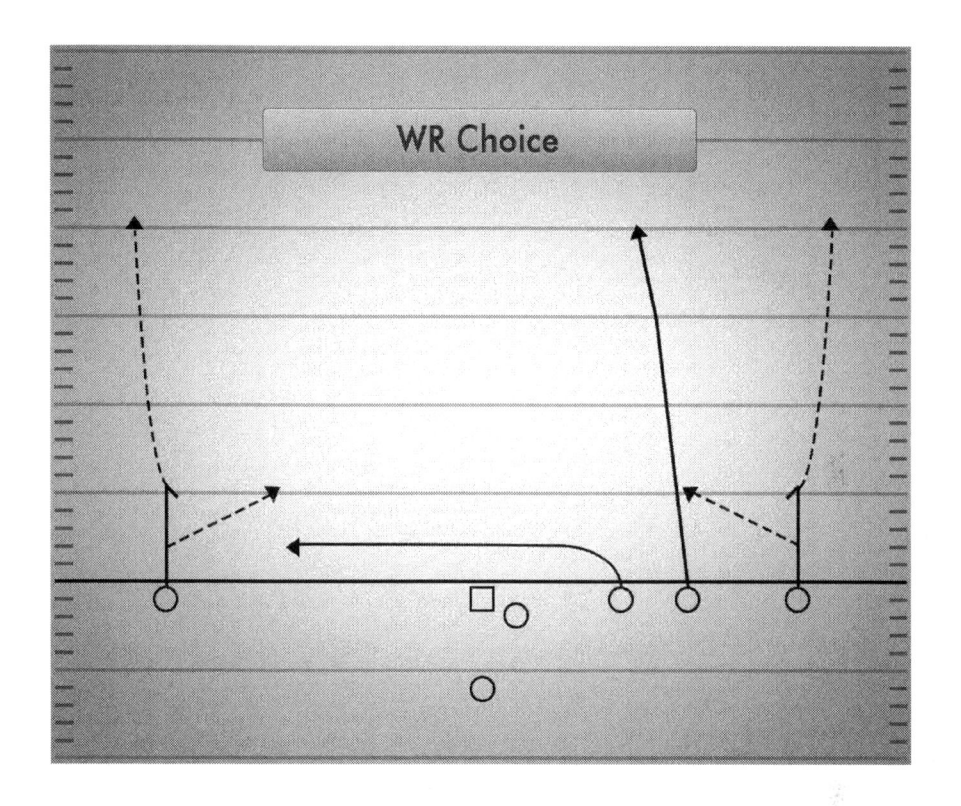

The WR Choice is meant to be a play that lets the Outside WR get open, no matter what the defense does. If the defender is playing inside, then the WR should run up the sideline on a fade. If the defender is playing outside, then the WR should jet to the inside on a slant. If the defense is giving the WR some space, then the WR should just settle down and wait for the ball on a stop route.

The Quarterback needs to have great chemistry with the WR so that they are on the same wavelength and can be expecting each other to make the same read.

FORMATION: **TRIPS FORMATION**

DISTANCE: **SHORT YARDAGE, LONG YARDAGE, MEDIUM YARDAGE**

ROUTES IN THIS PLAY: **SHALLOW CROSS, FADE, STOP, SLANT, SEAM**

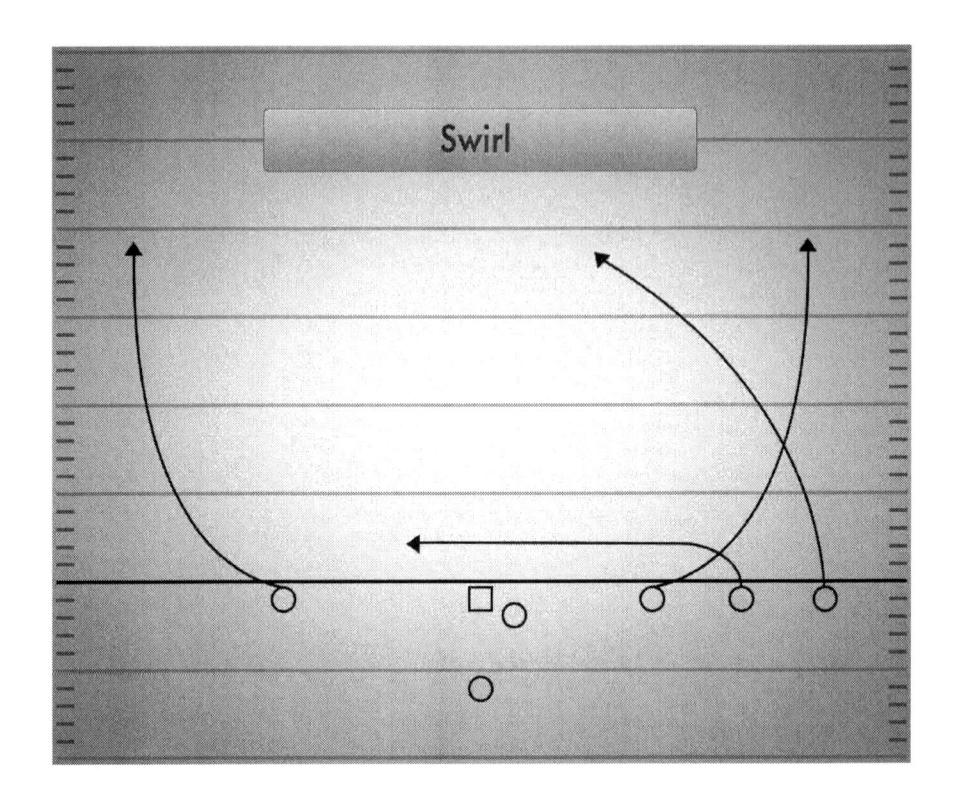

Swirl

The Swirl plays send the defense in a whirlwind by swirling the routes all around across the field. Unlike most plays, there are hardly no straight lines in the route patterns, as all the Wide Receivers are swirling their routes to get to their destination.

The switching and swirling pattern will make it hard for a man defense to keep up, and difficult for a zone defense to keep track.

FORMATION: **TRIPS FORMATION**

DISTANCE: **SHORT YARDAGE, LONG YARDAGE**

ROUTES IN THIS PLAY: **POST, SHALLOW CROSS, WHEEL**

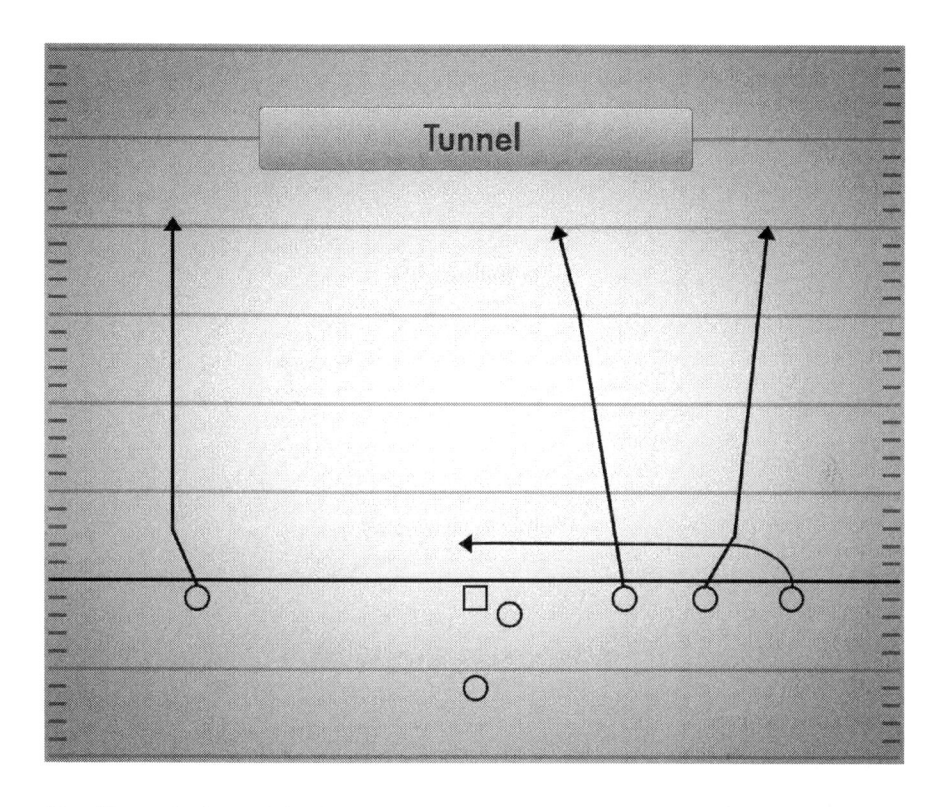

Tunnel

The Tunnel play might look like a deep play when drawn up, but it is really meant to be a play thrown to the Shallow Cross route that is "tunneling" underneath.

The other receivers are used primarily to run off the defense and take all the defenders deep downfield with them. After the defense has backed off, the shallow cross route should be open and have tons of room to run after the catch.

FORMATION: **TRIPS FORMATION**

DISTANCE: **SHORT YARDAGE**

ROUTES IN THIS PLAY: **SHALLOW CROSS, FADE, SEAM**

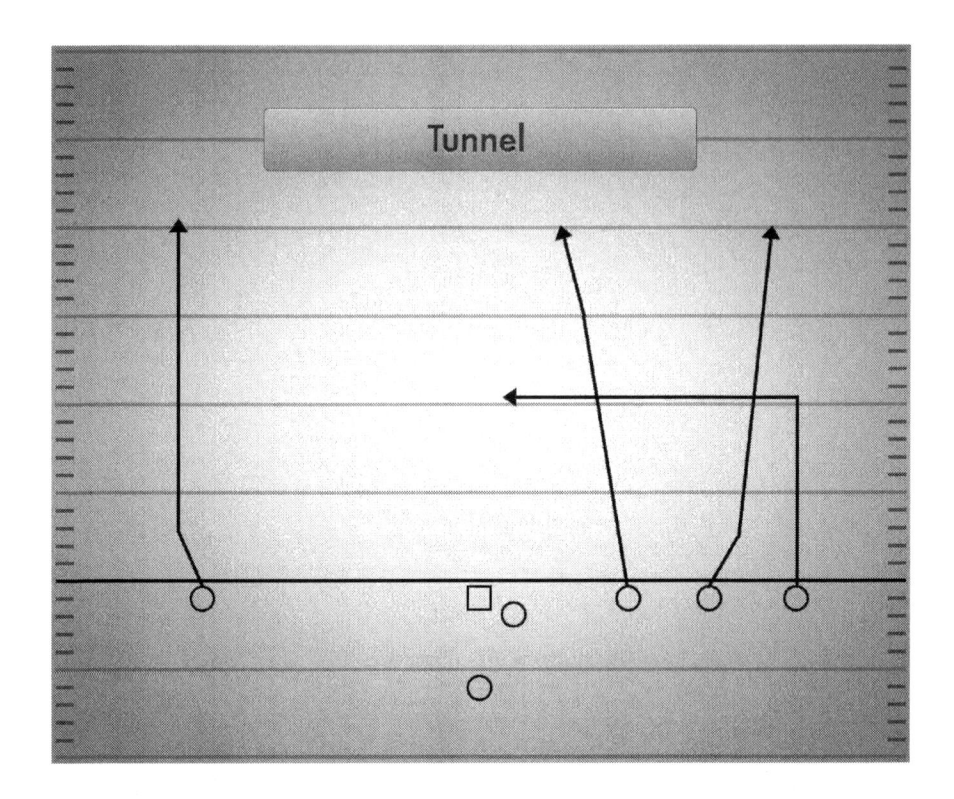

Tunnel

The primary focus of the Tunnel Deep play is to make the defense think that everybody is going deep, and then break off the outside receiver, and hit him coming across the field underneath the deep routes.

The other receivers are used primarily to run off the defense and take all the defenders deep downfield with them. After the defense has backed off, the In route should be open and have tons of room to run after the catch.

FORMATION: **TRIPS FORMATION**

DISTANCE: **LONG YARDAGE**

ROUTES IN THIS PLAY: **IN, FADE, SEAM**

Post Corner

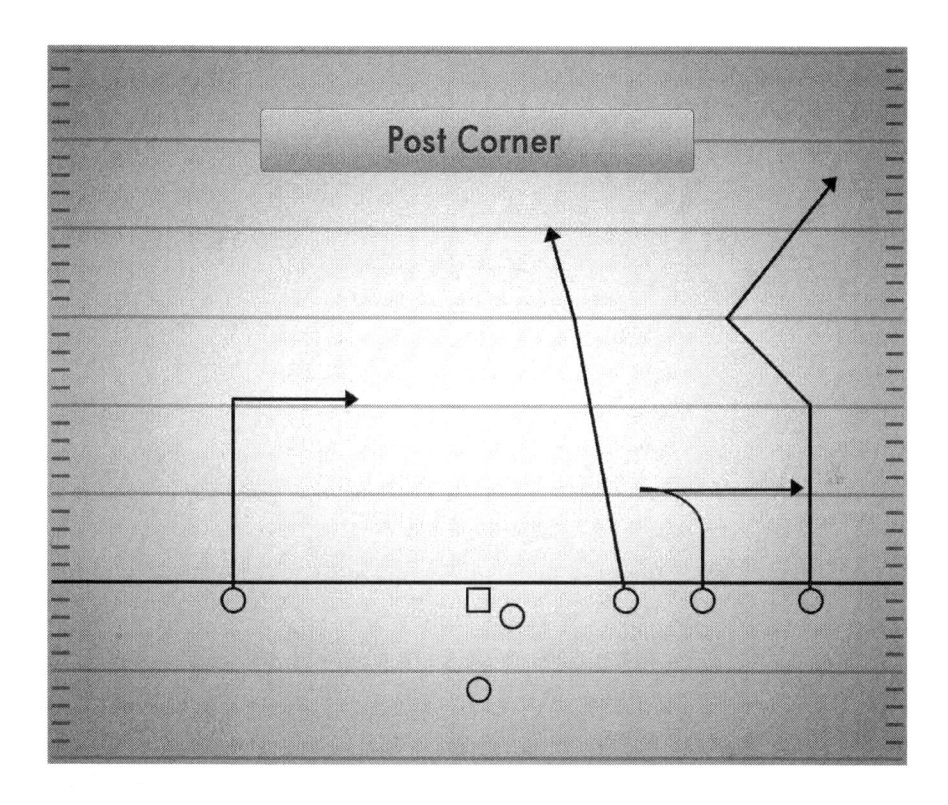

This play is all about setting up the Post-Corner route on the outside. The Receiver running the route has to make it look as if he is running the post, and as soon as he suckers the defense inside, he breaks to the outside and the Quarterback will hit him deep along the sideline.

The Whip route underneath, is used to keep the Cornerback from drifting back towards the Post-Corner. If the Cornerback does carry back deep and get in the way of the Post-Corner, then the Whip route should be open in the flats underneath.

FORMATION: **TRIPS FORMATION**

DISTANCE: **LONG YARDAGE, MEDIUM YARDAGE**

ROUTES IN THIS PLAY: **IN, WHIP, POST CORNER, SEAM**

Bubble

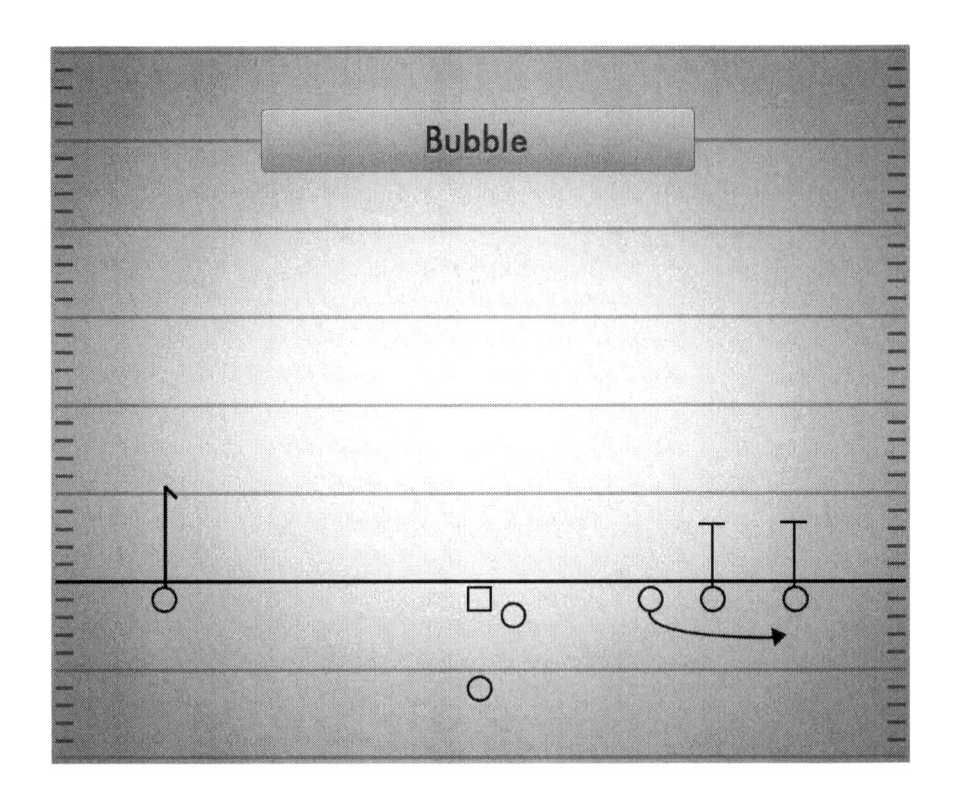

The Bubble play is a simple screen play. The Slot WR will bubble backwards with one step and proceed to drift towards the sideline. The block by the outside WR is critical to the success of the play.

Once the Quarterback delivers the ball the WR will read the block of the outside WR and sprint up the sideline.

FORMATION: **TRIPS FORMATION**

DISTANCE: **SHORT YARDAGE**

Bubble WR Pass

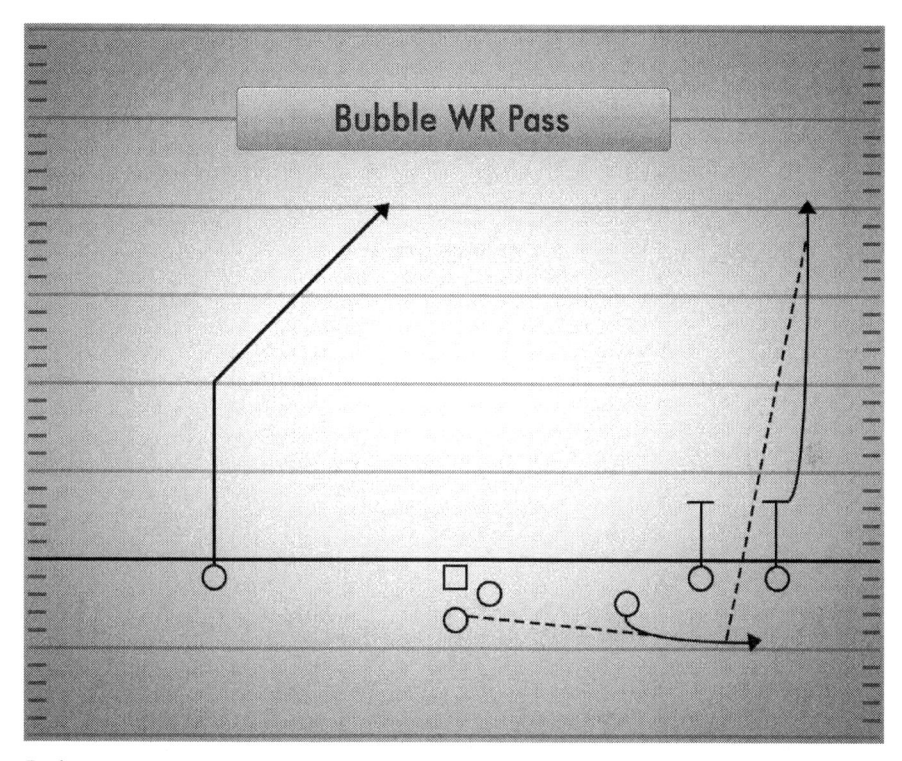

Before you can successfully pull off this double pass trick play, you first need to set it up with the normal Bubble play. After the defense is begins to cheat forward to guard the bubble, that's when you hit them with this Bubble WR Pass play.

The outside WR has to act as if he is going to block the defender like he normally does on the Bubble play, but as soon as he approaches, he needs to sidestep away and start jetting up the sideline. The inside WR needs to make a clean catch and quickly throw it over the defense to the WR who will be open downfield.

One key aspect of this play is that you have to remember that the first throw from the Quarterback has to be backwards, or else the second throw will be illegal. Therefore, the QB should scoot up a bit more than usual, and the WR should line up a little further back than usual, but both have to be done without making it obvious.

FORMATION: **TRIPS FORMATION**

DISTANCE: **LONG YARDAGE**

ROUTES IN THIS PLAY: **POST**

Hook and Ladder

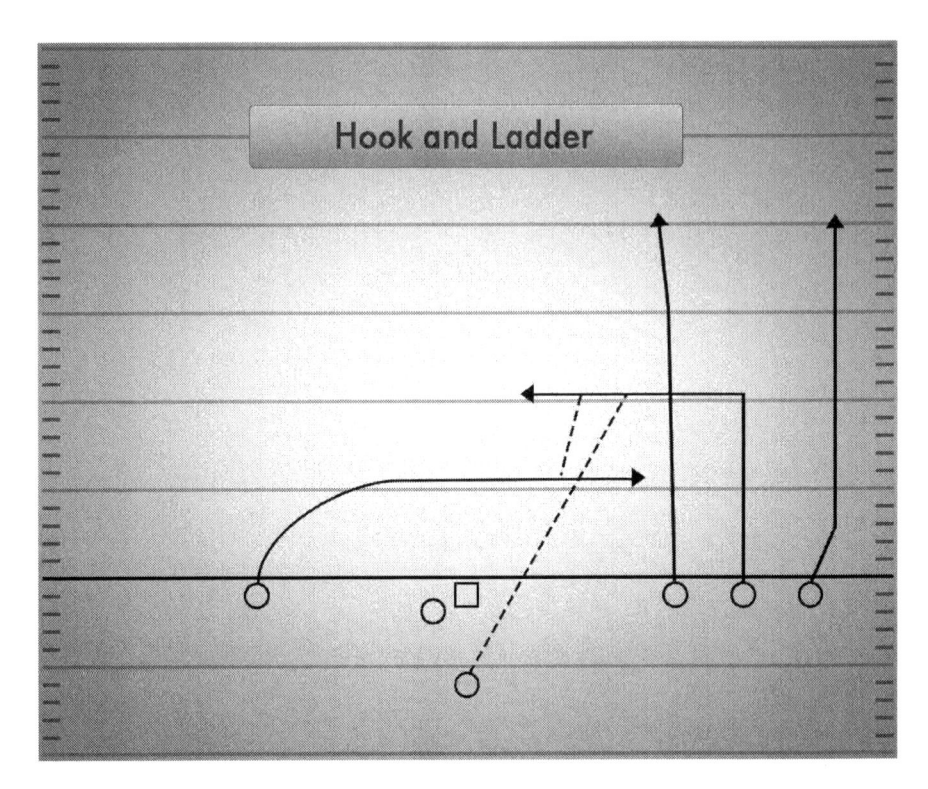

The Hook and Ladder is one of the greatest trick plays in any playbook. It involves incredible timing and perfectly performed maneuvers by multiple individuals, but can be a phenomenally successful play when all the moving parts come together correctly.

The QB must deliver the throw to the In route before he gets too far across the field. The WR running the Shallow Cross must time his crossing route so that he is running underneath the In route immediately after he catches the ball. Once caught, the In route has to quickly secure the ball, and then pitch it backwards to the shallow crosser. The defense will have been moving inwards towards the original receiver, and will be caught off guard when the shallow crosser receives the pitch and is sprinting outward towards the sideline.

FORMATION: **TRIPS FORMATION**

DISTANCE: **LONG YARDAGE**

ROUTES IN THIS PLAY: **IN, SHALLOW CROSS, FADE, SEAM**

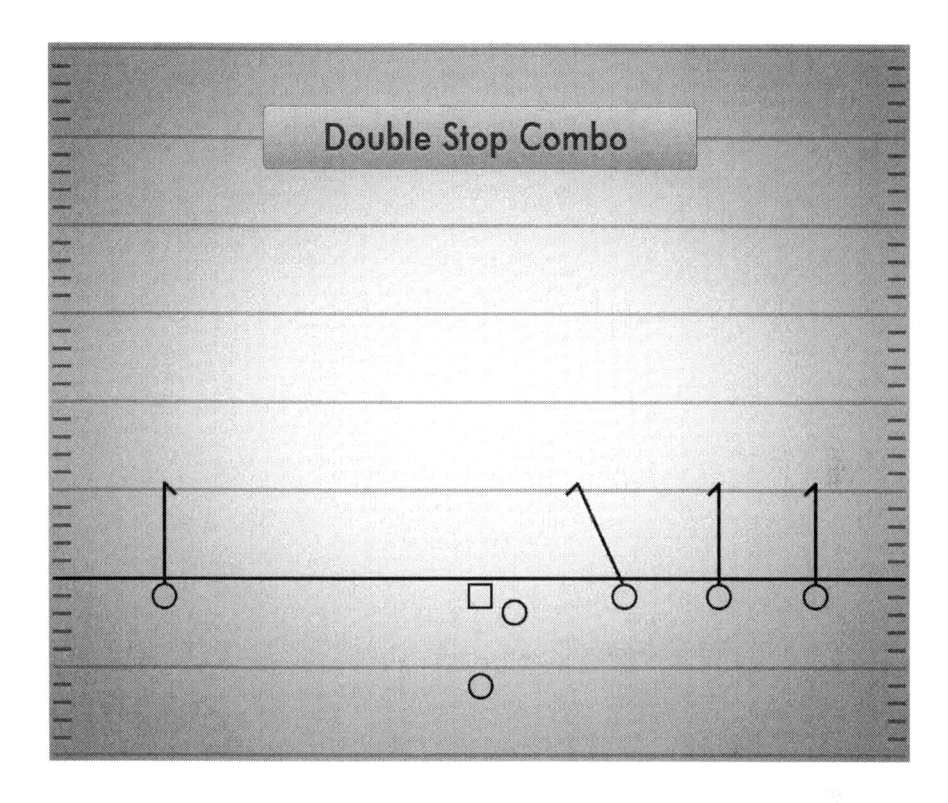

Double Stop Combo

The Double Stop Combo is one of the most fundamental plays of any spread offense passing tree. A simple route concept that quickly presents all the Wide Receivers on a quick 5-yard stop route.

This play can be called early in the game in order to help the QB get settled in, or it can be called in response to a defense that is playing far off the line of scrimmage.

FORMATION: **TRIPS FORMATION**

DISTANCE: **SHORT YARDAGE**

ROUTES IN THIS PLAY: **STOP**

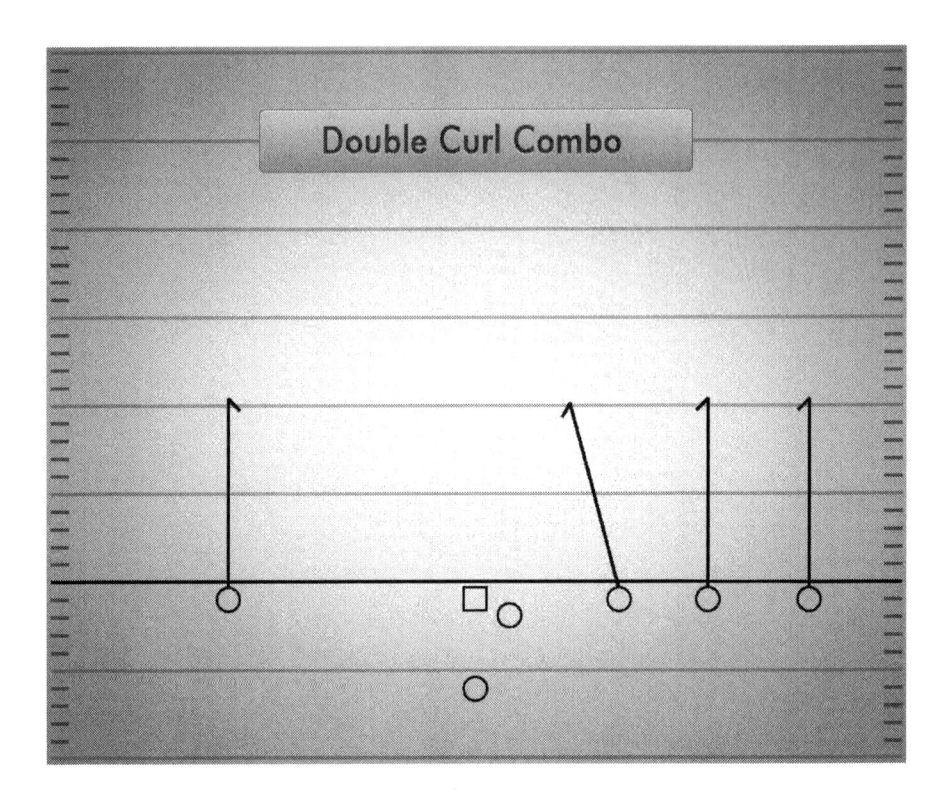

Double Curl Combo

The Double Curl Combo is an extended version of the Double Stop Combo play. It is a simple play for Medium Yardage.

Each Wide Receiver presses hard upfield for ten yards and quickly turns around, orienting their bodies toward the Quarterback who then takes his pick at the open man.

FORMATION: **TRIPS FORMATION**

DISTANCE: **MEDIUM YARDAGE**

ROUTES IN THIS PLAY: **CURL**

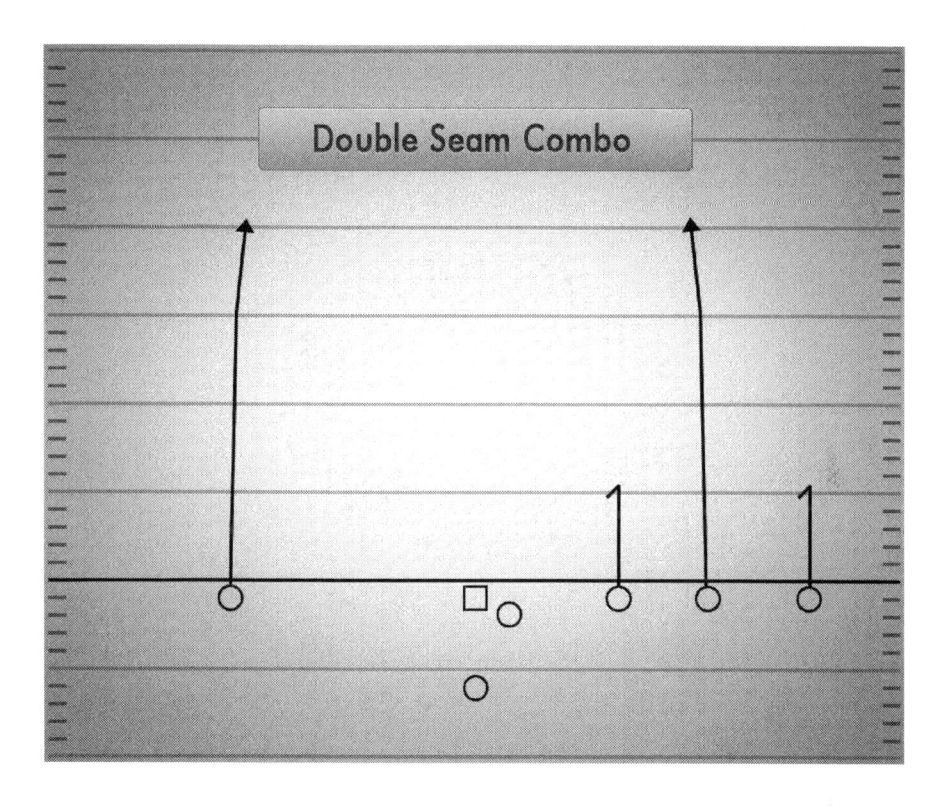

Double Seam Combo

Double Seam Combo is a play that places leverage on the defense up the seams. If the defense drops back to guard the seams, then the Quarterback should through the ball short to the 5-yard stop routes in the flats.

If it is a man-to-man defense, then consider throwing the seams over the top like a fade route, but run from an inside release. Safeties are not accustomed to guarding the fade route, and will therefore put your WR in better position to make the play.

FORMATION: **TRIPS FORMATION**

DISTANCE: **SHORT YARDAGE, LONG YARDAGE**

ROUTES IN THIS PLAY: **STOP, SEAM**

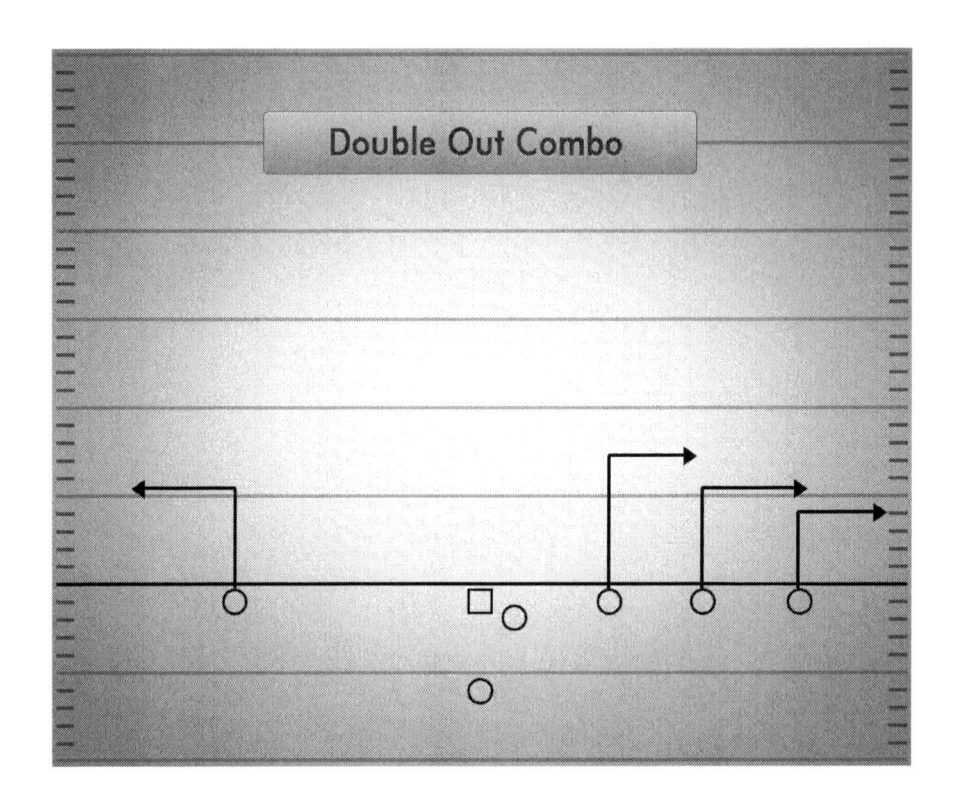

Double Out Combo

The Double Out Combo play places leverage on the outside of the defensive secondary. By attacking the flats with two players, the defender who is guarding the outside zone will be unable to guard both routes.

Versus a man to man defense, the QB must simply make a read based upon which WR makes a better move to the outside against the defender that is guarding him.

FORMATION: **TRIPS FORMATION**

DISTANCE: **SHORT YARDAGE**

ROUTES IN THIS PLAY: **OUT**

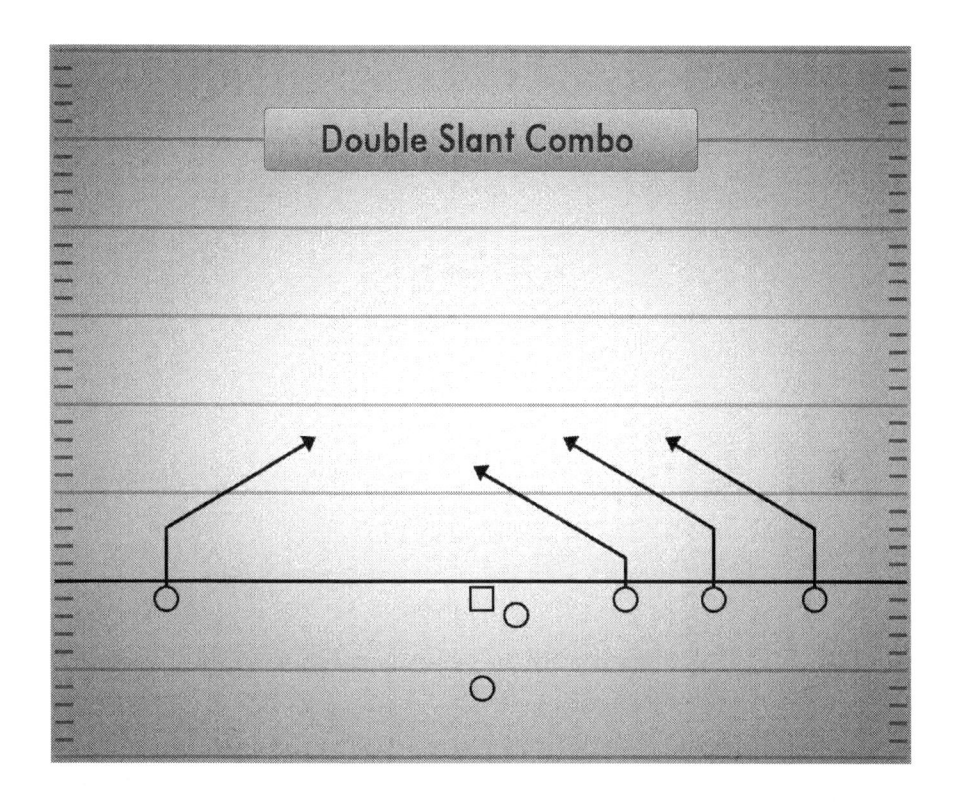

Double Slant Combo

The Double Slant Combo play is a great play to run in a short yardage situation if you have Wide Receivers who can run crisp routes. By making a clean cut to the inside, there will be a window of opportunity for the Quarterback to deliver the ball into the chest of the WR.

This play can also be used as a quick hitting play in the beginning of the game if the defense is playing far off the line of scrimmage. If the defense starts creeping up to guard against the short slant route, then hit them over the top by calling the Slant-and-Up Combo play.

FORMATION: **TRIPS FORMATION**

DISTANCE: **SHORT YARDAGE**

ROUTES IN THIS PLAY: **SLANT**

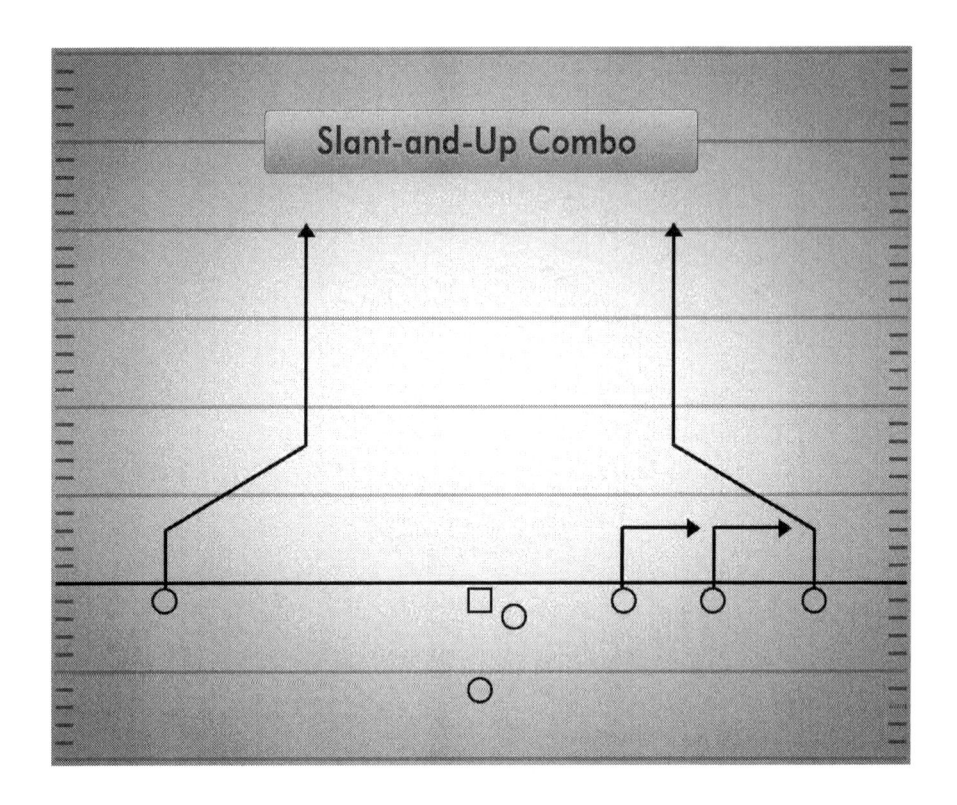

Slant-and-Up Combo

Slant-and-Up Combo is a companion play to the Out-Slant Combo play. By getting the defense used to seeing the Out-Slant combination routes, they will tend to cheat down. That is when you hit them over the top with this play.

As the defense makes a move to jump in front of the slant route, that is right when the WR turns it up field where the QB will throw it over the top for a long gain or a Touchdown.

FORMATION: **TRIPS FORMATION**

DISTANCE: **LONG YARDAGE**

ROUTES IN THIS PLAY: **OUT, SLANT**

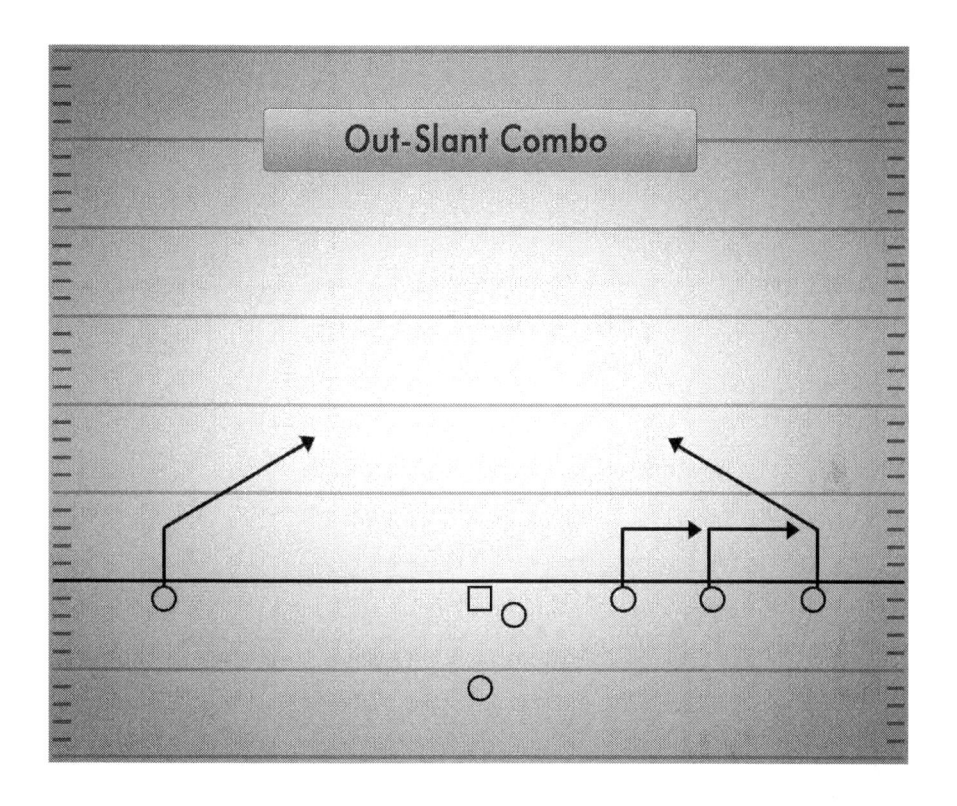

Out-Slant Combo

The Out-Slant Combo twists the defense around regardless of if they are playing man-to-man or zone. If they are playing zone, then the defense won't be able to keep track of the crossing patterns, and the man-to-man defense won't be able to keep up with the quick crossing cuts.

After the defense has gotten used to seeing this out-slant crossing pattern, mix things up by hitting them over the top with either the Slant-and-Up Combo play or the Out-and-Up Combo play.

FORMATION: **TRIPS FORMATION**

DISTANCE: **SHORT YARDAGE**

ROUTES IN THIS PLAY: **OUT, SLANT**

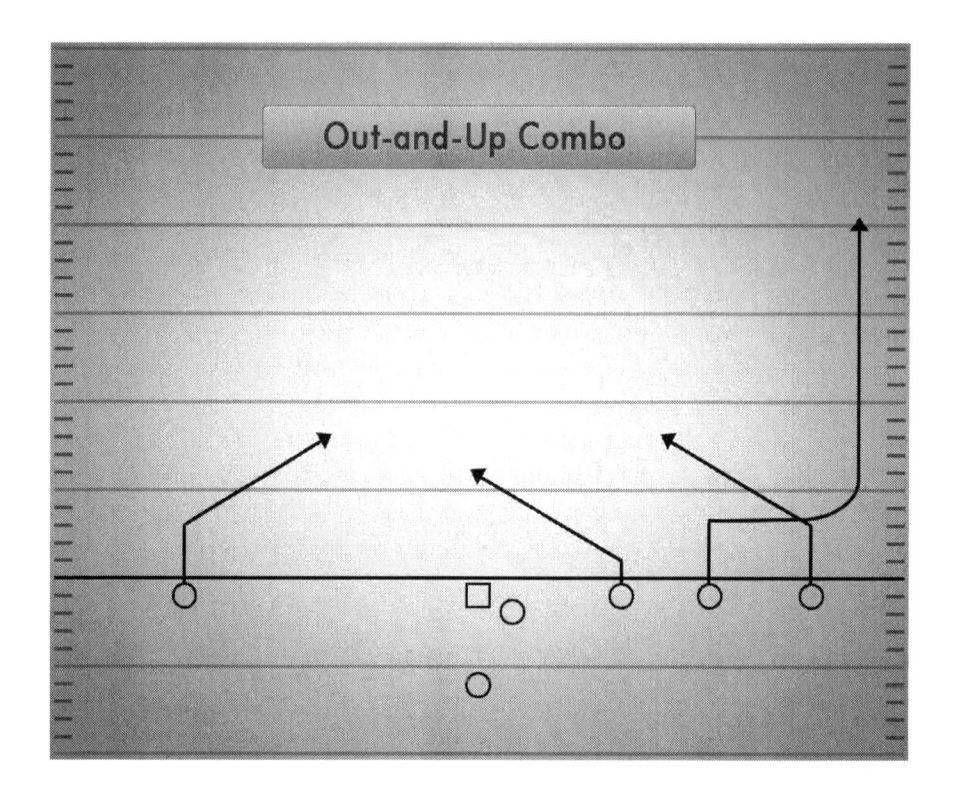

Out-and-Up Combo

The Out-and Up Combo is a companion play to the Out-Slant Combo play. After you have gotten the defense used to the shorter out route, hit them over the top with the Out-and-Up.

The part that makes this play extremely dangerous is against a man to man defense where the defender on the Out-and-Up route will have to run underneath the slant route, and will therefore be in a bad position to keep up with the inside WR who is now sprinting wide open up the sideline.

FORMATION: **TRIPS FORMATION**

DISTANCE: **LONG YARDAGE**

ROUTES IN THIS PLAY: **OUT, SLANT**

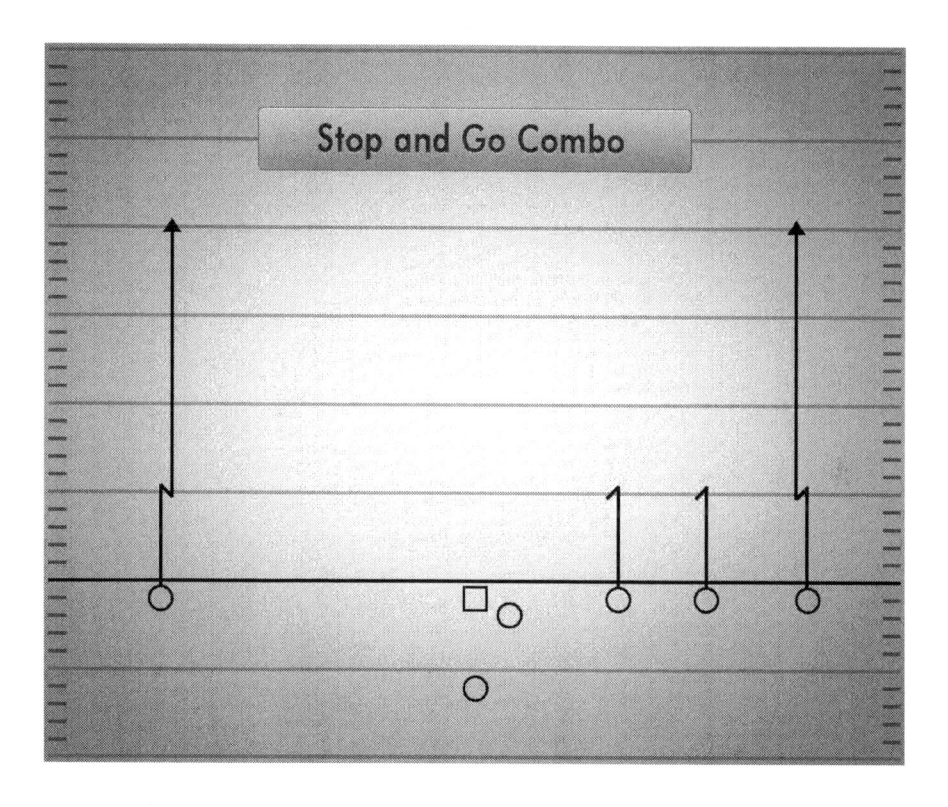

Stop and Go Combo

The Stop and Go route is one of the most famous double moves in all of football. After you have set up this play by repeatedly running the Double Stop Combo play, then surprise them with the Stop and Go and they won't know what hit them.

It is important that the Wide Receiver makes has break up the sideline after he stops. That way he is able to get passed the Cornerback easier.

FORMATION: **TRIPS FORMATION**

DISTANCE: **LONG YARDAGE**

ROUTES IN THIS PLAY: **STOP**

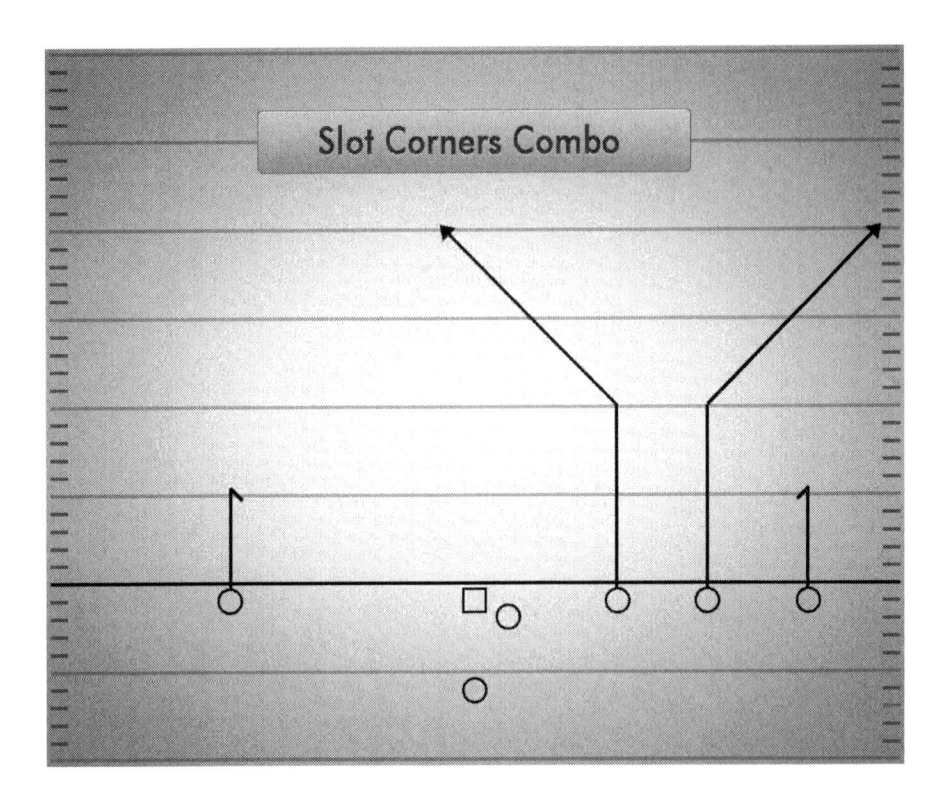

Slot Corners Combo

The Slot Corners play is a great play to use in order to isolate the Cornerback. The only thing that the Quarterback needs to read is how the Cornerback is positioning himself.

If the CB drops back underneath the Corner Route, then throw the ball to the stop on the outside. If the CB stay shallow in the flats, then throw over his head to the slot WR running the Corner route, making a break to the sideline.

FORMATION: **TRIPS FORMATION**

DISTANCE: **SHORT YARDAGE, MEDIUM YARDAGE**

ROUTES IN THIS PLAY: **CORNER, STOP**

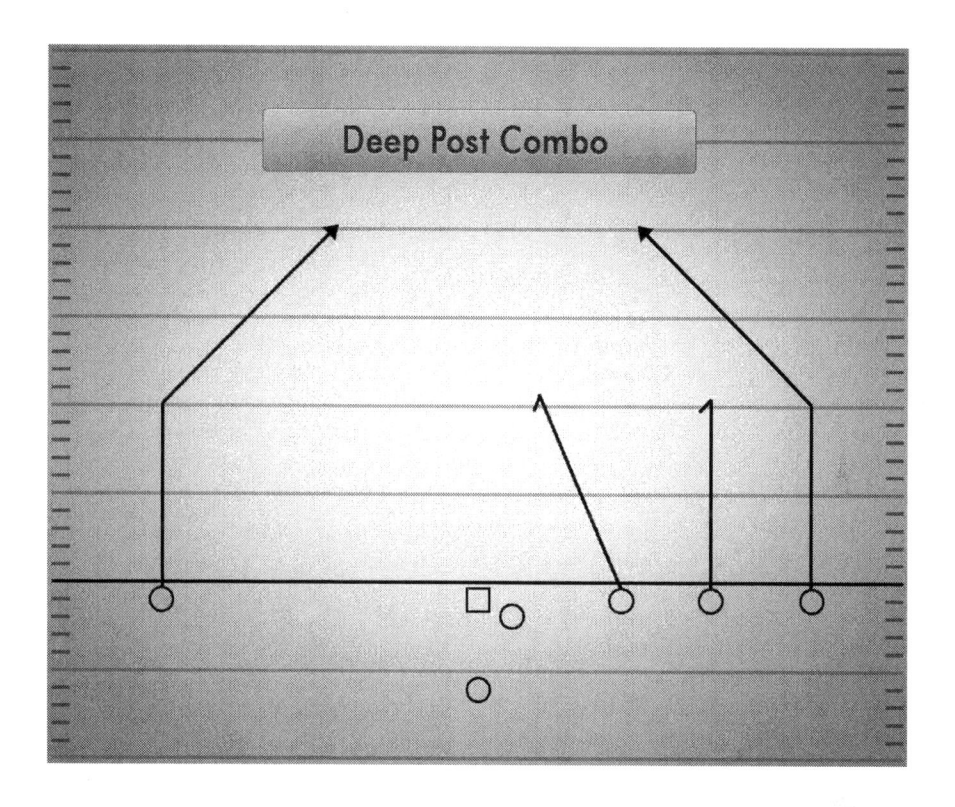

Deep Post Combo

The Deep Post Combo is a great way to attack downfield. The Post Route needs to be a skinny post with a trajectory that doesn't cross the middle of the field. The Slot Receiver needs to run his Curl Route in a way that grabs the attention of the Safety.

The Quarterback's read should be focused on the Safety. If the Safety stays high and guards the Post Route, then drop down and throw it to the Curl Route. If, however, the Safety is drawn down to the Slot Receiver running the Curl, then throw over his head to the Post running downfield.

FORMATION: **TRIPS FORMATION**

DISTANCE: **LONG YARDAGE, MEDIUM YARDAGE**

ROUTES IN THIS PLAY: **POST, CURL**

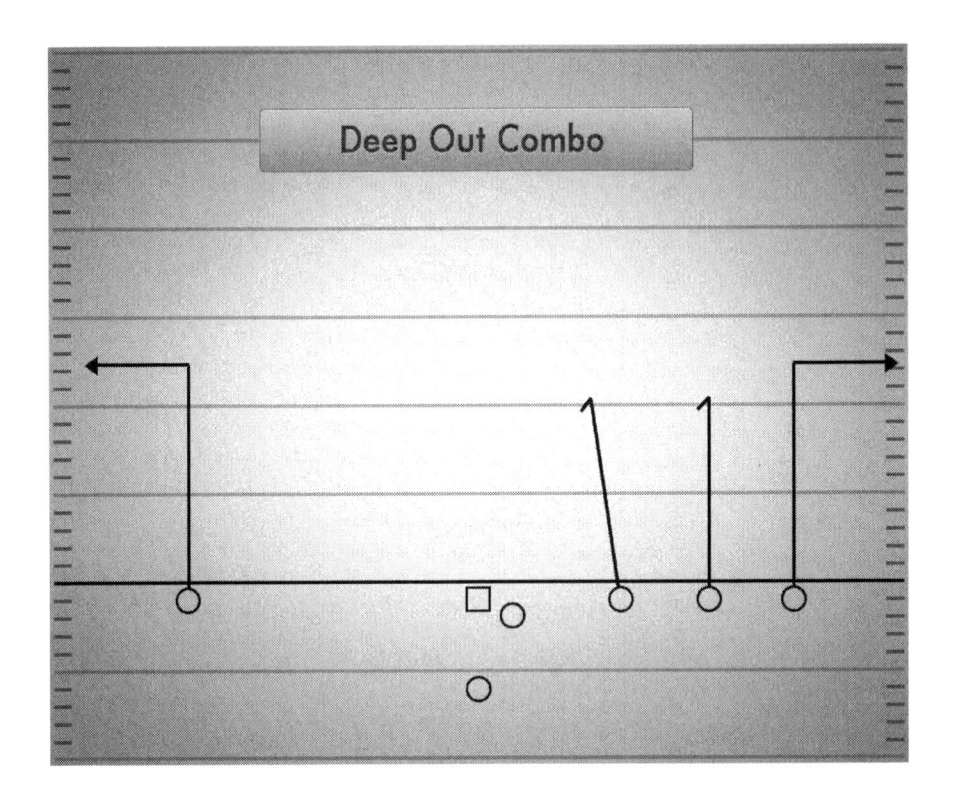

Deep Out Combo

The Deep Out Combo is similar to the Double Curl Combo play with a variation that send the outside WRs towards the sideline on a Deep Out Route.

The QB should make a pre-snap read to determine what side he is going to throw to. Once the side has been determined, then disregard the other half of the field and the read is locked into being between the Deep Out or the Curl Route.

FORMATION: **TRIPS FORMATION**

DISTANCE: **MEDIUM YARDAGE**

ROUTES IN THIS PLAY: **CURL, OUT**

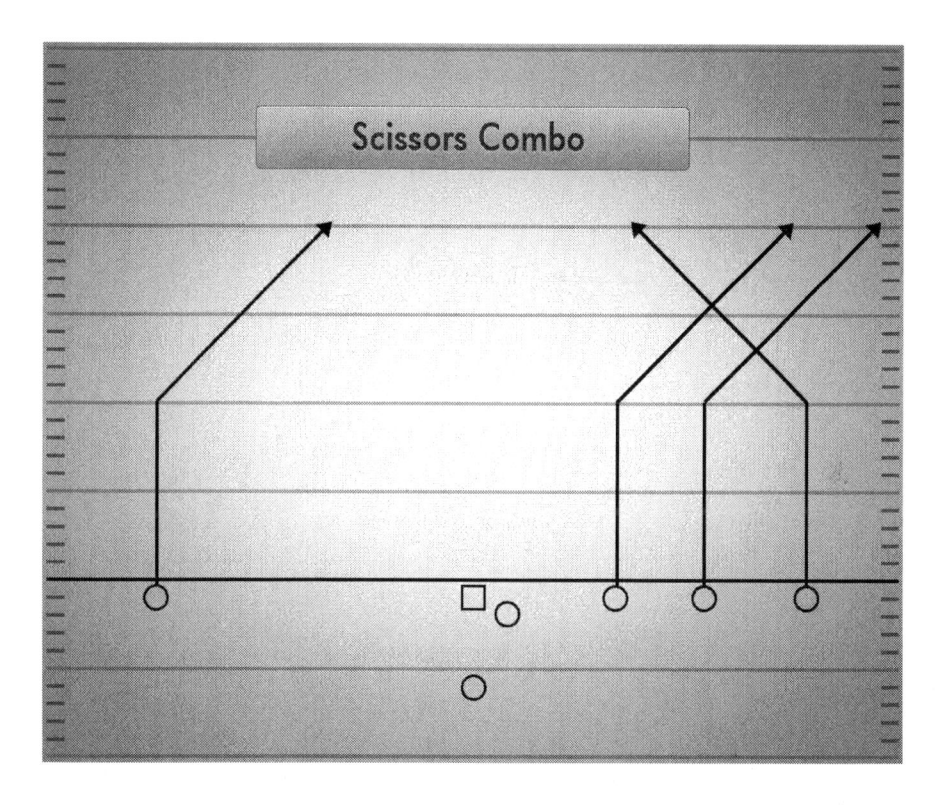

Scissors Combo

The Scissors Combo play is a mirrored play with the same route concept of a Post Route and a Corner Route on both sides.

The Wide Receivers need to cleanly run their routes by converging across each other at the point of the downfield cuts in order to disorient the defense and break free into the open field.

FORMATION: **TRIPS FORMATION**

DISTANCE: **LONG YARDAGE**

ROUTES IN THIS PLAY: **CORNER, POST**

Switchblade Combo

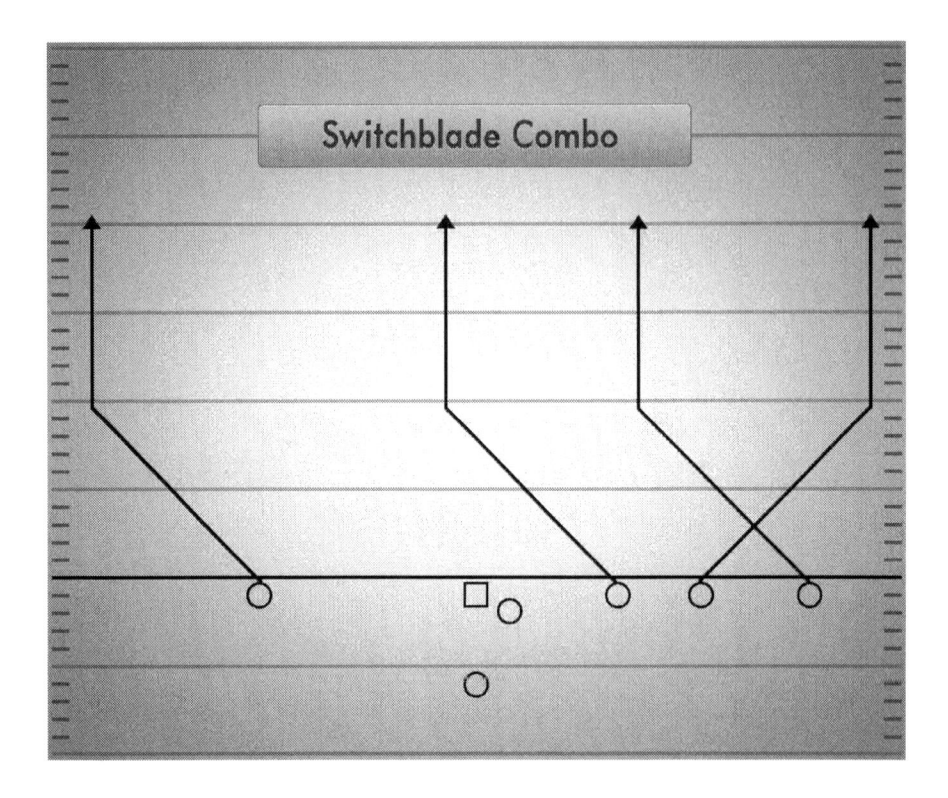

The Switchblade Combo play is intended to create a rub between the two combination receivers in order to break free from their defenders.

This play will work best against a man-to-man defense, because it is easy to lose the defenders when the Receivers cross and then break free going upfield.

FORMATION: TRIPS FORMATION

DISTANCE: LONG YARDAGE

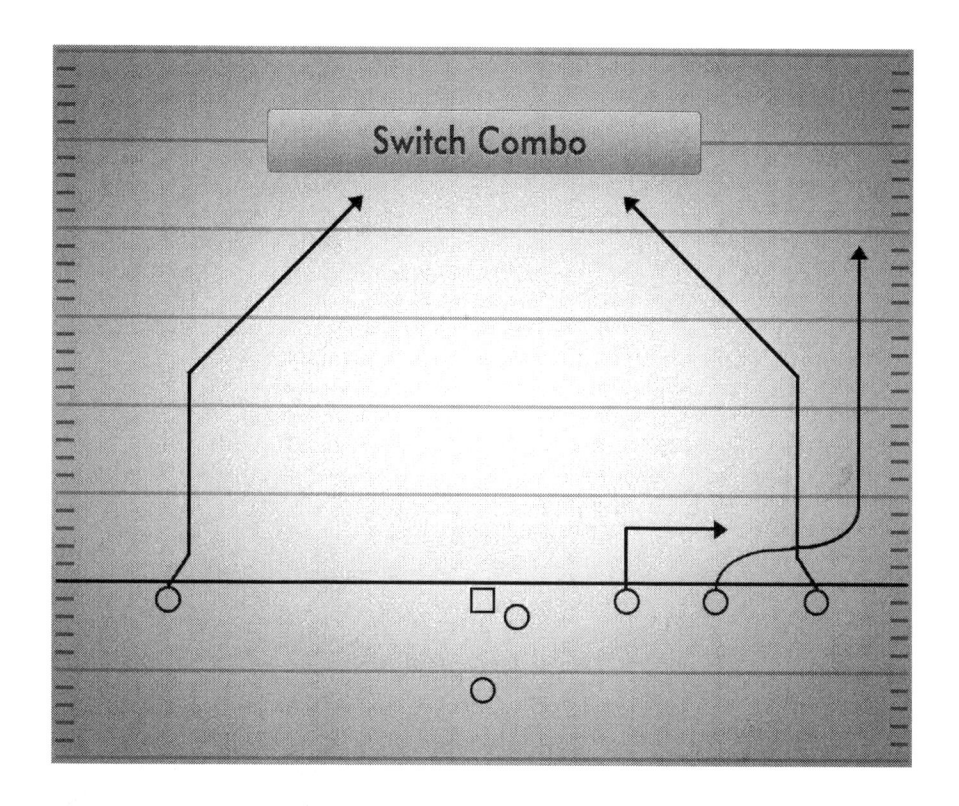

Switch Combo

Switch Combo is the classic switch play where the receivers use their routes to "switch" their positions on the field. The Outside Receiver gets upfield fast and runs a Post Route. The Slot Receiver goes underneath the Outside Receiver and then jets up the sideline.

The Quarterback should read the deep safeties. This play uses four players to attack zones that usually only have two, or maybe 3, defenders responsible for guarding them. Use your eyes to influence the defensive backs' movement, and then find the open WR running downfield.

FORMATION: **TRIPS FORMATION**

DISTANCE: **LONG YARDAGE**

ROUTES IN THIS PLAY: **POST**

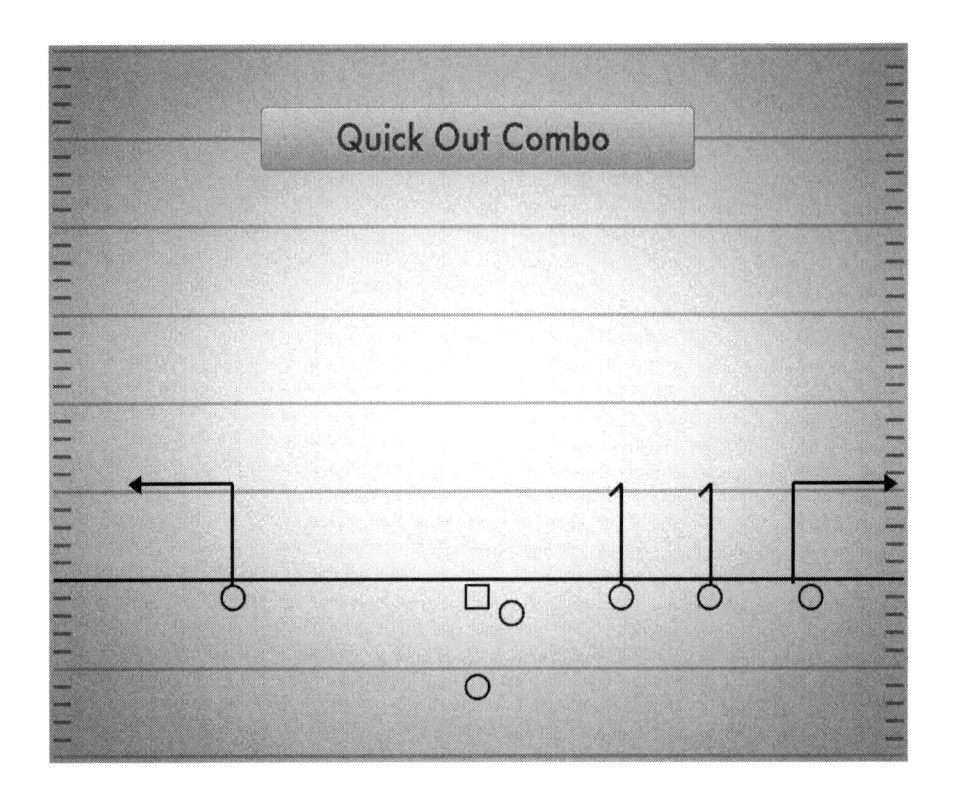

Quick Out Combo

Quick Cut Combo is a variation of the standard Double Stop Combo play, and a shorter version of the Deep Out Combo play.

The Quarterback should select one side of the field on the pre-snap read, and then as the play begins, determine which of the Wide Receivers gets in better position against the defense on his route.

FORMATION: **TRIPS FORMATION**

DISTANCE: **SHORT YARDAGE**

ROUTES IN THIS PLAY: **STOP, OUT**

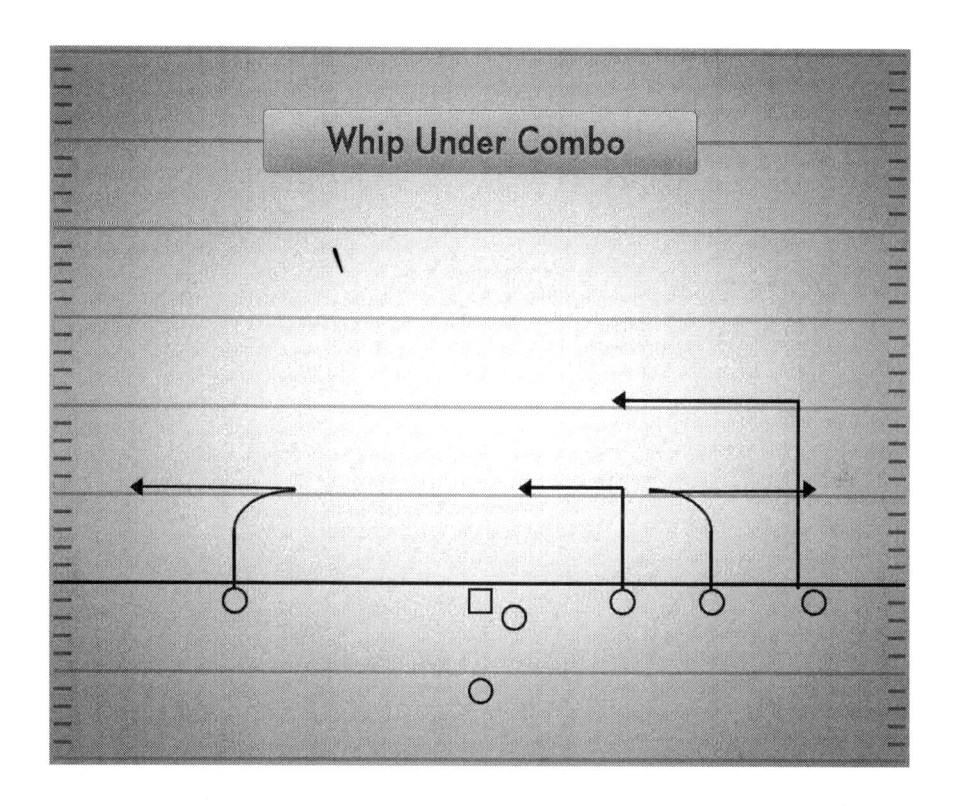

Whip Under Combo

The Whip Under Combo play is a great play to get some horizontal flow in your route concepts going. The crucial aspect of the play is the way in which the Whip Route is run by the Slot Receiver. The route must start of looking like an inside movement, but then the WR must plant his foot and spin (face toward the QB) and jet hard to the sideline.

If the Slot Receiver is not able to get open with the Whip Route, then the horizontal movement underneath should clear out to reveal the outside Receiver open on the In Route.

FORMATION: **TRIPS FORMATION**

DISTANCE: **SHORT YARDAGE, MEDIUM YARDAGE**

ROUTES IN THIS PLAY: **IN, OUT**

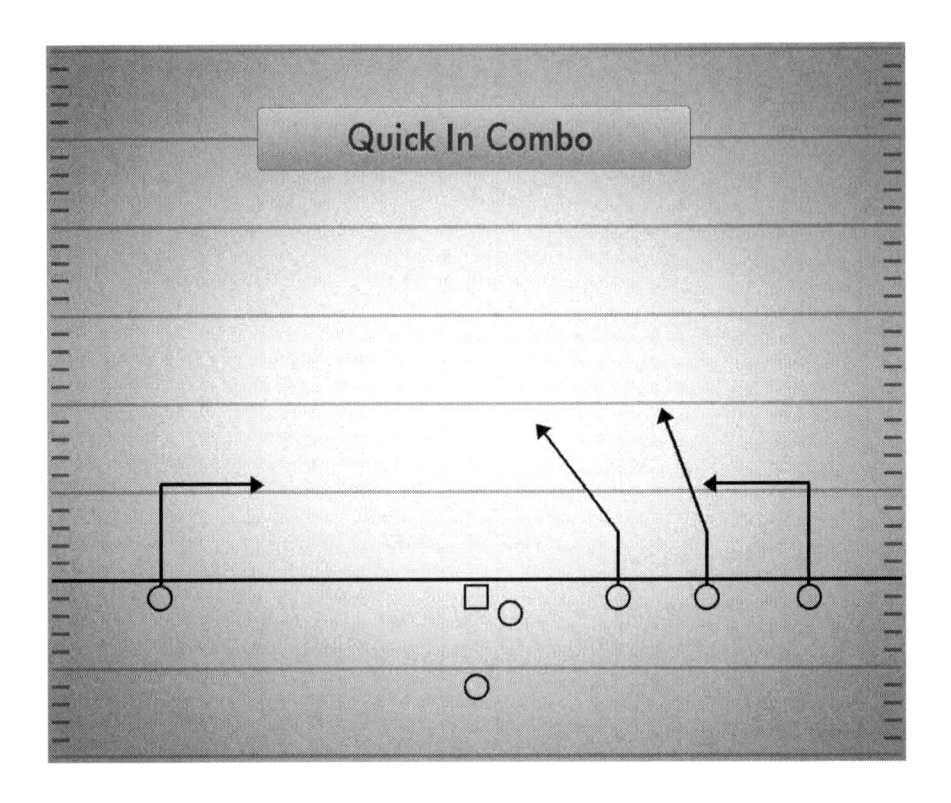

Quick In Combo

The Quick In Combo play is built to be a quick hitter. The Slot Receiver presses off the line of scrimmage in order to create space underneath for the Outside Receiver to be open for the In route.

The QB must make a pre-snap read to determine which side of the field is giving up the most position in the inside zone based upon formation alignment.

FORMATION: **TRIPS FORMATION**

DISTANCE: **SHORT YARDAGE**

ROUTES IN THIS PLAY: **IN, SEAM**

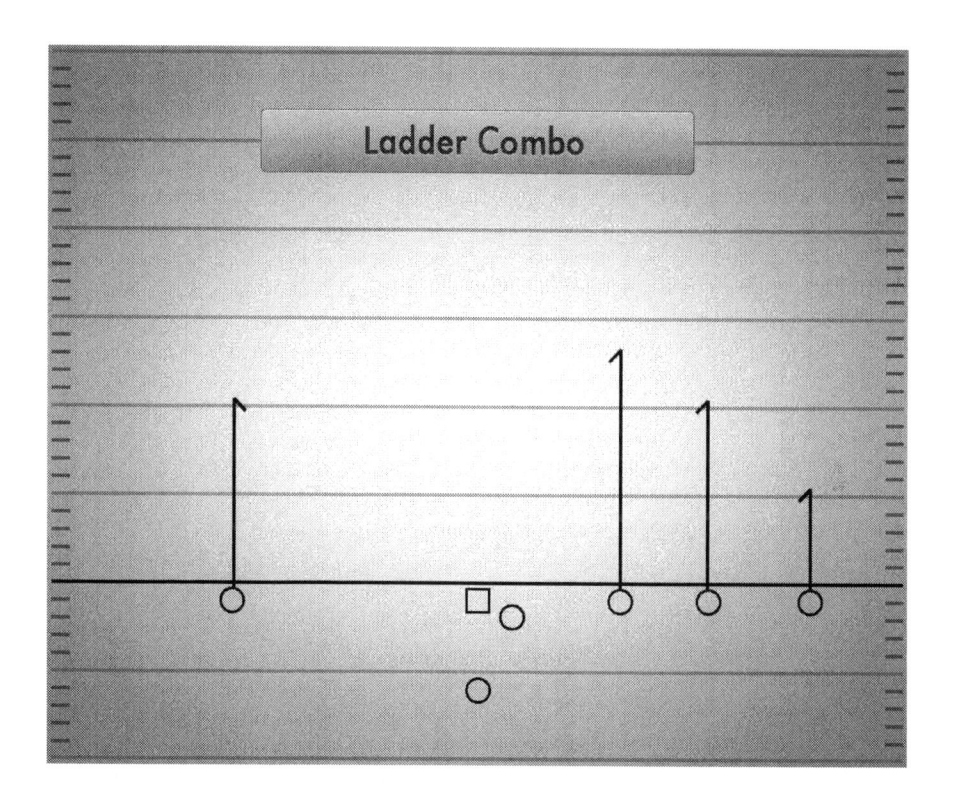

Ladder Combo

Ladder Combo is a play to hit the defense at varying vertical positions. All receivers run a stop and curl routes, but the lengths of the routes vary based upon their alignment.

The Quarterback should make his read just as if he is climbing up a "ladder." First look at the 5-Yard stop, and then work your way up to the 10-yard curl.

FORMATION: **TRIPS FORMATION**

DISTANCE: **SHORT YARDAGE, MEDIUM YARDAGE**

ROUTES IN THIS PLAY: **STOP, CURL**

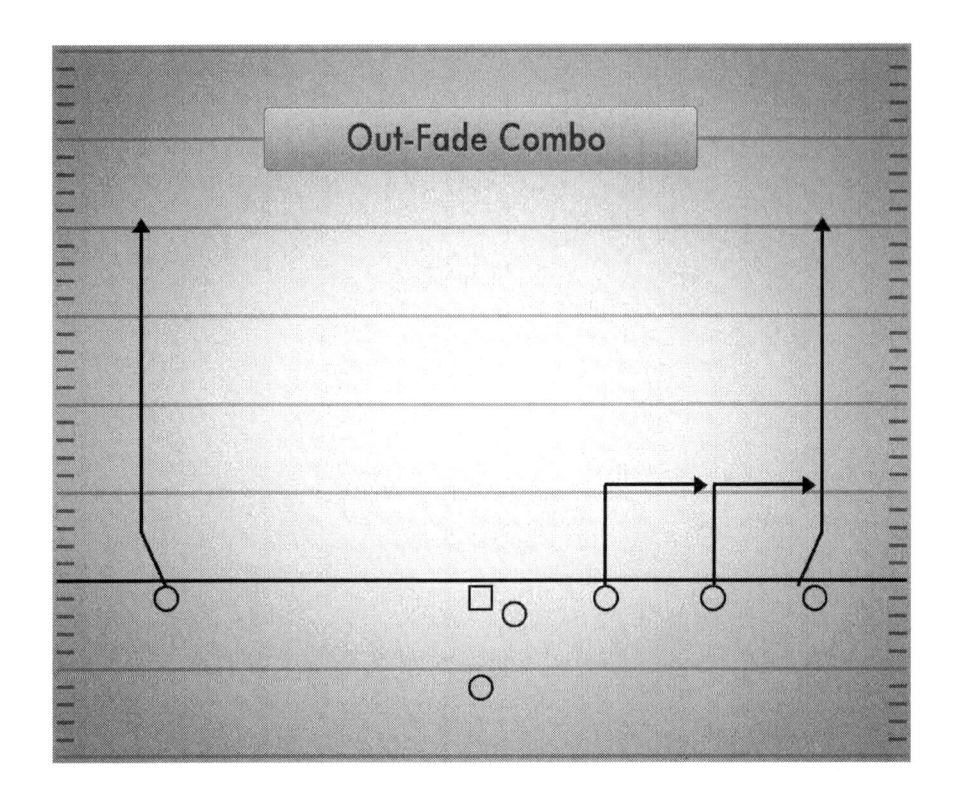

Out-Fade Combo

The Out-Fade route combination is one of the most popular route concepts in any football team's playbook. A Fade Route up the sideline on the outside combined with an Out Route from the Slot Receiver from the inside.

The Quarterback's read should be locked in on the defensive Cornerback. If the Cornerback drifts deep with the Fade, then throw the ball to the Out Route in the flats. If the Cornerback stays in the flats to jump on the Out, then throw it over the top to the Fade.

FORMATION: **TRIPS FORMATION**

DISTANCE: **SHORT YARDAGE, MEDIUM YARDAGE**

ROUTES IN THIS PLAY: **FADE, OUT**

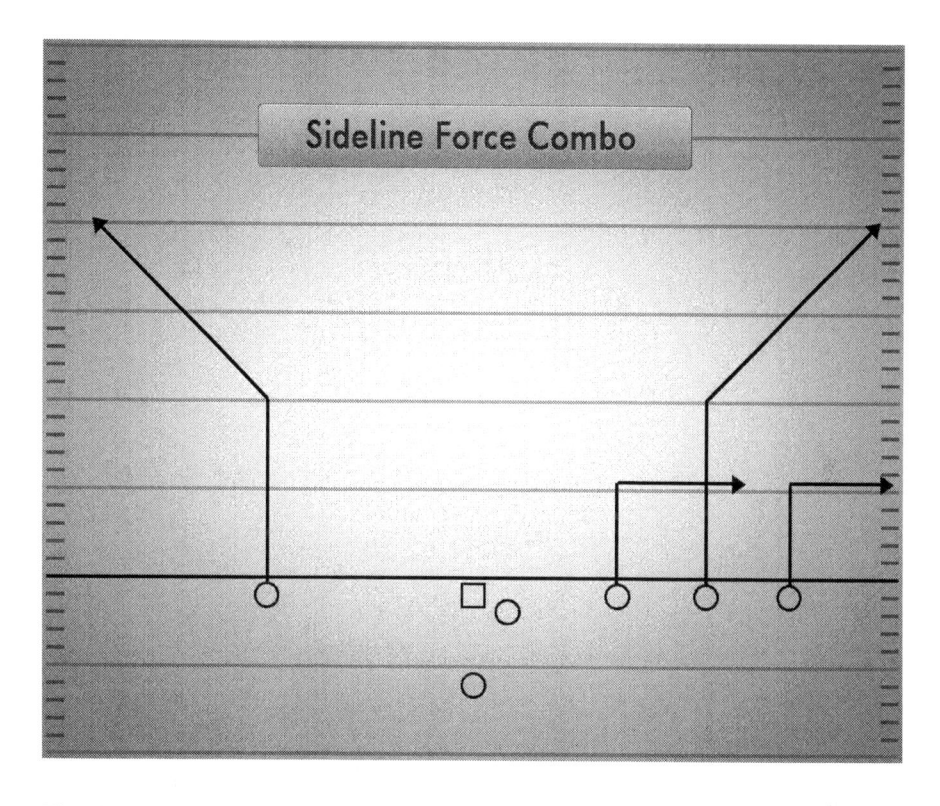

Sideline Force Combo

The Sideline Force Combo play is a shorter version of the Sideline Force Deep Combo play. The main goal of this play is to force the routes to the sideline.

This play is very effective when you need to manage the time on the clock because it allows the Receivers to quickly get out of bounds after the catch the ball.

FORMATION: **TRIPS FORMATION**

DISTANCE: **SHORT YARDAGE, MEDIUM YARDAGE**

ROUTES IN THIS PLAY: **CORNER, OUT**

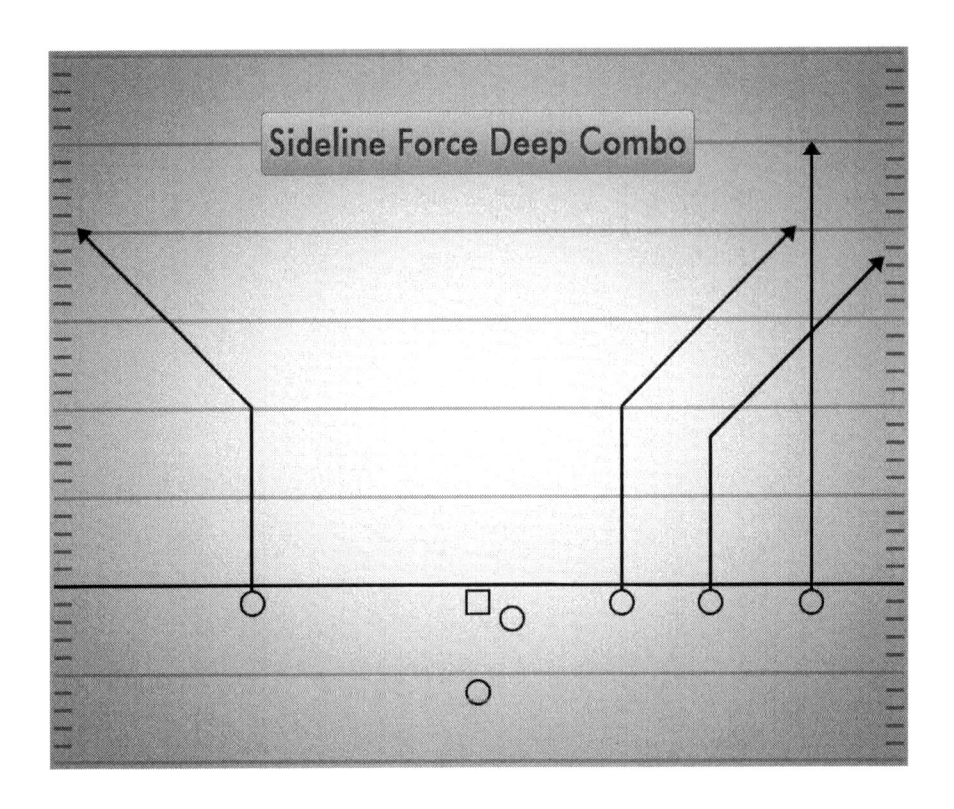

Sideline Force Deep Combo

The Sideline Force Deep Combo play is the deep version of the Sideline Force Combo play. The purpose of this play is to get the Wide Receivers in close proximity to the sideline while running deep downfield.

This play is very effective when you need to manage the time on the clock because it allows the Receivers to quickly get out of bounds after the catch the ball.

FORMATION: **TRIPS FORMATION**

DISTANCE: **LONG YARDAGE**

ROUTES IN THIS PLAY: **CORNER, STREAK**

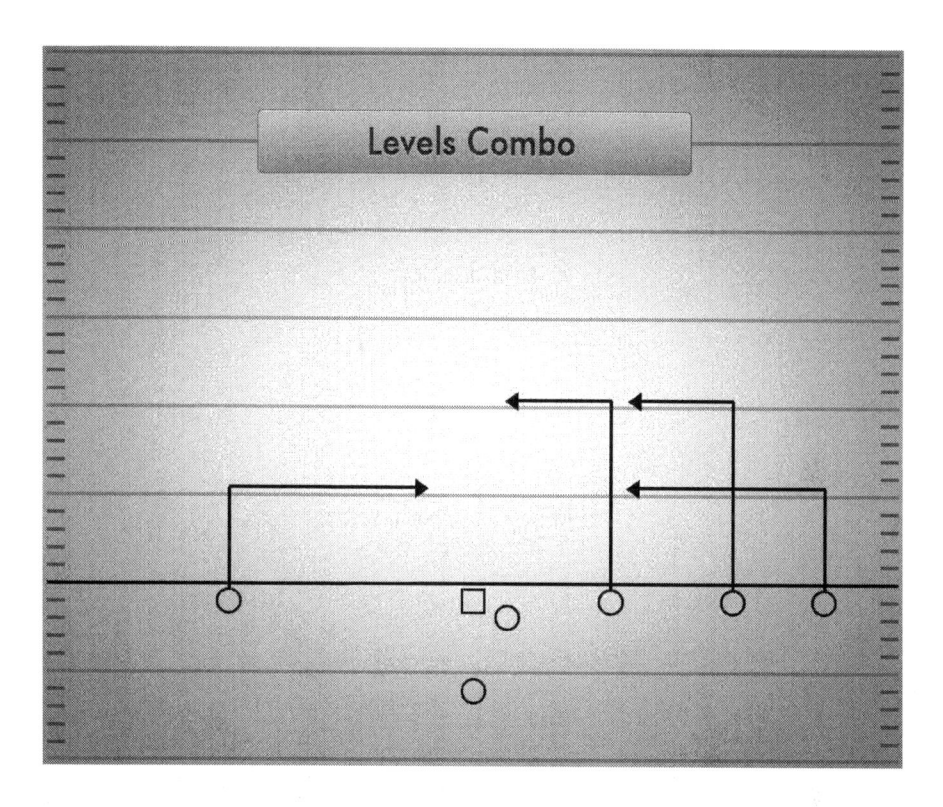

Levels Combo

The Levels Combo play is a great way to attack different vertical portions of the defensive secondary. The Wide Receivers run In Routes at varying distances down the field.

The horizontal movement should create a space for the Quarterback to find an opening to throw into, especially combined with the alternating vertical positioning of the routes.

FORMATION: **TRIPS FORMATION**

DISTANCE: **SHORT YARDAGE, MEDIUM YARDAGE**

ROUTES IN THIS PLAY: **IN**

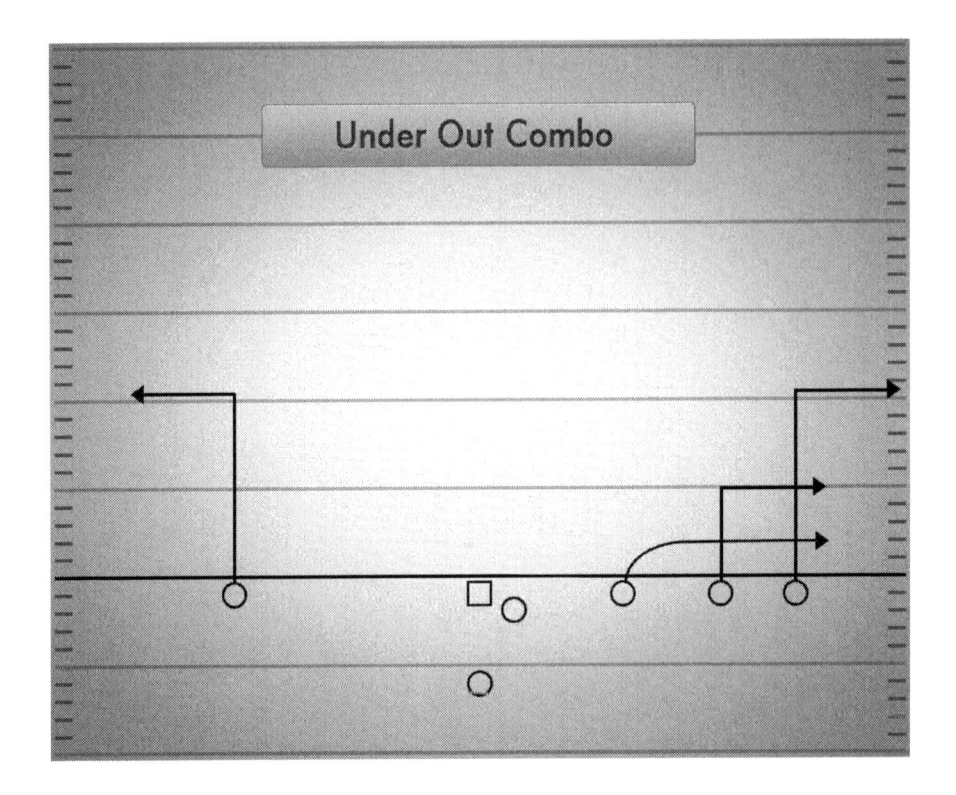

Under Out Combo

The Under Out Combo play positions the inside WR on a quick out underneath the deeper out. This places pressure on the flats of the defensive secondary by placing two WR on each side of the zone.

By splitting the responsibilities of the Cornerback, the Quarterback will have to see which one the Cornerback decides to guard, and then deliver the ball to the appropriate WR.

FORMATION: **TRIPS FORMATION**

DISTANCE: **SHORT YARDAGE, MEDIUM YARDAGE**

ROUTES IN THIS PLAY: **OUT**

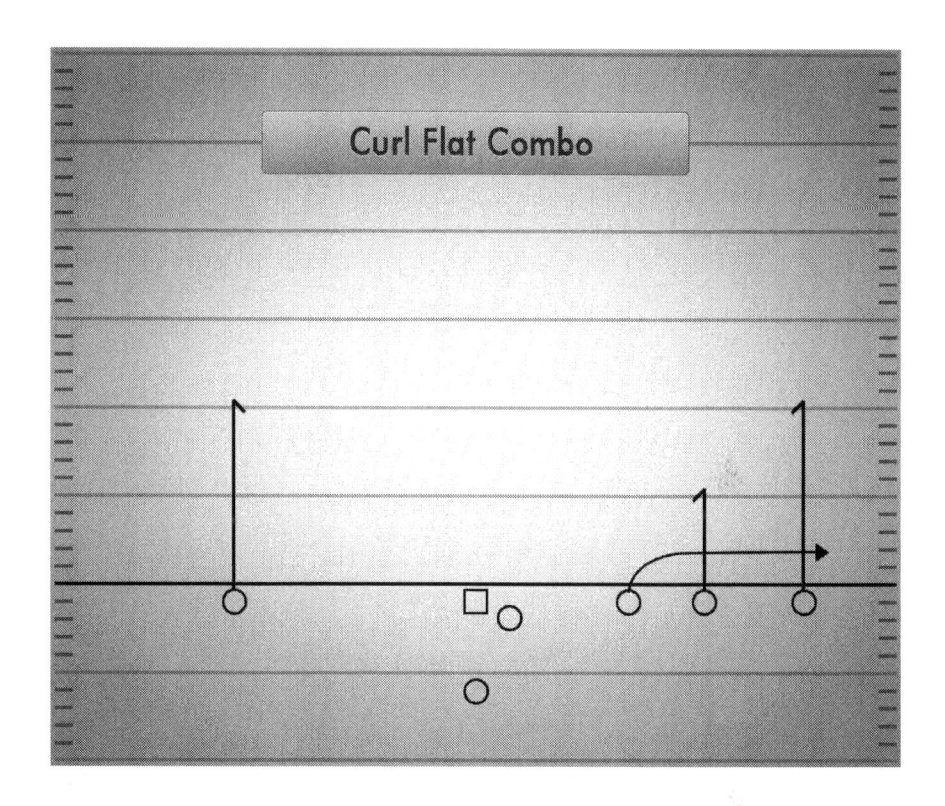

Curl Flat Combo

The Curl Flat Combo play attacks the defensive flat zone on the outside with a quick Out Route and a Curl Route over the top.

The Quarterback will want to look first at the quick out, and if the defense flowed fast to guard the out, then that means the curl route should be curling around in the open space right behind them.

FORMATION: **TRIPS FORMATION**

DISTANCE: **SHORT YARDAGE, MEDIUM YARDAGE**

ROUTES IN THIS PLAY: **CURL, OUT**

Plays

Stacks Formation

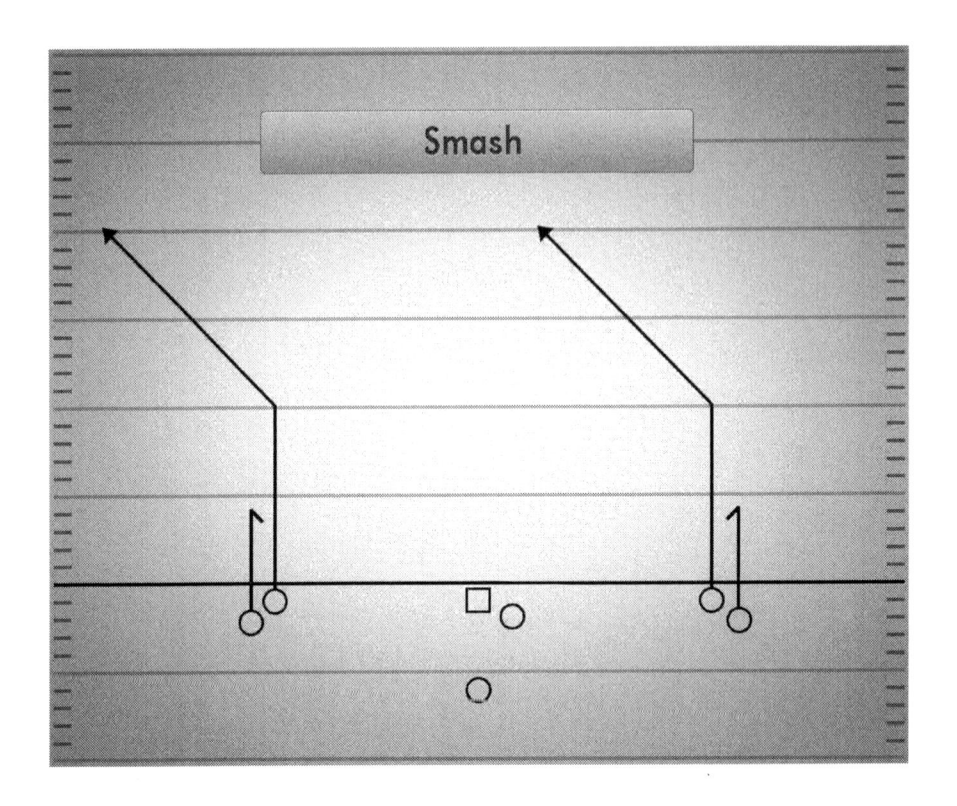

Smash

Utilizing the popular corner/stop route concept, the Smash play will attack many different zones in the defensive secondary. The first read that the Quarterback should make is to watch how the Cornerback plays the routes. If he stays low on the Stop route, then throw it over his head to the Corner route. If he stays high on the corner route, then throw it low to the Wide Receiver running the Stop route, who will be wide open in the flats. No outside linebacker will be able to run out there quick enough if the corner is dropping deep, and the Quarterback makes a quick read.

FORMATION: STACKS FORMATION

DISTANCE: SHORT YARDAGE, MEDIUM YARDAGE

ROUTES IN THIS PLAY: CORNER, POST, STOP

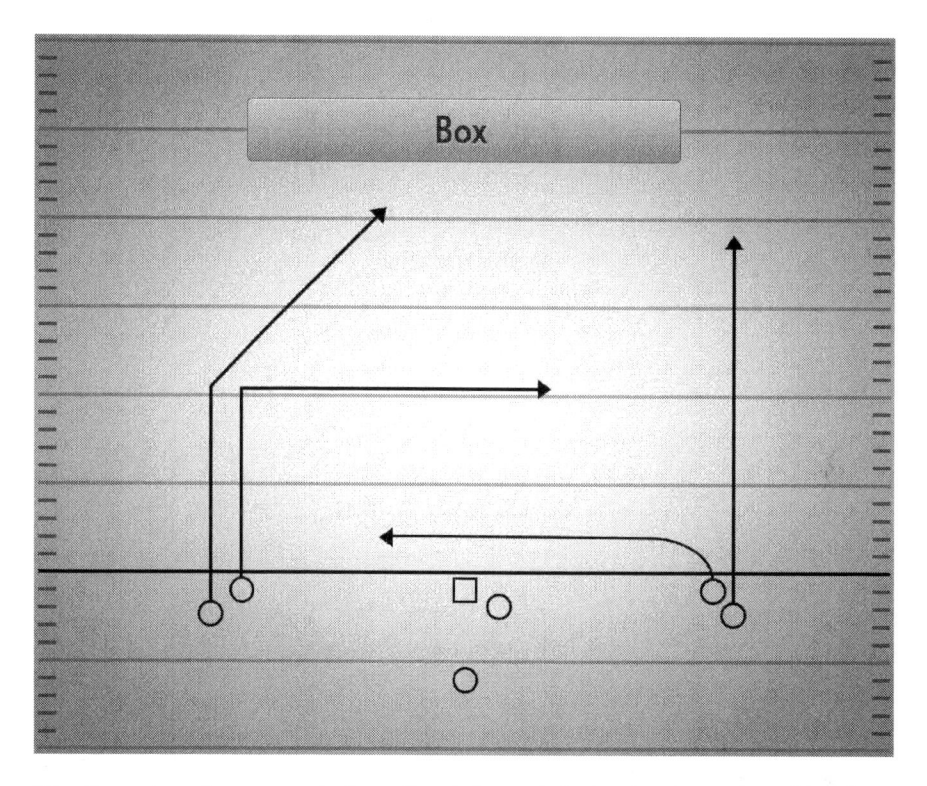

Box

The Box play allows you to trap the defense into having to make a high/low decision. In fact, there are two different high/low areas on the defense that this play attacks.

By singling out the safety, the Quarterback can make a "high/low" read based upon the combination of the Post route and the 10 yard In route. If the safety drops high to guard the Post, then throw it low to the In route. If the safety stays low on the In, then throw it high to the Post.

Additionally, another high/low read takes place at the level of the outside linebacker. The linebacker will have to make the decision to go high and guard the In route, or stay low and guard the Shallow Cross. The Quarterback's read progression should start by reading the Safety on the Post, and then moving down to the In route, and finally hitting the lowest shallow cross underneath, if everything higher is guarded.

FORMATION: STACKS FORMATION

DISTANCE: SHORT YARDAGE, LONG YARDAGE, MEDIUM YARDAGE

ROUTES IN THIS PLAY: POST, IN, SHALLOW CROSS, STREAK

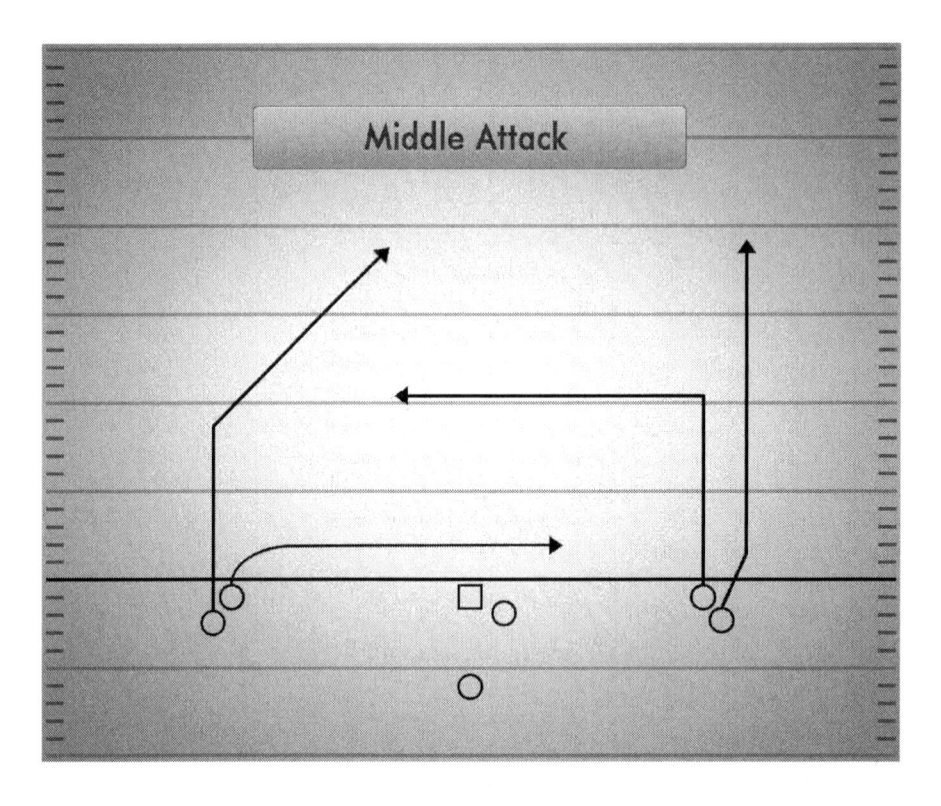

Middle Attack

The Middle Attack play attacks the middle of the defense with three different routes attacking three different levels in the defensive secondary. This allows the Quarterback to read the vertical flow of the defense in order to determine which of the three levels will be the open one. If the defense begins to crowd the middle of the field, then the outside receiver needs to get a wide release to run down the sideline on the fade route to stretch out the secondary.

Middle Attack is a variation of the Box play, but with a reversal of roles for the slot receivers.

FORMATION: STACKS FORMATION

DISTANCE: SHORT YARDAGE, LONG YARDAGE, MEDIUM YARDAGE

ROUTES IN THIS PLAY: POST, IN, SHALLOW CROSS, FADE

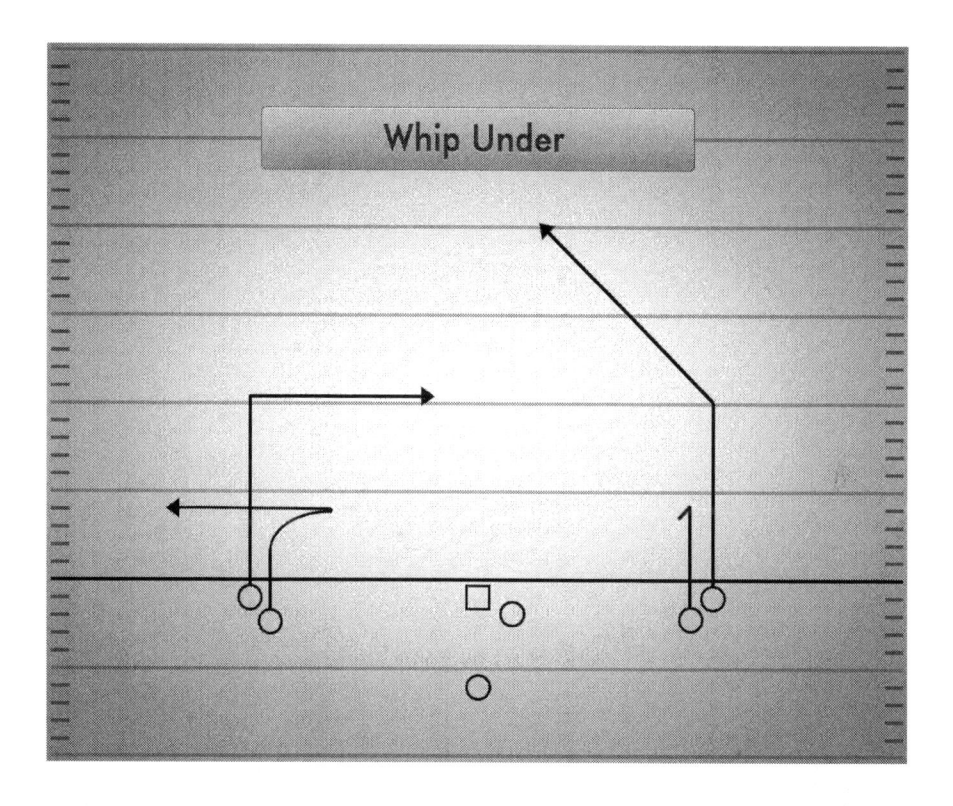

Whip Under

The Whip play is all about misdirection. The hard inside move gets the defense flowing inside, but the quick pivot outside is even more important for a quick move outside. If the inside receiver flowing underneath is covered up, then the outside receiver will be open coming inside over the top.

The Whip is best run in the second half of the game after setting up the defense with a sequence of successful slant plays. The defender will be ready to jump forward on the slant, but the wide out will plant hard and turn fast outside where he will be wide open running away from the defender.

FORMATION: **STACKS FORMATION**

DISTANCE: **SHORT YARDAGE, MEDIUM YARDAGE**

ROUTES IN THIS PLAY: **POST, IN, WHIP, STOP**

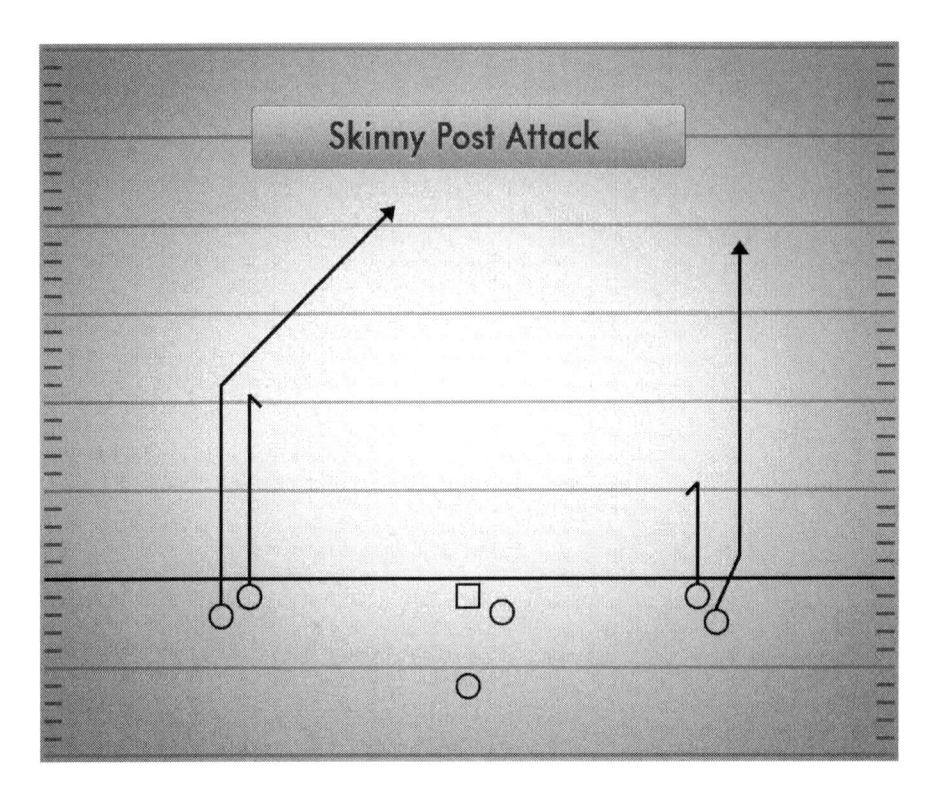

Skinny Post Attack

The Skinny Post Attack play requires special attention to detail. The main point of this play is to put the Safety in a tough situation by attacking his zone with two routes. The most critical route running in this play is the 10-yard Curl route, because it has to be run in a way that attracts the Safety's attention. If the slot receiver successfully gets the Safety to stay down and guard the curl, then the Post route will be wide open over the top.

If the Safety stays deep, however, then the Curl route needs to make sure that he is deep enough over the linebackers in order to be open 10-12 yards downfield. All in all, this play consists of a high/low read on the Safety by placing on route in the front of the Safety's zone, and the other over the top of the Safety's zone.

FORMATION: **STACKS FORMATION**

DISTANCE: **LONG YARDAGE, MEDIUM YARDAGE**

ROUTES IN THIS PLAY: **POST, FADE, STOP, CURL**

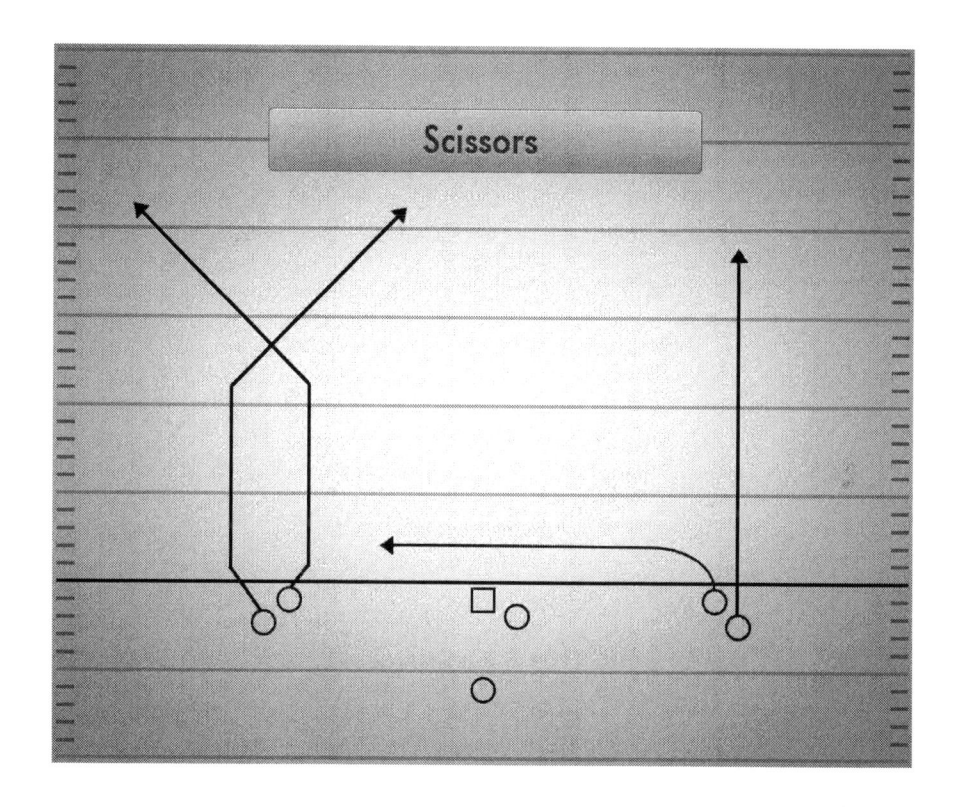

Scissors is a great play to cut through the defensive secondary by converging two receivers across each other on one half of the field. The Post route goes over the top of the Corner route. The Post is the first read coming across the top, followed up by the Corner cutting through below.

The most important aspect of the play is that both routes run quickly up field at the same time and cut across each other simultaneously to wreak havoc on the downfield defenders.

FORMATION: **STACKS FORMATION**

DISTANCE: **LONG YARDAGE**

ROUTES IN THIS PLAY: **CORNER, POST, SHALLOW CROSS, STREAK**

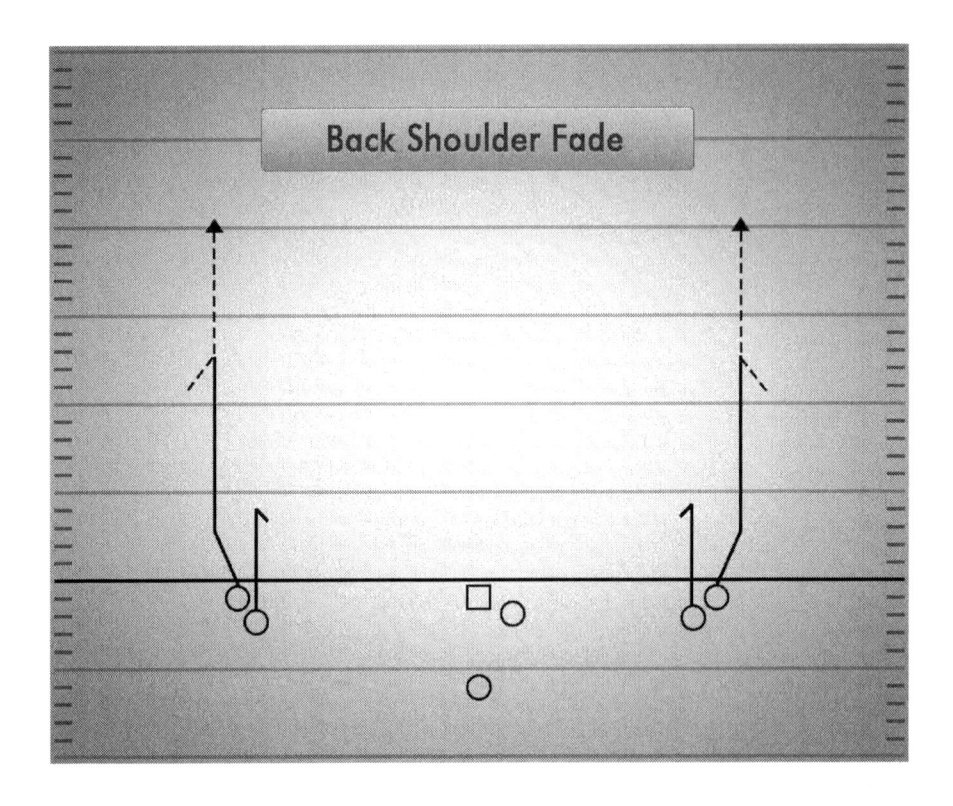

Back Shoulder Fade

The Back Shoulder fade is a go-to play for goal line situations. It gives the Receiver two options to choose from based upon how the defender guards him. If the Cornerback is guarding deep, then the Quarterback can throw the ball short, but if the Cornerback is play up close, then the Quarterback can throw the ball over the top.

Communication and chemistry between the Quarterback and the Receiver is of the utmost importance. Both the thrower and the route runner need to be on the same page to execute this play properly. Great chemistry will lead to great results on the Back Shoulder fade.

FORMATION: **STACKS FORMATION**

DISTANCE: **SHORT YARDAGE**

ROUTES IN THIS PLAY: **FADE, STOP**

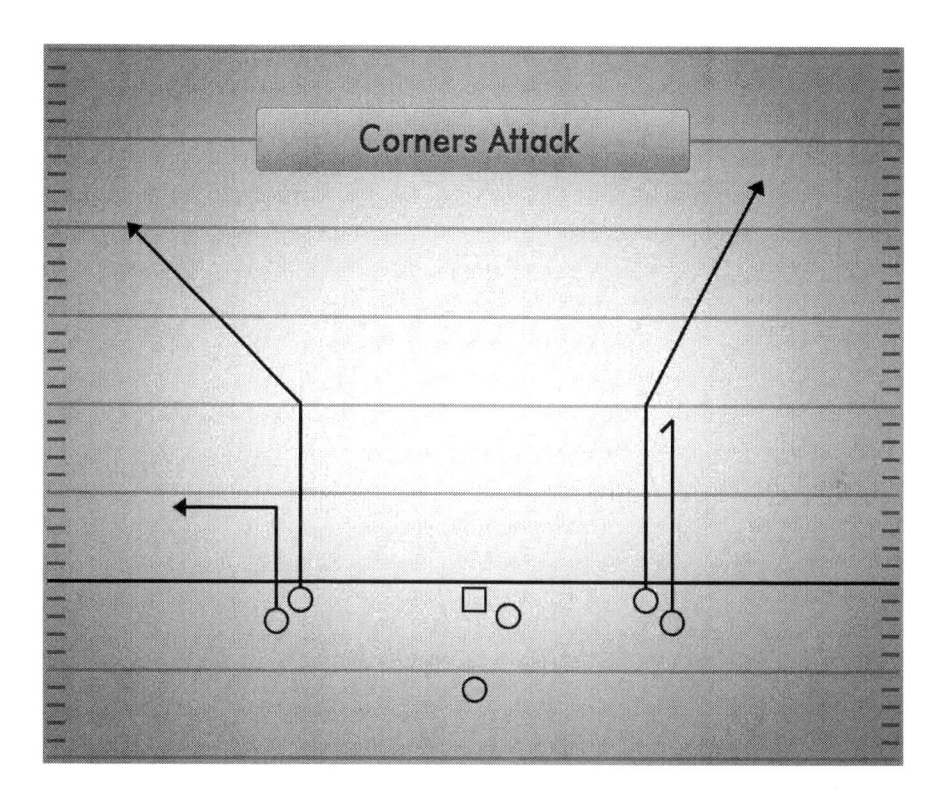

Corners Attack

Corners attack does just what its name says it does: Attack the Corners. The corner routes get depth into the corner of the defensive secondary, while the underneath routes wreak havoc in the flats. The slot receiver who runs the corner in combination with the 10-yard curl, has to make sure that he gets depth so that he is properly spaced over the top of the Curl route.

The Quarterback has to make a pre-snap decision on to select what side he wants to go to. Once that decision is made, read the Cornerback to see if he is staying on the deep corner, or cheating on the flat.

FORMATION: **STACKS FORMATION**

DISTANCE: **LONG YARDAGE**

ROUTES IN THIS PLAY: **CORNER, CURL, OUT**

Ridge Force

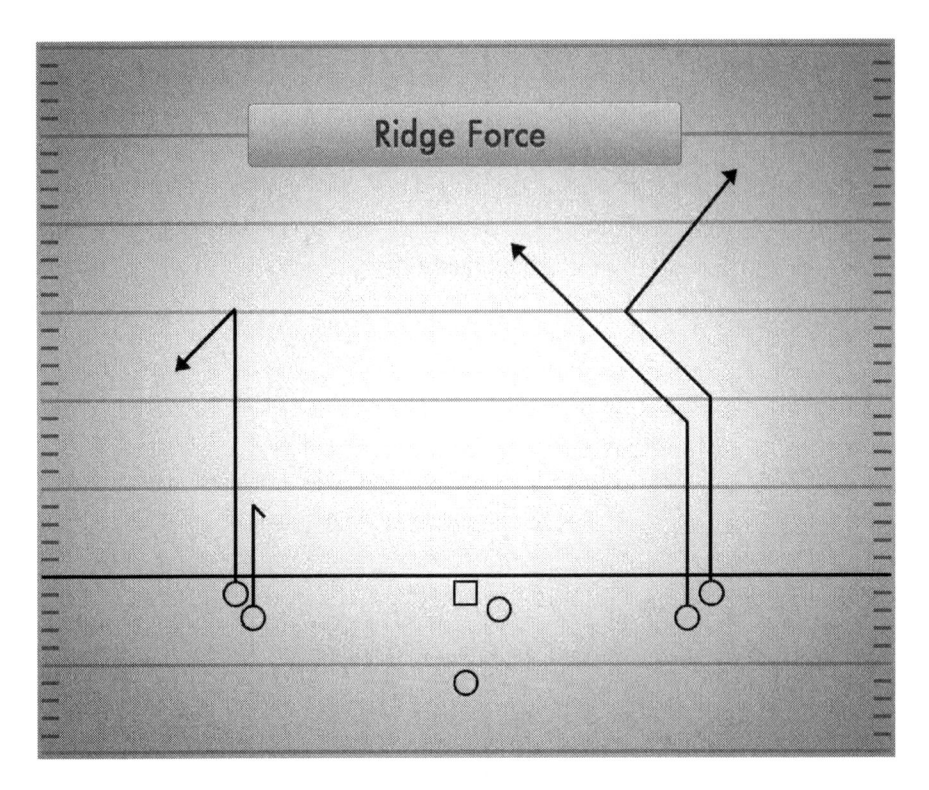

The Ridge Force play forces the defense to flow with the flow with the combination of the two post routes coming across the top ridge of the defensive secondary. Once the defenders start flowing with the combination of those routes, the outside receivers breaks hard to the outside on the Post Corner route.

The double move by the outside receiver will force the Safety into a hard decision if he is playing in a cover 2 zone, because he will be sitting right in the middle of two deep routes into his territory, but he can only choose to guard on of them.

If the defense is in a three deep formation and/or playing in a Cover three, then the QB will most likely want to drop down and hit the Comeback route on the other side of the field.

FORMATION: **STACKS FORMATION**

DISTANCE: **LONG YARDAGE**

ROUTES IN THIS PLAY: **POST, STOP, POST CORNER, COMEBACK**

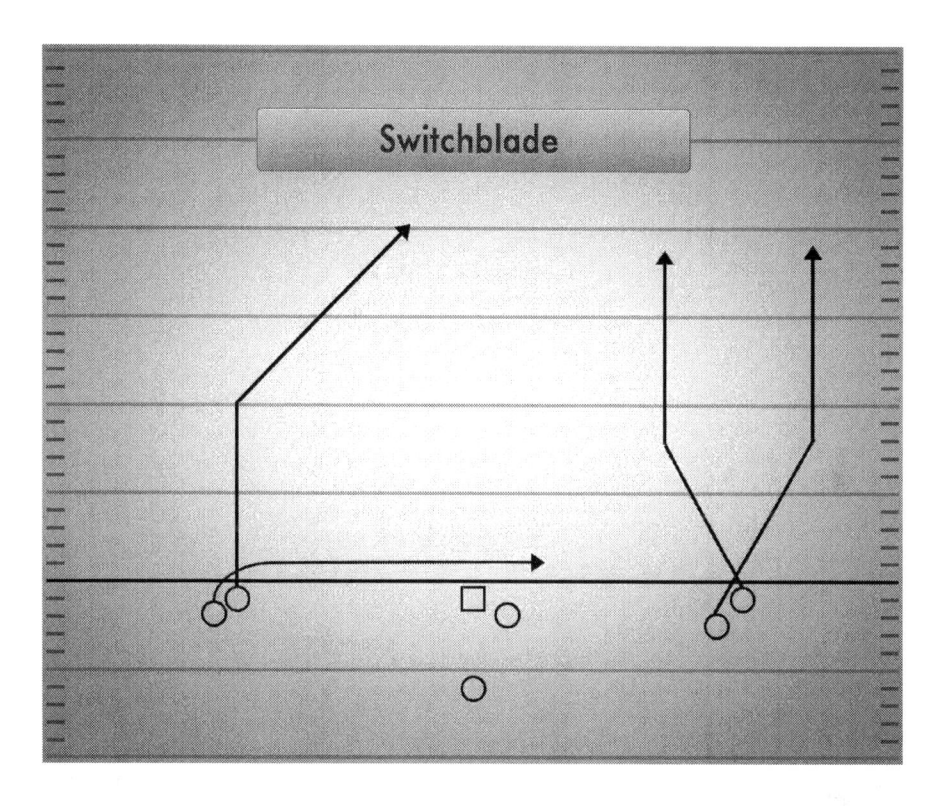

Switchblade

The Switchblade is a deadly combination route that cuts right through the defense by switching two receivers as they run their routes up field. A man-to-man defense will have trouble keeping up with both of the downfield receivers, and a zone defense will be thrown for a loop as the routes cut right through the zone.

The Quarterback has the option of cutting his losses if the deep routes aren't open, by checking down to the shallow cross underneath the switch route combination.

FORMATION: **STACKS FORMATION**

DISTANCE: **LONG YARDAGE**

ROUTES IN THIS PLAY: **POST, SHALLOW CROSS**

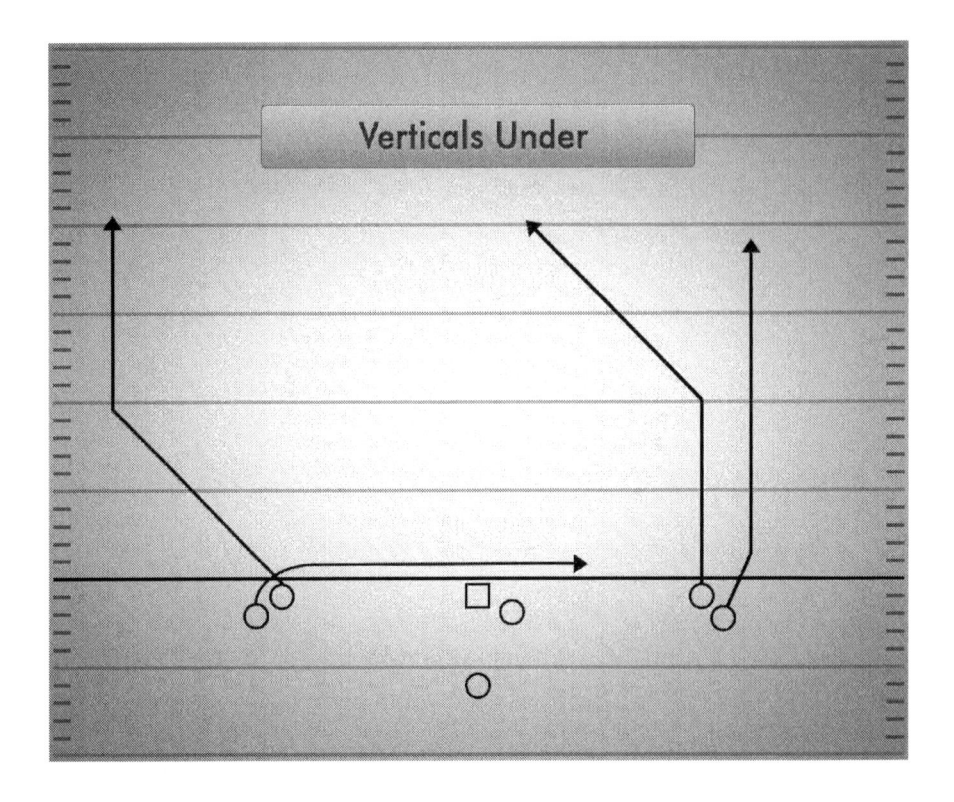

Verticals Under

The Verticals Under play sends the wide receivers up field in a shifted pattern that replaces the territory of the Receiver who is cutting underneath the Verticals.

By pushing the Vertical routes up field hard, it will distract the defense from the Shallow Cross coming underneath. Sometimes, however, the defense will lose track of the receiver taking the place of the underneath route, and he will be open down the sideline for a big gain.

FORMATION: **STACKS FORMATION**

DISTANCE: **SHORT YARDAGE, LONG YARDAGE**

ROUTES IN THIS PLAY: **SHALLOW CROSS, STREAK**

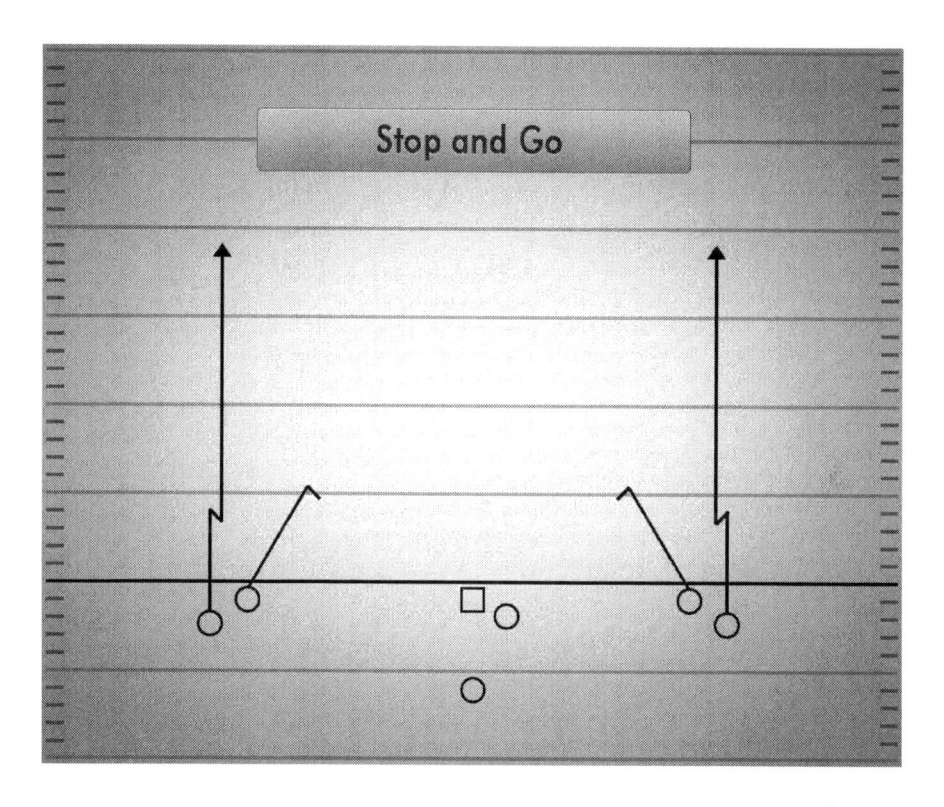

Stop and Go

The Stop and Go route is the most famous double move in all of football. The outside receiver will fake like he is running a 5 yard stop, but will twist and turn quickly up field.

It is imperative that the QB makes a good pump fake to sucker the defense in to jumping up on the short route. Once the pump fake is successfully completed, the QB must regather himself and get ready to throw the ball over the top of the defense to the receiver who is sprinting up field.

FORMATION: **STACKS FORMATION**

DISTANCE: **SHORT YARDAGE, LONG YARDAGE**

ROUTES IN THIS PLAY: **STOP**

Comebacks

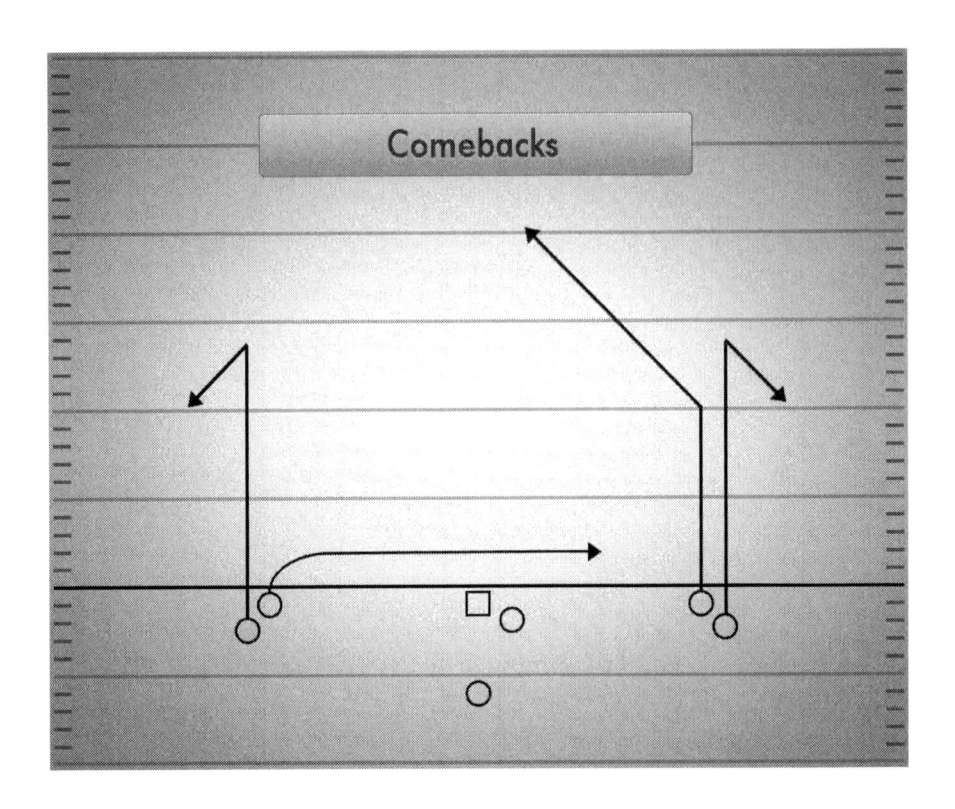

The Comeback route is a great route to run on a defense that is scared of getting beat deep. The way in which the Wide Receivers run the Comeback route is the most important part of the play. The WR will need to push up field hard as if he is running a Fade route or a Streak downfield. Once the defender is turned and running backwards, the WR needs to quickly turn around to the outside, as the QB plays a ball behind on the sideline.

After you scare the defense with the deep ball, the Comeback route is a great route to throw at them in order to pick up a chunk of yards.

FORMATION: **STACKS FORMATION**

DISTANCE: **MEDIUM YARDAGE**

ROUTES IN THIS PLAY: **POST, SHALLOW CROSS, COMEBACK**

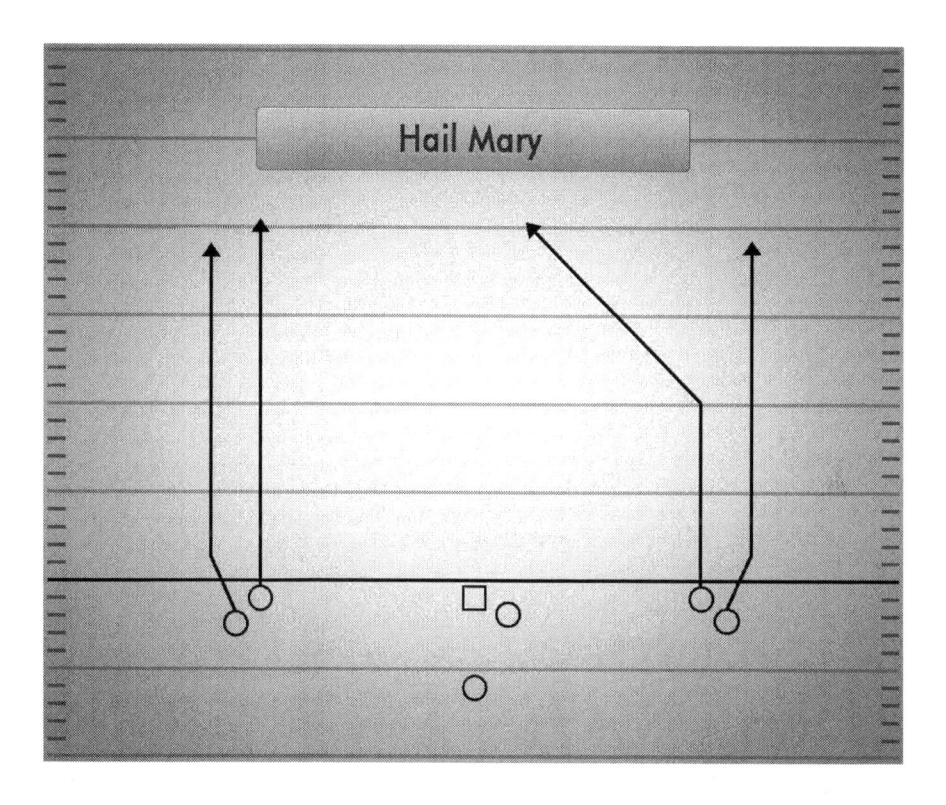

Hail Mary

Hail Mary time! You only need to pull out this play when you need a whole lot of yards all at once.

This version of the Hail Mary play is made to spread out the defense as much as possible, and potentially isolate a defender from the rest of his team. The Quarterback needs to find the WR who is able to get into a one-on-one match up and throw the ball up for a jump ball.

FORMATION: **STACKS FORMATION**

DISTANCE: **LONG YARDAGE**

ROUTES IN THIS PLAY: **POST, STREAK, FADE**

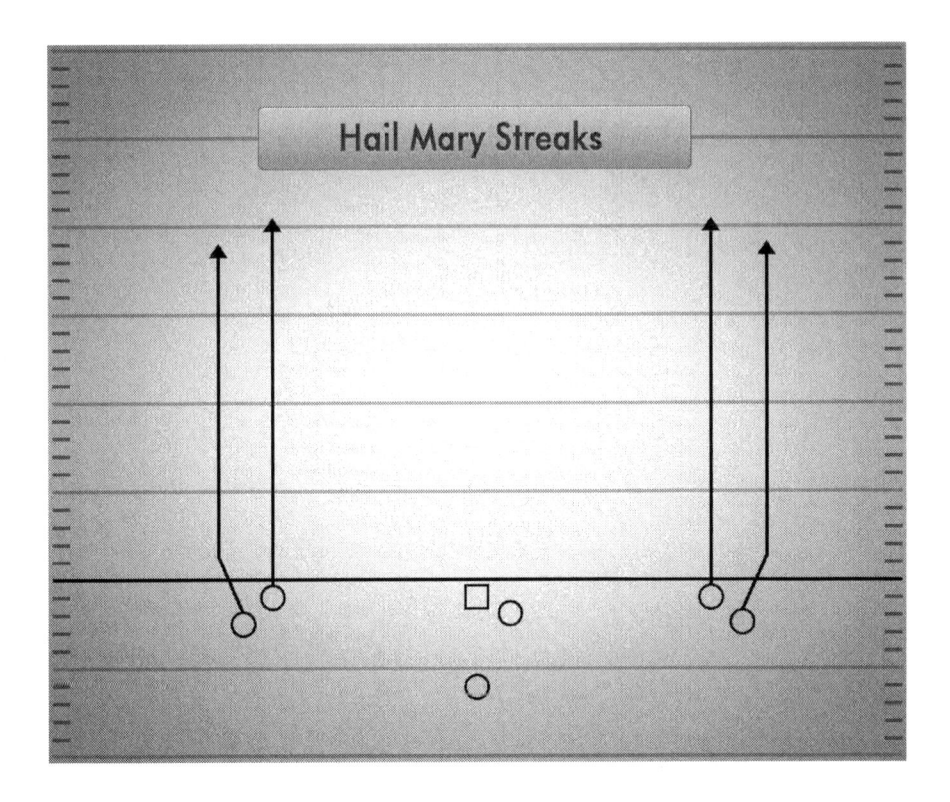

Hail Mary Streaks

Hail Mary time! You only need to pull out this play when you need a whole lot of yards all at once.

This version of the Hail Mary play simply send all the receivers downfield in a straight line in order to get as deep as possible, as fast as possible. Throw the ball up deep and hope for the best.

FORMATION: **STACKS FORMATION**

DISTANCE: **LONG YARDAGE**

ROUTES IN THIS PLAY: **STREAK**

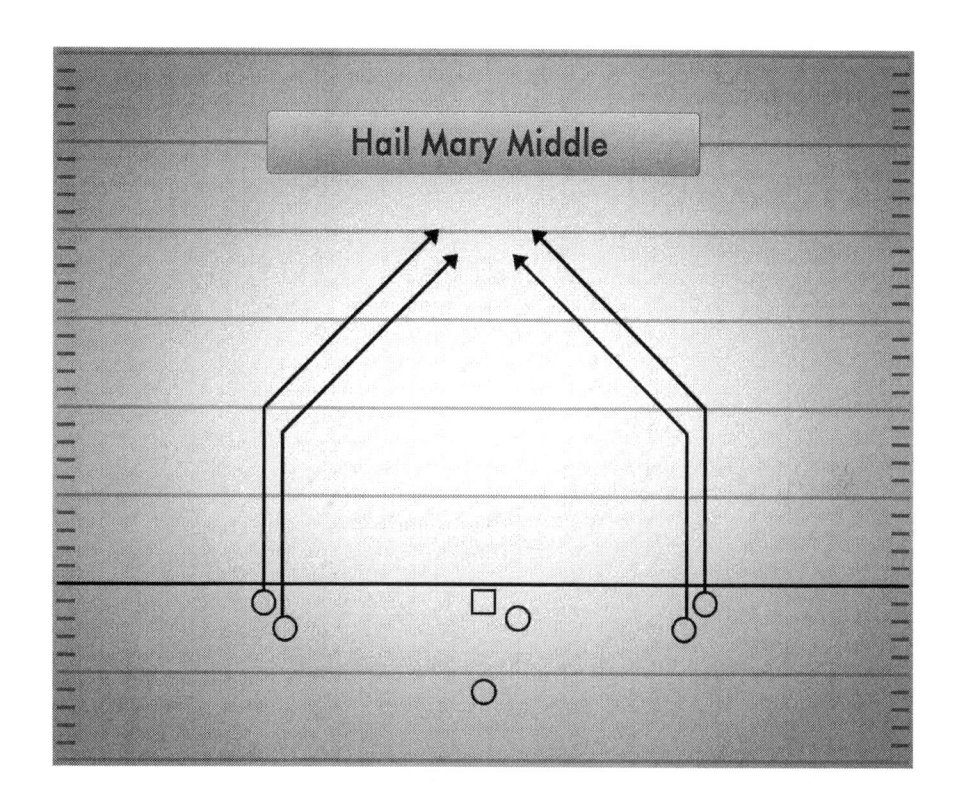

Hail Mary Middle

Hail Mary time! You only need to pull out this play when you need a whole lot of yards all at once.

This version of the Hail Mary play puts all your eggs in one basket by sending every Receiver to the middle of the field. Once all the Receivers are in position, the only thing left for the Quarterback to do is throw the ball as high as he can right into the middle of the field and hope that one of his own players comes down with it.

FORMATION: STACKS FORMATION

DISTANCE: LONG YARDAGE

ROUTES IN THIS PLAY: POST

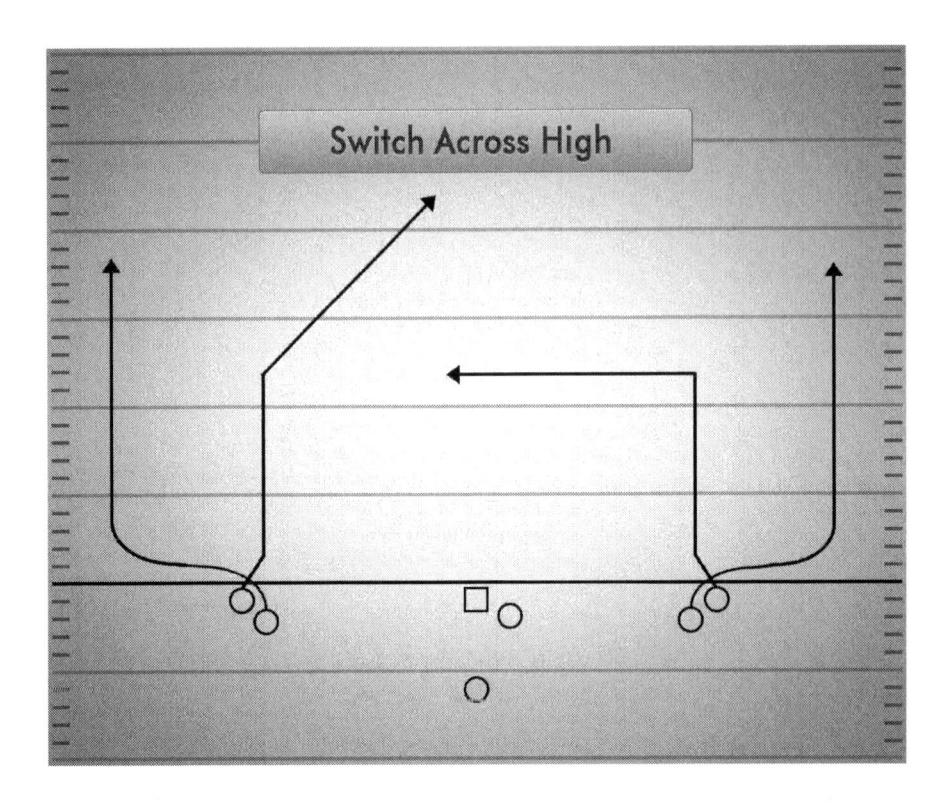

Switch Across High

This is the deeper variation of the Switch Across Low play. The key to this play is creating confusion for the defense at the very start of the play by having the receivers switch across each other on the way to their destination. This switch makes it hard for a zone defense to keep track of all the routes, and makes it very difficult for a man-to-man defense to keep up with the receiver amongst all the chaos going on.

FORMATION: **STACKS FORMATION**

DISTANCE: **LONG YARDAGE**

ROUTES IN THIS PLAY: **POST, IN, WHEEL**

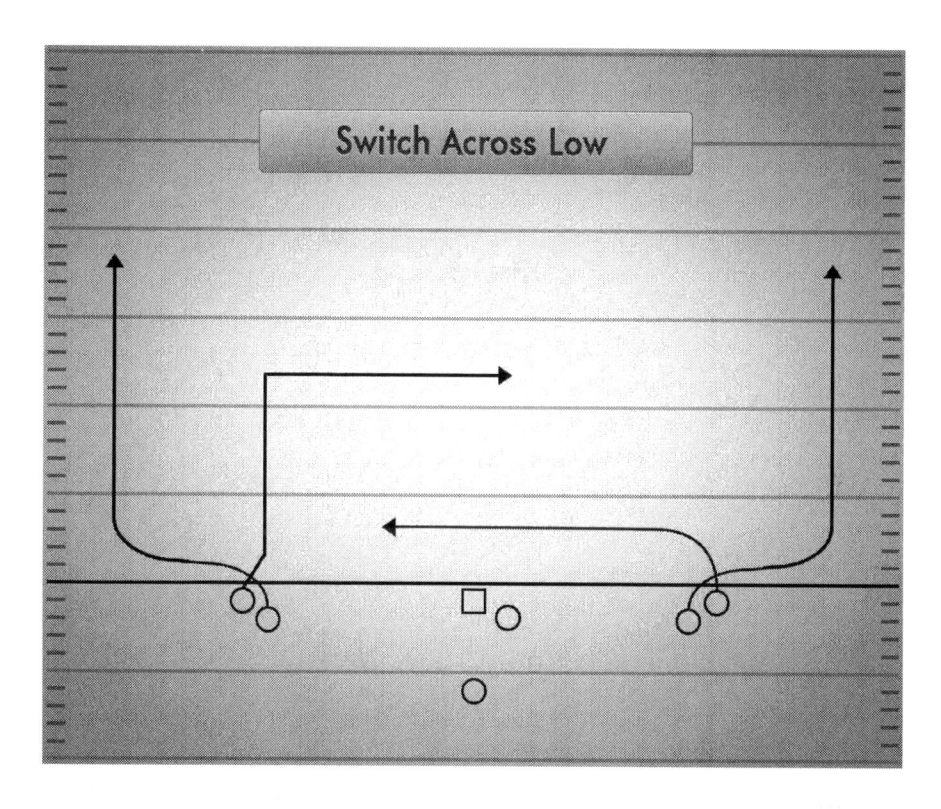

Switch Across Low

This is the shorter variation of the Switch Across High play. The key to this play is creating confusion for the defense at the very start of the play by having the receivers switch across each other on the way to their destination. This switch makes it hard for a zone defense to keep track of all the routes, and makes it very difficult for a man-to-man defense to keep up with the receiver amongst all the chaos going on.

FORMATION: **STACKS FORMATION**

DISTANCE: **SHORT YARDAGE, MEDIUM YARDAGE**

ROUTES IN THIS PLAY: **IN, SHALLOW CROSS, WHEEL**

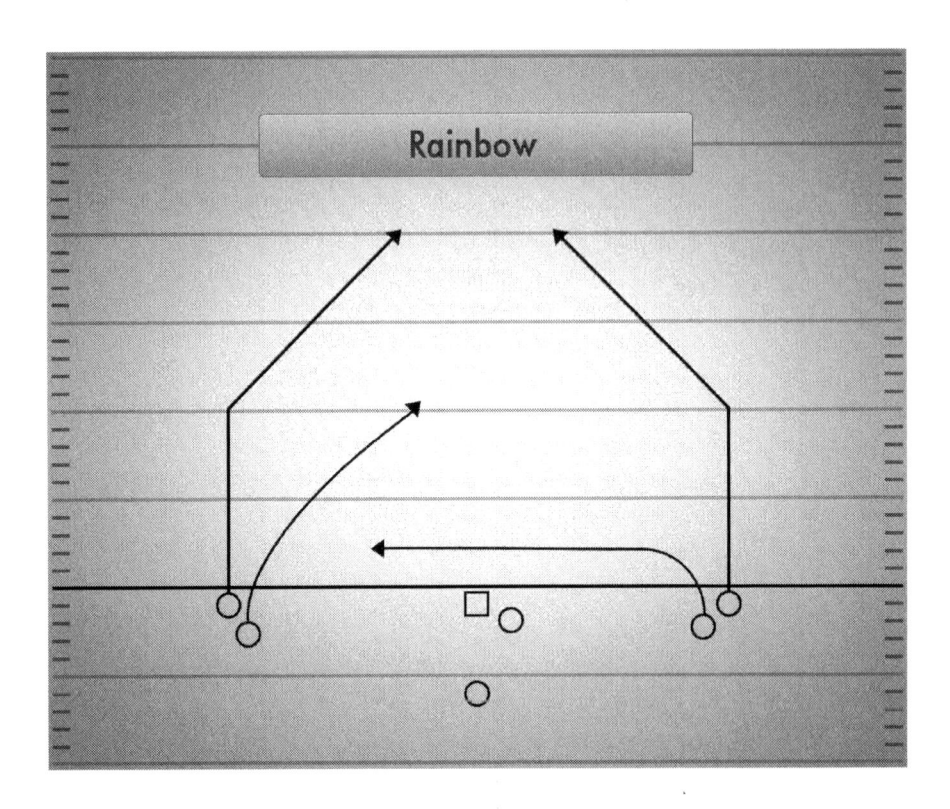

Rainbow

The Rainbow play allows the Wide Receivers to attack the defense by running arcs all across the middle of the field. Each arc is run at a different level of the defense, therefore, combining to create a Rainbow of manly intensity.

The Quarterback can choose to either read the arcs from low to high, or progress from high to low. Finding at least one open man in the Rainbow should be easy with so many routes hitting different levels in the middle of the field.

FORMATION: **STACKS FORMATION**

DISTANCE: **SHORT YARDAGE, LONG YARDAGE, MEDIUM YARDAGE**

ROUTES IN THIS PLAY: **POST, SHALLOW CROSS**

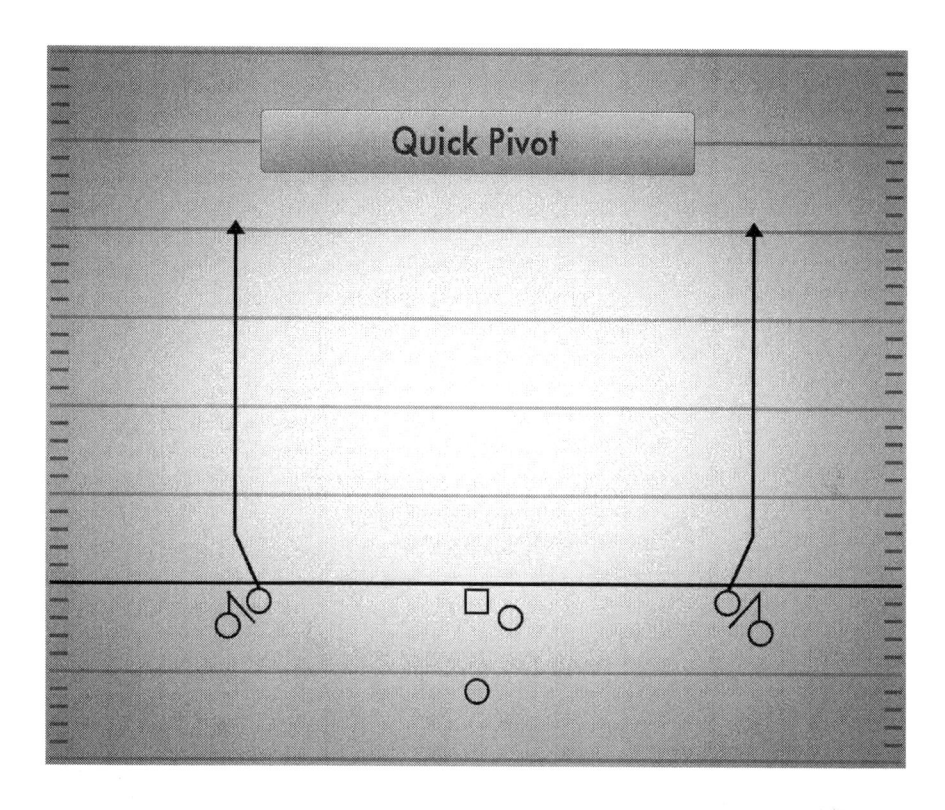

Quick Pivot

The Quick Pivot play is meant to be used as a play against a defense that is backing up off the line of scrimmage. If they are giving too much space to the Wide Receivers, then hit them with this quick pass to catch them off guard. If the Quarterback makes a quick throw to the Receiver, it will give the Receiver a chance to run with the ball in the open field and try to make a defender miss.

It is important that the Receivers push hard off the line of scrimmage for the first few steps, so that the defenders aren't immediately keyed into the fact that it is going to be a quick pass right at the line of scrimmage.

FORMATION: **STACKS FORMATION**

DISTANCE: **SHORT YARDAGE**

ROUTES IN THIS PLAY: **FADE**

WR Screen

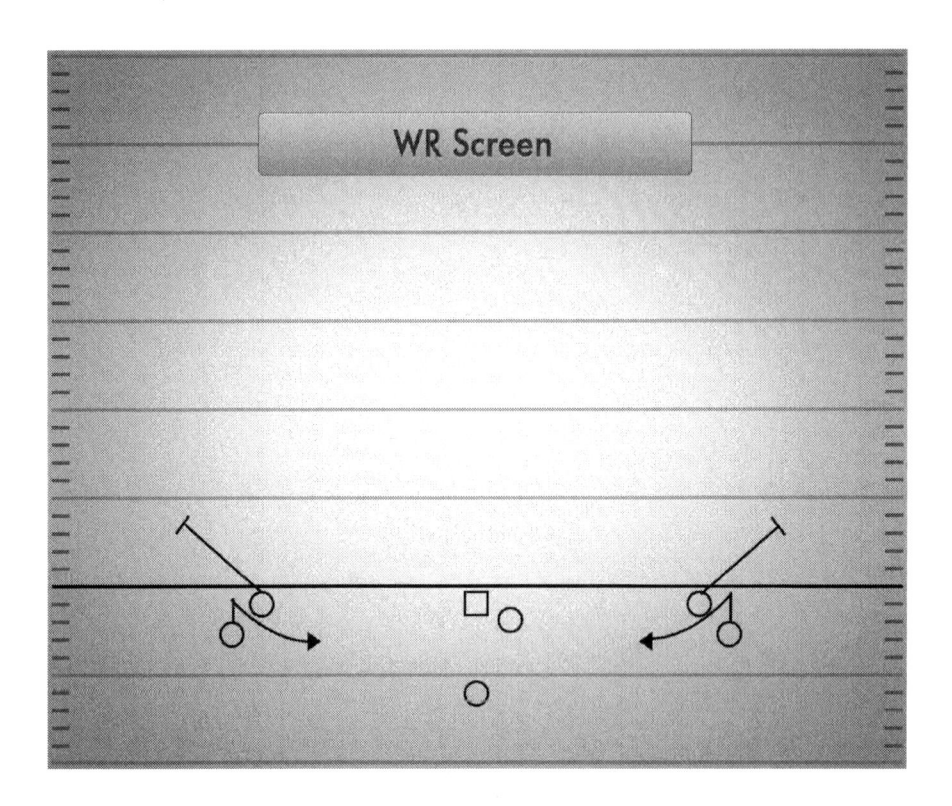

The WR Screen is a play that utilizes blocking by the inside Receivers to enable a running lane for the outside Receiver. The Wide Receiver running the screen route needs to push up field hard for two steps, and the quickly turn around for the ball. Timing is critical on the throw.

The inside Receiver needs to explode of the line of scrimmage directly at the guy who is guarding the outside Receiver. Once that defender turns around, quickly get in his way for the block, and the Receiver catching the screen will be off to the races.

FORMATION: **STACKS FORMATION**

DISTANCE: **SHORT YARDAGE**

WR Screen and Up

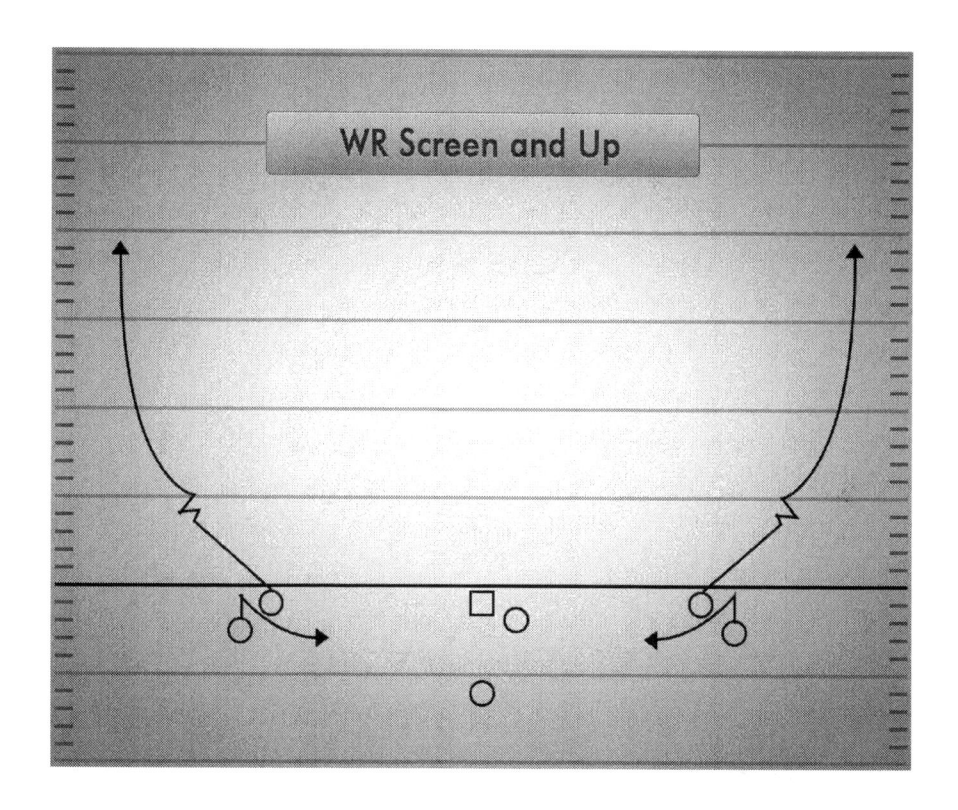

The WR Screen and Up play is a great trick play that takes some time to set up. You have to run the WR Screen play beforehand, and run it successfully. If you begin to hurt them with the Screen, then the defense will start to sneak up forward, and that is when you hit them with the Screen and Up.

The most important aspect of performing this play is the way in which the Wide Receiver fakes his block. He has to run out to the Cornerback as if he is going to block him, and as soon as the Cornerback makes a move to avoid the block, the Receiver then turns on the jets and runs up the sideline. The defense won't even know what hit them until the ball is flying over all their heads.

FORMATION: **STACKS FORMATION**

DISTANCE: **LONG YARDAGE**

Slot Choice

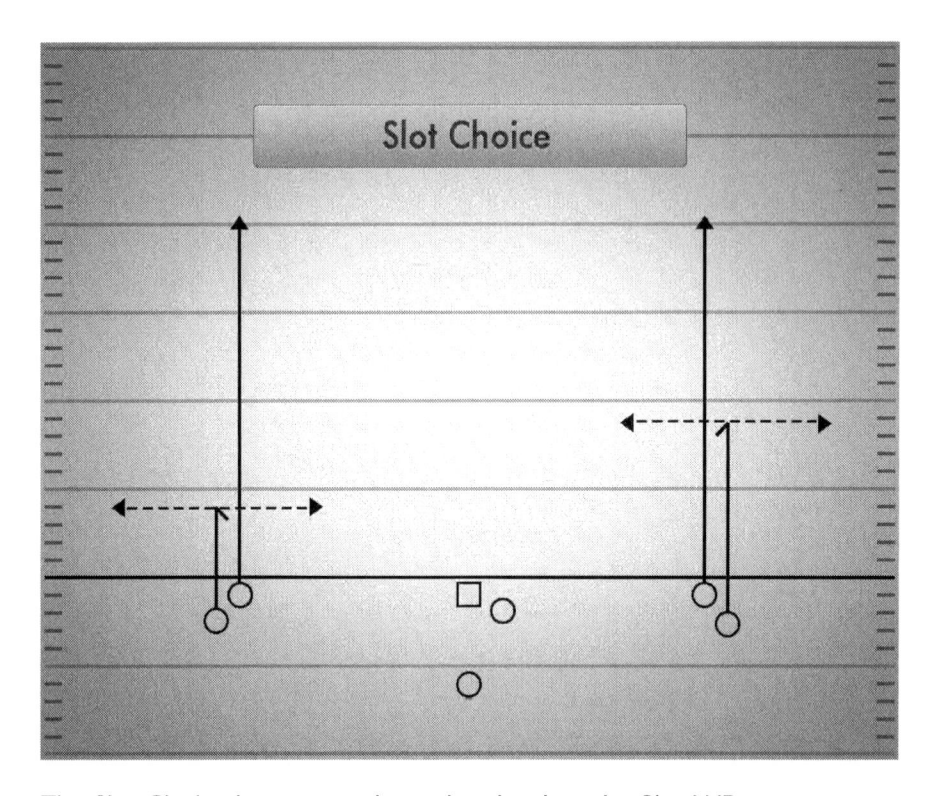

The Slot Choice is meant to be a play that lets the Slot WR get open, no matter what the defense does. The Choice route will either get to its mark and turn around for a stop in place, or it will jet out to the outside, or cut in to the inside.

If the defender is playing inside, then the WR should jet to the outside. If the defender is playing outside, then the WR should jet to the inside. If the defense is playing in a zone, and is giving the WR some space, then the WR should just settle down and wait for the ball.

The Quarterback needs to have great chemistry with the WR so that they are on the same wavelength and can be expecting each other to make the same read.

FORMATION: **STACKS FORMATION**

DISTANCE: **SHORT YARDAGE, MEDIUM YARDAGE**

ROUTES IN THIS PLAY: **IN, STREAK, STOP, OUT**

WR Choice

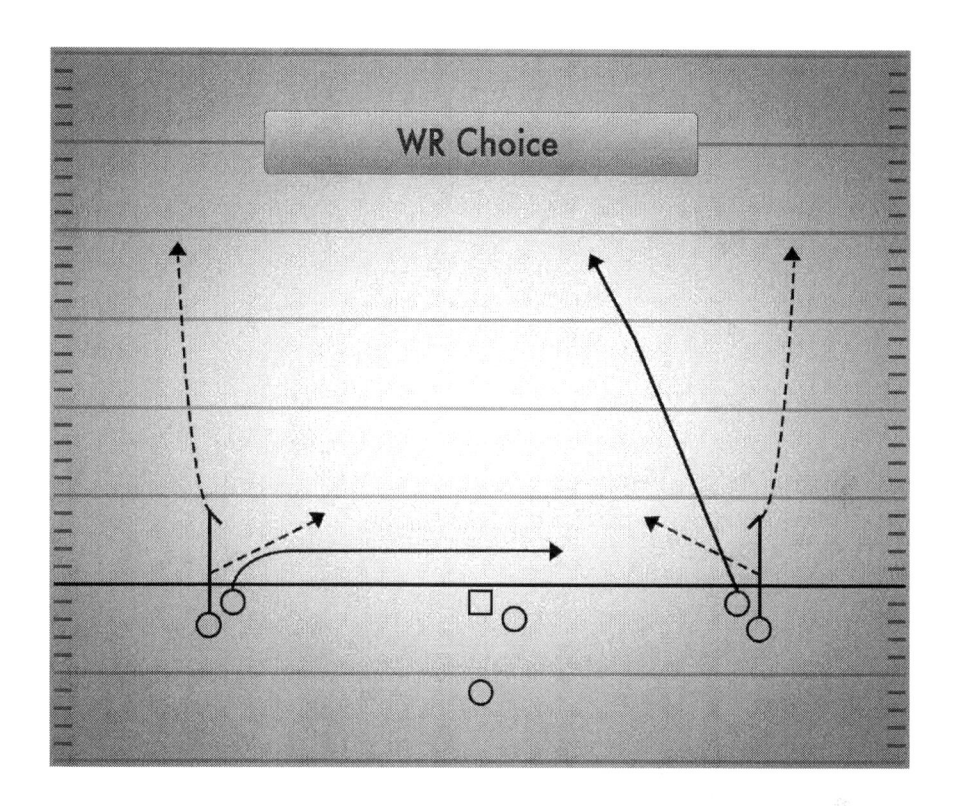

The WR Choice is meant to be a play that lets the Outside WR get open, no matter what the defense does. If the defender is playing inside, then the WR should run up the sideline on a fade. If the defender is playing outside, then the WR should jet to the inside on a slant. If the defense is giving the WR some space, then the WR should just settle down and wait for the ball on a stop route.

The Quarterback needs to have great chemistry with the WR so that they are on the same wavelength and can be expecting each other to make the same read.

FORMATION: STACKS FORMATION

DISTANCE: SHORT YARDAGE, LONG YARDAGE, MEDIUM YARDAGE

ROUTES IN THIS PLAY: SHALLOW CROSS, FADE, STOP, SLANT, SEAM

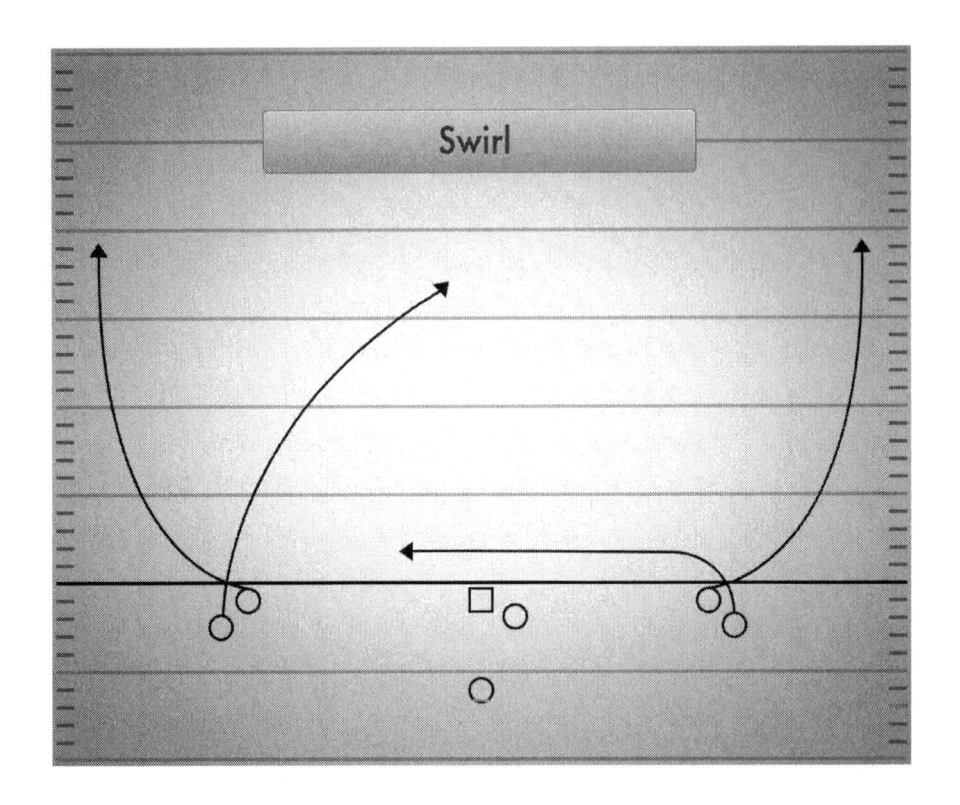

Swirl

The Swirl plays send the defense in a whirlwind by swirling the routes all around across the field. Unlike most plays, there are hardly no straight lines in the route patterns, as all the Wide Receivers are swirling their routes to get to their destination.

The switching and swirling pattern will make it hard for a man defense to keep up, and difficult for a zone defense to keep track.

FORMATION: **STACKS FORMATION**

DISTANCE: **SHORT YARDAGE, LONG YARDAGE**

ROUTES IN THIS PLAY: **POST, SHALLOW CROSS, WHEEL**

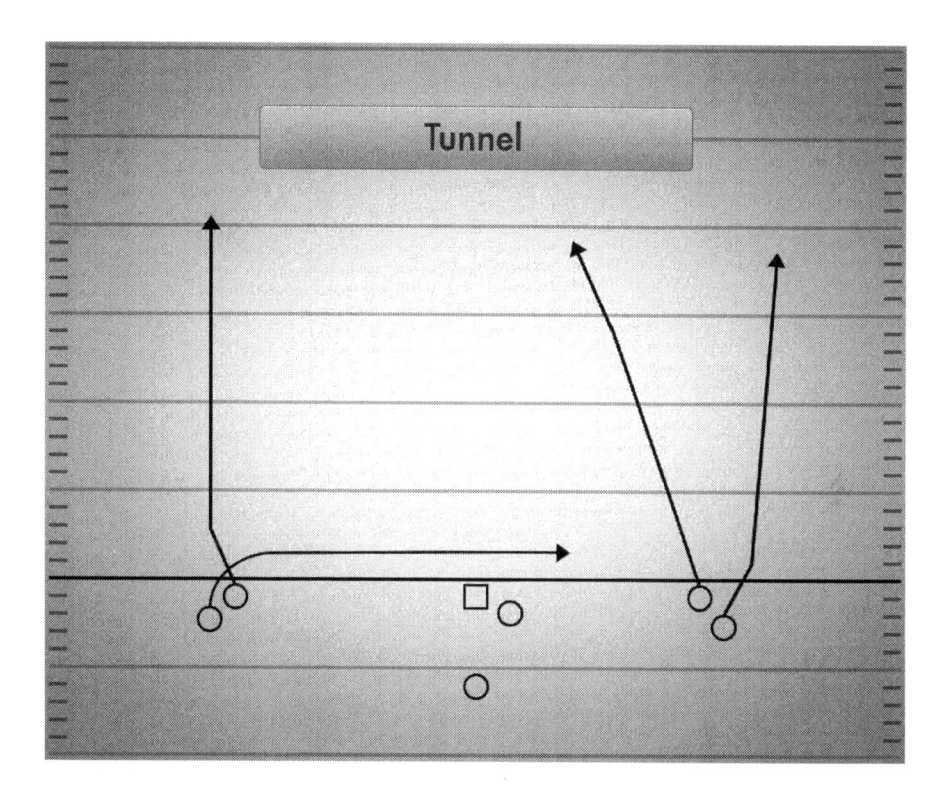

Tunnel

The Tunnel play might look like a deep play when drawn up, but it is really meant to be a play thrown to the Shallow Cross route that is "tunneling" underneath.

The other receivers are used primarily to run off the defense and take all the defenders deep downfield with them. After the defense has backed off, the shallow cross route should be open and have tons of room to run after the catch.

FORMATION: **STACKS FORMATION**

DISTANCE: **SHORT YARDAGE**

ROUTES IN THIS PLAY: **SHALLOW CROSS, FADE, SEAM**

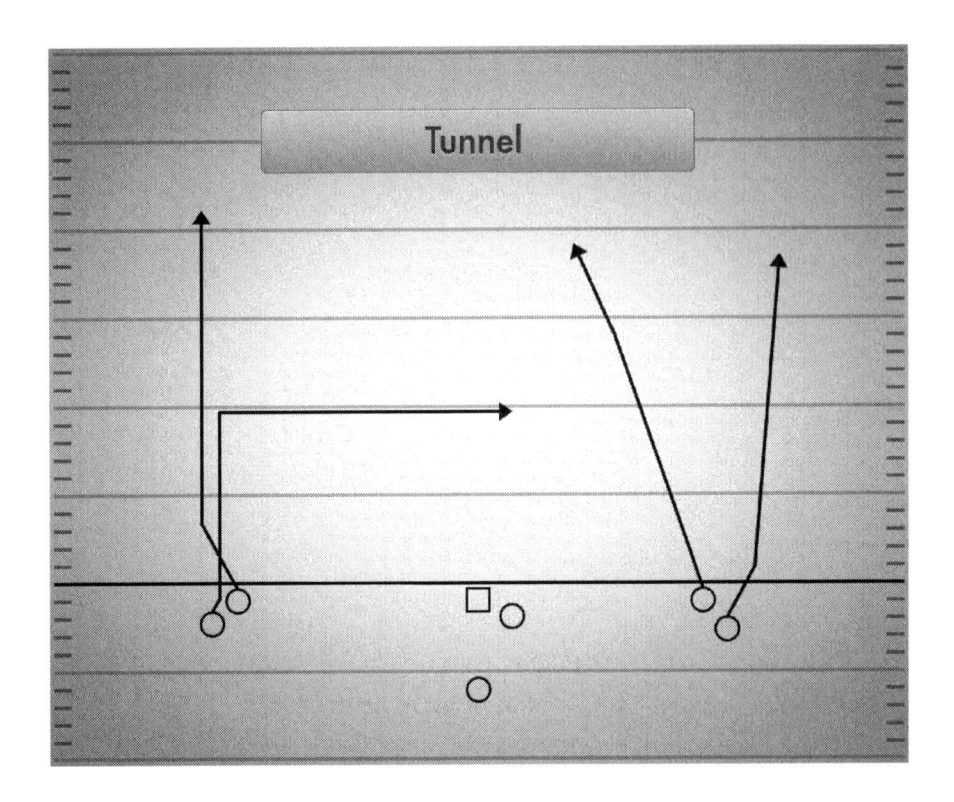

Tunnel

The primary focus of the Tunnel Deep play is to make the defense think that everybody is going deep, and then break off the outside receiver, and hit him coming across the field underneath the deep routes.

The other receivers are used primarily to run off the defense and take all the defenders deep downfield with them. After the defense has backed off, the In route should be open and have tons of room to run after the catch.

FORMATION: **STACKS FORMATION**

DISTANCE: **LONG YARDAGE**

ROUTES IN THIS PLAY: **IN, FADE, SEAM**

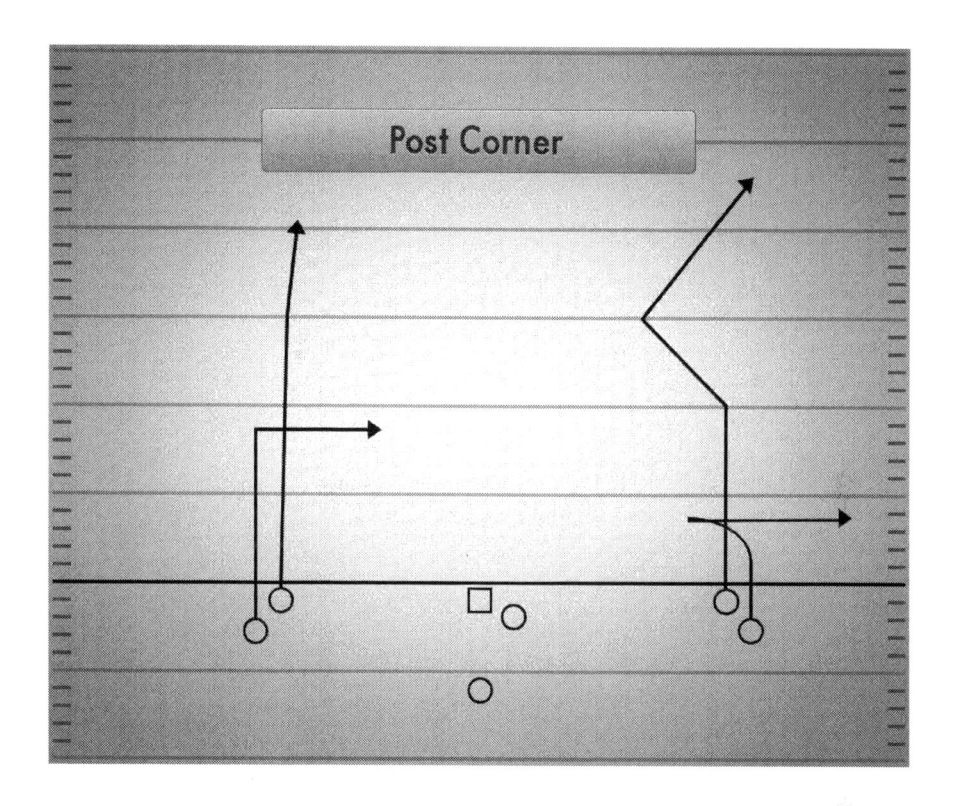

Post Corner

This play is all about setting up the Post-Corner route on the outside. The Receiver running the route has to make it look as if he is running the post, and as soon as he suckers the defense inside, he breaks to the outside and the Quarterback will hit him deep along the sideline.

The Whip route underneath, is used to keep the Cornerback from drifting back towards the Post-Corner. If the Cornerback does carry back deep and get in the way of the Post-Corner, then the Whip route should be open in the flats underneath.

FORMATION: **STACKS FORMATION**

DISTANCE: **LONG YARDAGE, MEDIUM YARDAGE**

ROUTES IN THIS PLAY: **IN, WHIP, POST CORNER, SEAM**

Bubble

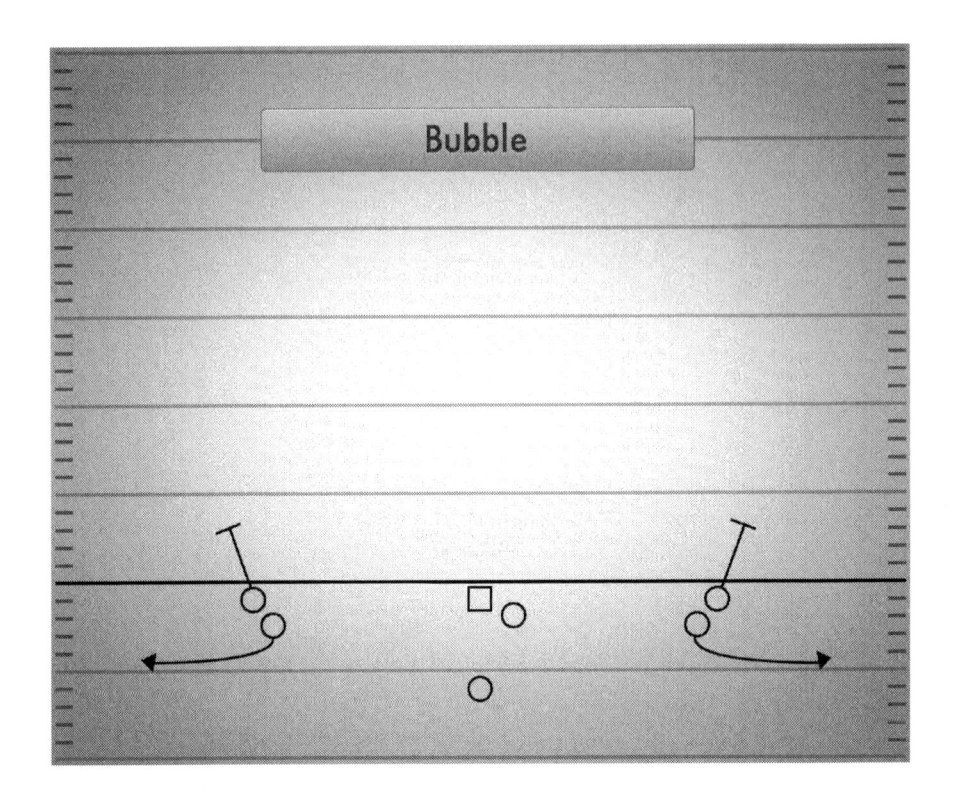

The Bubble play is a simple screen play. The Slot WR will bubble backwards with one step and proceed to drift towards the sideline. The block by the outside WR is critical to the success of the play.

Once the Quarterback delivers the ball the WR will read the block of the outside WR and sprint up the sideline.

FORMATION: **STACKS FORMATION**

DISTANCE: **SHORT YARDAGE**

Bubble WR Pass

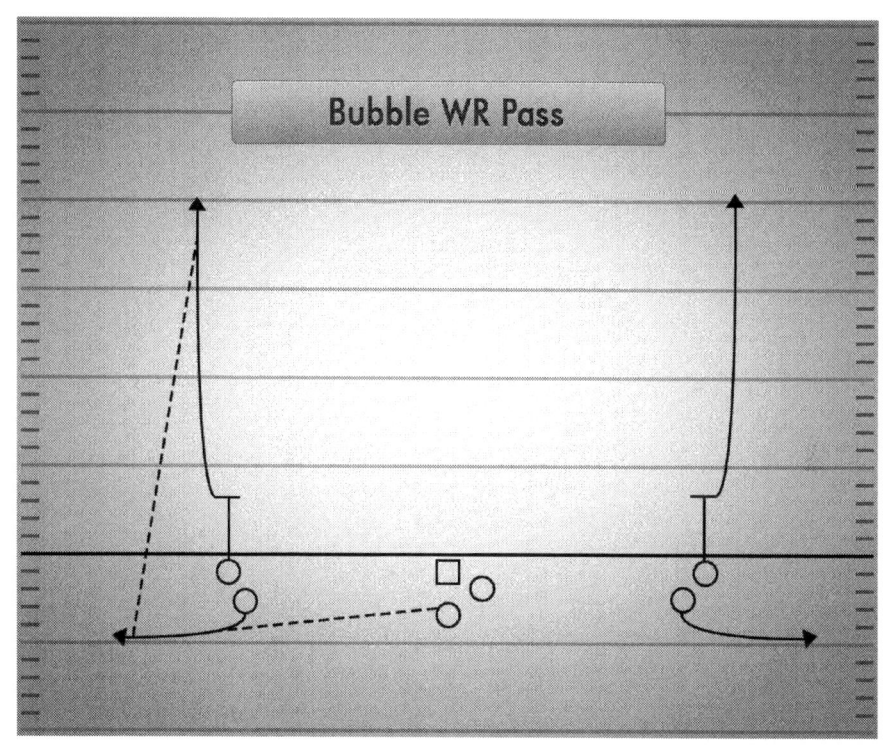

Before you can successfully pull off this double pass trick play, you first need to set it up with the normal Bubble play. After the defense is begins to cheat forward to guard the bubble, that's when you hit them with this Bubble WR Pass play.

The outside WR has to act as if he is going to block the defender like he normally does on the Bubble play, but as soon as he approaches, he needs to sidestep away and start jetting up the sideline. The inside WR needs to make a clean catch and quickly throw it over the defense to the WR who will be open downfield.

One key aspect of this play is that you have to remember that the first throw from the Quarterback has to be backwards, or else the second throw will be illegal. Therefore, the QB should scoot up a bit more than usual, and the WR should line up a little further back than usual, but both have to be done without making it obvious.

FORMATION: **STACKS FORMATION**

DISTANCE: **LONG YARDAGE**

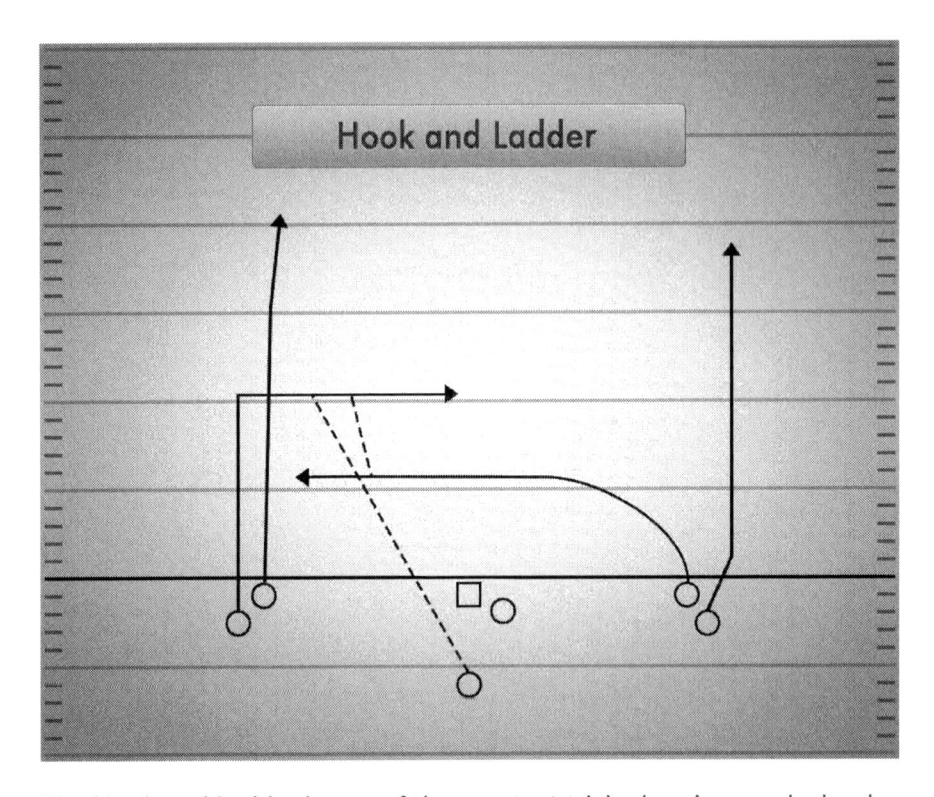

Hook and Ladder

The Hook and Ladder is one of the greatest trick plays in any playbook. It involves incredible timing and perfectly performed maneuvers by multiple individuals, but can be a phenomenally successful play when all the moving parts come together correctly.

The QB must deliver the throw to the In route before he gets too far across the field. The WR running the Shallow Cross must time his crossing route so that he is running underneath the In route immediately after he catches the ball. Once caught, the In route has to quickly secure the ball, and then pitch it backwards to the shallow crosser. The defense will have been moving inwards towards the original receiver, and will be caught off guard when the shallow crosser receives the pitch and is sprinting outward towards the sideline.

FORMATION: **STACKS FORMATION**

DISTANCE: **LONG YARDAGE**

ROUTES IN THIS PLAY: **IN, SHALLOW CROSS, FADE, SEAM**

Double Stop Combo

The Double Stop Combo is one of the most fundamental plays of any spread offense passing tree. A simple route concept that quickly presents all the Wide Receivers on a quick 5-yard stop route.

This play can be called early in the game in order to help the QB get settled in, or it can be called in response to a defense that is playing far off the line of scrimmage.

FORMATION: **STACKS FORMATION**

DISTANCE: **SHORT YARDAGE**

ROUTES IN THIS PLAY: **STOP**

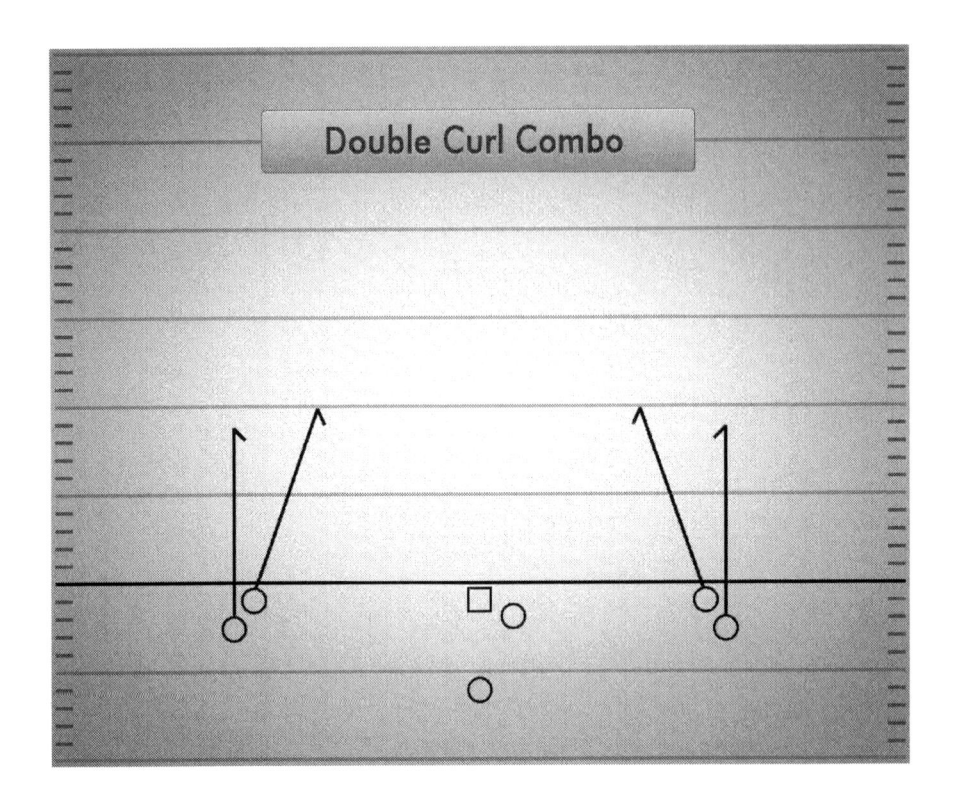

Double Curl Combo

The Double Curl Combo is an extended version of the Double Stop Combo play. It is a simple play for Medium Yardage.

Each Wide Receiver presses hard upfield for ten yards and quickly turns around, orienting their bodies toward the Quarterback who then takes his pick at the open man.

FORMATION: **STACKS FORMATION**

DISTANCE: **MEDIUM YARDAGE**

ROUTES IN THIS PLAY: **CURL**

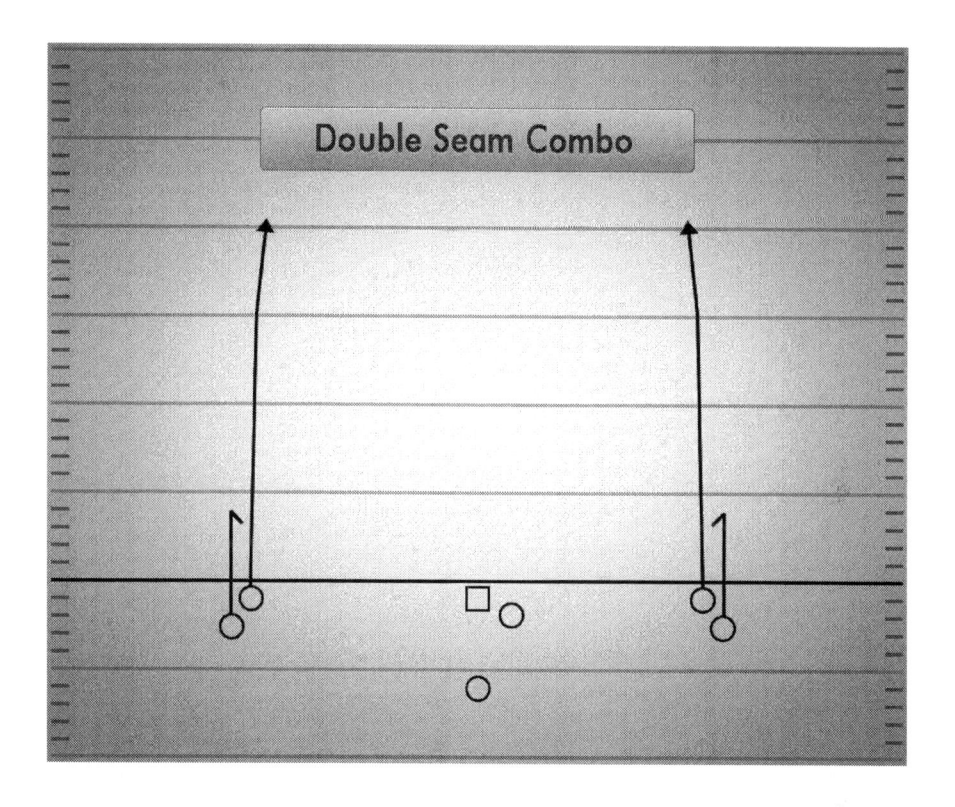

Double Seam Combo

Double Seam Combo is a play that places leverage on the defense up the seams. If the defense drops back to guard the seams, then the Quarterback should through the ball short to the 5-yard stop routes in the flats.

If it is a man-to-man defense, then consider throwing the seams over the top like a fade route, but run from an inside release. Safeties are not accustomed to guarding the fade route, and will therefore put your WR in better position to make the play.

FORMATION: **STACKS FORMATION**

DISTANCE: **SHORT YARDAGE, LONG YARDAGE**

ROUTES IN THIS PLAY: **STOP, SEAM**

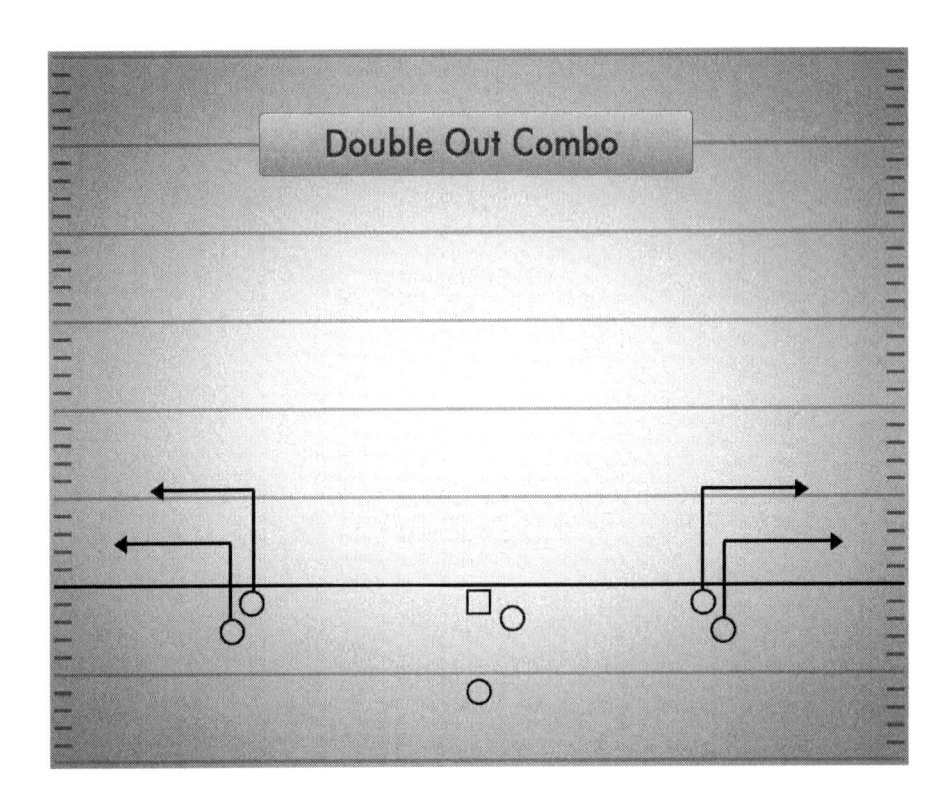

Double Out Combo

The Double Out Combo play places leverage on the outside of the defensive secondary. By attacking the flats with two players, the defender who is guarding the outside zone will be unable to guard both routes.

Versus a man to man defense, the QB must simply make a read based upon which WR makes a better move to the outside against the defender that is guarding him.

FORMATION: **STACKS FORMATION**

DISTANCE: **SHORT YARDAGE**

ROUTES IN THIS PLAY: **OUT**

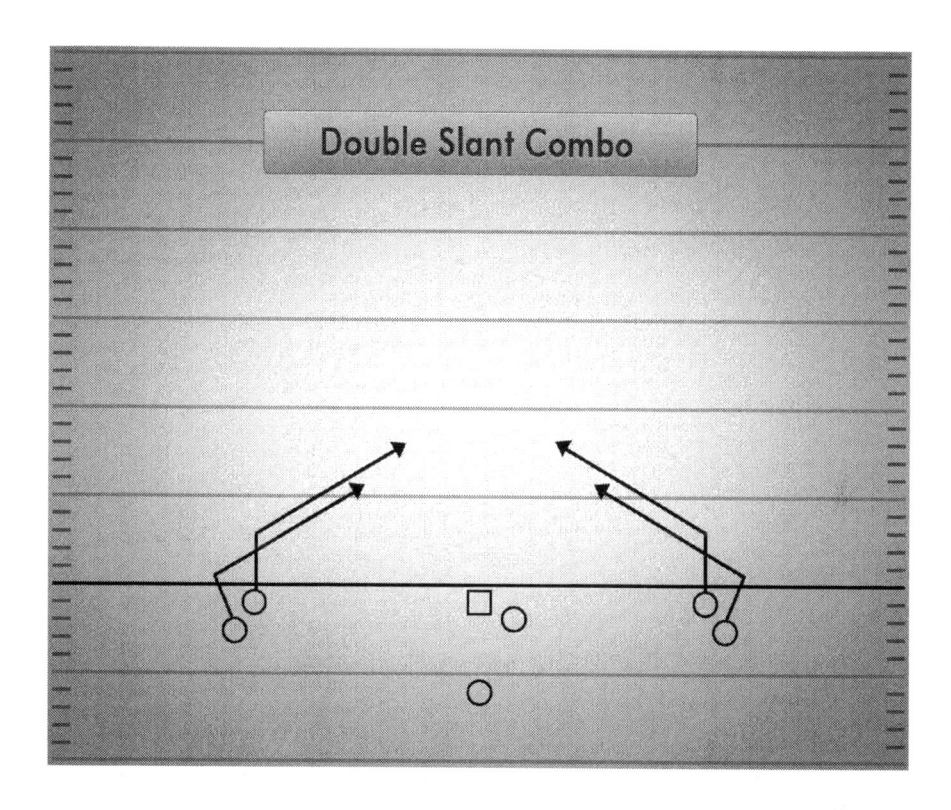

Double Slant Combo

The Double Slant Combo play is a great play to run in a short yardage situation if you have Wide Receivers who can run crisp routes. By making a clean cut to the inside, there will be a window of opportunity for the Quarterback to deliver the ball into the chest of the WR.

This play can also be used as a quick hitting play in the beginning of the game if the defense is playing far off the line of scrimmage. If the defense starts creeping up to guard against the short slant route, then hit them over the top by calling the Slant-and-Up Combo play.

FORMATION: **STACKS FORMATION**

DISTANCE: **SHORT YARDAGE**

ROUTES IN THIS PLAY: **SLANT**

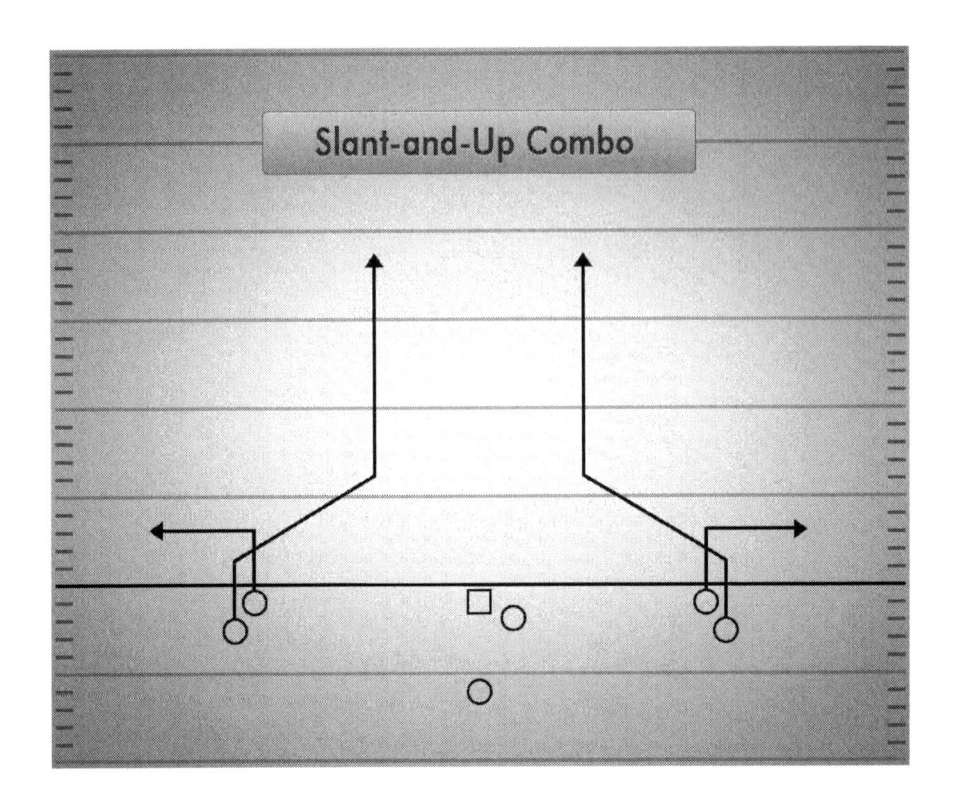

Slant-and-Up Combo

Slant-and-Up Combo is a companion play to the Out-Slant Combo play. By getting the defense used to seeing the Out-Slant combination routes, they will tend to cheat down. That is when you hit them over the top with this play.

As the defense makes a move to jump in front of the slant route, that is right when the WR turns it up field where the QB will throw it over the top for a long gain or a Touchdown.

FORMATION: **STACKS FORMATION**

DISTANCE: **LONG YARDAGE**

ROUTES IN THIS PLAY: **OUT, SLANT**

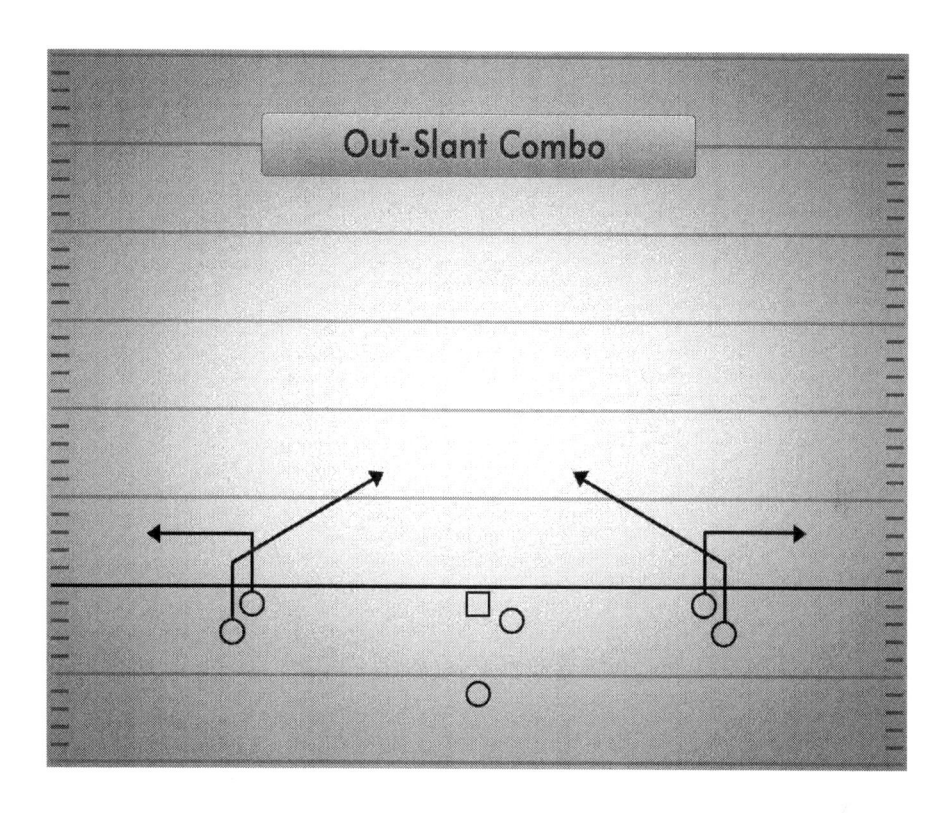

Out-Slant Combo

The Out-Slant Combo twists the defense around regardless of if they are playing man-to-man or zone. If they are playing zone, then the defense won't be able to keep track of the crossing patterns, and the man-to-man defense won't be able to keep up with the quick crossing cuts.

After the defense has gotten used to seeing this out-slant crossing pattern, mix things up by hitting them over the top with either the Slant-and-Up Combo play or the Out-and-Up Combo play.

FORMATION: **STACKS FORMATION**

DISTANCE: **SHORT YARDAGE**

ROUTES IN THIS PLAY: **OUT, SLANT**

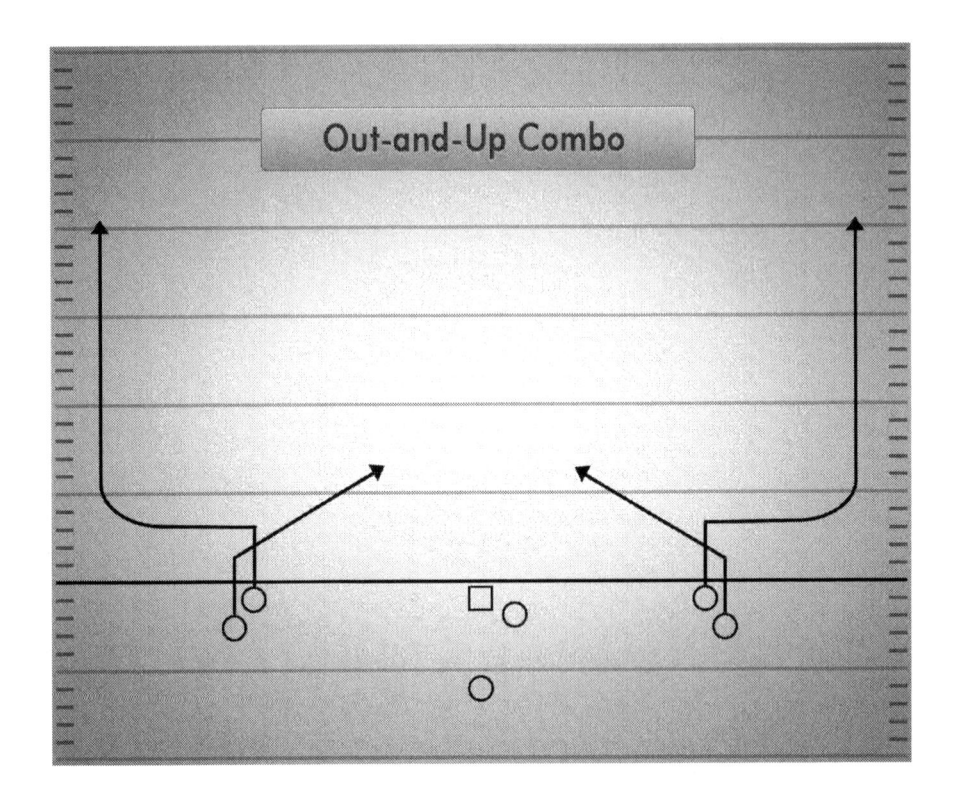

Out-and-Up Combo

The Out-and Up Combo is a companion play to the Out-Slant Combo play. After you have gotten the defense used to the shorter out route, hit them over the top with the Out-and-Up.

The part that makes this play extremely dangerous is against a man to man defense where the defender on the Out-and-Up route will have to run underneath the slant route, and will therefore be in a bad position to keep up with the inside WR who is now sprinting wide open up the sideline.

FORMATION: **STACKS FORMATION**

DISTANCE: **LONG YARDAGE**

ROUTES IN THIS PLAY: **OUT, SLANT**

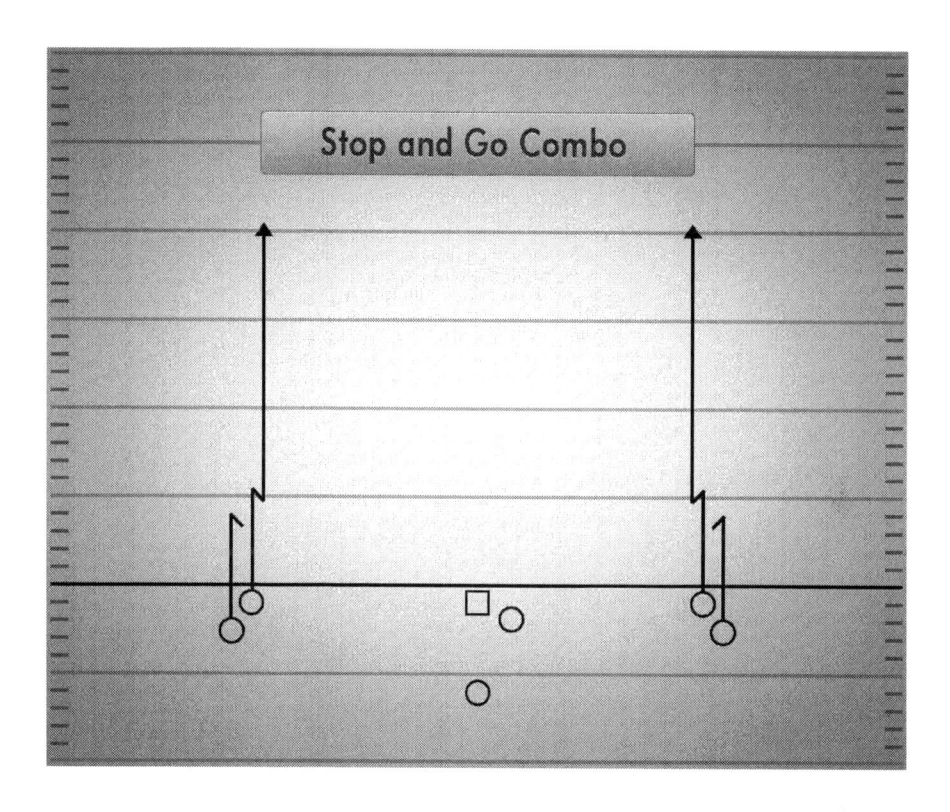

Stop and Go Combo

The Stop and Go route is one of the most famous double moves in all of football. After you have set up this play by repeatedly running the Double Stop Combo play, then surprise them with the Stop and Go and they won't know what hit them.

It is important that the Wide Receiver makes has break up the sideline after he stops. That way he is able to get passed the Cornerback easier.

FORMATION: **STACKS FORMATION**

DISTANCE: **LONG YARDAGE**

ROUTES IN THIS PLAY: **STOP**

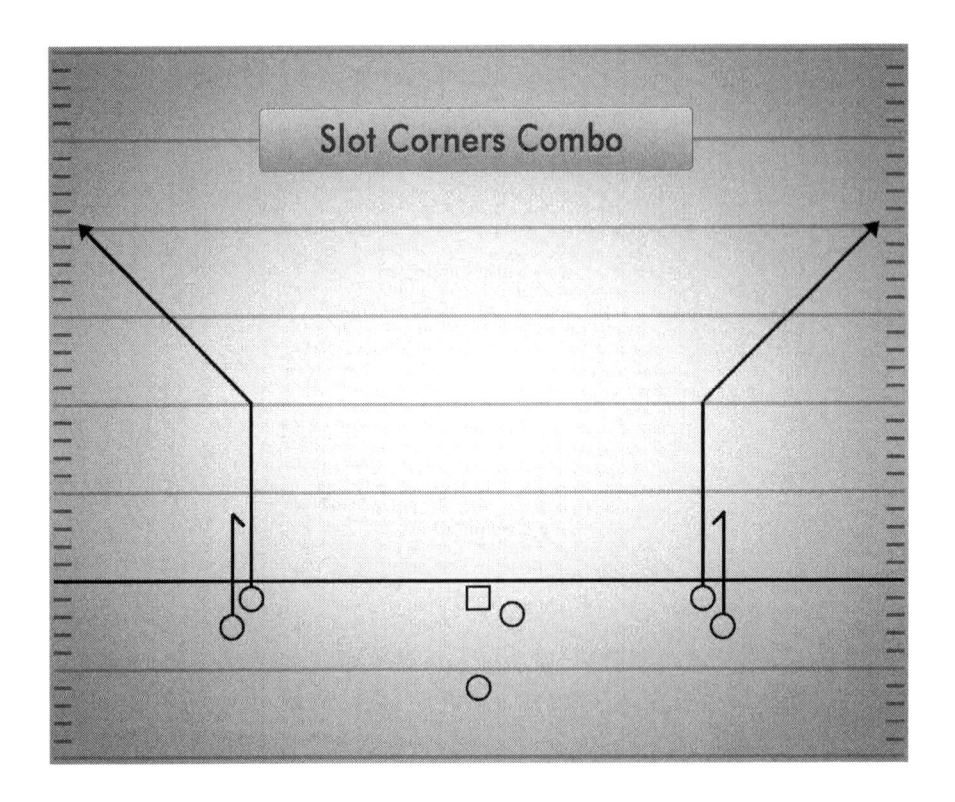

Slot Corners Combo

The Slot Corners play is a great play to use in order to isolate the Cornerback. The only thing that the Quarterback needs to read is how the Cornerback is positioning himself.

If the CB drops back underneath the Corner Route, then throw the ball to the stop on the outside. If the CB stay shallow in the flats, then throw over his head to the slot WR running the Corner route, making a break to the sideline.

FORMATION: **STACKS FORMATION**

DISTANCE: **SHORT YARDAGE, MEDIUM YARDAGE**

ROUTES IN THIS PLAY: **CORNER, STOP**

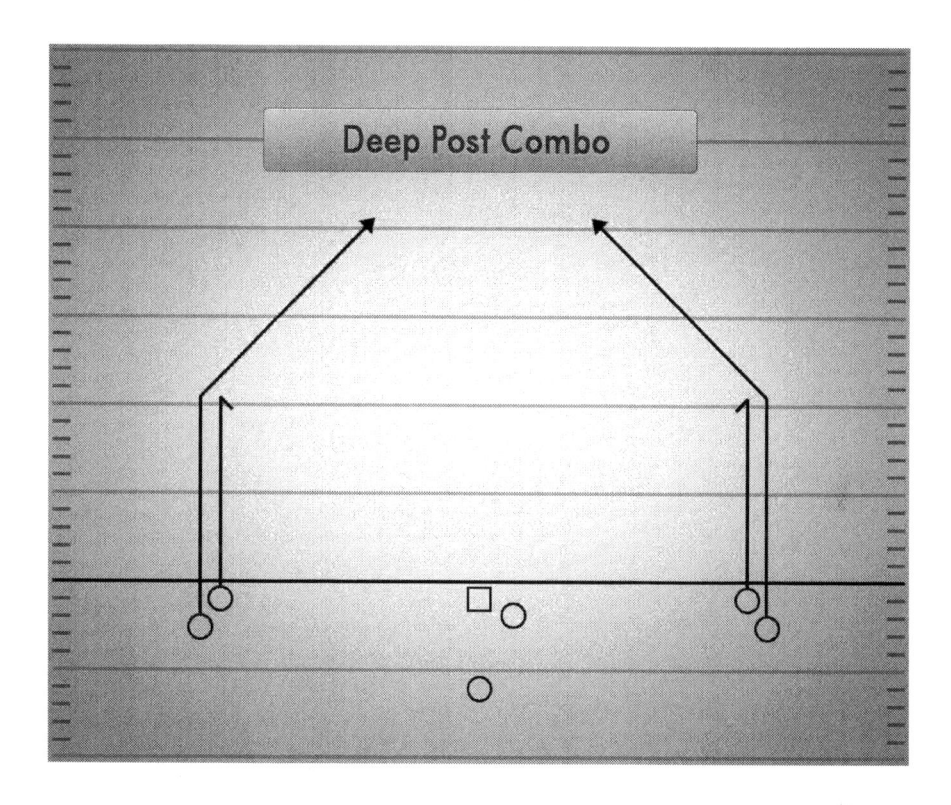

Deep Post Combo

The Deep Post Combo is a great way to attack downfield. The Post Route needs to be a skinny post with a trajectory that doesn't cross the middle of the field. The Slot Receiver needs to run his Curl Route in a way that grabs the attention of the Safety.

The Quarterback's read should be focused on the Safety. If the Safety stays high and guards the Post Route, then drop down and throw it to the Curl Route. If, however, the Safety is drawn down to the Slot Receiver running the Curl, then throw over his head to the Post running downfield.

FORMATION: **STACKS FORMATION**

DISTANCE: **LONG YARDAGE, MEDIUM YARDAGE**

ROUTES IN THIS PLAY: **POST, CURL**

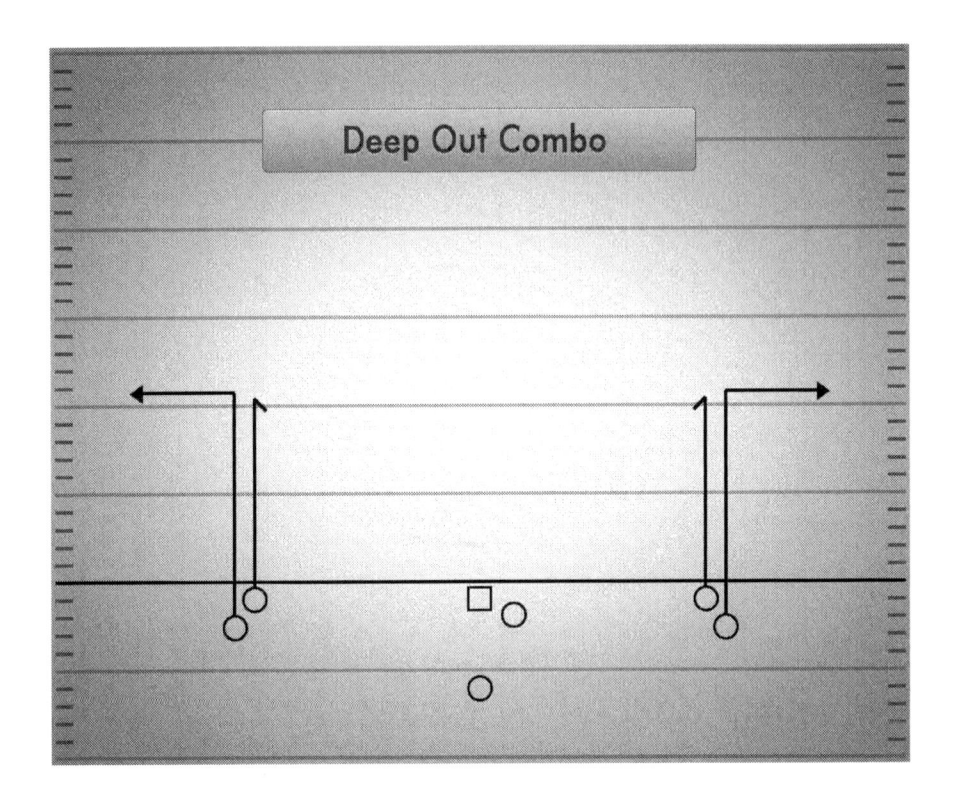

Deep Out Combo

The Deep Out Combo is similar to the Double Curl Combo play with a variation that send the outside WRs towards the sideline on a Deep Out Route.

The QB should make a pre-snap read to determine what side he is going to throw to. Once the side has been determined, then disregard the other half of the field and the read is locked into being between the Deep Out or the Curl Route.

FORMATION: **STACKS FORMATION**

DISTANCE: **MEDIUM YARDAGE**

ROUTES IN THIS PLAY: **CURL, OUT**

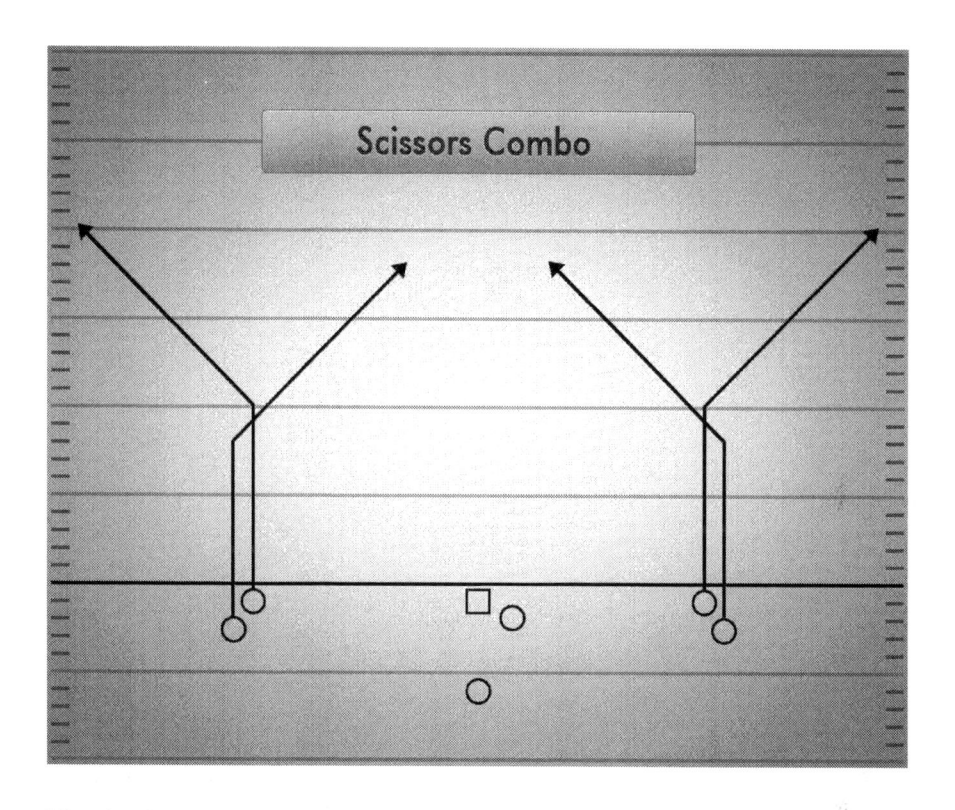

Scissors Combo

The Scissors Combo play is a mirrored play with the same route concept of a Post Route and a Corner Route on both sides.

The Wide Receivers need to cleanly run their routes by converging across each other at the point of the downfield cuts in order to disorient the defense and break free into the open field.

FORMATION: **STACKS FORMATION**

DISTANCE: **LONG YARDAGE**

ROUTES IN THIS PLAY: **CORNER, POST**

Switchblade Combo

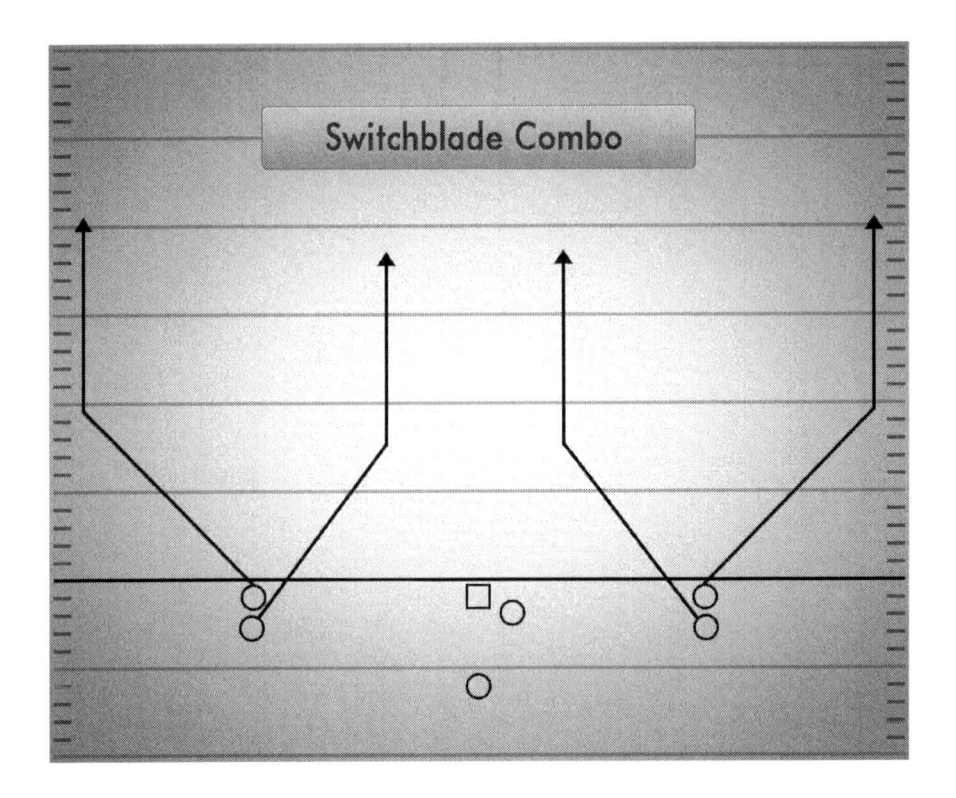

The Switchblade Combo play is intended to create a rub between the two combination receivers in order to break free from their defenders.

This play will work best against a man-to-man defense, because it is easy to lose the defenders when the Receivers cross and then break free going upfield.

FORMATION: STACKS FORMATION

DISTANCE: LONG YARDAGE

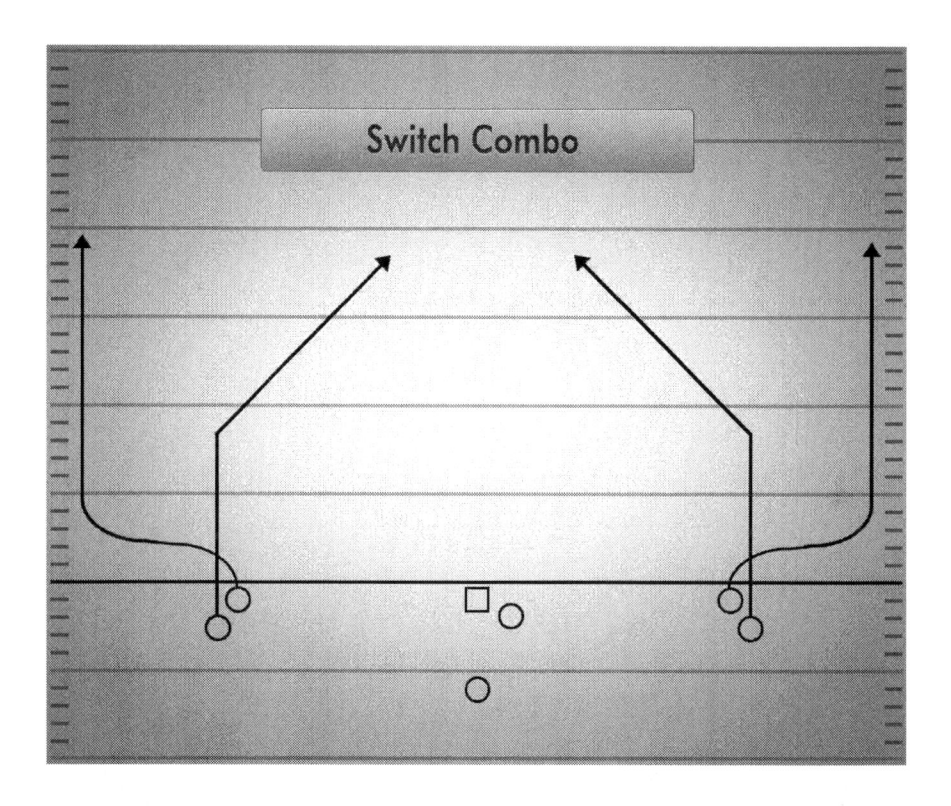

Switch Combo

Switch Combo is the classic switch play where the receivers use their routes to "switch" their positions on the field. The Outside Receiver gets upfield fast and runs a Post Route. The Slot Receiver goes underneath the Outside Receiver and then jets up the sideline.

The Quarterback should read the deep safeties. This play uses four players to attack zones that usually only have two, or maybe 3, defenders responsible for guarding them. Use your eyes to influence the defensive backs' movement, and then find the open WR running downfield.

FORMATION: **STACKS FORMATION**

DISTANCE: **LONG YARDAGE**

ROUTES IN THIS PLAY: **POST**

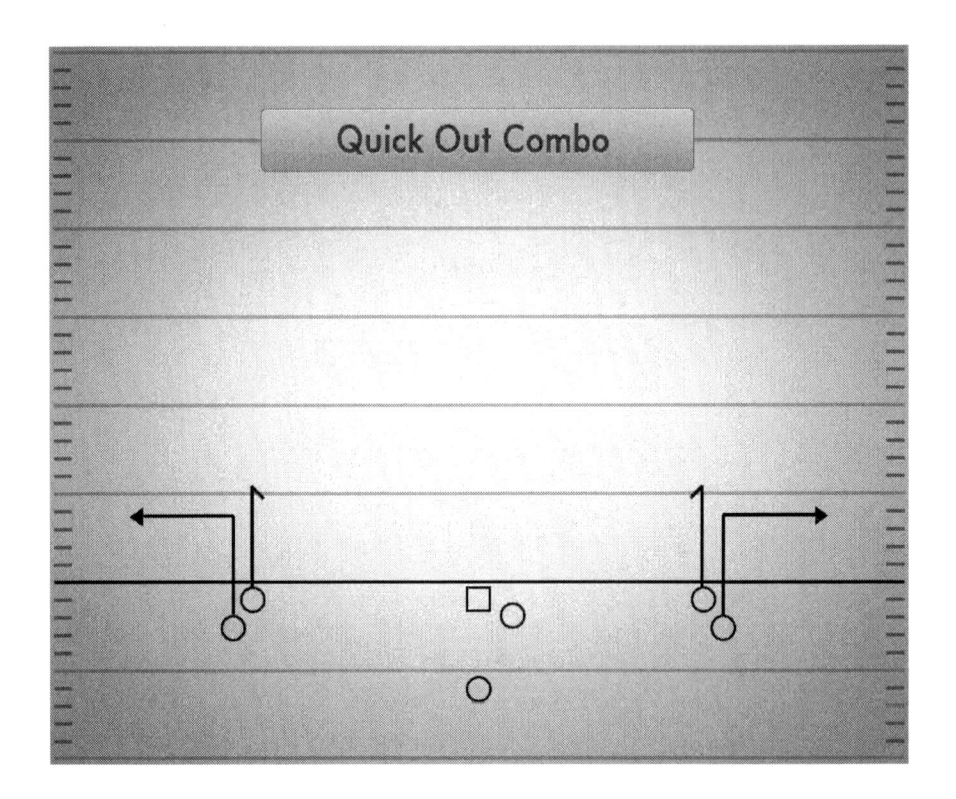

Quick Out Combo

Quick Cut Combo is a variation of the standard Double Stop Combo play, and a shorter version of the Deep Out Combo play.

The Quarterback should select one side of the field on the pre-snap read, and then as the play begins, determine which of the Wide Receivers gets in better position against the defense on his route.

FORMATION: **STACKS FORMATION**

DISTANCE: **SHORT YARDAGE**

ROUTES IN THIS PLAY: **STOP, OUT**

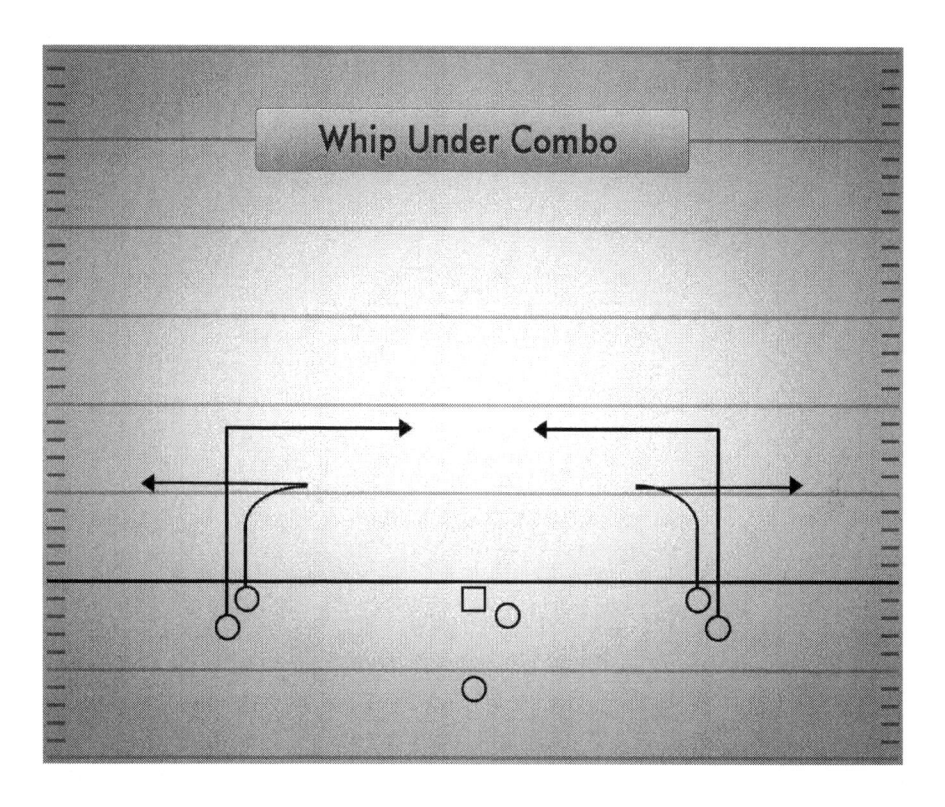

Whip Under Combo

The Whip Under Combo play is a great play to get some horizontal flow in your route concepts going. The crucial aspect of the play is the way in which the Whip Route is run by the Slot Receiver. The route must start of looking like an inside movement, but then the WR must plant his foot and spin (face toward the QB) and jet hard to the sideline.

If the Slot Receiver is not able to get open with the Whip Route, then the horizontal movement underneath should clear out to reveal the outside Receiver open on the In Route.

FORMATION: **STACKS FORMATION**

DISTANCE: **SHORT YARDAGE, MEDIUM YARDAGE**

ROUTES IN THIS PLAY: **IN, OUT**

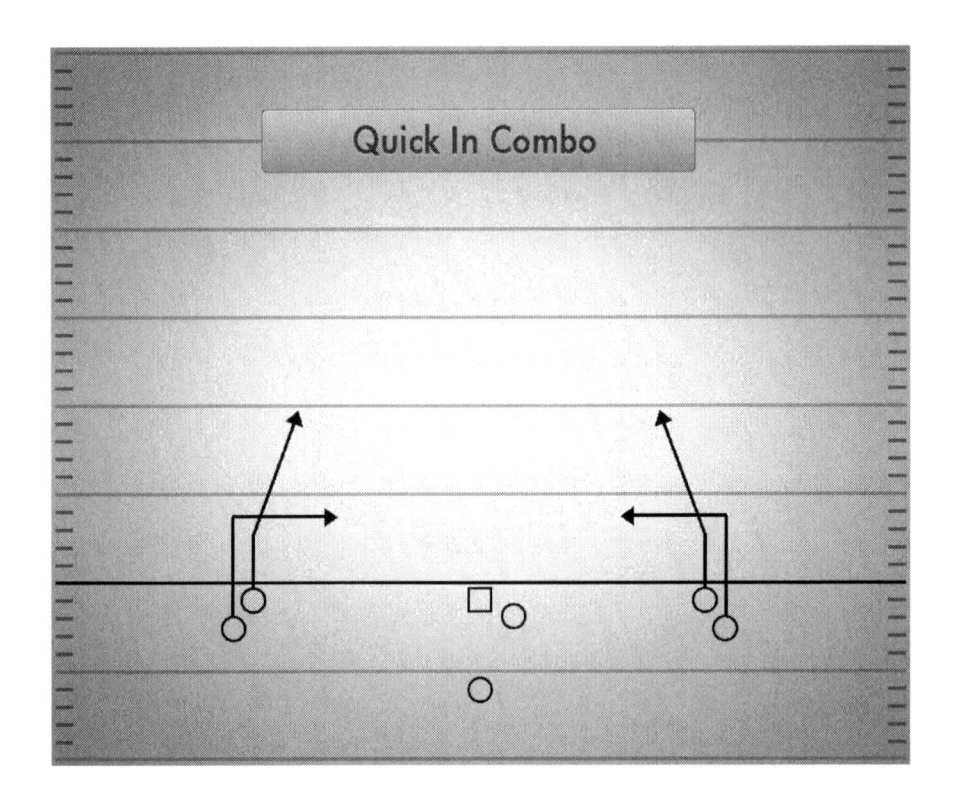

Quick In Combo

The Quick In Combo play is built to be a quick hitter. The Slot Receiver presses off the line of scrimmage in order to create space underneath for the Outside Receiver to be open for the In route.

The QB must make a pre-snap read to determine which side of the field is giving up the most position in the inside zone based upon formation alignment.

FORMATION: STACKS FORMATION

DISTANCE: SHORT YARDAGE

ROUTES IN THIS PLAY: IN, SEAM

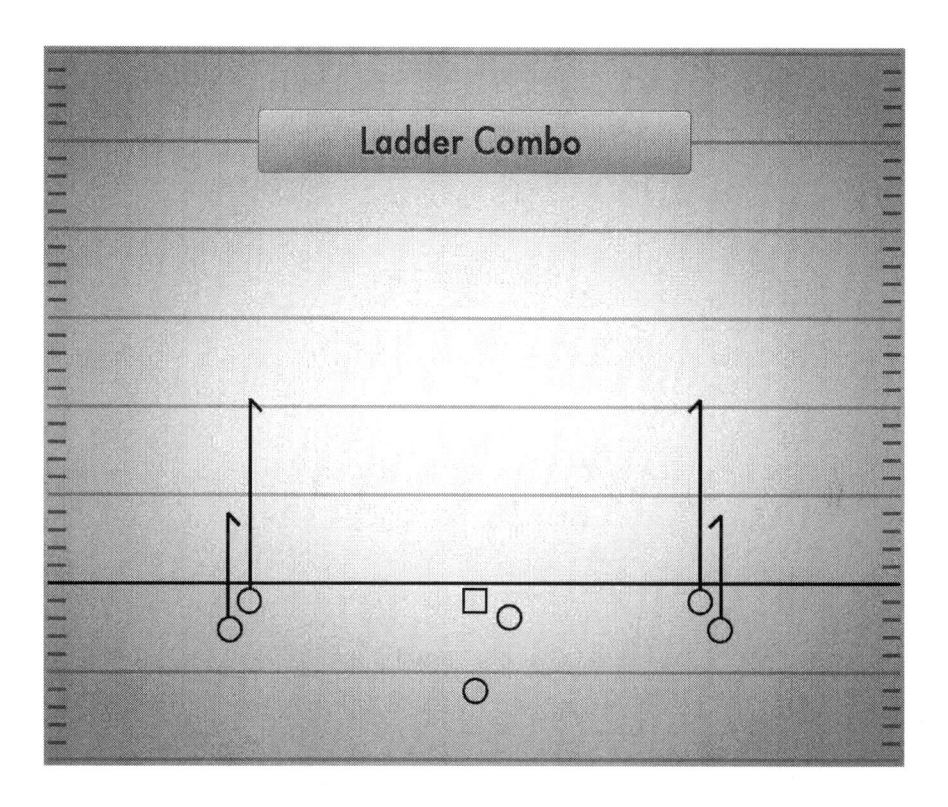

Ladder Combo

Ladder Combo is a play to hit the defense at varying vertical positions. All receivers run a stop and curl routes, but the lengths of the routes vary based upon their alignment.

The Quarterback should make his read just as if he is climbing up a "ladder." First look at the 5-Yard stop, and then work your way up to the 10-yard curl.

FORMATION: STACKS FORMATION

DISTANCE: SHORT YARDAGE, MEDIUM YARDAGE

ROUTES IN THIS PLAY: STOP, CURL

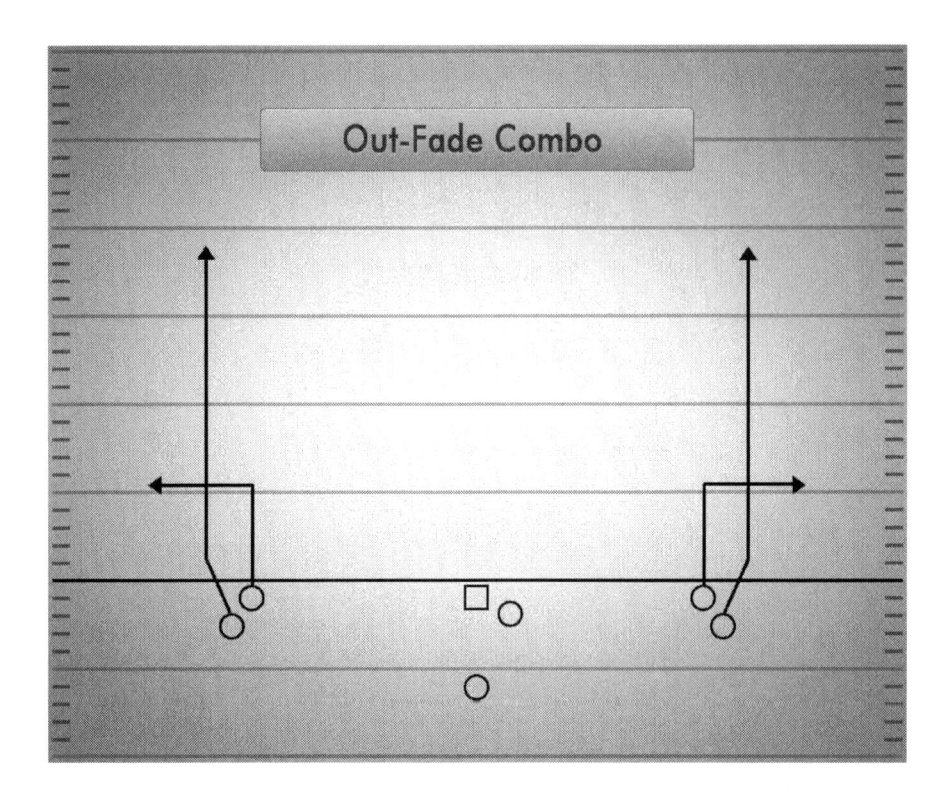

Out-Fade Combo

The Out-Fade route combination is one of the most popular route concepts in any football team's playbook. A Fade Route up the sideline on the outside combined with an Out Route from the Slot Receiver from the inside.

The Quarterback's read should be locked in on the defensive Cornerback. If the Cornerback drifts deep with the Fade, then throw the ball to the Out Route in the flats. If the Cornerback stays in the flats to jump on the Out, then throw it over the top to the Fade.

FORMATION: **STACKS FORMATION**

DISTANCE: **SHORT YARDAGE, MEDIUM YARDAGE**

ROUTES IN THIS PLAY: **FADE, OUT**

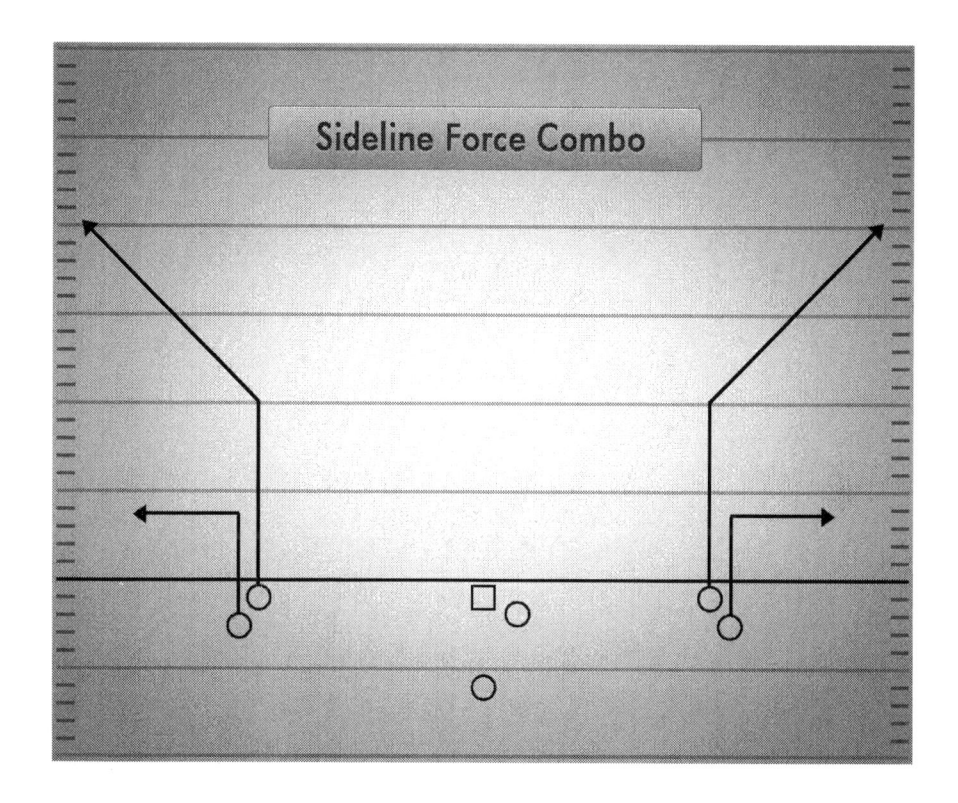

Sideline Force Combo

The Sideline Force Combo play is a shorter version of the Sideline Force Deep Combo play. The main goal of this play is to force the routes to the sideline.

This play is very effective when you need to manage the time on the clock because it allows the Receivers to quickly get out of bounds after the catch the ball.

FORMATION: **STACKS FORMATION**

DISTANCE: **SHORT YARDAGE, MEDIUM YARDAGE**

ROUTES IN THIS PLAY: **CORNER, OUT**

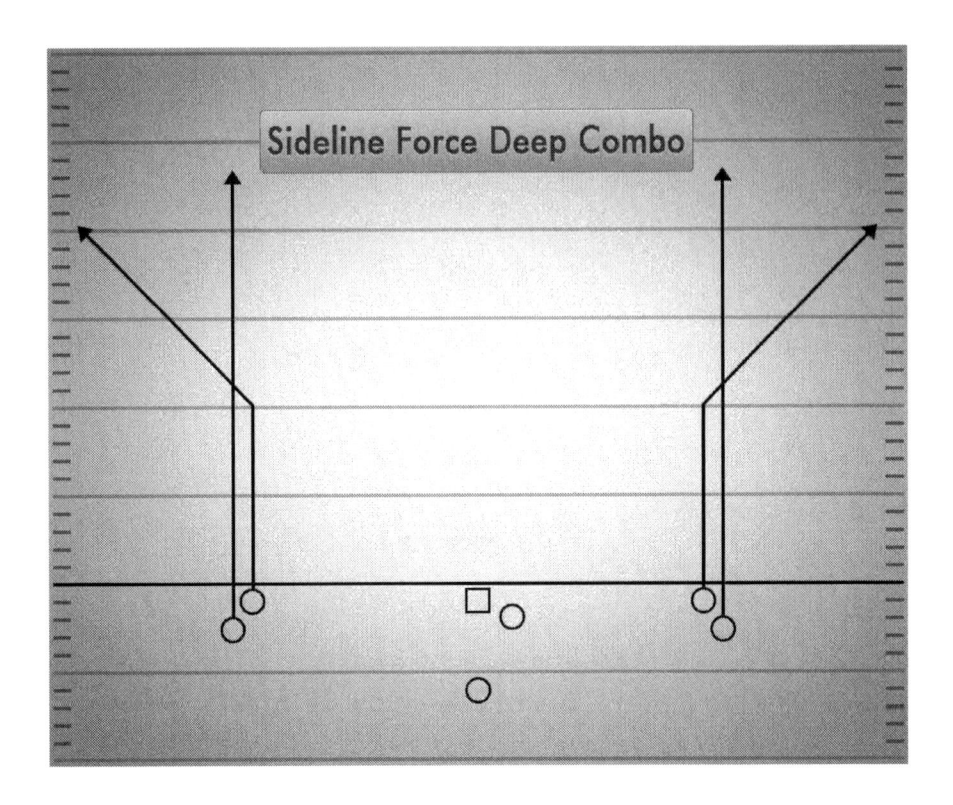

Sideline Force Deep Combo

The Sideline Force Deep Combo play is the deep version of the Sideline Force Combo play. The purpose of this play is to get the Wide Receivers in close proximity to the sideline while running deep downfield.

This play is very effective when you need to manage the time on the clock because it allows the Receivers to quickly get out of bounds after the catch the ball.

FORMATION: **STACKS FORMATION**

DISTANCE: **LONG YARDAGE**

ROUTES IN THIS PLAY: **CORNER, STREAK**

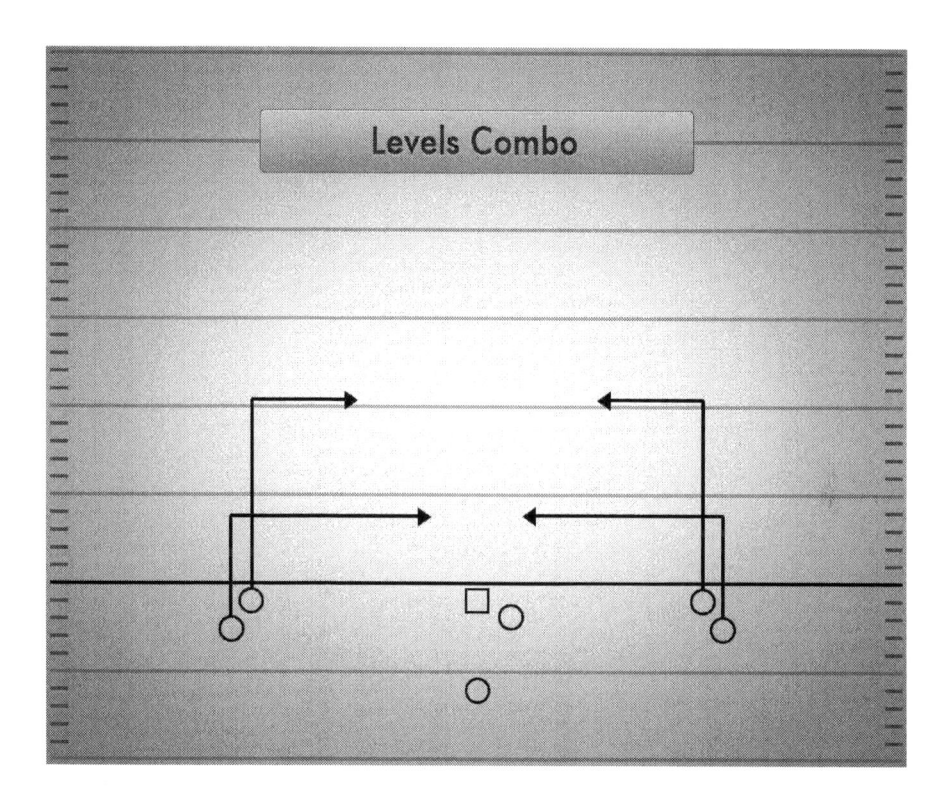

Levels Combo

The Levels Combo play is a great way to attack different vertical portions of the defensive secondary. The Wide Receivers run In Routes at varying distances down the field.

The horizontal movement should create a space for the Quarterback to find an opening to throw into, especially combined with the alternating vertical positioning of the routes.

FORMATION: **STACKS FORMATION**

DISTANCE: **SHORT YARDAGE, MEDIUM YARDAGE**

ROUTES IN THIS PLAY: **IN**

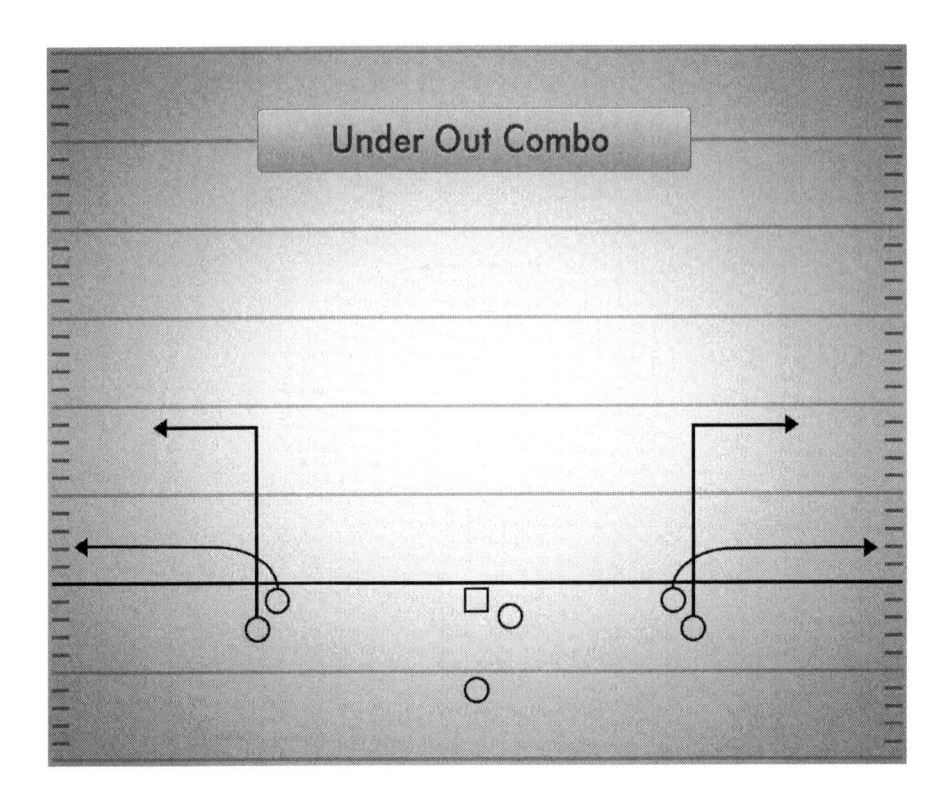

Under Out Combo

The Under Out Combo play positions the inside WR on a quick out underneath the deeper out. This places pressure on the flats of the defensive secondary by placing two WR on each side of the zone.

By splitting the responsibilities of the Cornerback, the Quarterback will have to see which one the Cornerback decides to guard, and then deliver the ball to the appropriate WR.

FORMATION: **STACKS FORMATION**

DISTANCE: **SHORT YARDAGE, MEDIUM YARDAGE**

ROUTES IN THIS PLAY: **OUT**

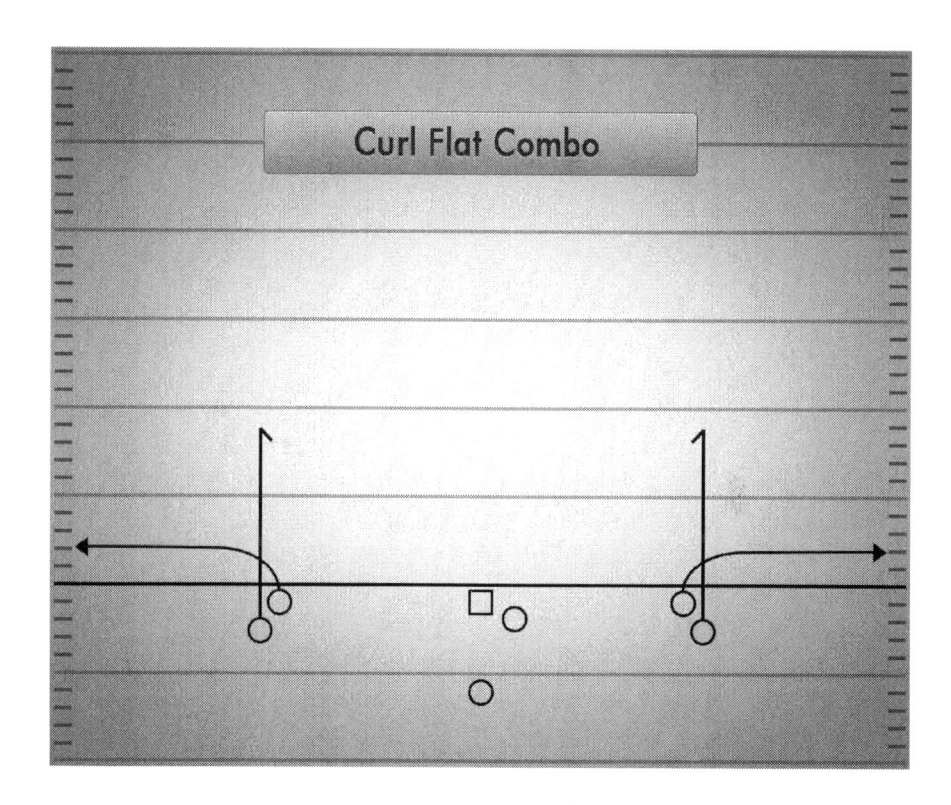

Curl Flat Combo

The Curl Flat Combo play attacks the defensive flat zone on the outside with a quick Out Route and a Curl Route over the top.

The Quarterback will want to look first at the quick out, and if the defense flowed fast to guard the out, then that means the curl route should be curling around in the open space right behind them.

FORMATION: **STACKS FORMATION**

DISTANCE: **SHORT YARDAGE, MEDIUM YARDAGE**

ROUTES IN THIS PLAY: **CURL, OUT**

Plays
Bunch Formation

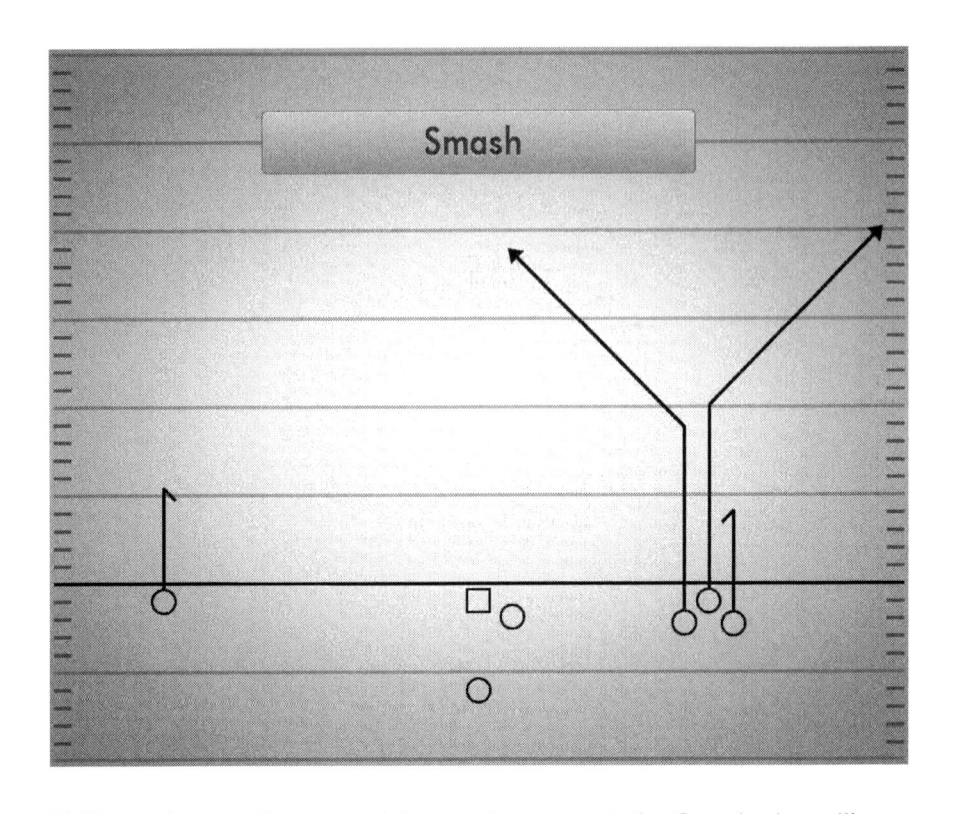

Smash

Utilizing the popular corner/stop route concept, the Smash play will attack many different zones in the defensive secondary. The first read that the Quarterback should make is to watch how the Cornerback plays the routes. If he stays low on the Stop route, then throw it over his head to the Corner route. If he stays high on the corner route, then throw it low to the Wide Receiver running the Stop route, who will be wide open in the flats. No outside linebacker will be able to run out there quick enough if the corner is dropping deep, and the Quarterback makes a quick read.

FORMATION: **BUNCH FORMATION**

DISTANCE: **SHORT YARDAGE, MEDIUM YARDAGE**

ROUTES IN THIS PLAY: **CORNER, POST, STOP**

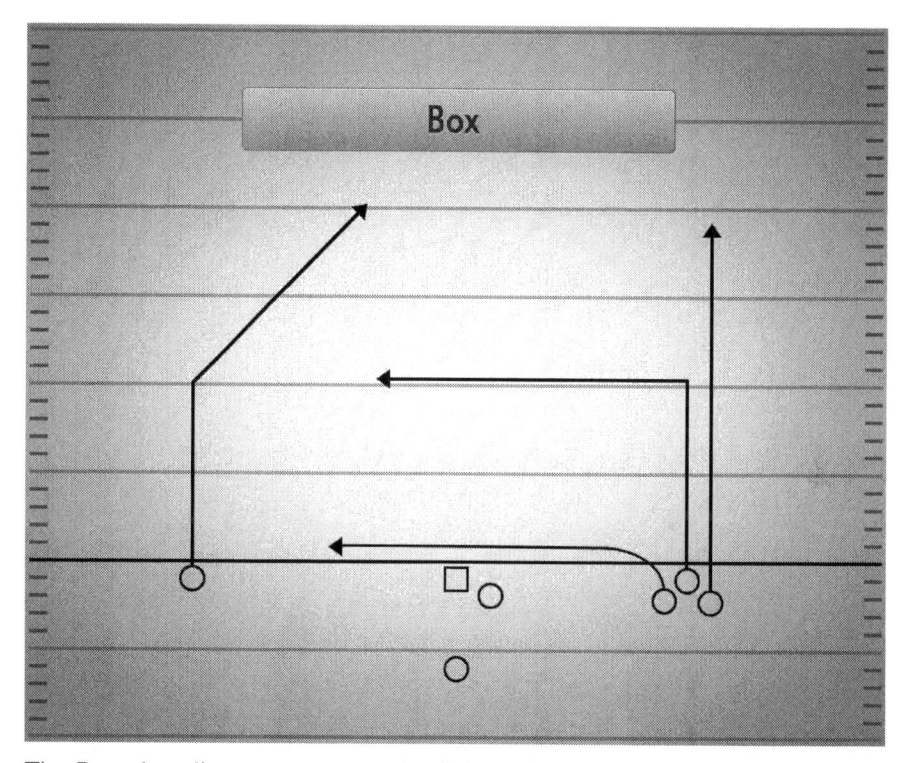

Box

The Box play allows you to trap the defense into having to make a high/low decision. In fact, there are two different high/low areas on the defense that this play attacks.

By singling out the safety, the Quarterback can make a "high/low" read based upon the combination of the Post route and the 10 yard In route. If the safety drops high to guard the Post, then throw it low to the In route. If the safety stays low on the In, then throw it high to the Post.

Additionally, another high/low read takes place at the level of the outside linebacker. The linebacker will have to make the decision to go high and guard the In route, or stay low and guard the Shallow Cross. The Quarterback's read progression should start by reading the Safety on the Post, and then moving down to the In route, and finally hitting the lowest shallow cross underneath, if everything higher is guarded.

FORMATION: **BUNCH FORMATION**

DISTANCE: **SHORT YARDAGE, LONG YARDAGE, MEDIUM YARDAGE**

ROUTES IN THIS PLAY: **POST, IN, SHALLOW CROSS, STREAK**

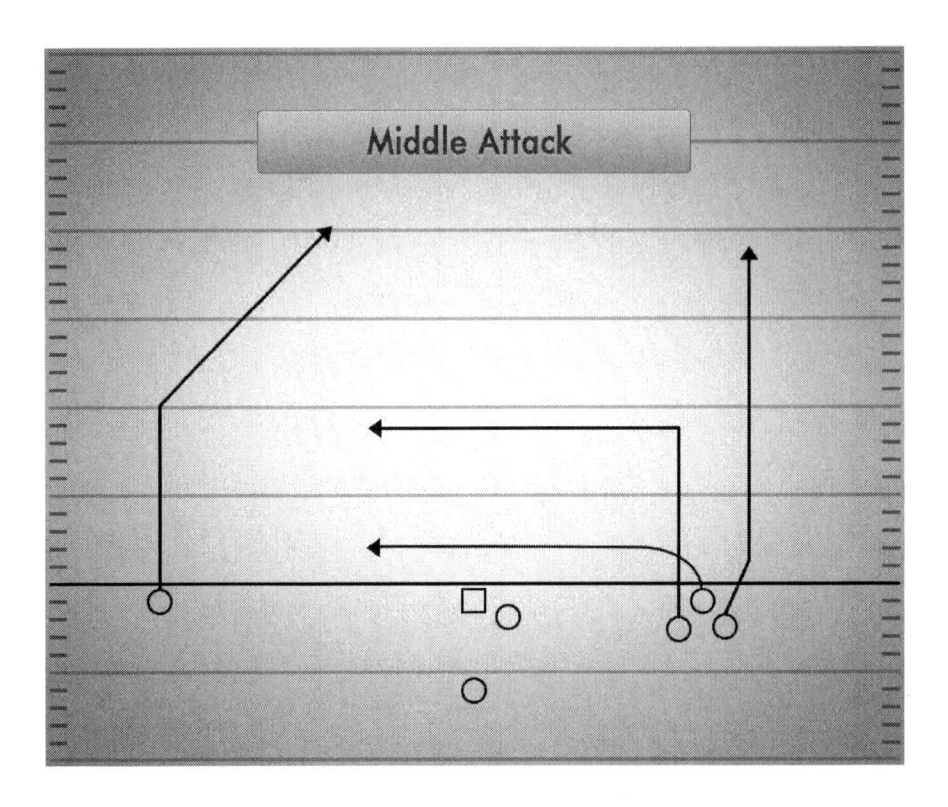

Middle Attack

The Middle Attack play attacks the middle of the defense with three different routes attacking three different levels in the defensive secondary. This allows the Quarterback to read the vertical flow of the defense in order to determine which of the three levels will be the open one. If the defense begins to crowd the middle of the field, then the outside receiver needs to get a wide release to run down the sideline on the fade route to stretch out the secondary.

Middle Attack is a variation of the Box play, but with a reversal of roles for the slot receivers.

FORMATION: **BUNCH FORMATION**

DISTANCE: **SHORT YARDAGE, LONG YARDAGE, MEDIUM YARDAGE**

ROUTES IN THIS PLAY: **POST, IN, SHALLOW CROSS, FADE**

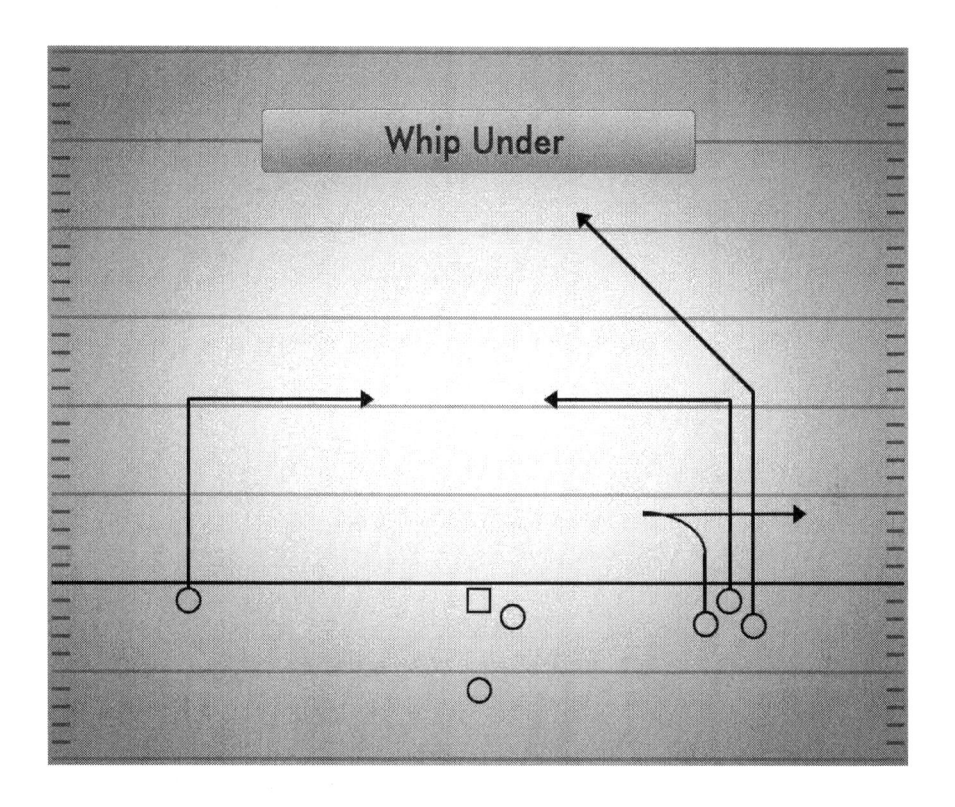

Whip Under

The Whip play is all about misdirection. The hard inside move gets the defense flowing inside, but the quick pivot outside is even more important for a quick move outside. If the inside receiver flowing underneath is covered up, then the outside receiver will be open coming inside over the top.

The Whip is best run in the second half of the game after setting up the defense with a sequence of successful slant plays. The defender will be ready to jump forward on the slant, but the wide out will plant hard and turn fast outside where he will be wide open running away from the defender.

FORMATION: **BUNCH FORMATION**

DISTANCE: **SHORT YARDAGE, MEDIUM YARDAGE**

ROUTES IN THIS PLAY: **POST, IN, WHIP, STOP**

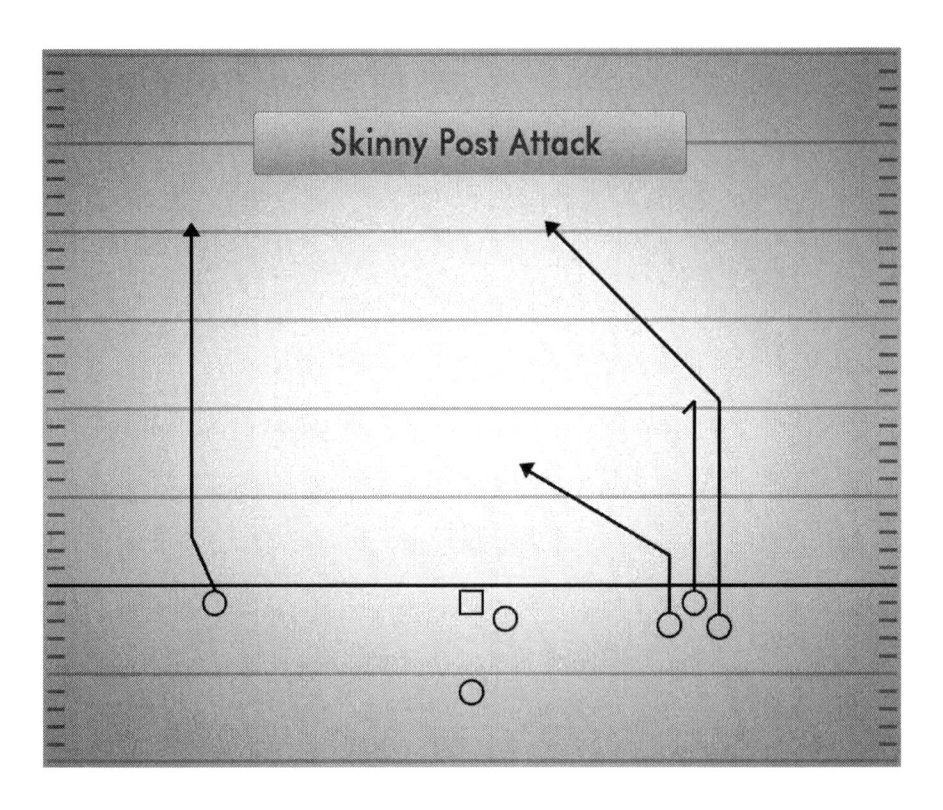

Skinny Post Attack

The Skinny Post Attack play requires special attention to detail. The main point of this play is to put the Safety in a tough situation by attacking his zone with two routes. The most critical route running in this play is the 10-yard Curl route, because it has to be run in a way that attracts the Safety's attention. If the slot receiver successfully gets the Safety to stay down and guard the curl, then the Post route will be wide open over the top.

If the Safety stays deep, however, then the Curl route needs to make sure that he is deep enough over the linebackers in order to be open 10-12 yards downfield. All in all, this play consists of a high/low read on the Safety by placing on route in the front of the Safety's zone, and the other over the top of the Safety's zone.

FORMATION: **BUNCH FORMATION**

DISTANCE: **LONG YARDAGE, MEDIUM YARDAGE**

ROUTES IN THIS PLAY: **POST, FADE, STOP, CURL**

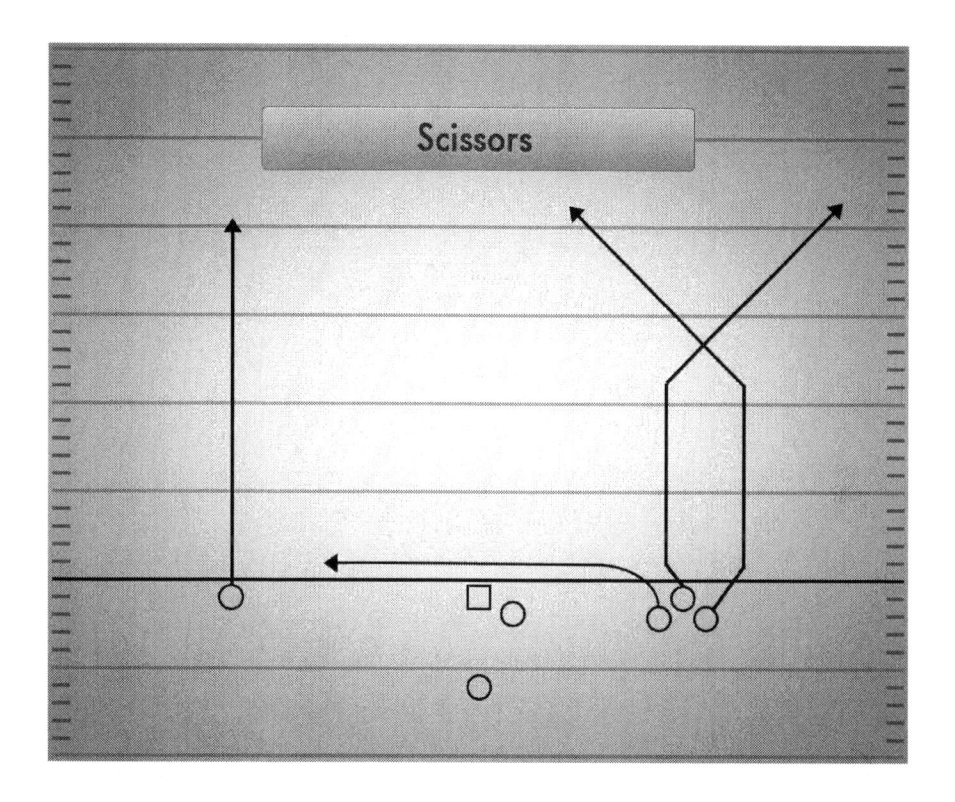

Scissors

Scissors is a great play to cut through the defensive secondary by converging two receivers across each other on one half of the field. The Post route goes over the top of the Corner route. The Post is the first read coming across the top, followed up by the Corner cutting through below.

The most important aspect of the play is that both routes run quickly up field at the same time and cut across each other simultaneously to wreak havoc on the downfield defenders.

FORMATION: **BUNCH FORMATION**

DISTANCE: **LONG YARDAGE**

ROUTES IN THIS PLAY: **CORNER, POST, SHALLOW CROSS, STREAK**

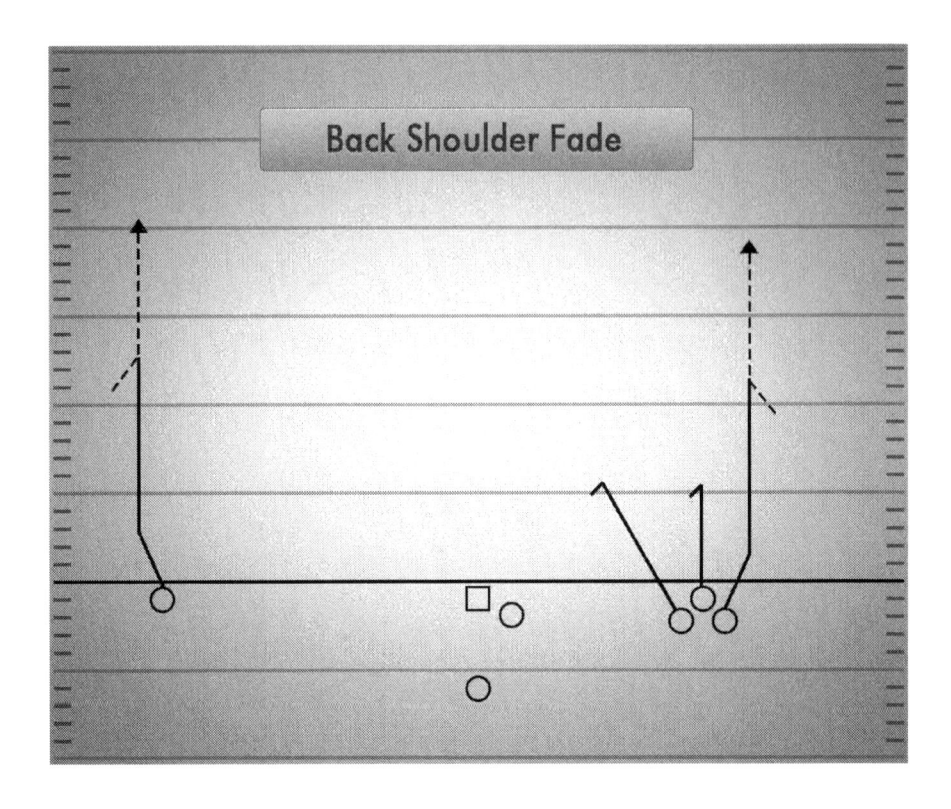

Back Shoulder Fade

The Back Shoulder fade is a go-to play for goal line situations. It gives the Receiver two options to choose from based upon how the defender guards him. If the Cornerback is guarding deep, then the Quarterback can throw the ball short, but if the Cornerback is play up close, then the Quarterback can throw the ball over the top.

Communication and chemistry between the Quarterback and the Receiver is of the utmost importance. Both the thrower and the route runner need to be on the same page to execute this play properly. Great chemistry will lead to great results on the Back Shoulder fade.

FORMATION: **BUNCH FORMATION**

DISTANCE: **SHORT YARDAGE**

ROUTES IN THIS PLAY: **FADE, STOP**

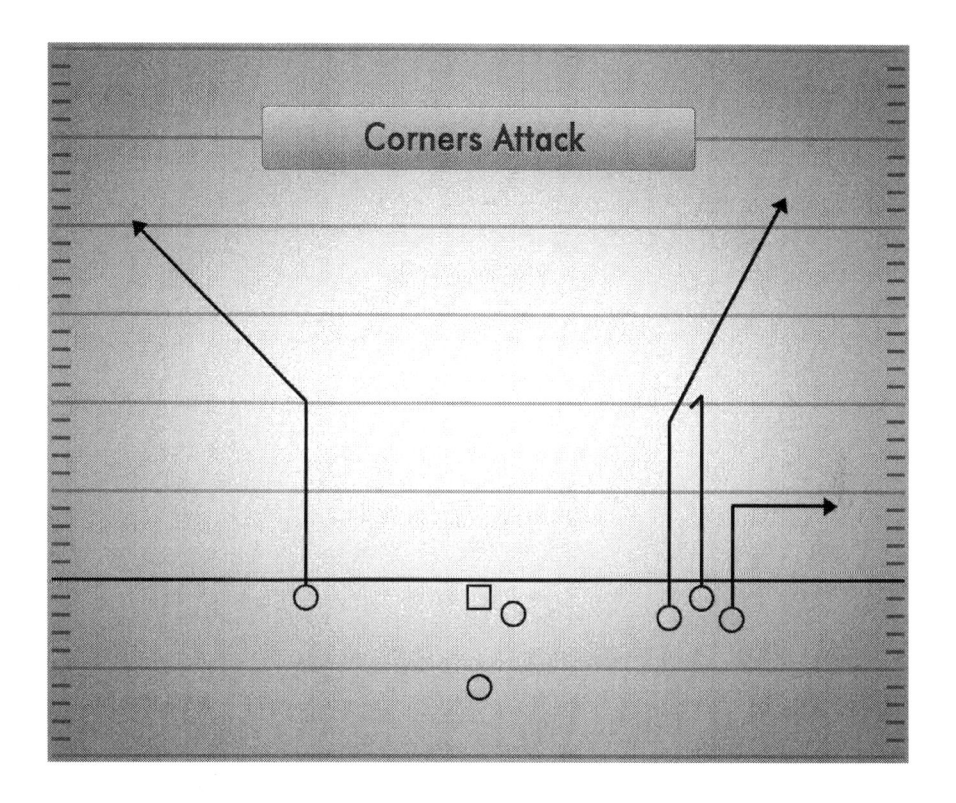

Corners Attack

Corners attack does just what its name says it does: Attack the Corners. The corner routes get depth into the corner of the defensive secondary, while the underneath routes wreak havoc in the flats. The slot receiver who runs the corner in combination with the 10-yard curl, has to make sure that he gets depth so that he is properly spaced over the top of the Curl route.

The Quarterback has to make a pre-snap decision on to select what side he wants to go to. Once that decision is made, read the Cornerback to see if he is staying on the deep corner, or cheating on the flat.

FORMATION: **BUNCH FORMATION**

DISTANCE: **LONG YARDAGE**

ROUTES IN THIS PLAY: **CORNER, CURL, OUT**

Ridge Force

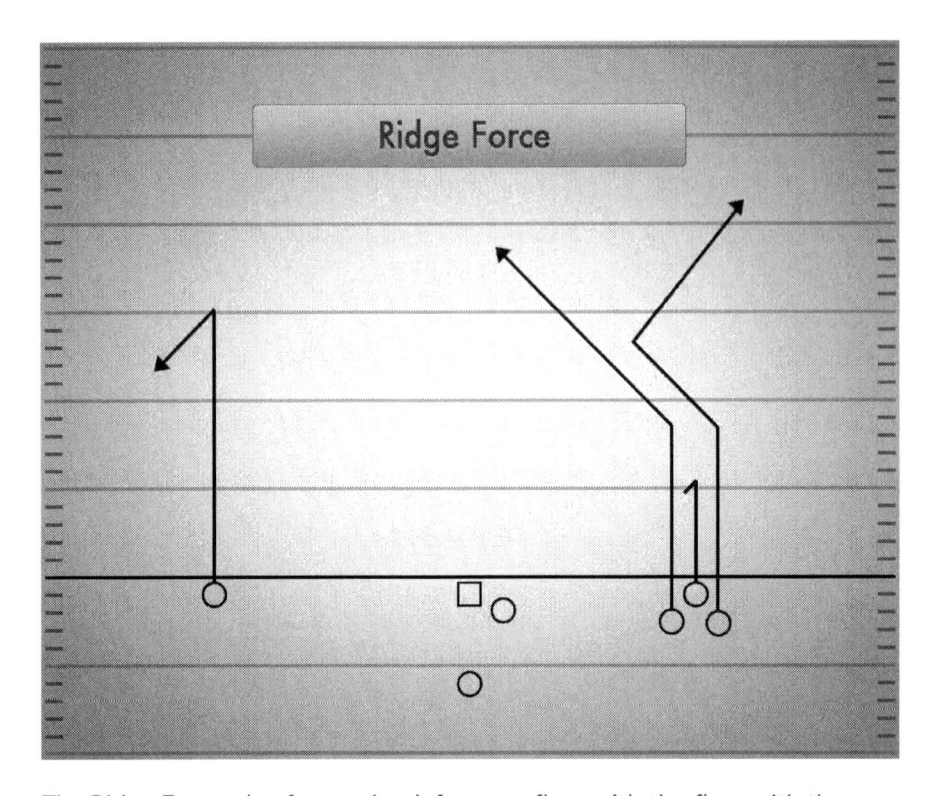

The Ridge Force play forces the defense to flow with the flow with the combination of the two post routes coming across the top ridge of the defensive secondary. Once the defenders start flowing with the combination of those routes, the outside receivers breaks hard to the outside on the Post Corner route.

The double move by the outside receiver will force the Safety into a hard decision if he is playing in a cover 2 zone, because he will be sitting right in the middle of two deep routes into his territory, but he can only choose to guard on of them.

If the defense is in a three deep formation and/or playing in a Cover three, then the QB will most likely want to drop down and hit the Comeback route on the other side of the field.

FORMATION: **BUNCH FORMATION**

DISTANCE: **LONG YARDAGE**

ROUTES IN THIS PLAY: **POST, STOP, POST CORNER, COMEBACK**

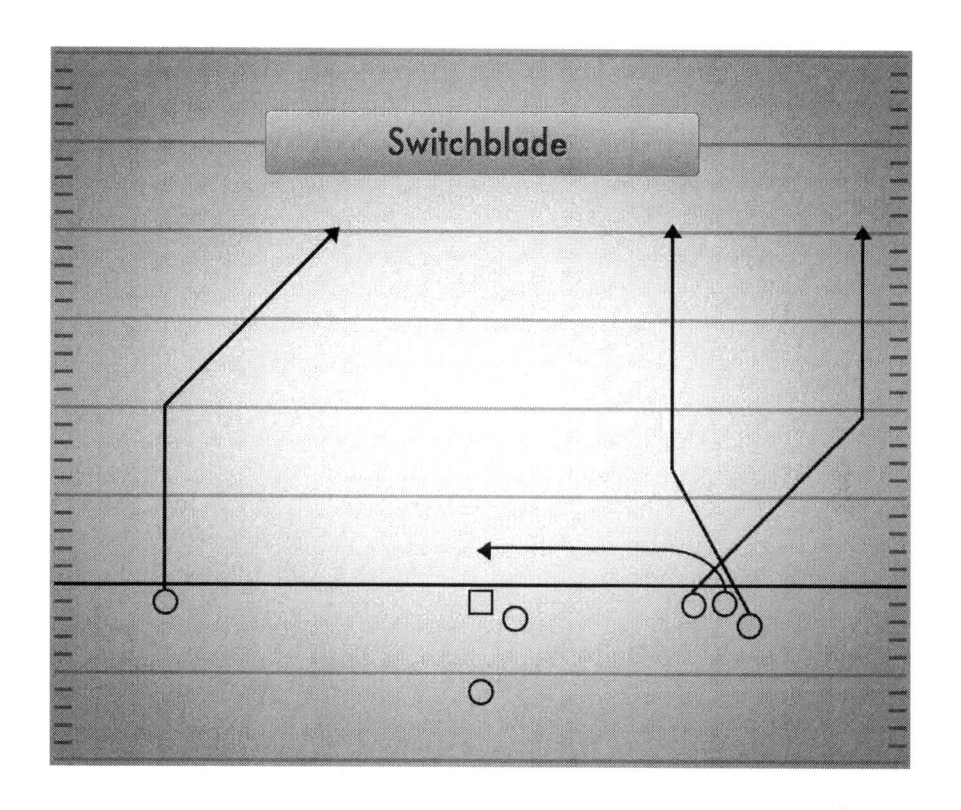

Switchblade

The Switchblade is a deadly combination route that cuts right through the defense by switching two receivers as they run their routes up field. A man-to-man defense will have trouble keeping up with both of the downfield receivers, and a zone defense will be thrown for a loop as the routes cut right through the zone.

The Quarterback has the option of cutting his losses if the deep routes aren't open, by checking down to the shallow cross underneath the switch route combination.

FORMATION: **BUNCH FORMATION**

DISTANCE: **LONG YARDAGE**

ROUTES IN THIS PLAY: **POST, SHALLOW CROSS**

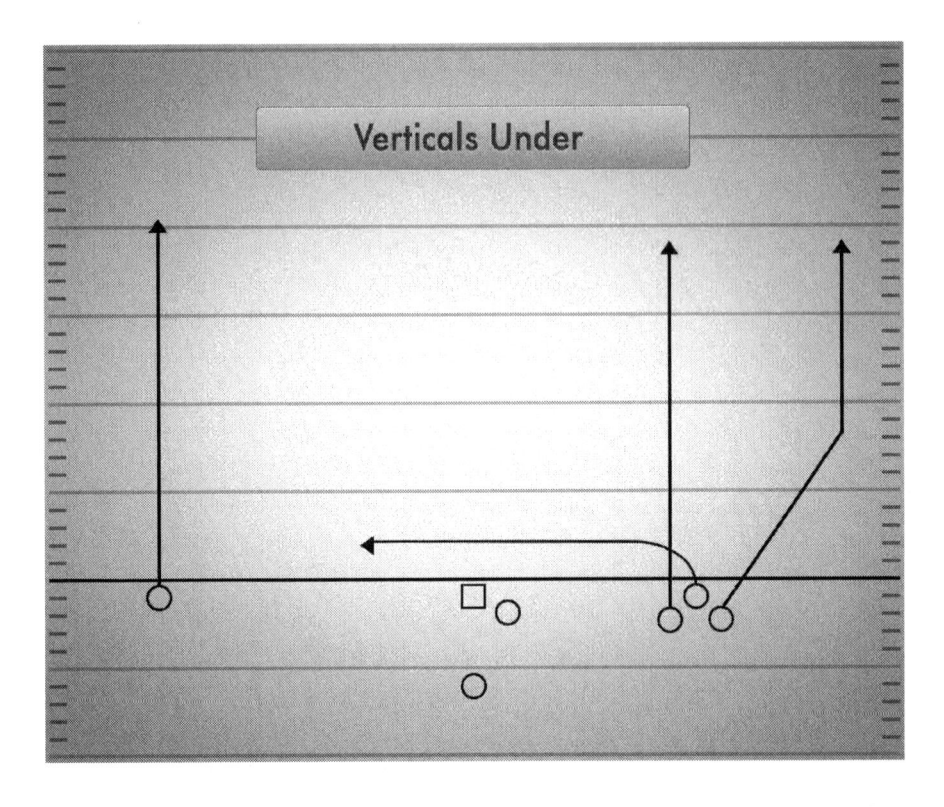

Verticals Under

The Verticals Under play sends the wide receivers up field in a shifted pattern that replaces the territory of the Receiver who is cutting underneath the Verticals.

By pushing the Vertical routes up field hard, it will distract the defense from the Shallow Cross coming underneath. Sometimes, however, the defense will lose track of the receiver taking the place of the underneath route, and he will be open down the sideline for a big gain.

FORMATION: **BUNCH FORMATION**

DISTANCE: **SHORT YARDAGE, LONG YARDAGE**

ROUTES IN THIS PLAY: **SHALLOW CROSS, STREAK**

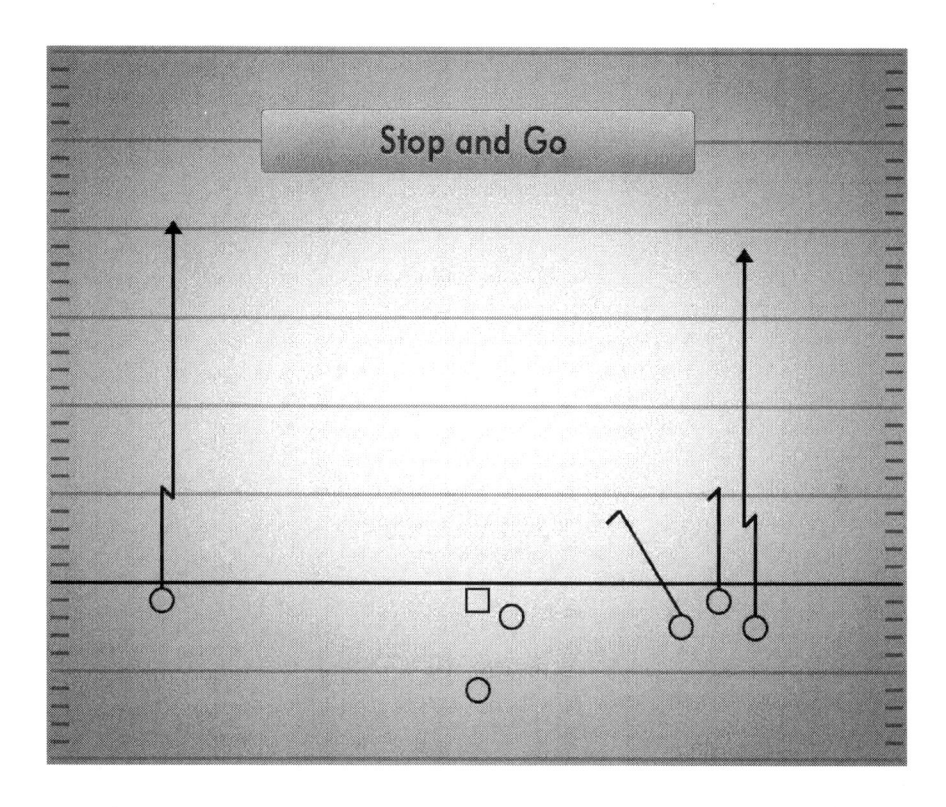

Stop and Go

The Stop and Go route is the most famous double move in all of football. The outside receiver will fake like he is running a 5 yard stop, but will twist and turn quickly up field.

It is imperative that the QB makes a good pump fake to sucker the defense in to jumping up on the short route. Once the pump fake is successfully completed, the QB must regather himself and get ready to throw the ball over the top of the defense to the receiver who is sprinting up field.

FORMATION: **BUNCH FORMATION**

DISTANCE: **SHORT YARDAGE, LONG YARDAGE**

ROUTES IN THIS PLAY: **STOP**

Comebacks

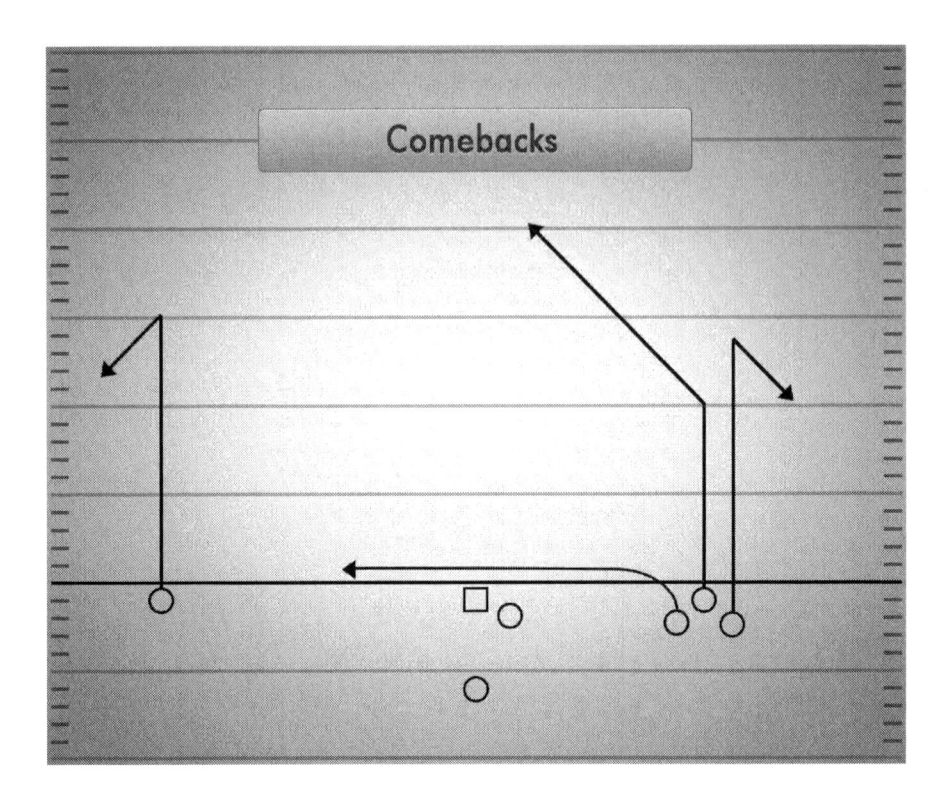

The Comeback route is a great route to run on a defense that is scared of getting beat deep. The way in which the Wide Receivers run the Comeback route is the most important part of the play. The WR will need to push up field hard as if he is running a Fade route or a Streak downfield. Once the defender is turned and running backwards, the WR needs to quickly turn around to the outside, as the QB plays a ball behind on the sideline.

After you scare the defense with the deep ball, the Comeback route is a great route to throw at them in order to pick up a chunk of yards.

FORMATION: **BUNCH FORMATION**

DISTANCE: **MEDIUM YARDAGE**

ROUTES IN THIS PLAY: **POST, SHALLOW CROSS, COMEBACK**

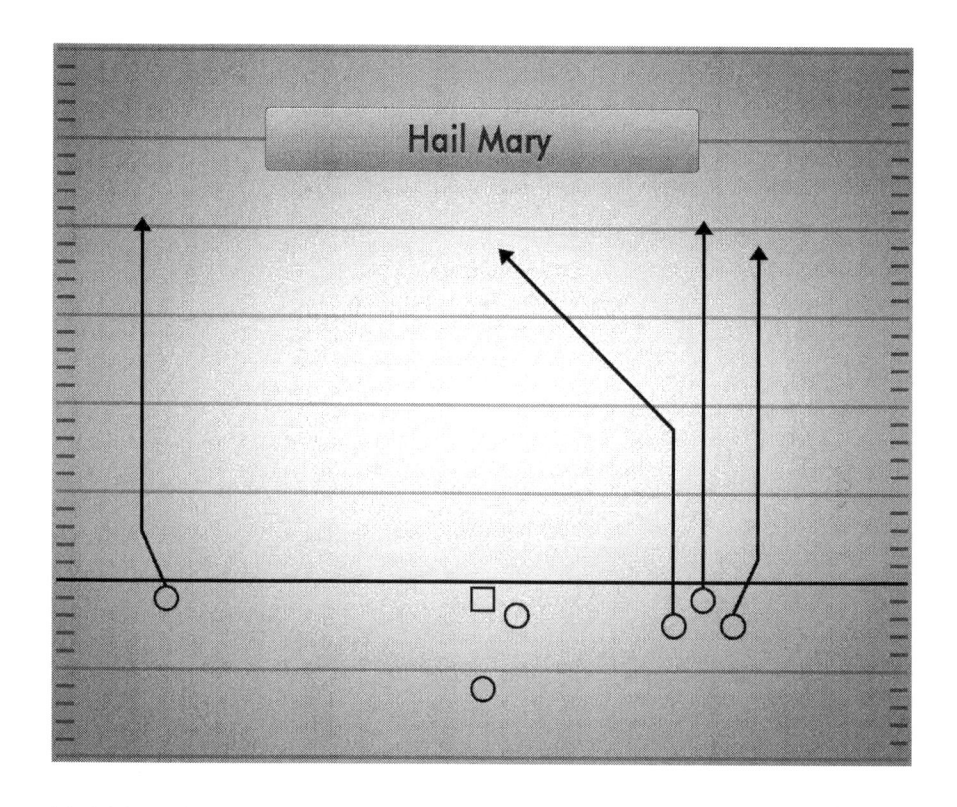

Hail Mary

Hail Mary time! You only need to pull out this play when you need a whole lot of yards all at once.

This version of the Hail Mary play is made to spread out the defense as much as possible, and potentially isolate a defender from the rest of his team. The Quarterback needs to find the WR who is able to get into a one-on-one match up and throw the ball up for a jump ball.

FORMATION: **BUNCH FORMATION**

DISTANCE: **LONG YARDAGE**

ROUTES IN THIS PLAY: **POST, STREAK, FADE**

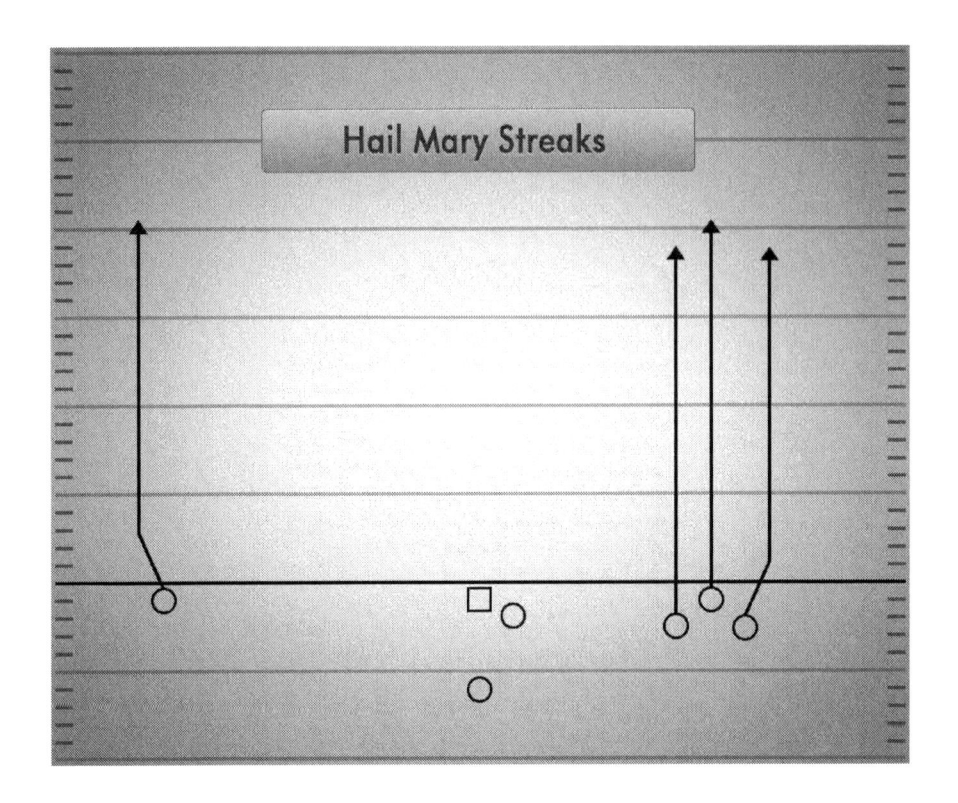

Hail Mary Streaks

Hail Mary time! You only need to pull out this play when you need a whole lot of yards all at once.

This version of the Hail Mary play simply send all the receivers downfield in a straight line in order to get as deep as possible, as fast as possible. Throw the ball up deep and hope for the best.

FORMATION: **BUNCH FORMATION**

DISTANCE: **LONG YARDAGE**

ROUTES IN THIS PLAY: **STREAK**

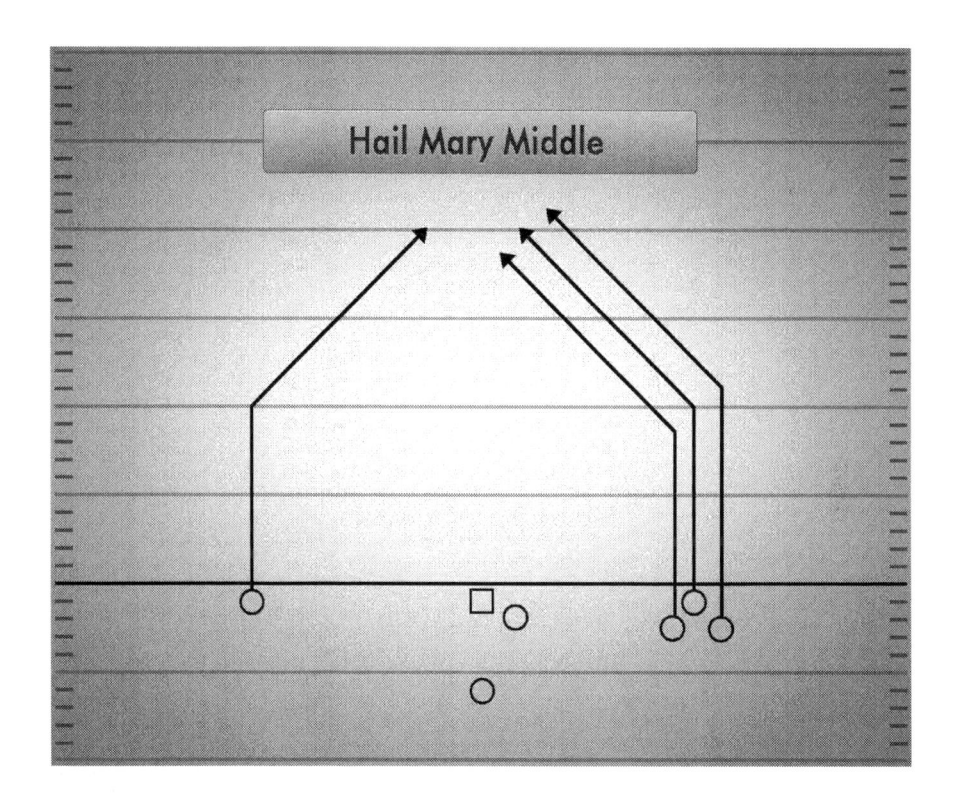

Hail Mary Middle

Hail Mary time! You only need to pull out this play when you need a whole lot of yards all at once.

This version of the Hail Mary play puts all your eggs in one basket by sending every Receiver to the middle of the field. Once all the Receivers are in position, the only thing left for the Quarterback to do is throw the ball as high as he can right into the middle of the field and hope that one of his own players comes down with it.

FORMATION: **BUNCH FORMATION**

DISTANCE: **LONG YARDAGE**

ROUTES IN THIS PLAY: **POST**

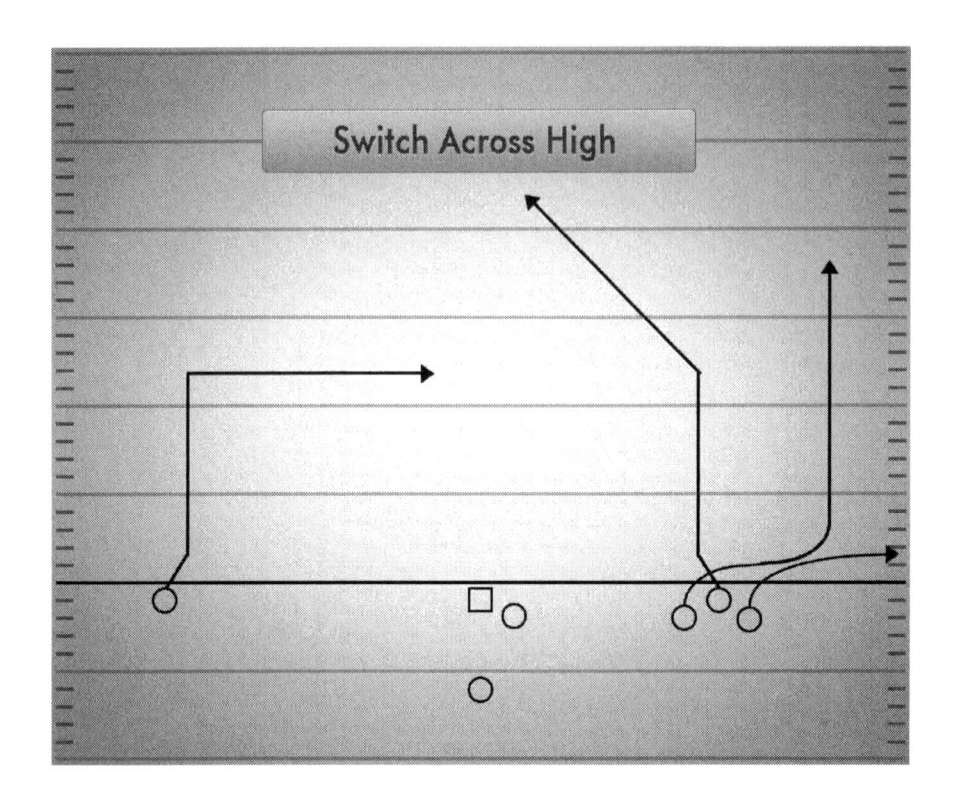

Switch Across High

This is the deeper variation of the Switch Across Low play. The key to this play is creating confusion for the defense at the very start of the play by having the receivers switch across each other on the way to their destination. This switch makes it hard for a zone defense to keep track of all the routes, and makes it very difficult for a man-to-man defense to keep up with the receiver amongst all the chaos going on.

FORMATION: **BUNCH FORMATION**

DISTANCE: **LONG YARDAGE**

ROUTES IN THIS PLAY: **POST, IN, WHEEL**

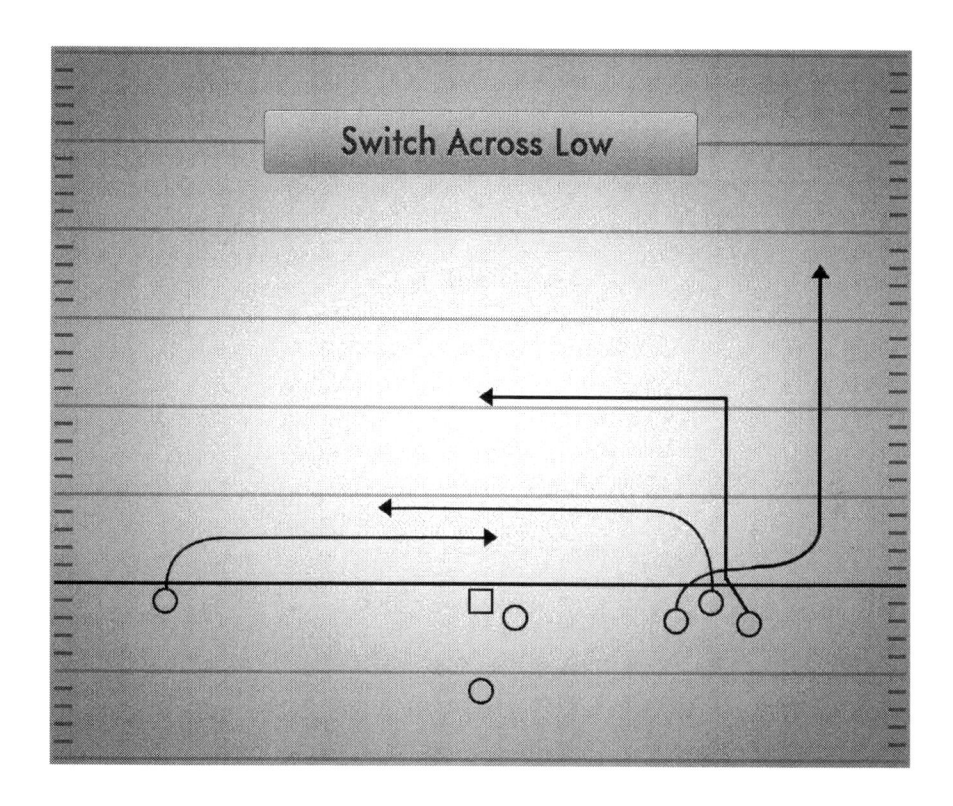

Switch Across Low

This is the shorter variation of the Switch Across High play. The key to this play is creating confusion for the defense at the very start of the play by having the receivers switch across each other on the way to their destination. This switch makes it hard for a zone defense to keep track of all the routes, and makes it very difficult for a man-to-man defense to keep up with the receiver amongst all the chaos going on.

FORMATION: **BUNCH FORMATION**

DISTANCE: **SHORT YARDAGE, MEDIUM YARDAGE**

ROUTES IN THIS PLAY: **IN, SHALLOW CROSS, WHEEL**

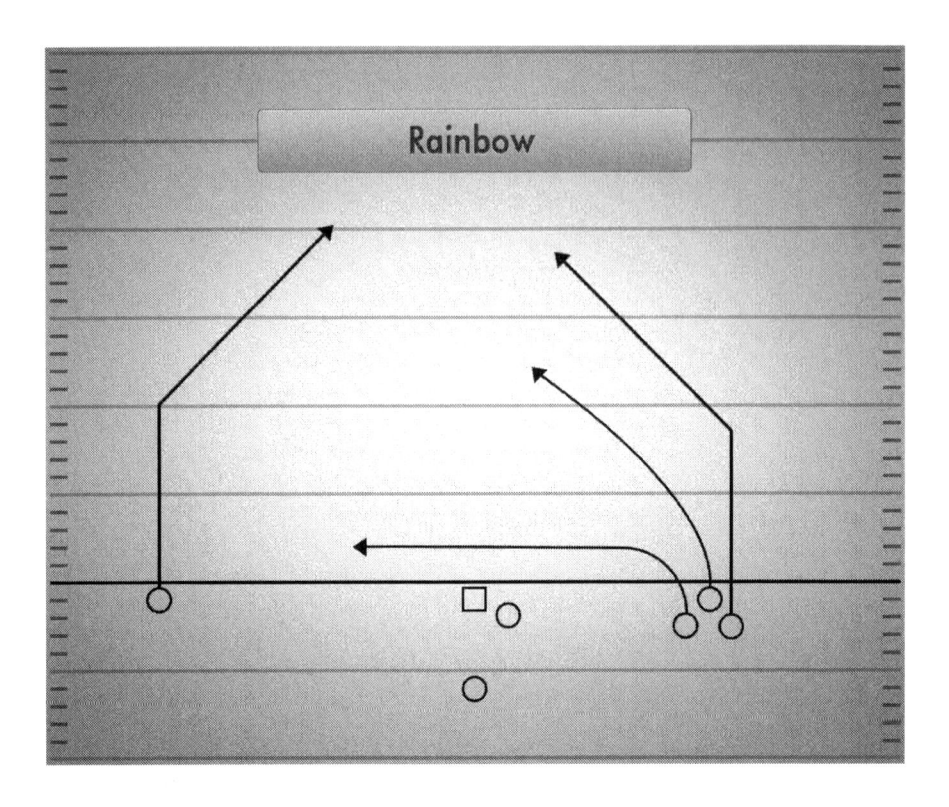

Rainbow

The Rainbow play allows the Wide Receivers to attack the defense by running arcs all across the middle of the field. Each arc is run at a different level of the defense, therefore, combining to create a Rainbow of manly intensity.

The Quarterback can choose to either read the arcs from low to high, or progress from high to low. Finding at least one open man in the Rainbow should be easy with so many routes hitting different levels in the middle of the field.

FORMATION: **BUNCH FORMATION**

DISTANCE: **SHORT YARDAGE, LONG YARDAGE, MEDIUM YARDAGE**

ROUTES IN THIS PLAY: **POST, SHALLOW CROSS**

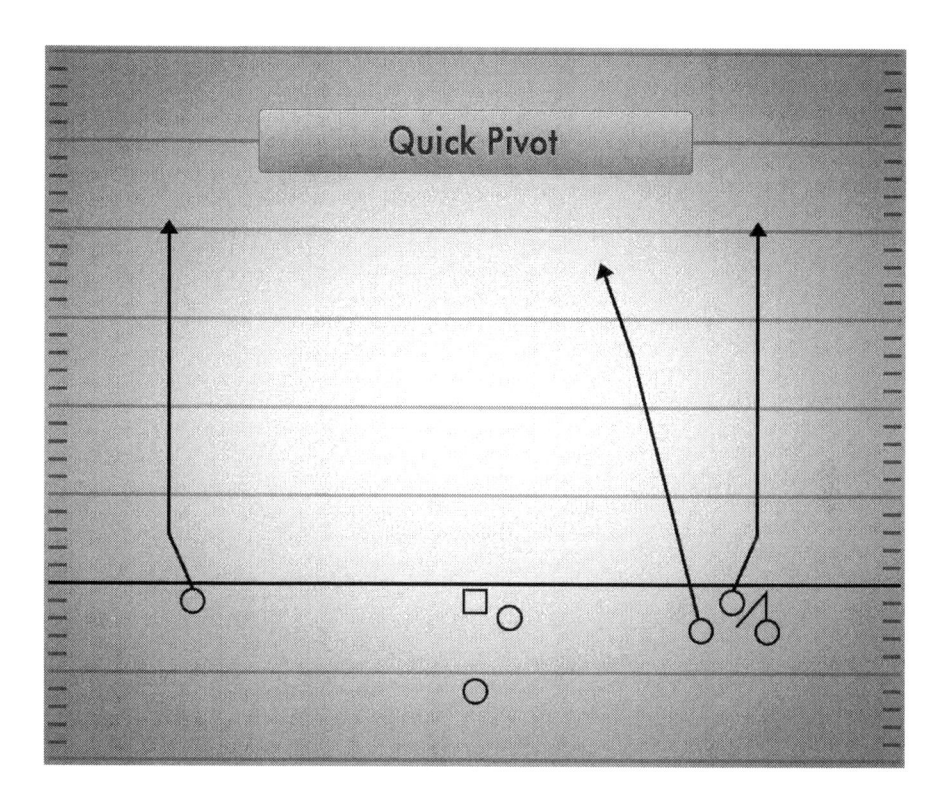

Quick Pivot

The Quick Pivot play is meant to be used as a play against a defense that is backing up off the line of scrimmage. If they are giving too much space to the Wide Receivers, then hit them with this quick pass to catch them off guard. If the Quarterback makes a quick throw to the Receiver, it will give the Receiver a chance to run with the ball in the open field and try to make a defender miss.

It is important that the Receivers push hard off the line of scrimmage for the first few steps, so that the defenders aren't immediately keyed into the fact that it is going to be a quick pass right at the line of scrimmage.

FORMATION: **BUNCH FORMATION**

DISTANCE: **SHORT YARDAGE**

ROUTES IN THIS PLAY: **FADE**

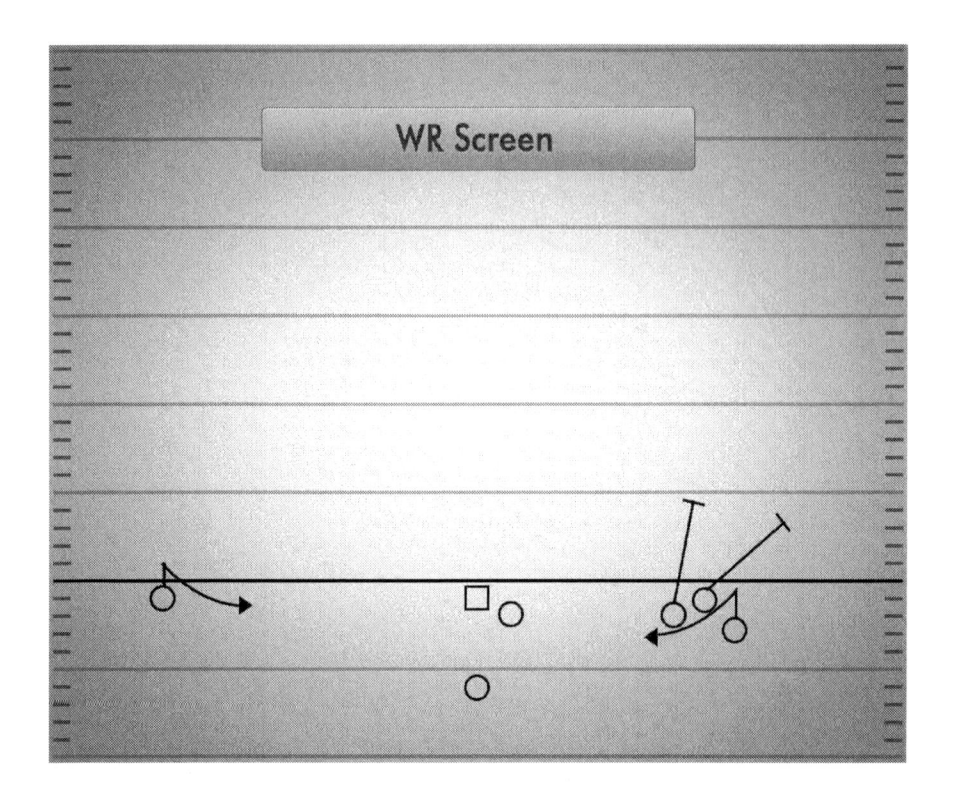

WR Screen

The WR Screen is a play that utilizes blocking by the inside Receivers to enable a running lane for the outside Receiver. The Wide Receiver running the screen route needs to push up field hard for two steps, and the quickly turn around for the ball. Timing is critical on the throw.

The inside Receiver needs to explode of the line of scrimmage directly at the guy who is guarding the outside Receiver. Once that defender turns around, quickly get in his way for the block, and the Receiver catching the screen will be off to the races.

FORMATION: **BUNCH FORMATION**

DISTANCE: **SHORT YARDAGE**

WR Screen and Up

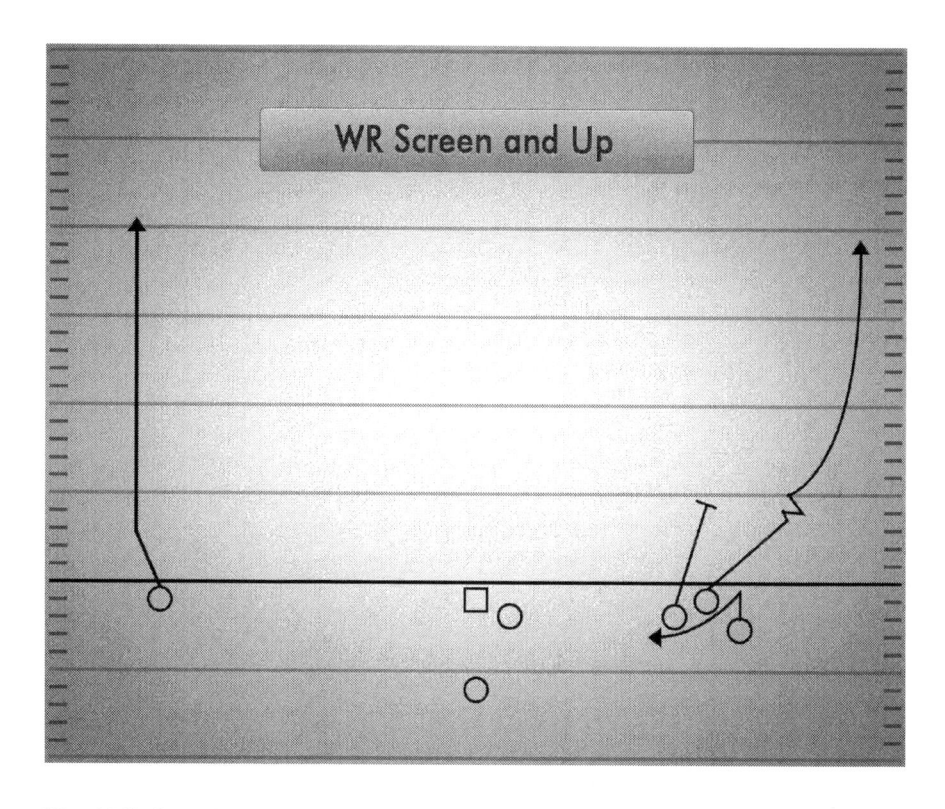

The WR Screen and Up play is a great trick play that takes some time to set up. You have to run the WR Screen play beforehand, and run it successfully. If you begin to hurt them with the Screen, then the defense will start to sneak up forward, and that is when you hit them with the Screen and Up.

The most important aspect of performing this play is the way in which the Wide Receiver fakes his block. He has to run out to the Cornerback as if he is going to block him, and as soon as the Cornerback makes a move to avoid the block, the Receiver then turns on the jets and runs up the sideline. The defense won't even know what hit them until the ball is flying over all their heads.

FORMATION: BUNCH FORMATION

DISTANCE: LONG YARDAGE

Slot Choice

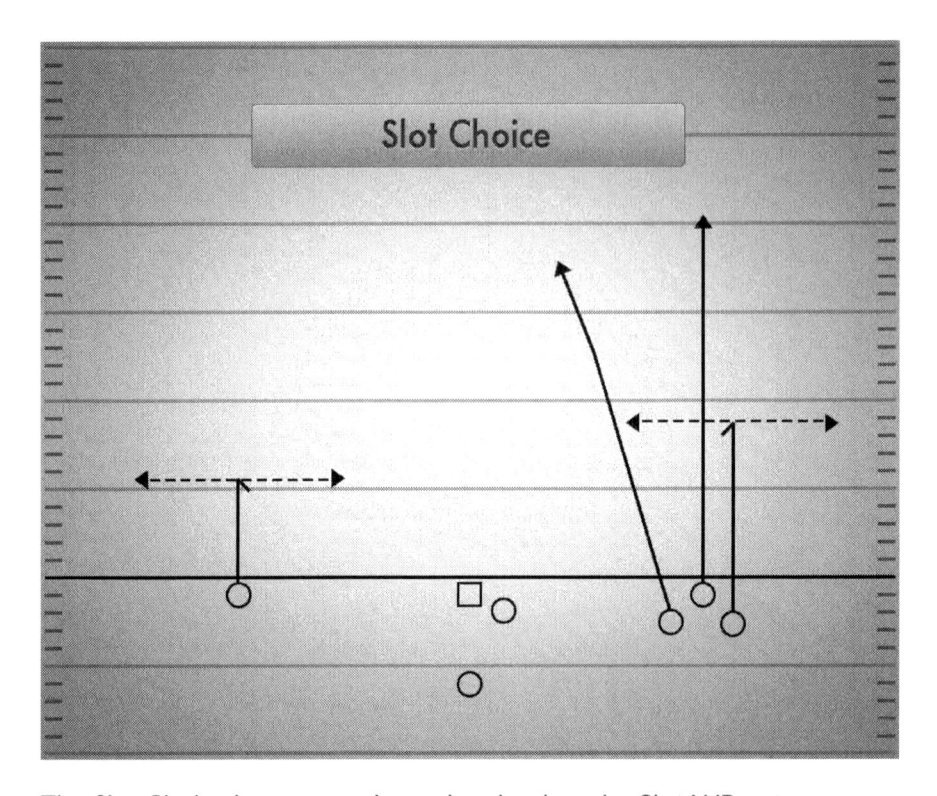

The Slot Choice is meant to be a play that lets the Slot WR get open, no matter what the defense does. The Choice route will either get to its mark and turn around for a stop in place, or it will jet out to the outside, or cut in to the inside.

If the defender is playing inside, then the WR should jet to the outside. If the defender is playing outside, then the WR should jet to the inside. If the defense is playing in a zone, and is giving the WR some space, then the WR should just settle down and wait for the ball.

The Quarterback needs to have great chemistry with the WR so that they are on the same wavelength and can be expecting each other to make the same read.

FORMATION: **BUNCH FORMATION**

DISTANCE: **SHORT YARDAGE, MEDIUM YARDAGE**

ROUTES IN THIS PLAY: **IN, STREAK, STOP, OUT**

WR Choice

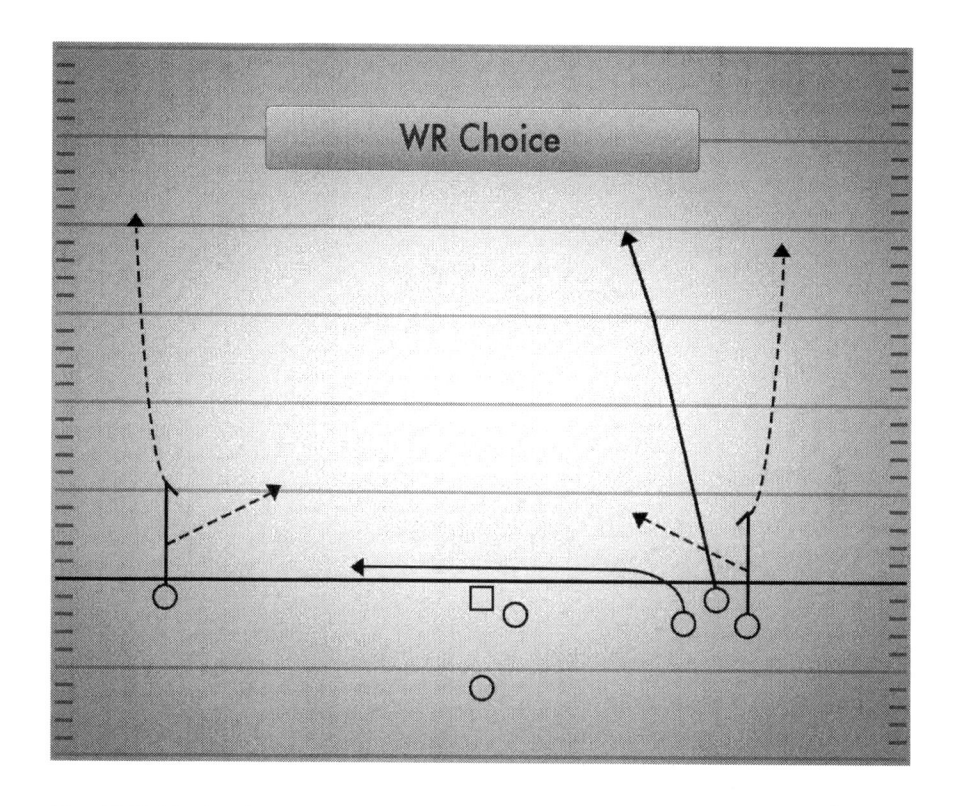

The WR Choice is meant to be a play that lets the Outside WR get open, no matter what the defense does. If the defender is playing inside, then the WR should run up the sideline on a fade. If the defender is playing outside, then the WR should jet to the inside on a slant. If the defense is giving the WR some space, then the WR should just settle down and wait for the ball on a stop route.

The Quarterback needs to have great chemistry with the WR so that they are on the same wavelength and can be expecting each other to make the same read.

FORMATION: **BUNCH FORMATION**

DISTANCE: **SHORT YARDAGE, LONG YARDAGE, MEDIUM YARDAGE**

ROUTES IN THIS PLAY: **SHALLOW CROSS, FADE, STOP, SLANT, SEAM**

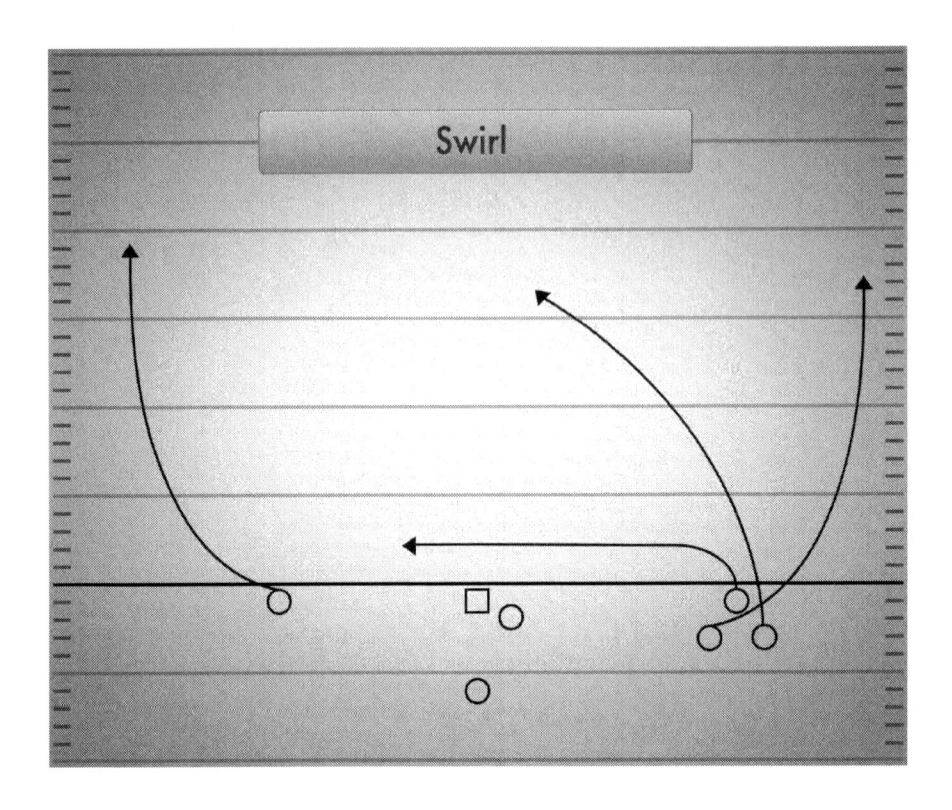

Swirl

The Swirl plays send the defense in a whirlwind by swirling the routes all around across the field. Unlike most plays, there are hardly no straight lines in the route patterns, as all the Wide Receivers are swirling their routes to get to their destination.

The switching and swirling pattern will make it hard for a man defense to keep up, and difficult for a zone defense to keep track.

FORMATION: **BUNCH FORMATION**

DISTANCE: **SHORT YARDAGE, LONG YARDAGE**

ROUTES IN THIS PLAY: **POST, SHALLOW CROSS, WHEEL**

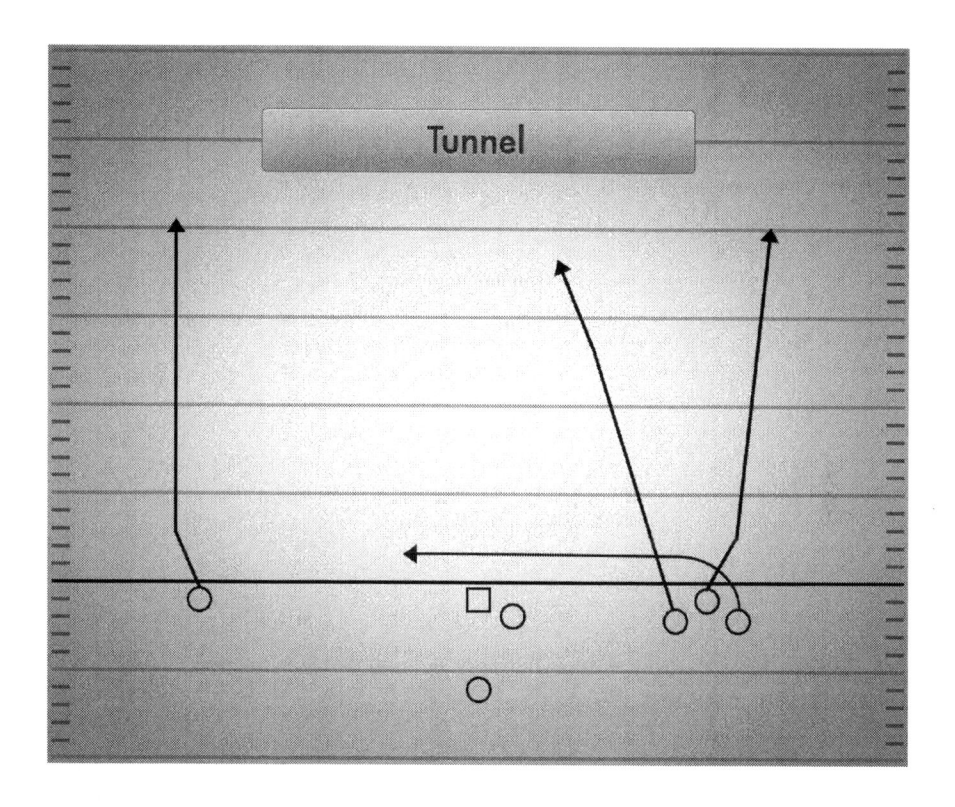

Tunnel

The Tunnel play might look like a deep play when drawn up, but it is really meant to be a play thrown to the Shallow Cross route that is "tunneling" underneath.

The other receivers are used primarily to run off the defense and take all the defenders deep downfield with them. After the defense has backed off, the shallow cross route should be open and have tons of room to run after the catch.

FORMATION: **BUNCH FORMATION**

DISTANCE: **SHORT YARDAGE**

ROUTES IN THIS PLAY: **SHALLOW CROSS, FADE, SEAM**

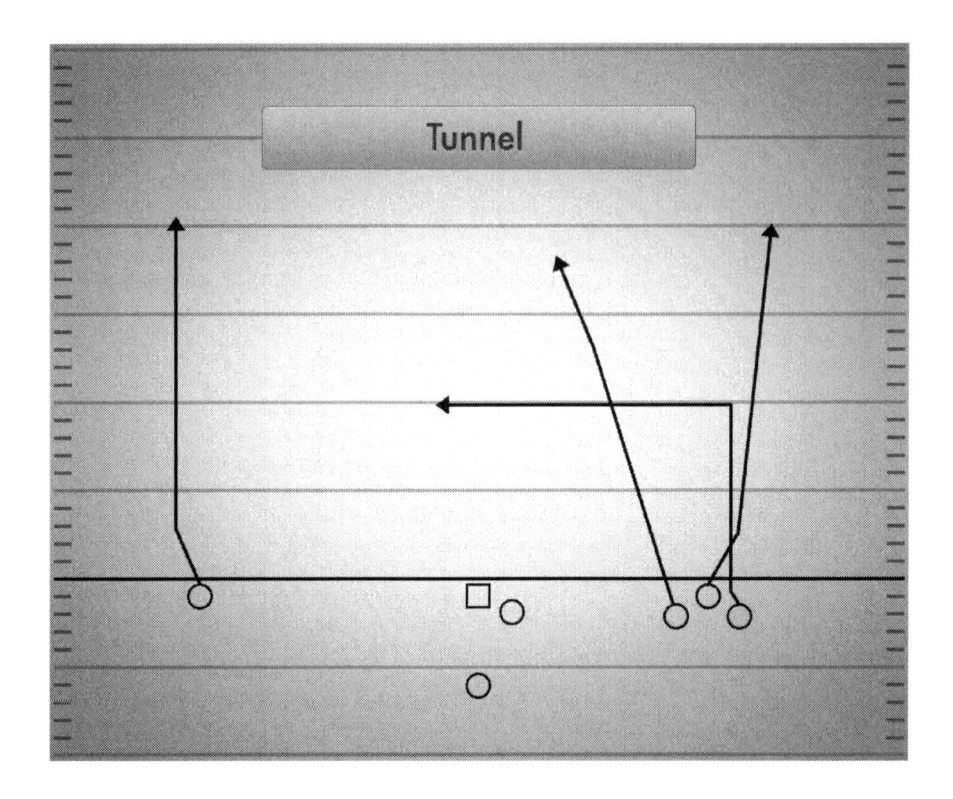

Tunnel

The primary focus of the Tunnel Deep play is to make the defense think that everybody is going deep, and then break off the outside receiver, and hit him coming across the field underneath the deep routes.

The other receivers are used primarily to run off the defense and take all the defenders deep downfield with them. After the defense has backed off, the In route should be open and have tons of room to run after the catch.

FORMATION: **BUNCH FORMATION**

DISTANCE: **LONG YARDAGE**

ROUTES IN THIS PLAY: **IN, FADE, SEAM**

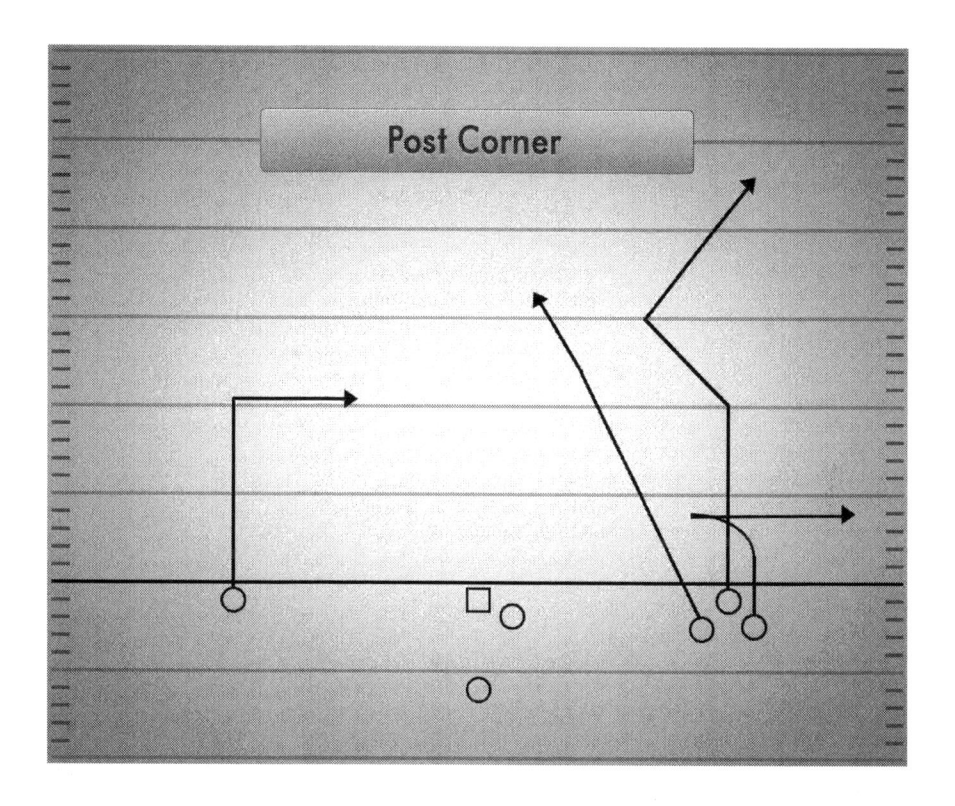

Post Corner

This play is all about setting up the Post-Corner route on the outside. The Receiver running the route has to make it look as if he is running the post, and as soon as he suckers the defense inside, he breaks to the outside and the Quarterback will hit him deep along the sideline.

The Whip route underneath, is used to keep the Cornerback from drifting back towards the Post-Corner. If the Cornerback does carry back deep and get in the way of the Post-Corner, then the Whip route should be open in the flats underneath.

FORMATION: **BUNCH FORMATION**

DISTANCE: **LONG YARDAGE, MEDIUM YARDAGE**

ROUTES IN THIS PLAY: **IN, WHIP, POST CORNER, SEAM**

Bubble

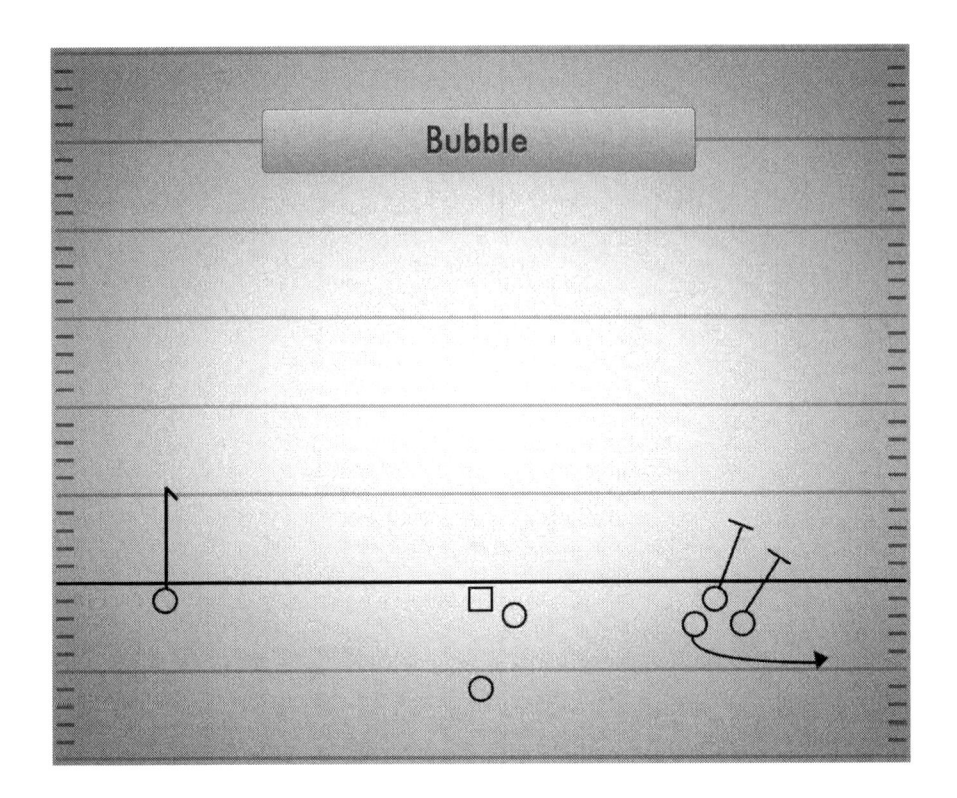

The Bubble play is a simple screen play. The Slot WR will bubble backwards with one step and proceed to drift towards the sideline. The block by the outside WR is critical to the success of the play.

Once the Quarterback delivers the ball the WR will read the block of the outside WR and sprint up the sideline.

FORMATION: **BUNCH FORMATION**

DISTANCE: **SHORT YARDAGE**

Bubble WR Pass

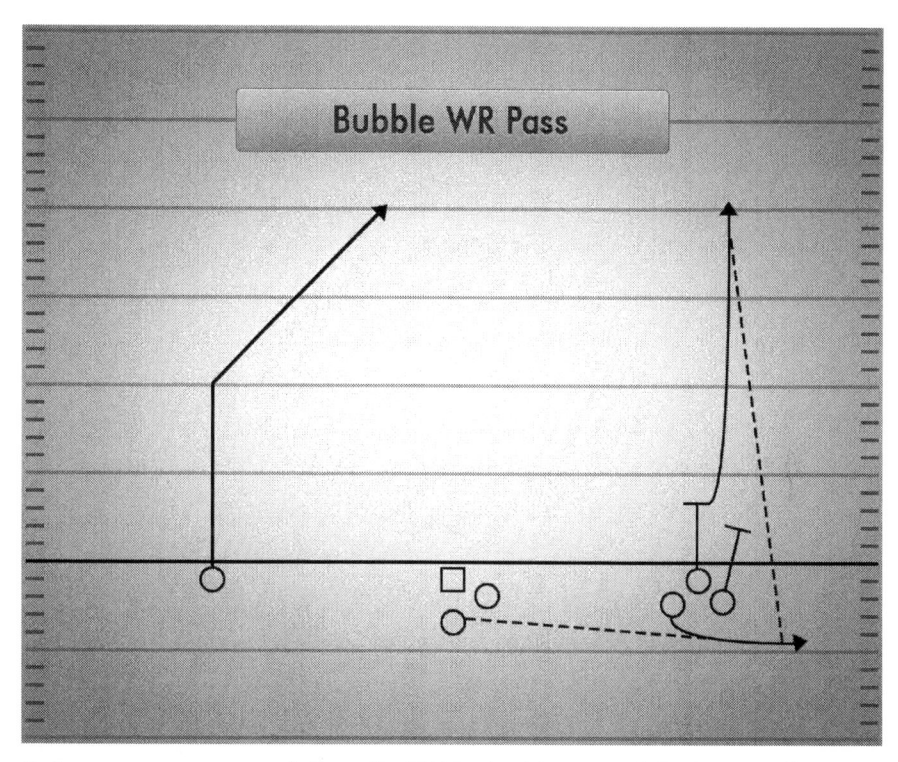

Before you can successfully pull off this double pass trick play, you first need to set it up with the normal Bubble play. After the defense is begins to cheat forward to guard the bubble, that's when you hit them with this Bubble WR Pass play.

The outside WR has to act as if he is going to block the defender like he normally does on the Bubble play, but as soon as he approaches, he needs to sidestep away and start jetting up the sideline. The inside WR needs to make a clean catch and quickly throw it over the defense to the WR who will be open downfield.

One key aspect of this play is that you have to remember that the first throw from the Quarterback has to be backwards, or else the second throw will be illegal. Therefore, the QB should scoot up a bit more than usual, and the WR should line up a little further back than usual, but both have to be done without making it obvious.

FORMATION: **BUNCH FORMATION**

DISTANCE: **LONG YARDAGE**

ROUTES IN THIS PLAY: **POST**

Hook and Ladder

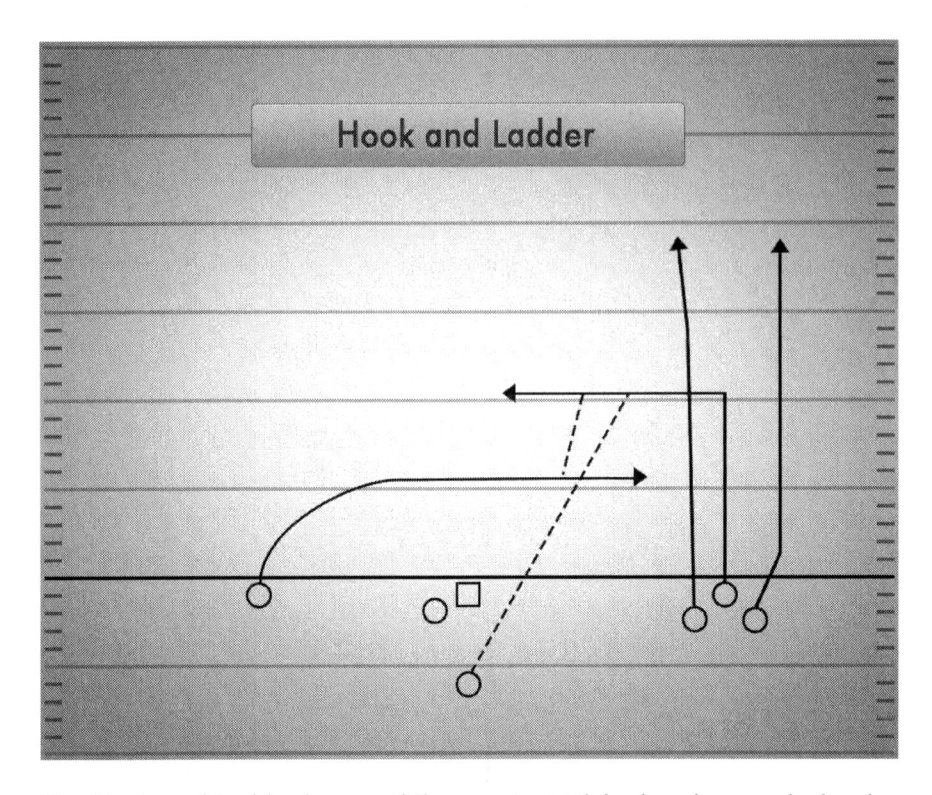

The Hook and Ladder is one of the greatest trick plays in any playbook. It involves incredible timing and perfectly performed maneuvers by multiple individuals, but can be a phenomenally successful play when all the moving parts come together correctly.

The QB must deliver the throw to the In route before he gets too far across the field. The WR running the Shallow Cross must time his crossing route so that he is running underneath the In route immediately after he catches the ball. Once caught, the In route has to quickly secure the ball, and then pitch it backwards to the shallow crosser. The defense will have been moving inwards towards the original receiver, and will be caught off guard when the shallow crosser receives the pitch and is sprinting outward towards the sideline.

FORMATION: **BUNCH FORMATION**

DISTANCE: **LONG YARDAGE**

ROUTES IN THIS PLAY: **IN, SHALLOW CROSS, FADE, SEAM**

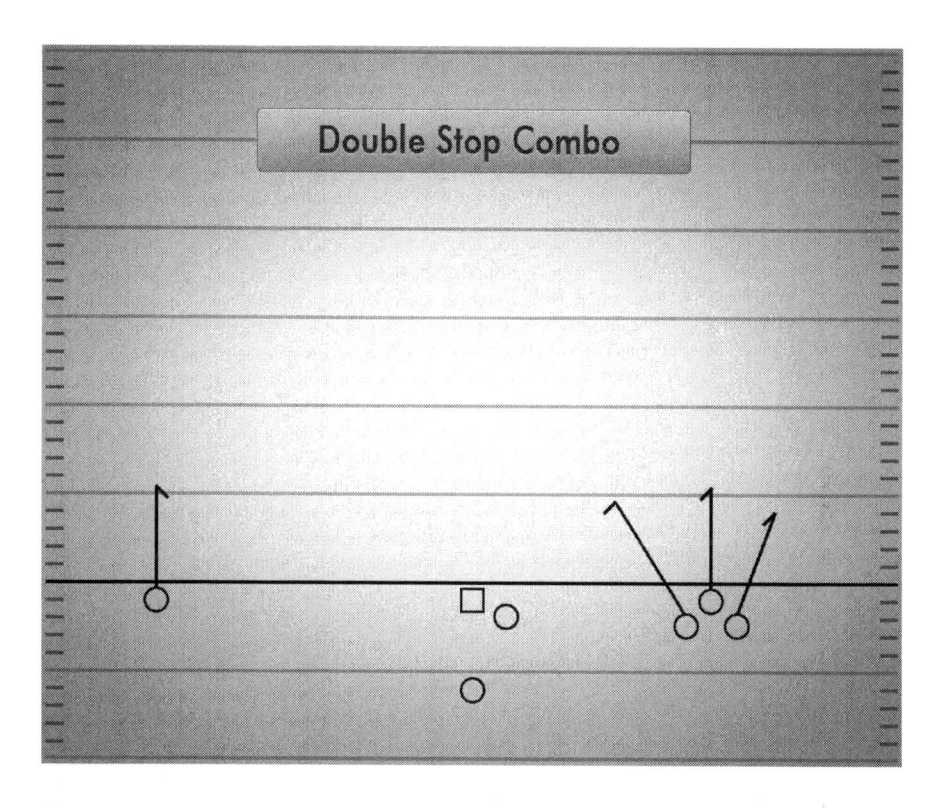

Double Stop Combo

The Double Stop Combo is one of the most fundamental plays of any spread offense passing tree. A simple route concept that quickly presents all the Wide Receivers on a quick 5-yard stop route.

This play can be called early in the game in order to help the QB get settled in, or it can be called in response to a defense that is playing far off the line of scrimmage.

FORMATION: **BUNCH FORMATION**

DISTANCE: **SHORT YARDAGE**

ROUTES IN THIS PLAY: **STOP**

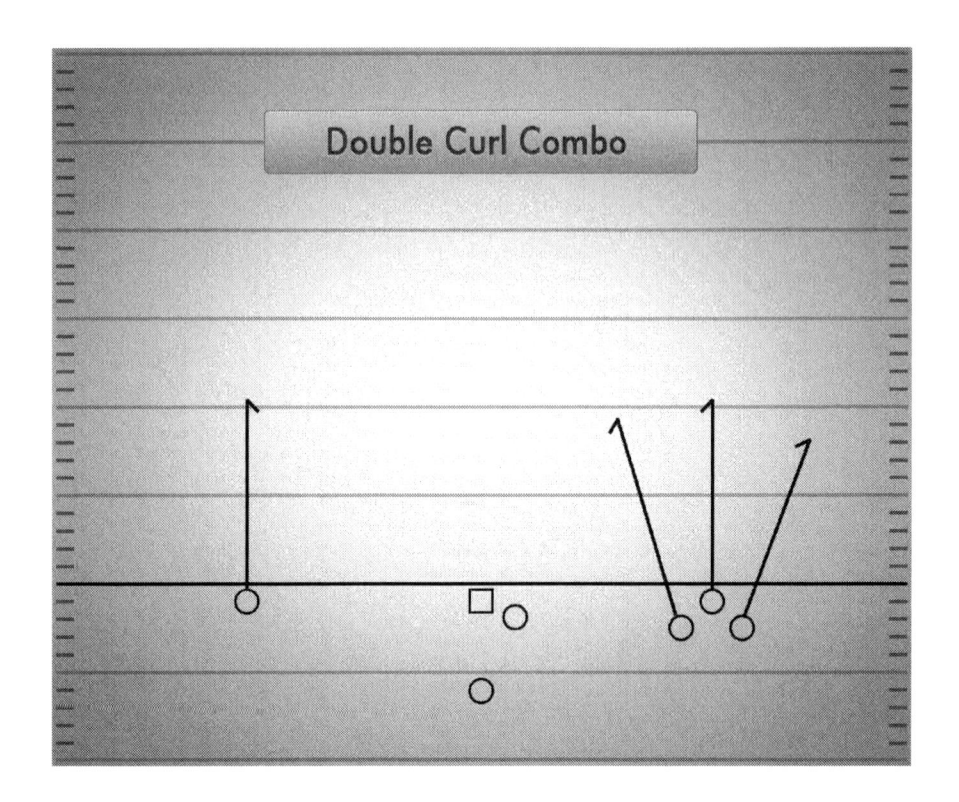

Double Curl Combo

The Double Curl Combo is an extended version of the Double Stop Combo play. It is a simple play for Medium Yardage.

Each Wide Receiver presses hard upfield for ten yards and quickly turns around, orienting their bodies toward the Quarterback who then takes his pick at the open man.

FORMATION: **BUNCH FORMATION**

DISTANCE: **MEDIUM YARDAGE**

ROUTES IN THIS PLAY: **CURL**

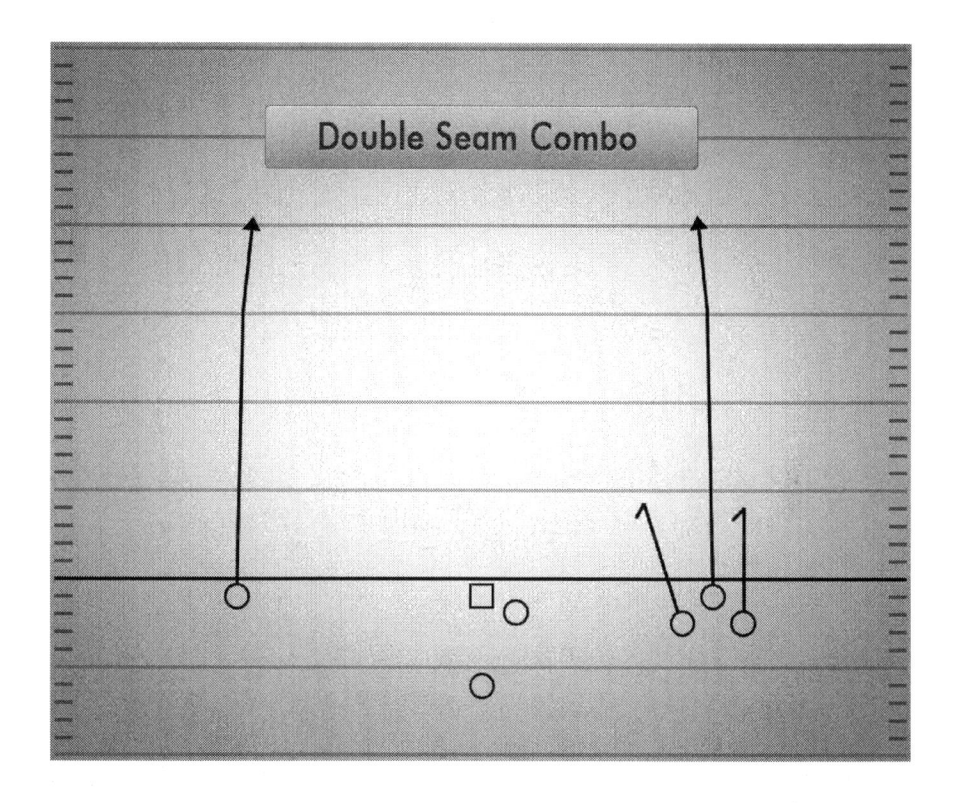

Double Seam Combo

Double Seam Combo is a play that places leverage on the defense up the seams. If the defense drops back to guard the seams, then the Quarterback should through the ball short to the 5-yard stop routes in the flats.

If it is a man-to-man defense, then consider throwing the seams over the top like a fade route, but run from an inside release. Safeties are not accustomed to guarding the fade route, and will therefore put your WR in better position to make the play.

FORMATION: **BUNCH FORMATION**

DISTANCE: **SHORT YARDAGE, LONG YARDAGE**

ROUTES IN THIS PLAY: **STOP, SEAM**

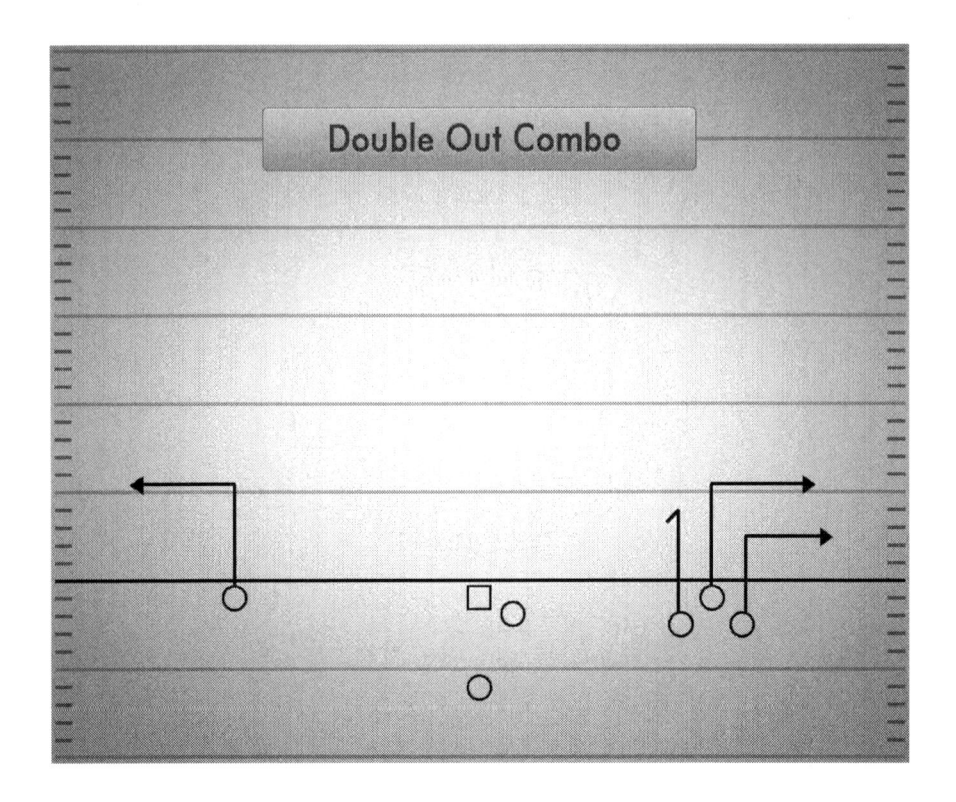

Double Out Combo

The Double Out Combo play places leverage on the outside of the defensive secondary. By attacking the flats with two players, the defender who is guarding the outside zone will be unable to guard both routes.

Versus a man to man defense, the QB must simply make a read based upon which WR makes a better move to the outside against the defender that is guarding him.

FORMATION: **BUNCH FORMATION**

DISTANCE: **SHORT YARDAGE**

ROUTES IN THIS PLAY: **OUT**

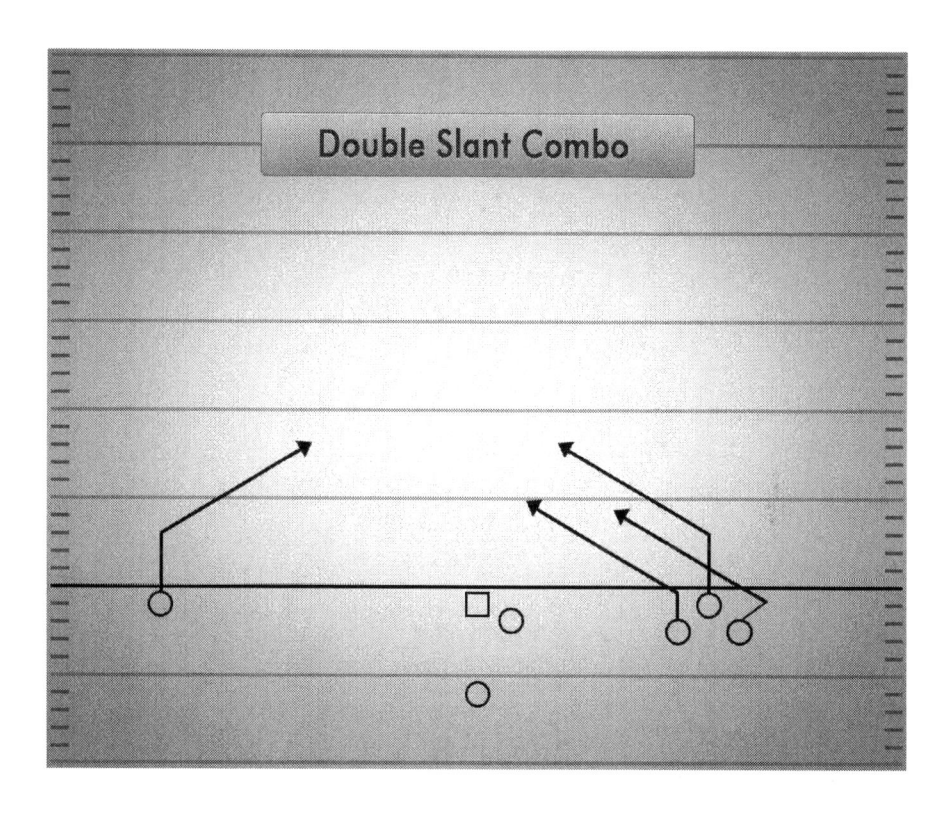

Double Slant Combo

The Double Slant Combo play is a great play to run in a short yardage situation if you have Wide Receivers who can run crisp routes. By making a clean cut to the inside, there will be a window of opportunity for the Quarterback to deliver the ball into the chest of the WR.

This play can also be used as a quick hitting play in the beginning of the game if the defense is playing far off the line of scrimmage. If the defense starts creeping up to guard against the short slant route, then hit them over the top by calling the Slant-and-Up Combo play.

FORMATION: **BUNCH FORMATION**

DISTANCE: **SHORT YARDAGE**

ROUTES IN THIS PLAY: **SLANT**

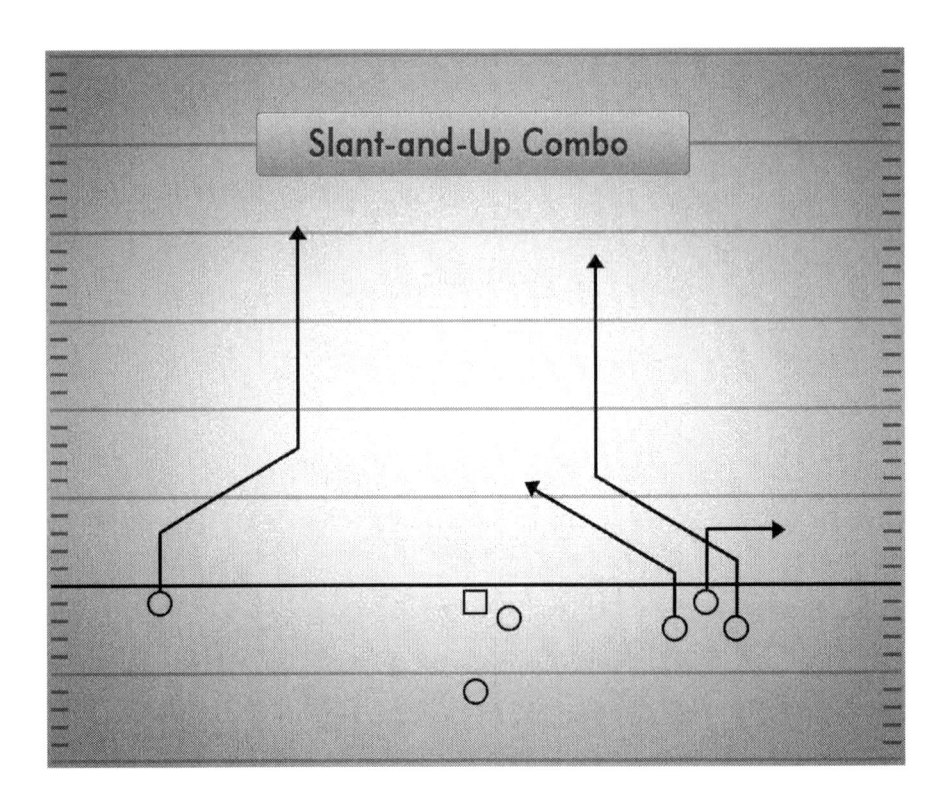

Slant-and-Up Combo

Slant-and-Up Combo is a companion play to the Out-Slant Combo play. By getting the defense used to seeing the Out-Slant combination routes, they will tend to cheat down. That is when you hit them over the top with this play.

As the defense makes a move to jump in front of the slant route, that is right when the WR turns it up field where the QB will throw it over the top for a long gain or a Touchdown.

FORMATION: **BUNCH FORMATION**

DISTANCE: **LONG YARDAGE**

ROUTES IN THIS PLAY: **OUT, SLANT**

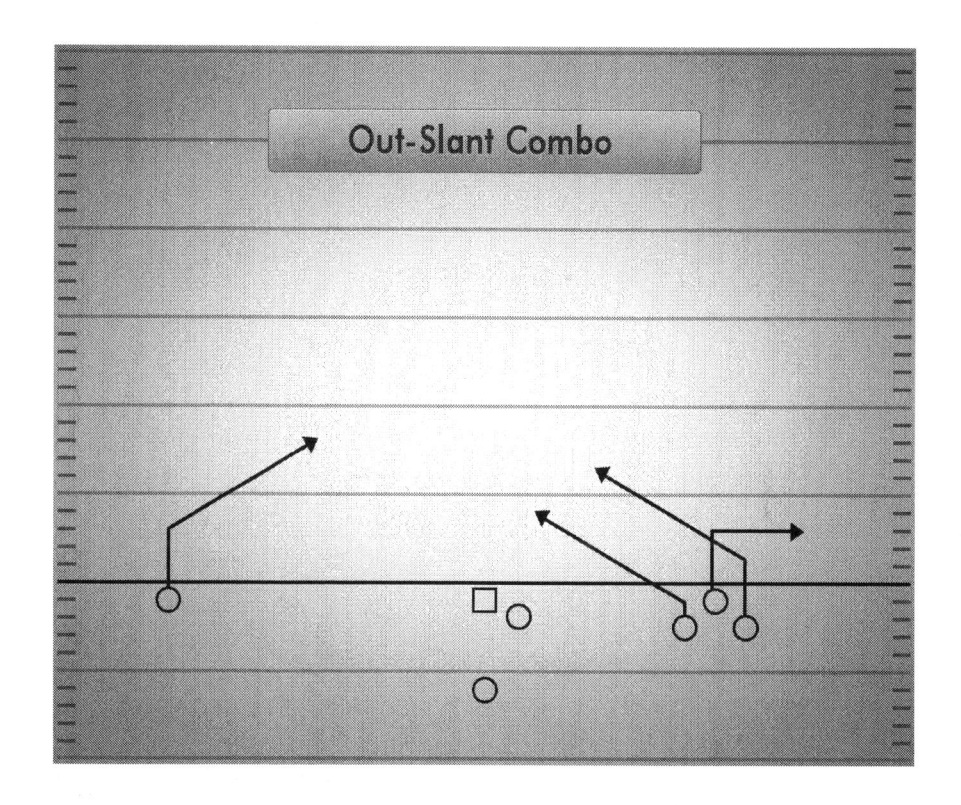

Out-Slant Combo

The Out-Slant Combo twists the defense around regardless of if they are playing man-to-man or zone. If they are playing zone, then the defense won't be able to keep track of the crossing patterns, and the man-to-man defense won't be able to keep up with the quick crossing cuts.

After the defense has gotten used to seeing this out-slant crossing pattern, mix things up by hitting them over the top with either the Slant-and-Up Combo play or the Out-and-Up Combo play.

FORMATION: **BUNCH FORMATION**

DISTANCE: **SHORT YARDAGE**

ROUTES IN THIS PLAY: **OUT, SLANT**

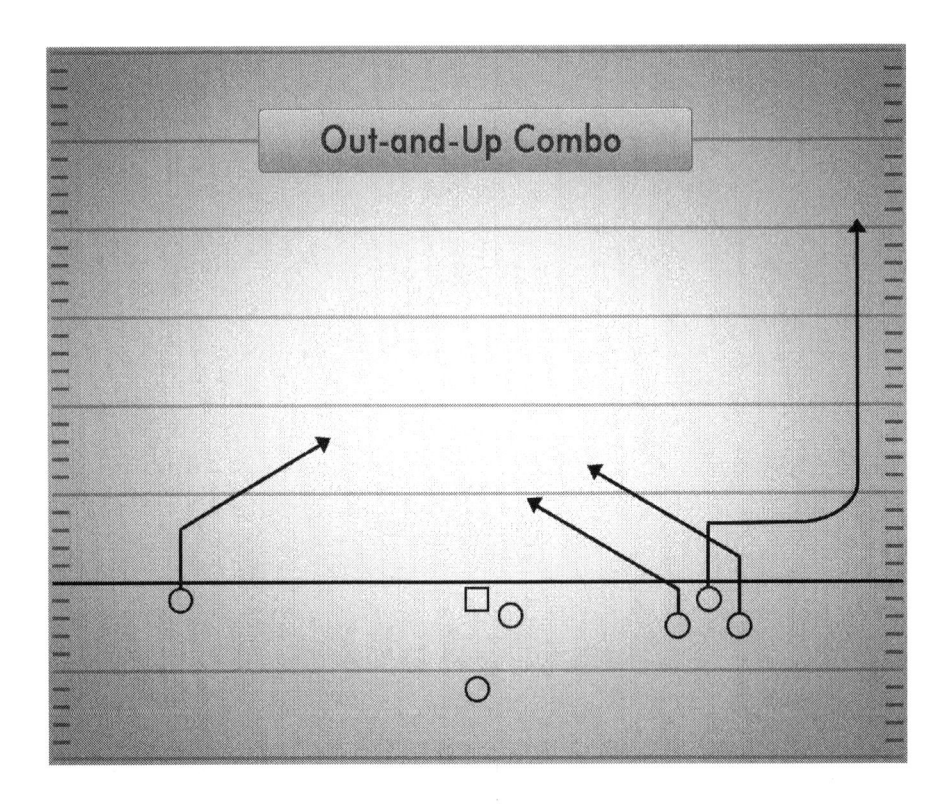

Out-and-Up Combo

The Out-and Up Combo is a companion play to the Out-Slant Combo play. After you have gotten the defense used to the shorter out route, hit them over the top with the Out-and-Up.

The part that makes this play extremely dangerous is against a man to man defense where the defender on the Out-and-Up route will have to run underneath the slant route, and will therefore be in a bad position to keep up with the inside WR who is now sprinting wide open up the sideline.

FORMATION: **BUNCH FORMATION**

DISTANCE: **LONG YARDAGE**

ROUTES IN THIS PLAY: **OUT, SLANT**

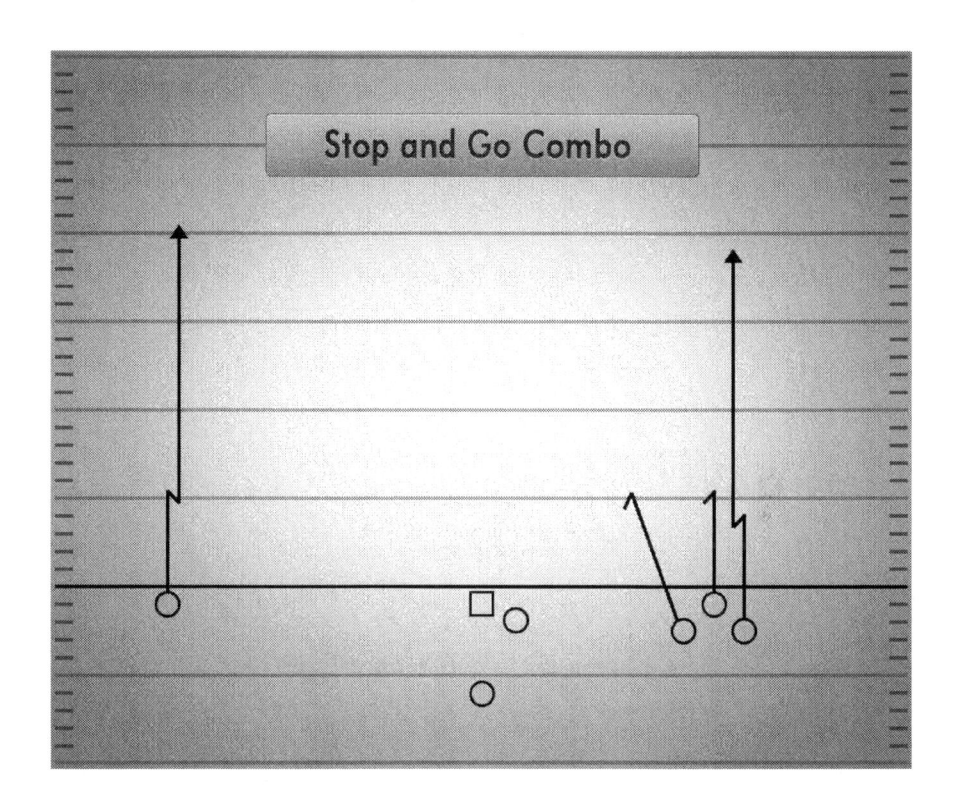

Stop and Go Combo

The Stop and Go route is one of the most famous double moves in all of football. After you have set up this play by repeatedly running the Double Stop Combo play, then surprise them with the Stop and Go and they won't know what hit them.

It is important that the Wide Receiver makes has break up the sideline after he stops. That way he is able to get passed the Cornerback easier.

FORMATION: **BUNCH FORMATION**

DISTANCE: **LONG YARDAGE**

ROUTES IN THIS PLAY: **STOP**

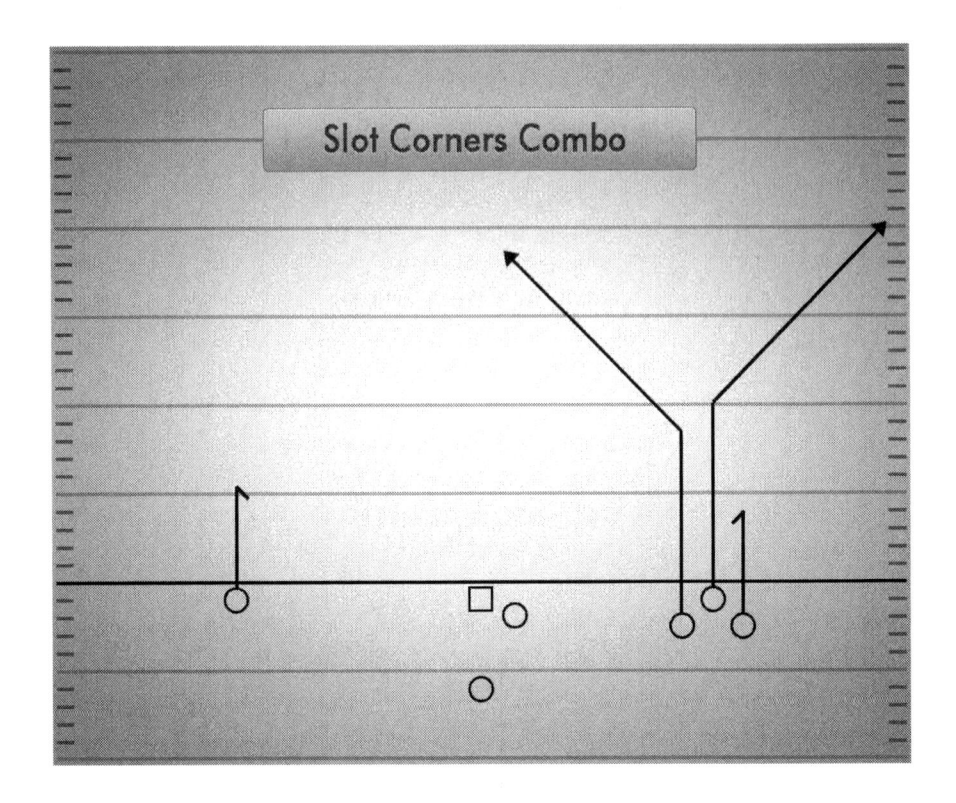

Slot Corners Combo

The Slot Corners play is a great play to use in order to isolate the Cornerback. The only thing that the Quarterback needs to read is how the Cornerback is positioning himself.

If the CB drops back underneath the Corner Route, then throw the ball to the stop on the outside. If the CB stay shallow in the flats, then throw over his head to the slot WR running the Corner route, making a break to the sideline.

FORMATION: **BUNCH FORMATION**

DISTANCE: **SHORT YARDAGE, MEDIUM YARDAGE**

ROUTES IN THIS PLAY: **CORNER, STOP**

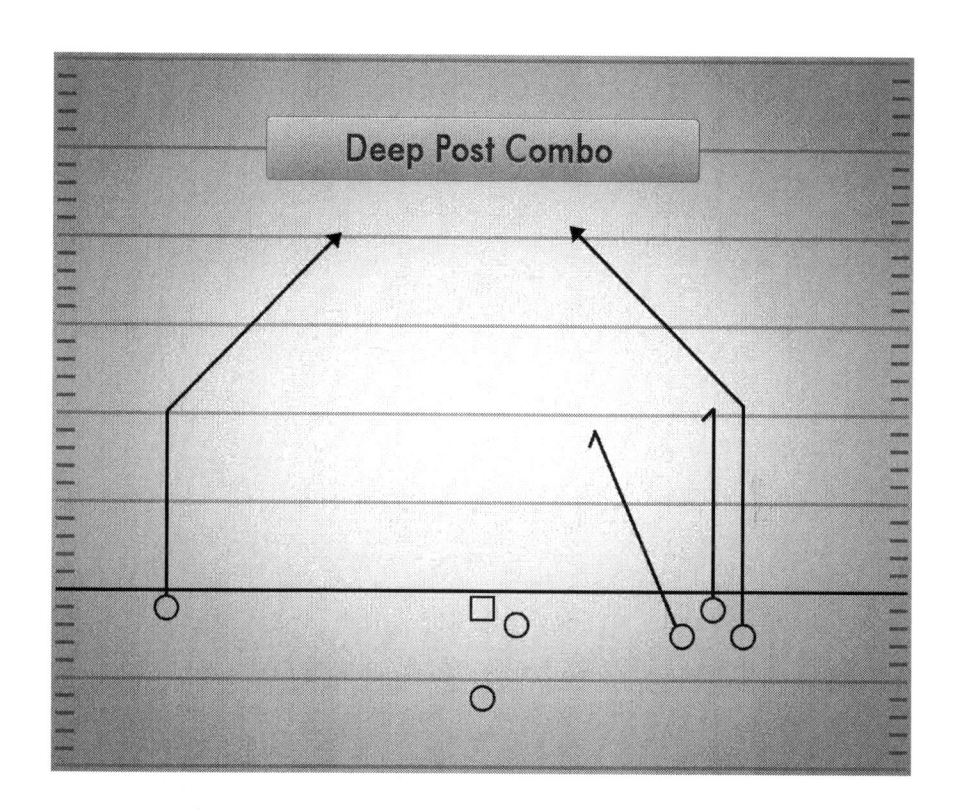

Deep Post Combo

The Deep Post Combo is a great way to attack downfield. The Post Route needs to be a skinny post with a trajectory that doesn't cross the middle of the field. The Slot Receiver needs to run his Curl Route in a way that grabs the attention of the Safety.

The Quarterback's read should be focused on the Safety. If the Safety stays high and guards the Post Route, then drop down and throw it to the Curl Route. If, however, the Safety is drawn down to the Slot Receiver running the Curl, then throw over his head to the Post running downfield.

FORMATION: **BUNCH FORMATION**

DISTANCE: **LONG YARDAGE, MEDIUM YARDAGE**

ROUTES IN THIS PLAY: **POST, CURL**

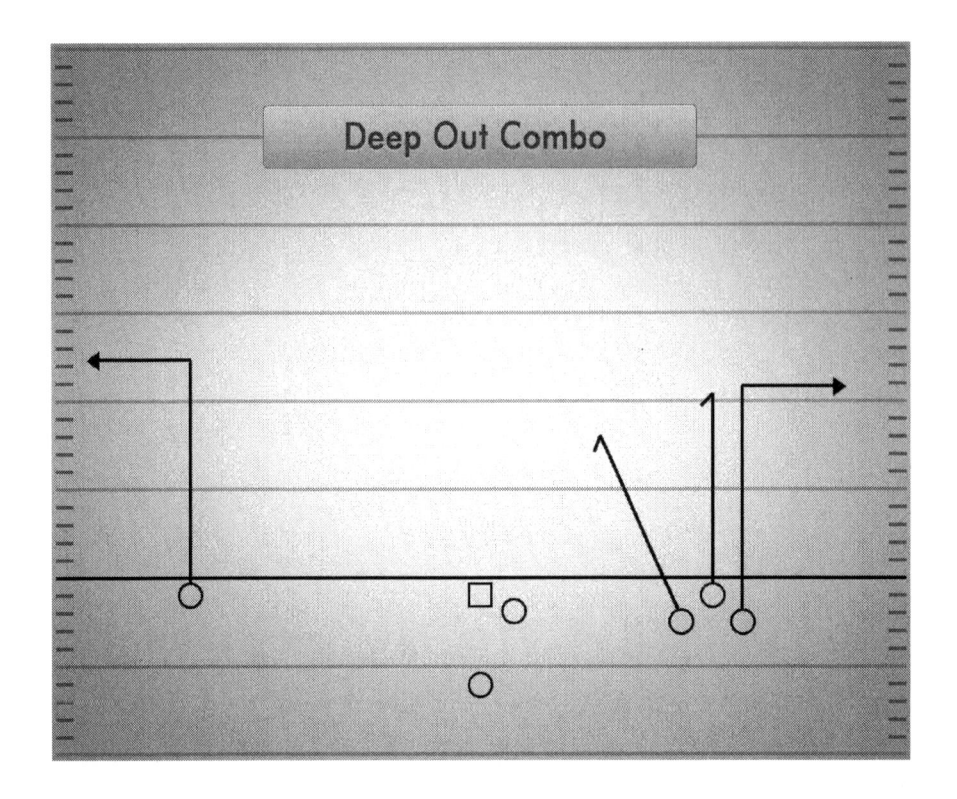

Deep Out Combo

The Deep Out Combo is similar to the Double Curl Combo play with a variation that send the outside WRs towards the sideline on a Deep Out Route.

The QB should make a pre-snap read to determine what side he is going to throw to. Once the side has been determined, then disregard the other half of the field and the read is locked into being between the Deep Out or the Curl Route.

FORMATION: **BUNCH FORMATION**

DISTANCE: **MEDIUM YARDAGE**

ROUTES IN THIS PLAY: **CURL, OUT**

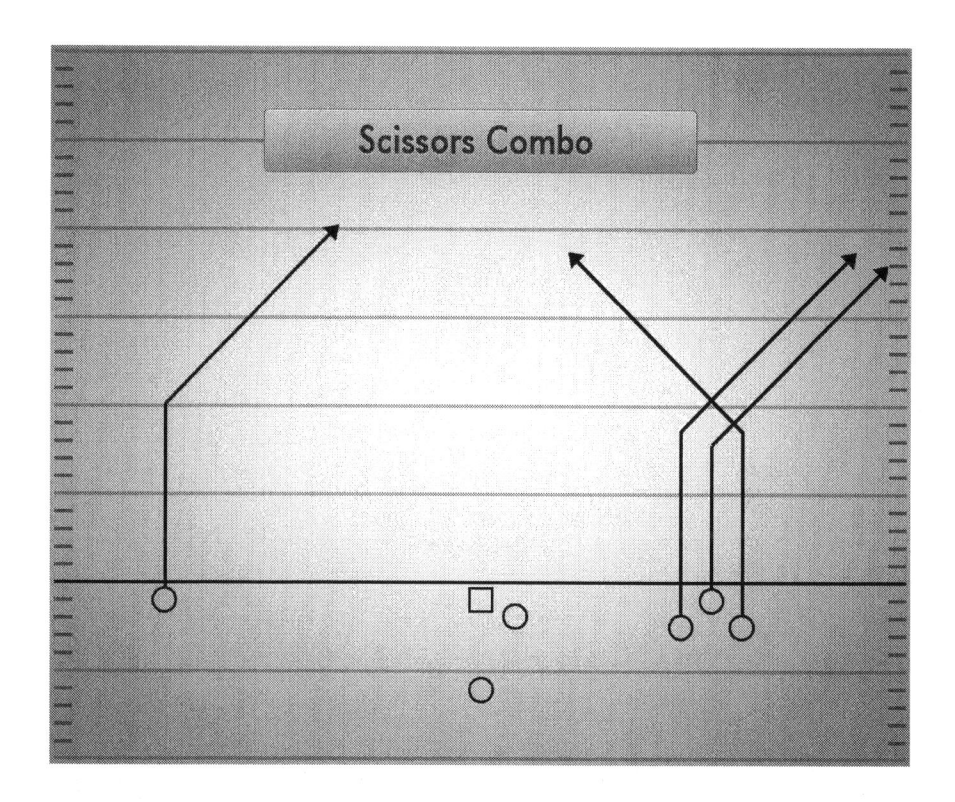

Scissors Combo

The Scissors Combo play is a mirrored play with the same route concept of a Post Route and a Corner Route on both sides.

The Wide Receivers need to cleanly run their routes by converging across each other at the point of the downfield cuts in order to disorient the defense and break free into the open field.

FORMATION: **BUNCH FORMATION**

DISTANCE: **LONG YARDAGE**

ROUTES IN THIS PLAY: **CORNER, POST**

Switchblade Combo

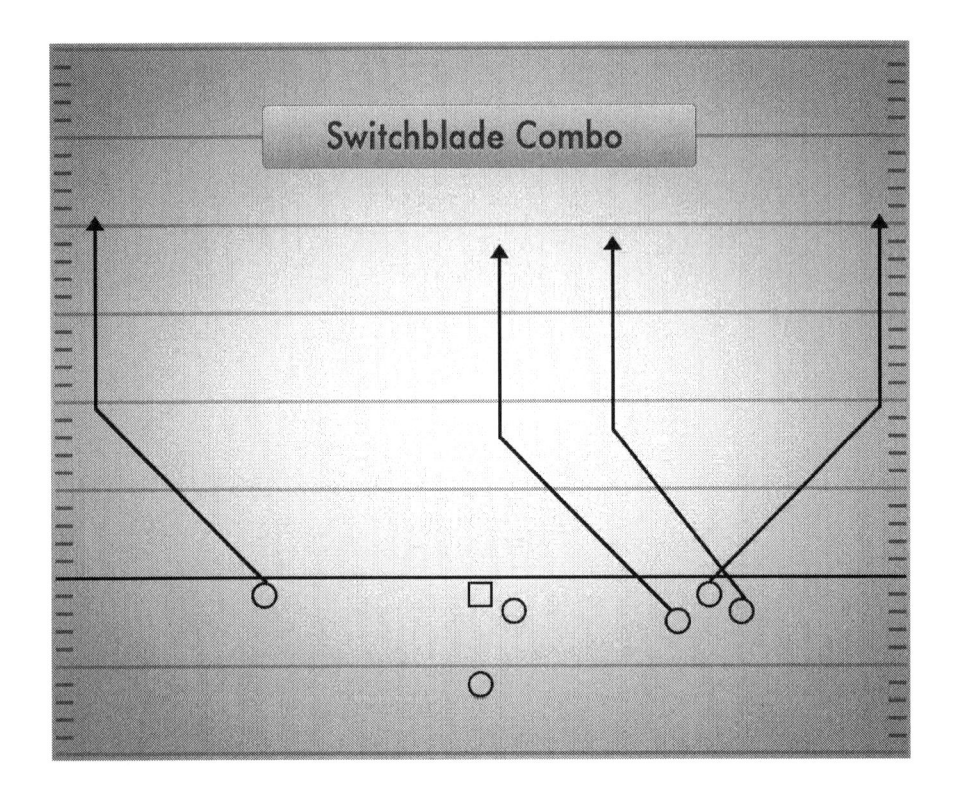

The Switchblade Combo play is intended to create a rub between the two combination receivers in order to break free from their defenders.

This play will work best against a man-to-man defense, because it is easy to lose the defenders when the Receivers cross and then break free going upfield.

FORMATION: **BUNCH FORMATION**

DISTANCE: **LONG YARDAGE**

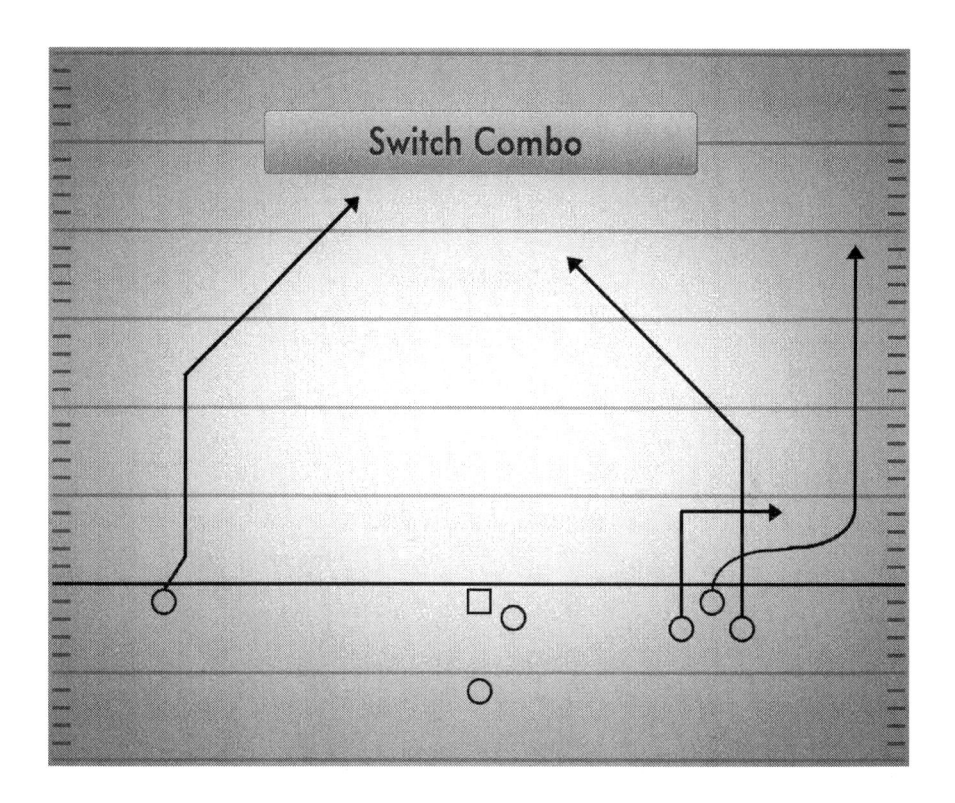

Switch Combo

Switch Combo is the classic switch play where the receivers use their routes to "switch" their positions on the field. The Outside Receiver gets upfield fast and runs a Post Route. The Slot Receiver goes underneath the Outside Receiver and then jets up the sideline.

The Quarterback should read the deep safeties. This play uses four players to attack zones that usually only have two, or maybe 3, defenders responsible for guarding them. Use your eyes to influence the defensive backs' movement, and then find the open WR running downfield.

FORMATION: **BUNCH FORMATION**

DISTANCE: **LONG YARDAGE**

ROUTES IN THIS PLAY: **POST**

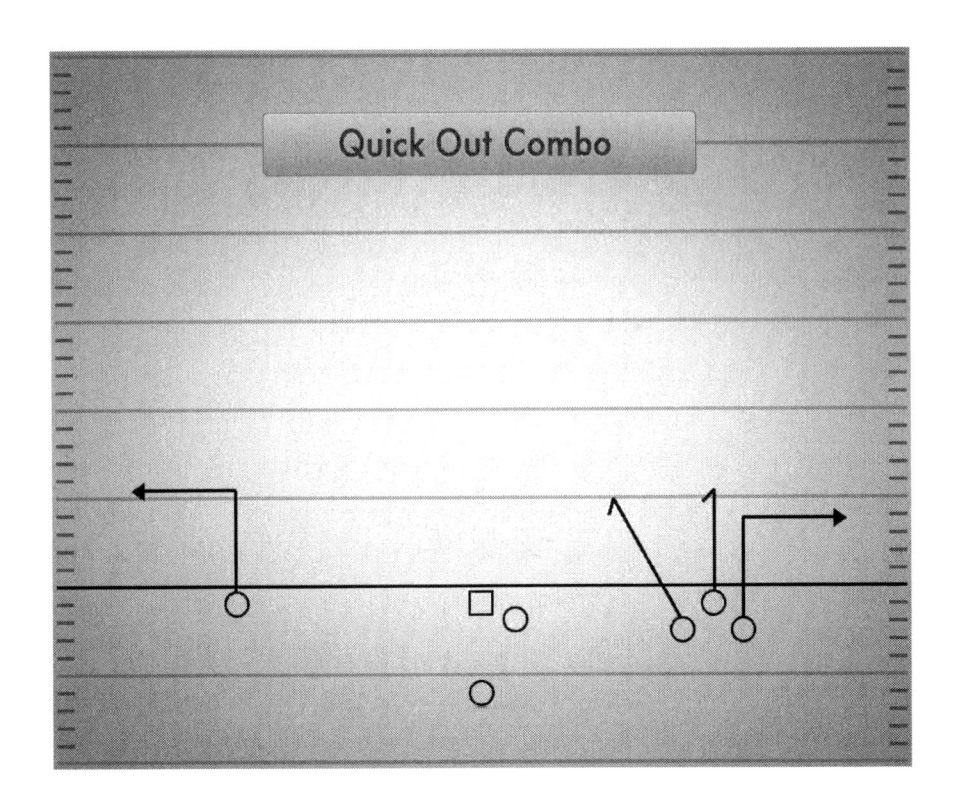

Quick Out Combo

Quick Cut Combo is a variation of the standard Double Stop Combo play, and a shorter version of the Deep Out Combo play.

The Quarterback should select one side of the field on the pre-snap read, and then as the play begins, determine which of the Wide Receivers gets in better position against the defense on his route.

FORMATION: **BUNCH FORMATION**

DISTANCE: **SHORT YARDAGE**

ROUTES IN THIS PLAY: **STOP, OUT**

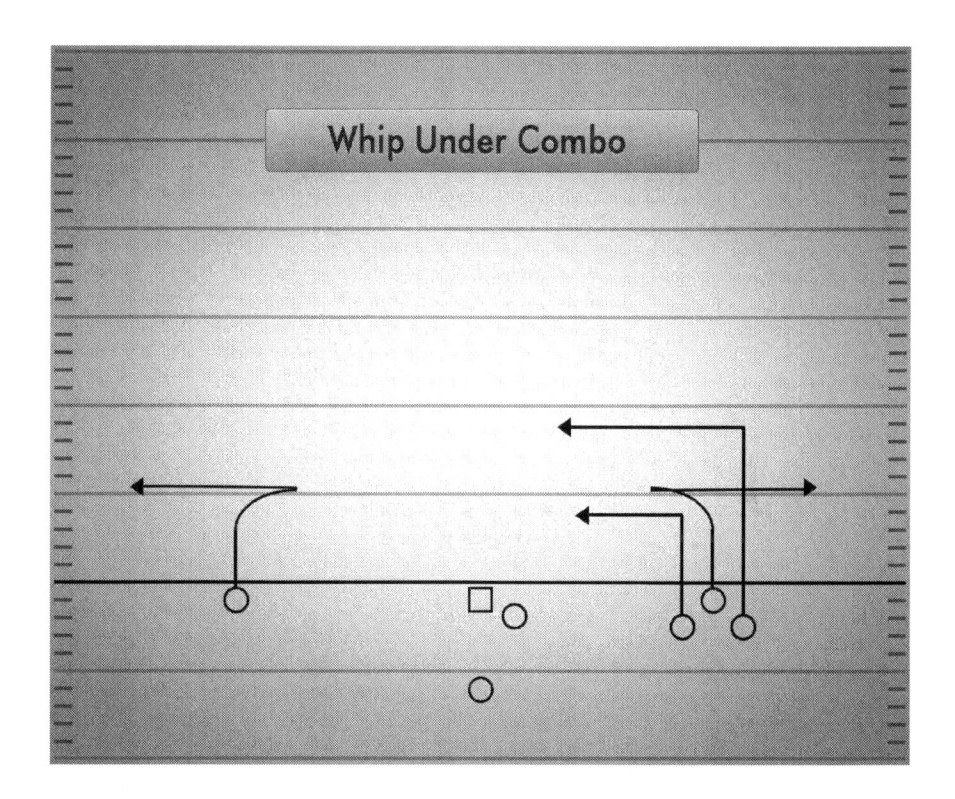

Whip Under Combo

The Whip Under Combo play is a great play to get some horizontal flow in your route concepts going. The crucial aspect of the play is the way in which the Whip Route is run by the Slot Receiver. The route must start of looking like an inside movement, but then the WR must plant his foot and spin (face toward the QB) and jet hard to the sideline.

If the Slot Receiver is not able to get open with the Whip Route, then the horizontal movement underneath should clear out to reveal the outside Receiver open on the In Route.

FORMATION: **BUNCH FORMATION**

DISTANCE: **SHORT YARDAGE, MEDIUM YARDAGE**

ROUTES IN THIS PLAY: **IN, OUT**

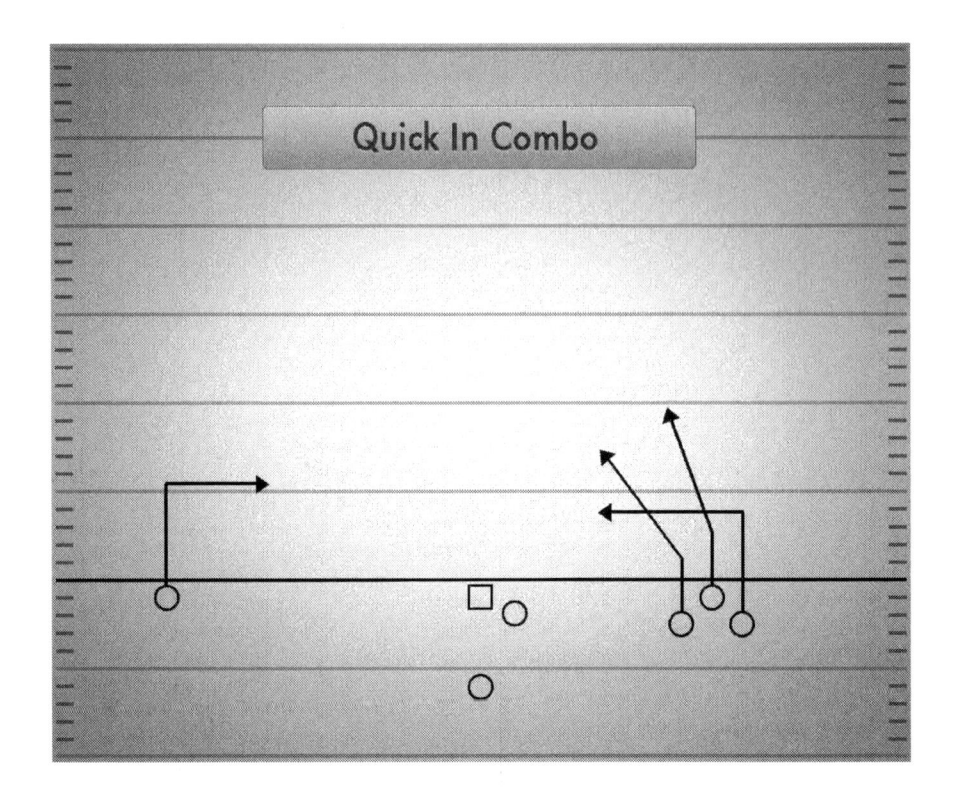

Quick In Combo

The Quick In Combo play is built to be a quick hitter. The Slot Receiver presses off the line of scrimmage in order to create space underneath for the Outside Receiver to be open for the In route.

The QB must make a pre-snap read to determine which side of the field is giving up the most position in the inside zone based upon formation alignment.

FORMATION: **BUNCH FORMATION**

DISTANCE: **SHORT YARDAGE**

ROUTES IN THIS PLAY: **IN, SEAM**

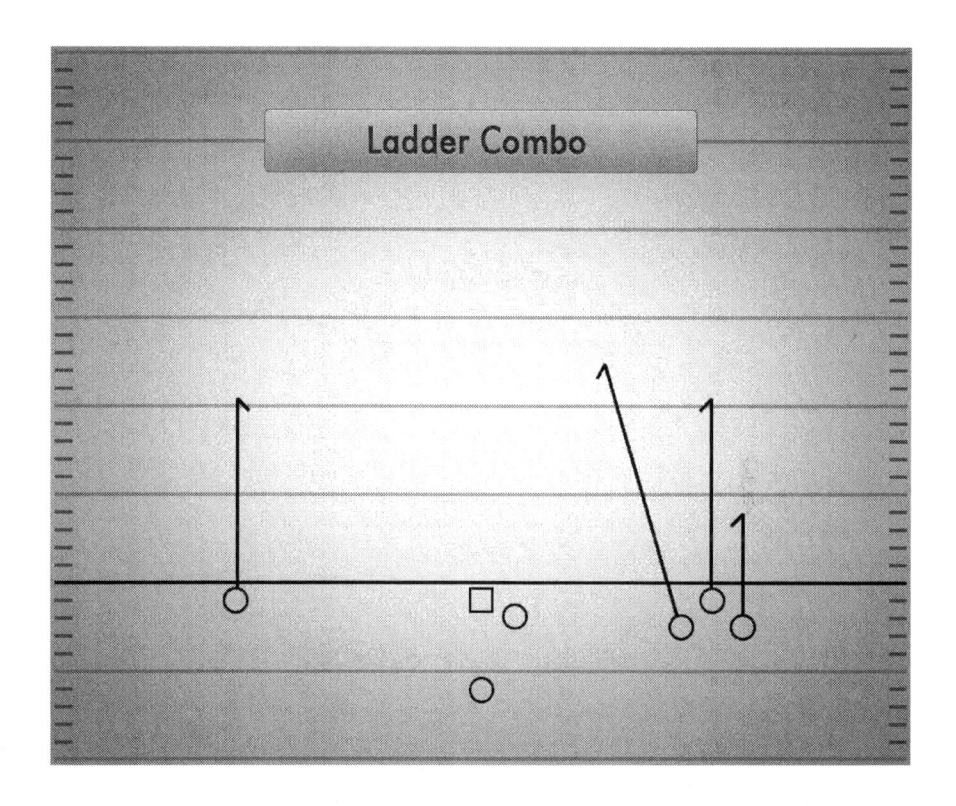

Ladder Combo

Ladder Combo is a play to hit the defense at varying vertical positions. All receivers run a stop and curl routes, but the lengths of the routes vary based upon their alignment.

The Quarterback should make his read just as if he is climbing up a "ladder." First look at the 5-Yard stop, and then work your way up to the 10-yard curl.

FORMATION: **BUNCH FORMATION**

DISTANCE: **SHORT YARDAGE, MEDIUM YARDAGE**

ROUTES IN THIS PLAY: **STOP, CURL**

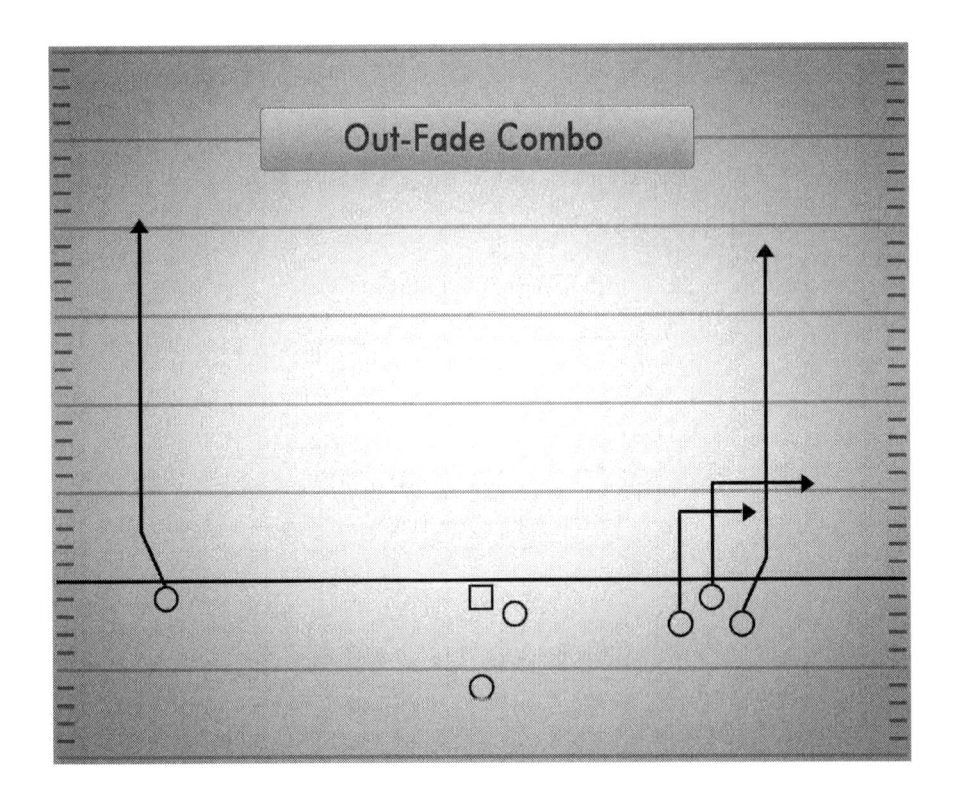

Out-Fade Combo

The Out-Fade route combination is one of the most popular route concepts in any football team's playbook. A Fade Route up the sideline on the outside combined with an Out Route from the Slot Receiver from the inside.

The Quarterback's read should be locked in on the defensive Cornerback. If the Cornerback drifts deep with the Fade, then throw the ball to the Out Route in the flats. If the Cornerback stays in the flats to jump on the Out, then throw it over the top to the Fade.

FORMATION: **BUNCH FORMATION**

DISTANCE: **SHORT YARDAGE, MEDIUM YARDAGE**

ROUTES IN THIS PLAY: **FADE, OUT**

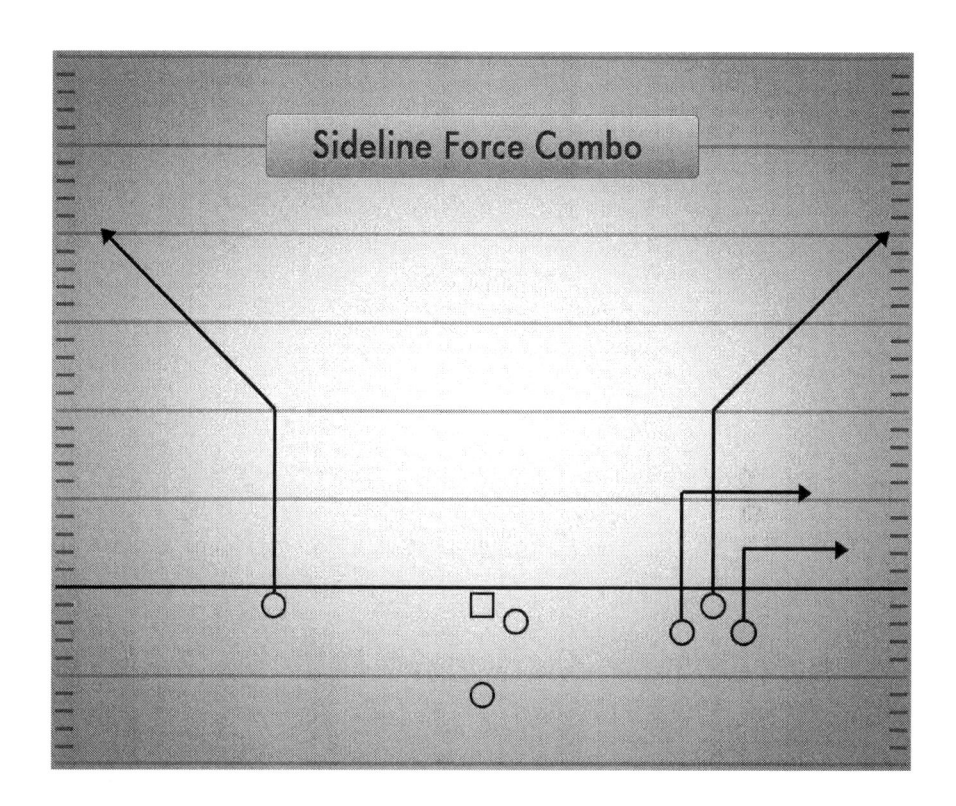

Sideline Force Combo

The Sideline Force Combo play is a shorter version of the Sideline Force Deep Combo play. The main goal of this play is to force the routes to the sideline.

This play is very effective when you need to manage the time on the clock because it allows the Receivers to quickly get out of bounds after the catch the ball.

FORMATION: **BUNCH FORMATION**

DISTANCE: **SHORT YARDAGE, MEDIUM YARDAGE**

ROUTES IN THIS PLAY: **CORNER, OUT**

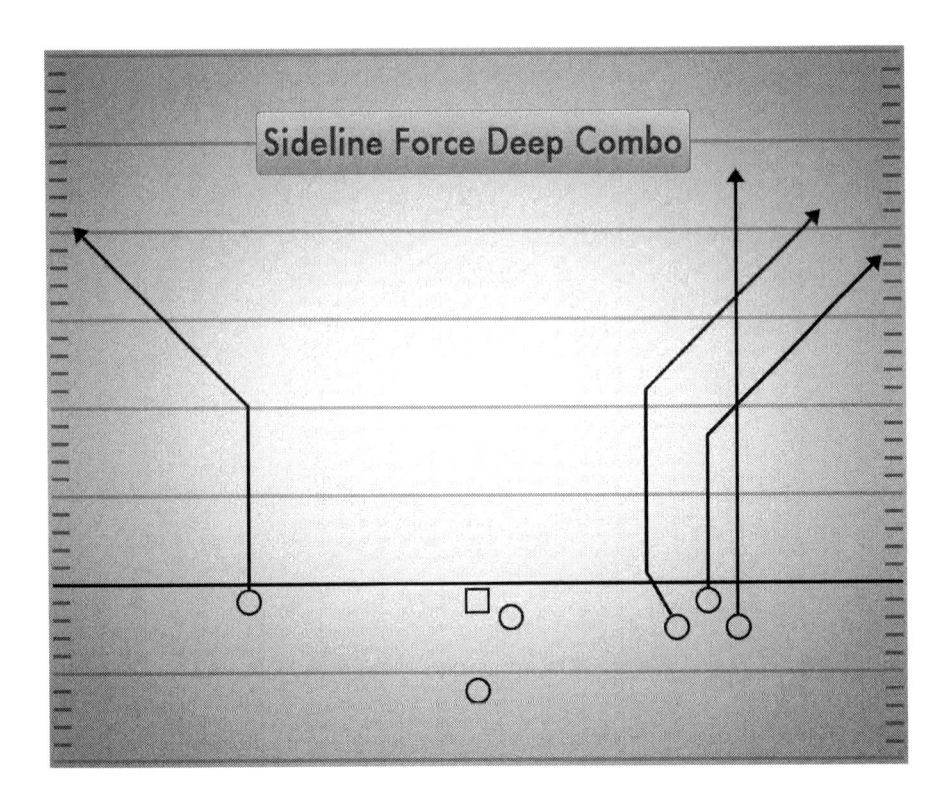

Sideline Force Deep Combo

The Sideline Force Deep Combo play is the deep version of the Sideline Force Combo play. The purpose of this play is to get the Wide Receivers in close proximity to the sideline while running deep downfield.

This play is very effective when you need to manage the time on the clock because it allows the Receivers to quickly get out of bounds after the catch the ball.

FORMATION: **BUNCH FORMATION**

DISTANCE: **LONG YARDAGE**

ROUTES IN THIS PLAY: **CORNER, STREAK**

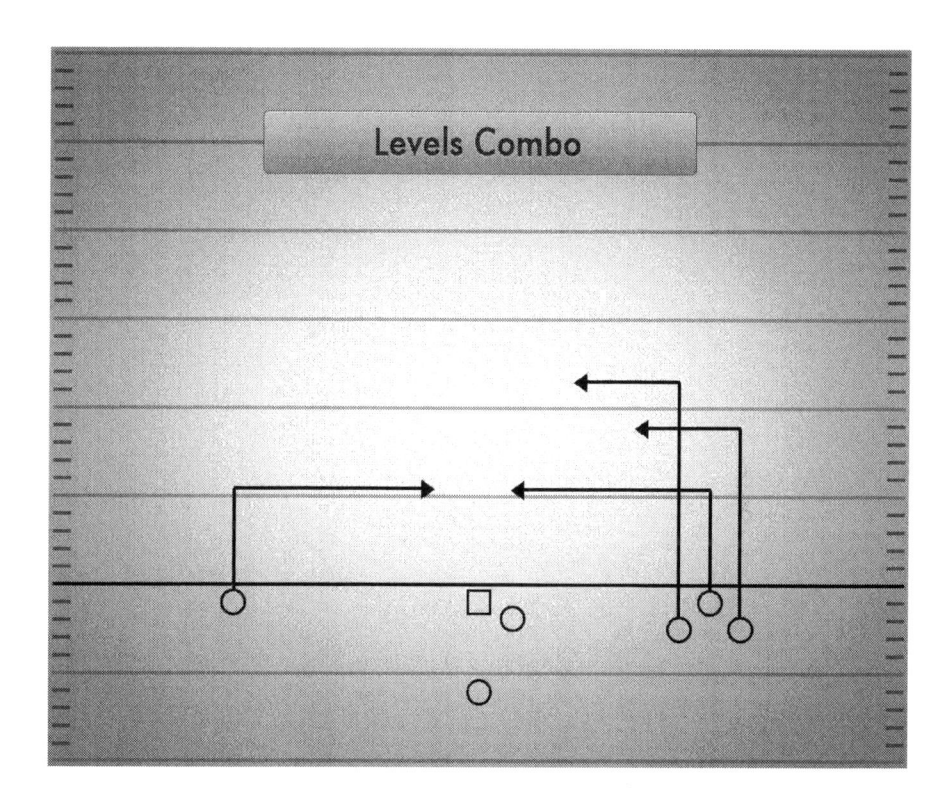

Levels Combo

The Levels Combo play is a great way to attack different vertical portions of the defensive secondary. The Wide Receivers run In Routes at varying distances down the field.

The horizontal movement should create a space for the Quarterback to find an opening to throw into, especially combined with the alternating vertical positioning of the routes.

FORMATION: **BUNCH FORMATION**

DISTANCE: **SHORT YARDAGE, MEDIUM YARDAGE**

ROUTES IN THIS PLAY: **IN**

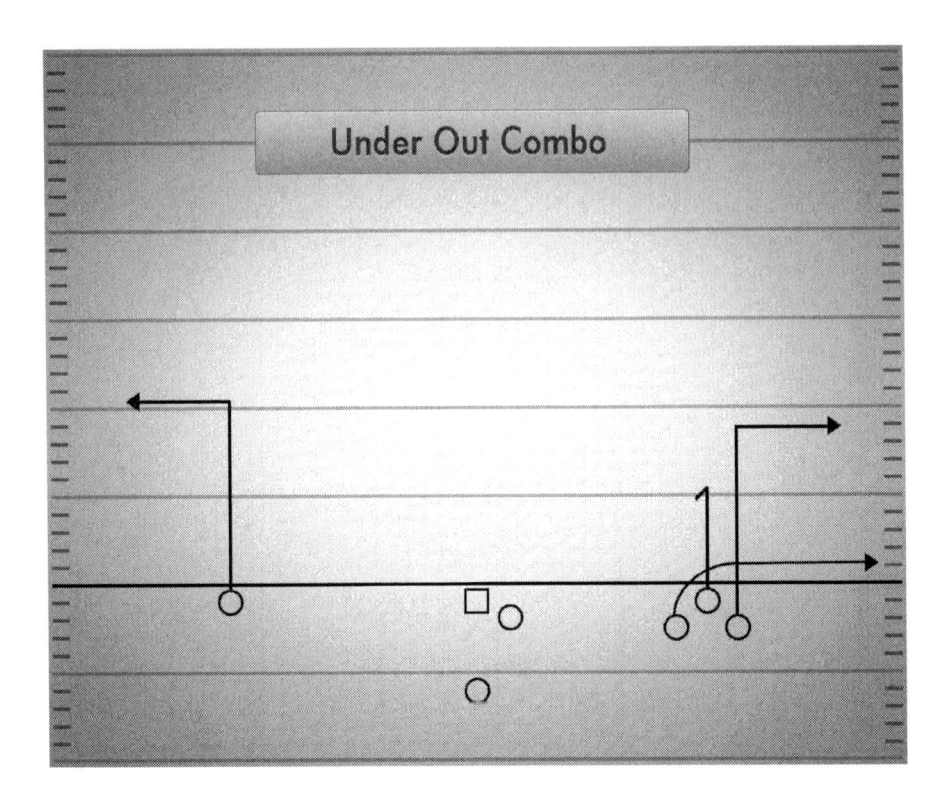

Under Out Combo

The Under Out Combo play positions the inside WR on a quick out underneath the deeper out. This places pressure on the flats of the defensive secondary by placing two WR on each side of the zone.

By splitting the responsibilities of the Cornerback, the Quarterback will have to see which one the Cornerback decides to guard, and then deliver the ball to the appropriate WR.

FORMATION: **BUNCH FORMATION**

DISTANCE: **SHORT YARDAGE, MEDIUM YARDAGE**

ROUTES IN THIS PLAY: **OUT**

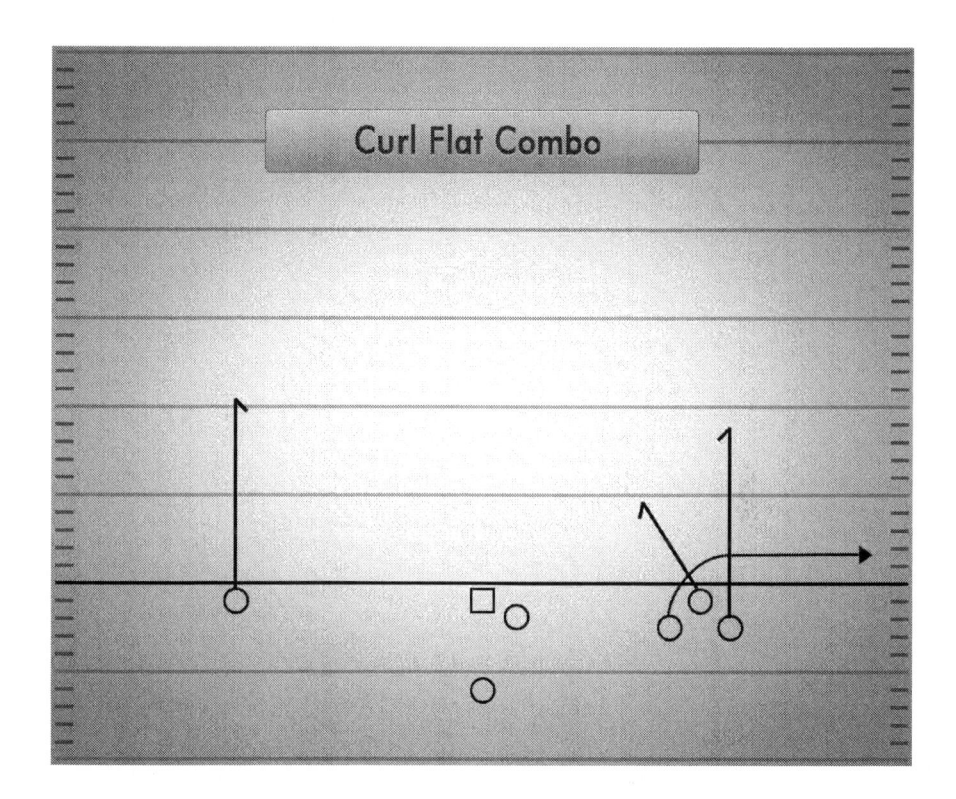

Curl Flat Combo

The Curl Flat Combo play attacks the defensive flat zone on the outside with a quick Out Route and a Curl Route over the top.

The Quarterback will want to look first at the quick out, and if the defense flowed fast to guard the out, then that means the curl route should be curling around in the open space right behind them.

FORMATION: **BUNCH FORMATION**

DISTANCE: **SHORT YARDAGE, MEDIUM YARDAGE**

ROUTES IN THIS PLAY: **CURL, OUT**

Advanced Strategies

Formations and Alignment

Different leagues will have different rules and regulations for proper alignment. For example, a standard 7 on 7 league will typically require at least 3 players to be on the line of scrimmage, and up to 4 players can be behind that line of Scrimmage.

In leagues where blocking is legal, it would be wise to place the lineman behind the line of scrimmage. This is valuable for two reasons. One, it allows the Wide Receivers to all be on the line of scrimmage in order to have a faster start downfield. Two, it allows the lineman to take a step of the line in order to better position themselves to get in front of the rushing defenders.

This playbook has been put together with reference to standardization, meaning that all plays found in offset formations, where there are more players on one side of the field than the other (such as Trips, Bunch, and 3-Wide) will all be presented in the same way. For example, all Trips Formations plays will have the three Wide Receivers on the right side of the field. However, in game situations, these plays can also be used by flipping which side of the field the Trips side is on. The flipping shouldn't be random, though. You should flip a play in order to have more players on the side of the field that has the most space. For instance, if the ball is placed towards the right side of the field, then the three receivers of the Trips or Bunch formation should line up on the left side, and flip the routes that each person would run.

Motion

In the Sport of football, the concept of "motion" is when an offensive player is moving along the line of scrimmage before the play starts. You can snap the ball while the player is moving in order to start the play before the defense can readjust. The plays in this Playbook do not have any motion specifically designed into them because no motion is required for the play to be successful. However, all plays can be equipped with motion in order to add on additional confusion for the defense.

The best way to go about adding on motion is to call the play in a particular formation, but then tell one of the Wide Receivers to line up on the opposite side of the field of where he is supposed to be on the play. Then have the Quarterback give him the signal to go into motion, and snap the ball once he gets into the proper place. Motion is most useful by making the formation appear to be another formation (for example Trips) and then moving the Wide Receiver from the Trips side to the other side (to make it the standard 4-Wide formation). Or you can start with two Receivers on each side, and then motion one over to the other side to create a Trips formation, and snap the ball before the defense has time to adjust.

Shifts

A "shift" is similar to a "motion," however, instead of only moving one player, a shift will move multiple players. For example, a great formations shift that can be used with the plays in this playbook is to shift from a Trips formation into a Bunch formation. The Trips formation will have three receivers evenly spread out on one side of the field, but the Bunch formation has the all tightly packed together so that they can rub their routes closely off of each other in order to make it hard for the defense to stay organized. A shift can be implemented to switch between this two variations of formations in order to quickly catch the defense off guard.

One note to remember when it comes to shifts is that once a shift has been started, all players have to be reset still for at least one second before you can snap the ball. Otherwise, the shift will result in a penalty.

Blocking

Flag Football games will have two different variations on the rules for blocking. Some leagues will not allow any blocking whatsoever. When blocking is legal, however, it is typically limited to the chest. The lineman will shuffle there feet in order to stay in front of the defenders in order to keep them from reaching the Quarterback. The lineman are required to either place their hands behind their back, or clasped together in front of their chest without extending them out.

The Flag Football Plays on this website, and in the Best Flag Football Playbook, are designed with both forms of blocking in mind. In games where blocking is allowed, the formations will provide both a center as well as one or two lineman. Upon snapping the ball, these players can be used to block the defense, or go out on passing routes, depending on the rules for the game. Either way, these plays will be beneficial for any form of Flag Football rules.

Running Plays

The ability for the Quarterback to run past the line of scrimmage is another variation in the rules that some games will allow and others will not. Some leagues will allow the Quarterback to run after a certain amount of time, or immediately upon the start of the play, or not at all.

The plays in this playbook do not have any explicate running plays diagrammed into them, because runs in Flag Football are usually ad libbed plays made up on the fly depending on how the play is turning out.

Index
Routes

Comeback

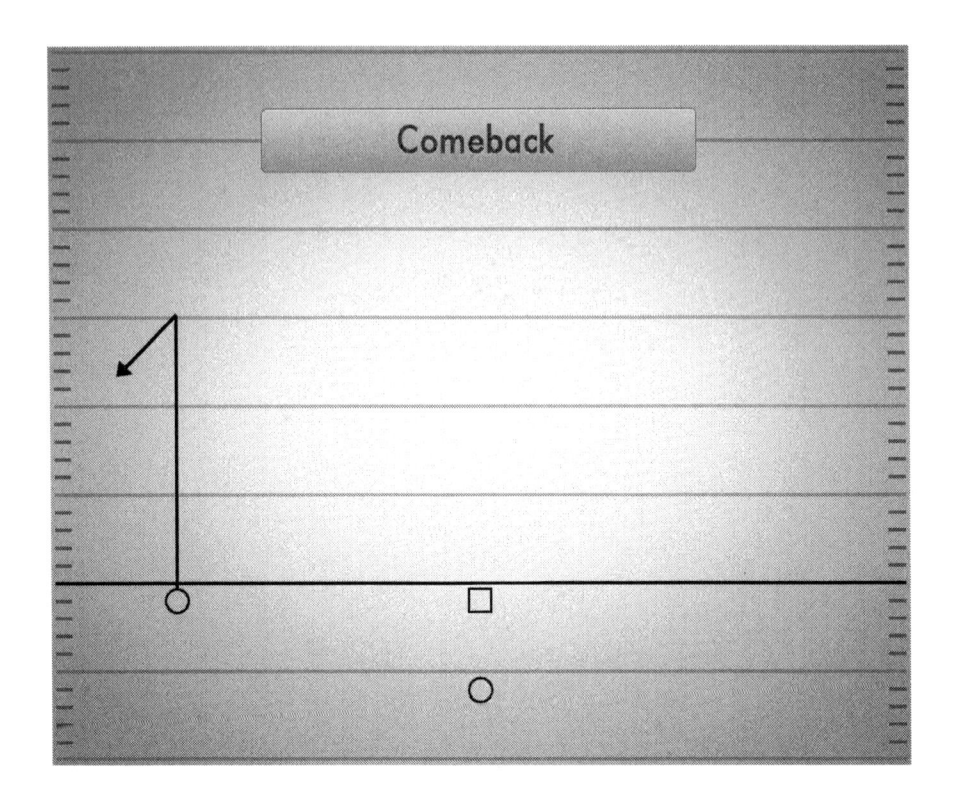

ROUTE DESCRIPTION

The Comeback route is the quintessential hard cut route. You want to push up field to the defender's outside in order to make it look like you are going deep on a Fade or Streak Route. Once the defender turns around to run downfield with you, break off hard to the outside. It differs from a Stop or Curl route due to the fact that the break is to the outside towards the sideline, instead of to the inside towards the Quarterback. Therefore, the cut must be made with even more force in order to get your head turned all the way around in time to see the ball flying for you.

*Plays containing the **Comeback** Route:*

14, 18, 72, 76, 130, 134, 188, 192, 246, 250

ROUTE DESCRIPTION

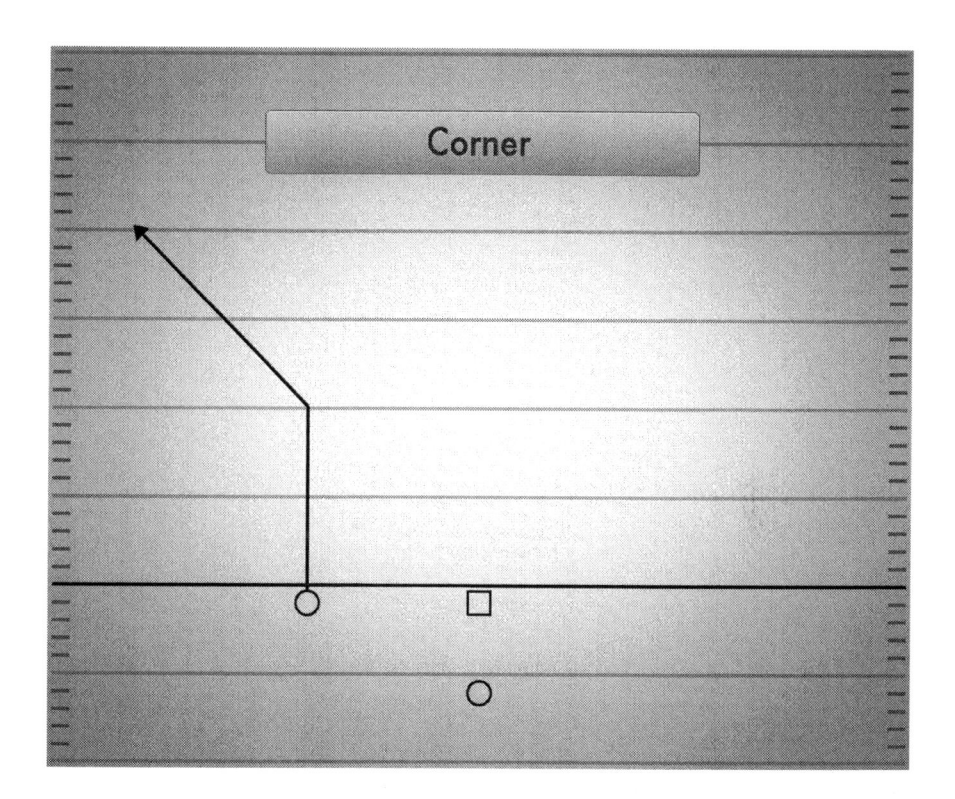

The Corner route is the inverse of the Post route on paper, however, there are a few intricacies that differentiates the way the route is run. Instead of breaking off at a 45 degree angle to the middle of the field, you break off at a 45 degree angle towards the sideline or the "corner" of the field. At this point, you will be running directly away from the Quarterback, so you will want to turn your head all the way around so that you are facing the line of scrimmage and in position to adjust to the trajectory of the throw.

*Plays containing the **Corner** Route:*

6, 11, 13, 46, 49, 57, 58, 64, 69, 71, 104, 107, 115, 116, 122, 127, 129, 162, 165, 173, 174, 180, 185, 187, 220, 223, 231, 232, 238, 243, 245, 278, 281, 289, 290

ROUTE DESCRIPTION

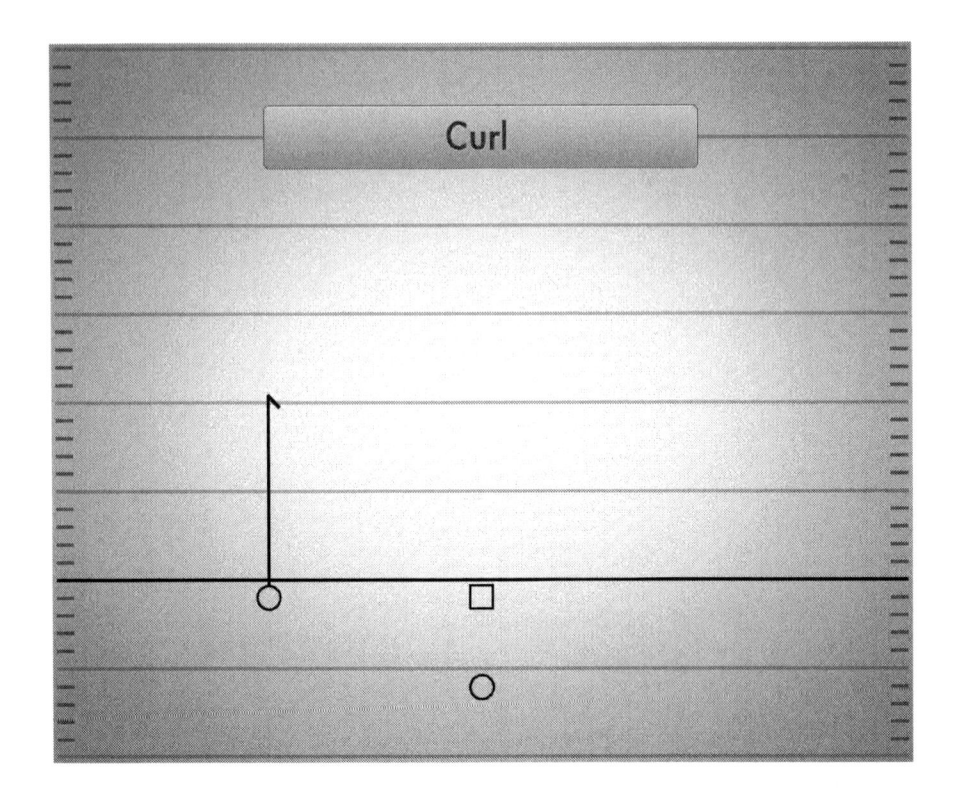

The Curl route is identical to the Stop route but run at the depth of 10-12 yards downfield. Due to the fact that the receiver is further away from the Quarterback, the ball will take longer to travel to the destination. Therefore, the WR will need to be ready to come back towards the ball as it is in the air so that the defense will not be able to jump in front for the interception.

Plays containing the **Curl** *Route:*

10, 13, 38, 47, 48, 55, 61, 68, 71, 96, 105, 106, 113, 119, 126, 129, 154, 163, 164, 171, 177, 184, 187, 212, 221, 222, 229, 235, 242, 245, 270, 279, 280, 287, 293

Fade

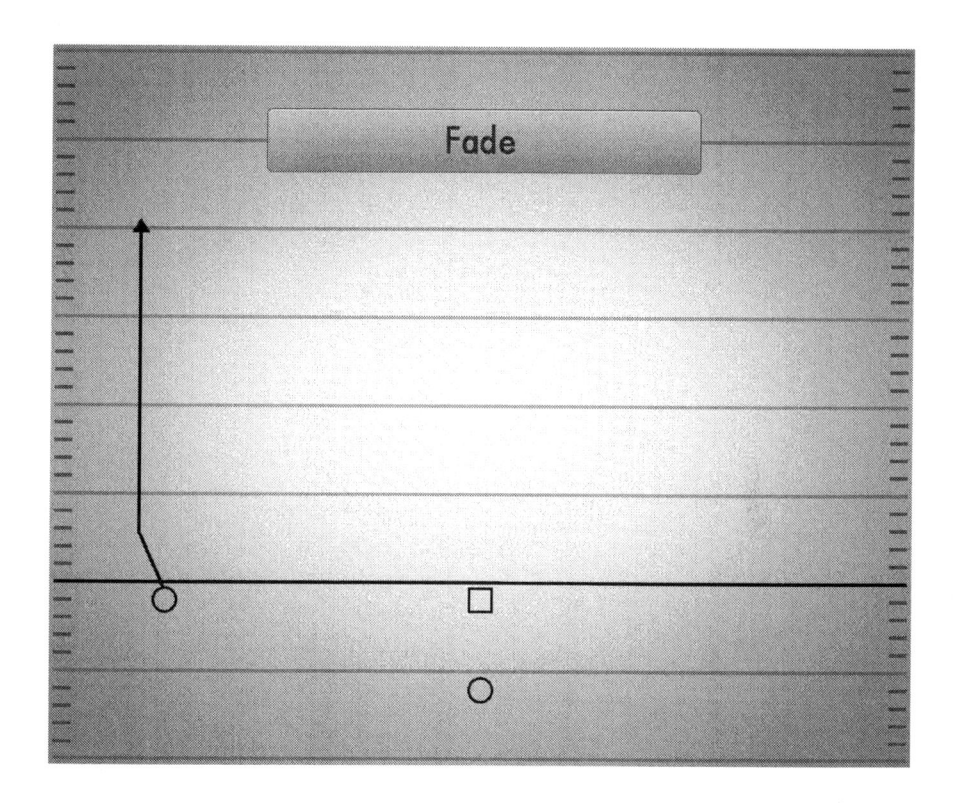

ROUTE DESCRIPTION

The Fade route is similar to the Streak route in the sense that it is a deep pattern up the sideline, however, it has one crucial difference. The release off the line of scrimmage has to be to the outside of the defender, because the QB will usually throw the fade ball up higher to the sideline in hopes that the WR is in good position to go jump up and catch it.

*Plays containing the **Fade** Route:*

8, 10, 12, 19, 25, 29, 31, 32, 36, 56, 66, 68, 70, 77, 83, 87, 89, 90, 114, 124, 126, 128, 135, 141, 145, 147, 148, 152, 172, 182, 184, 186, 193, 199, 203, 205, 206, 210, 230, 240, 242, 244, 251, 257, 261, 263, 264, 268, 288

ROUTE DESCRIPTION

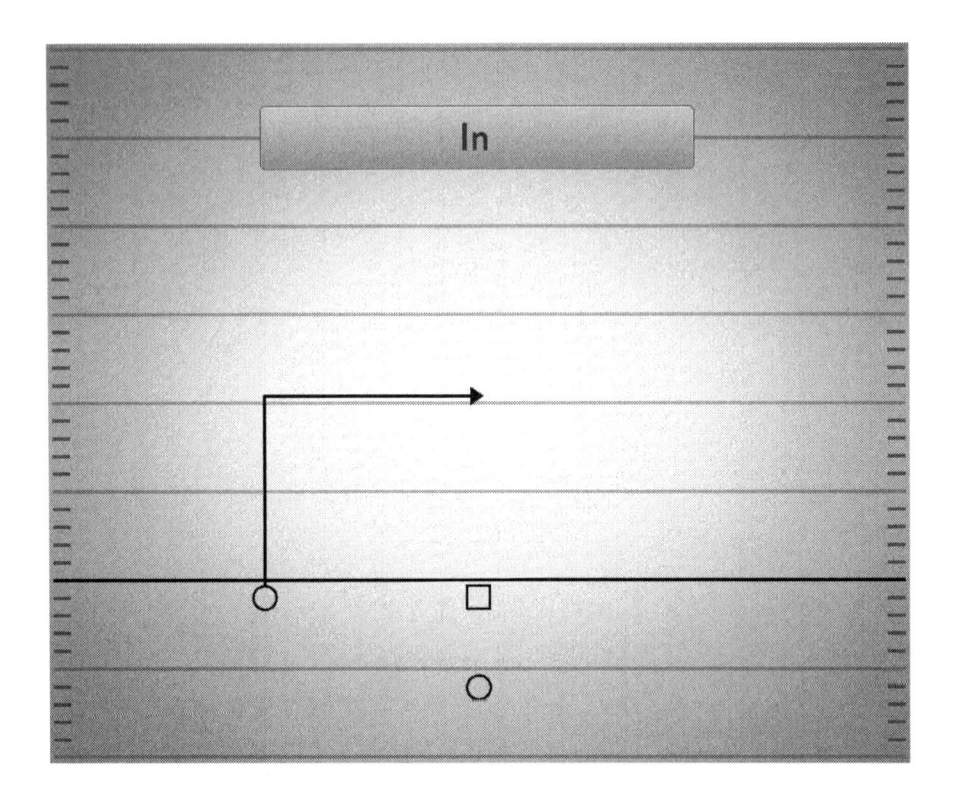

The In route is a hard 90 degree cut to the inside of the field. It can be run at 5 or 10 yard distances. Make sure that the cut is not rounded, and that it is directly to the inside so that the defense cannot jump in front of it.

Plays containing the In Route:

7, 8, 9, 22, 23, 28, 32, 33, 36, 53, 54, 59, 65, 66, 67, 80, 81, 86, 90, 91, 94, 111, 112, 117, 123, 124, 125, 138, 139, 144, 148, 149, 152, 169, 170, 175, 181, 182, 183, 196, 197, 202, 206, 207, 210, 227, 228, 233, 239, 240, 241, 254, 255, 260, 264, 265, 268, 285, 286, 291

ROUTE DESCRIPTION

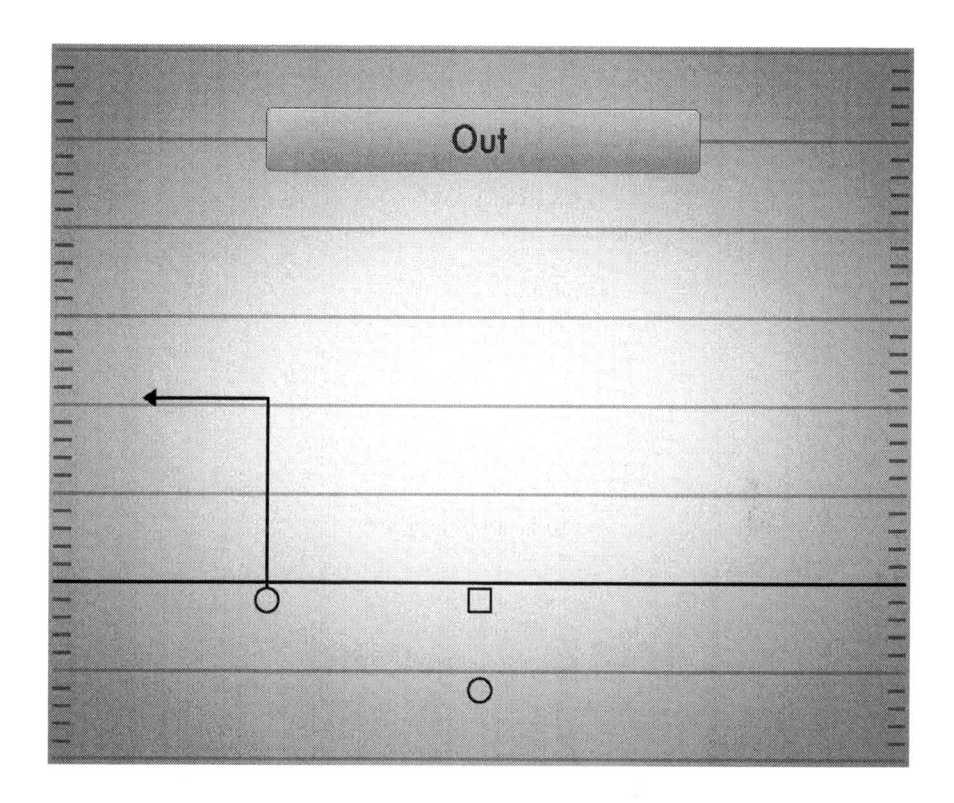

The Out route is a hard 90 degree cut to the outside of the field. It can be run at 5, 10, or 15 yard distances. Make sure that the cut is not rounded, and that it is directly to the sideline so that the defense cannot jump in front of it.

*Plays containing the **Out** Route:*

13, 28, 40, 42, 43, 44, 48, 52, 53, 56, 57, 60, 61, 71, 86, 98, 100, 101, 102, 106, 110, 111, 114, 115, 118, 119, 129, 144, 156, 158, 159, 160, 164, 168, 169, 172, 173, 176, 177, 187, 202, 214, 216, 217, 218, 222, 226, 227, 230, 231, 234, 235, 245, 260, 272, 274, 275, 276, 280, 284, 285, 288, 289, 292, 293

ROUTE DESCRIPTION

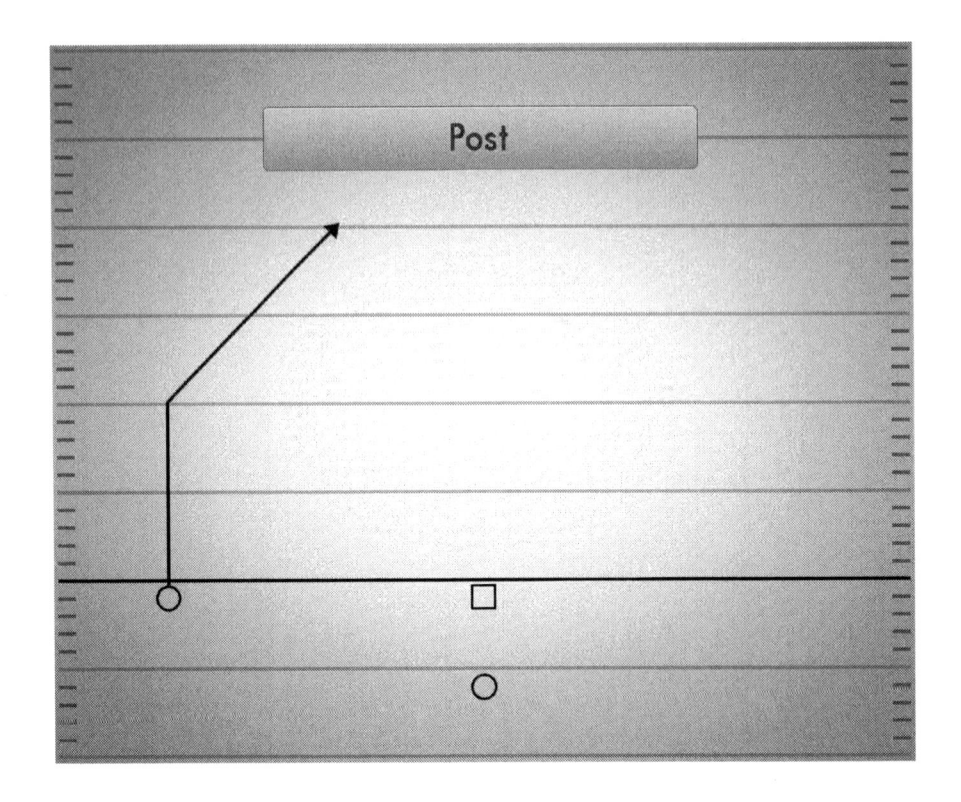

The Post route is run 10 yards up field, and then breaks off at a 45 degree angle to the inside. It is called a "post" because when you make your cut, you should be aiming for the goal post in the end zone.

*Plays containing the **Post** Route:*

6, 7, 8, 9, 10, 11, 14, 15, 18, 19, 21, 22, 24, 30, 47, 49, 51, 64, 65, 66, 67, 68, 69, 72, 73, 76, 77, 79, 80, 82, 88, 93, 105, 107, 109, 122, 123, 124, 125, 126, 127, 130, 131, 134, 135, 137, 138, 140, 146, 151, 163, 165, 167, 180, 181, 182, 183, 184, 185, 188, 189, 192, 193, 195, 196, 198, 204, 221, 223, 225, 238, 239, 240, 241, 242, 243, 246, 247, 250, 251, 253, 254, 256, 262, 267, 279, 281, 283

Post Corner

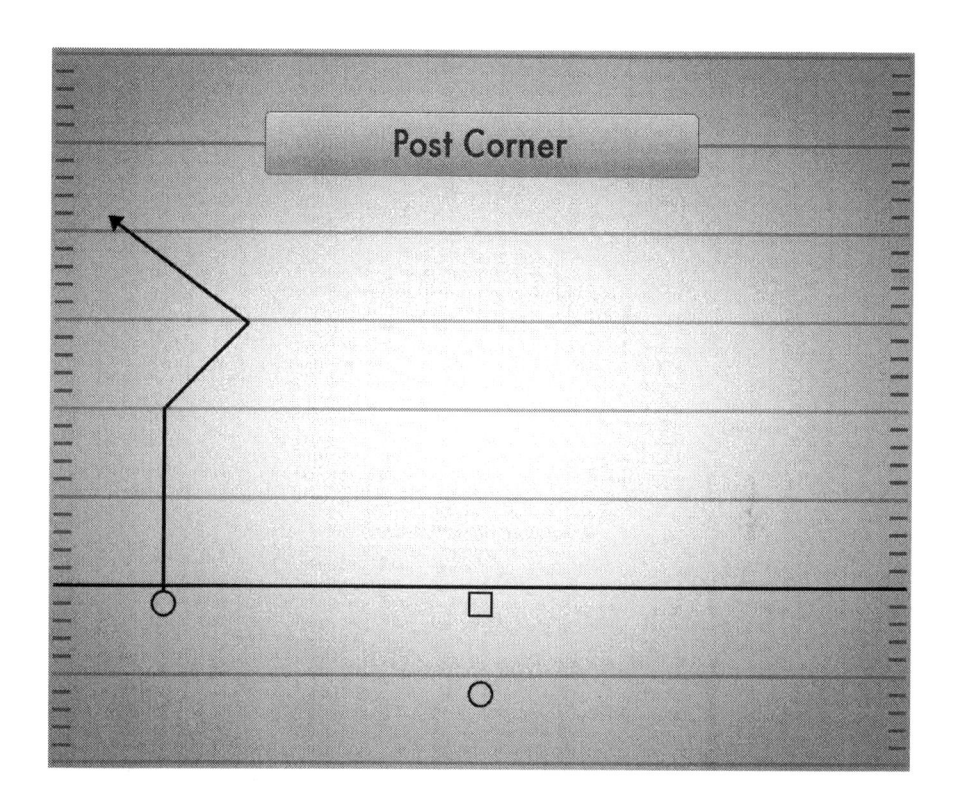

ROUTE DESCRIPTION

The Post Corner is a deep double move route. The route should be run identically to the Post route in order to make the defense think that the route will be run inside. At the last second, however, the WR should break off to the outside corner for a deep throw towards the sideline.

*Plays containing the **Post Corner** Route:*

14, 33, 72, 91, 130, 149, 188, 207, 246, 265

ROUTE DESCRIPTION

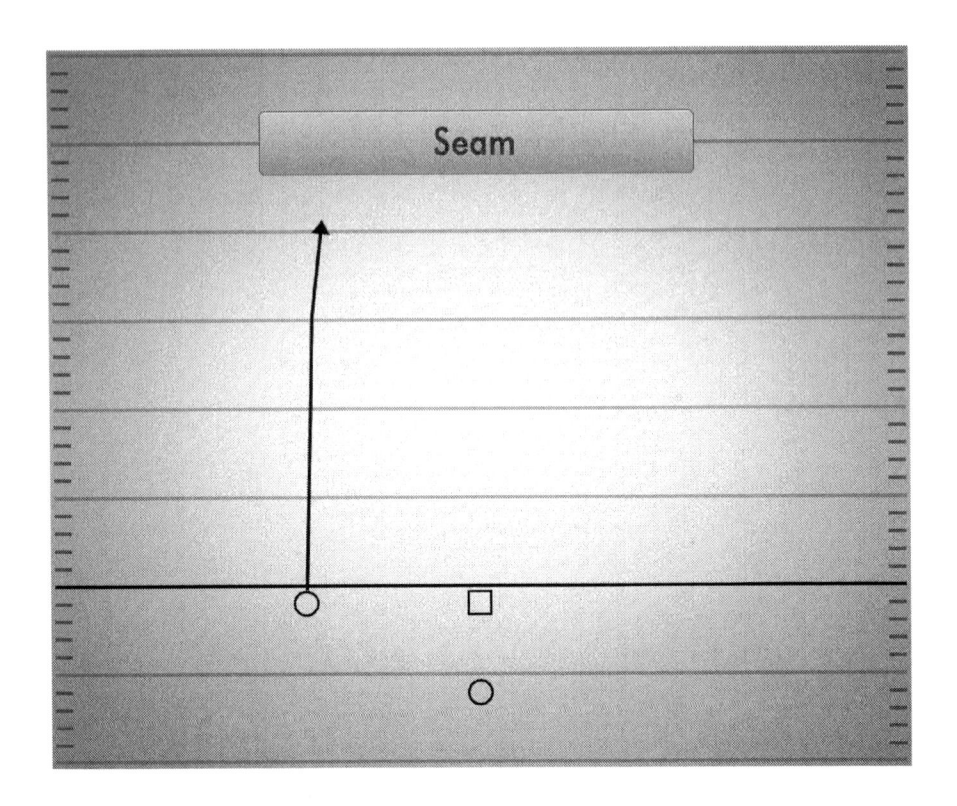

The Seam route differs from a fade or streak route because it is always run by the inside receiver who angles the trajectory slightly to the inside of the field. By shading the route to the inside, it creates an opportunity for a pass to be made inside of the downfield safeties. This does not need to be a deep throw, however, the Quarterback merely needs to wait for the WR to clear the depth of the linebackers underneath.

*Plays containing the **Seam** Route:*

29, 31, 32, 33, 36, 39, 54, 87, 89, 90, 94, 97, 112, 145, 147, 148, 149, 152, 155, 170, 203, 205, 206, 207, 210, 213, 228, 261, 263, 264, 265, 268, 271, 286

Shallow Cross

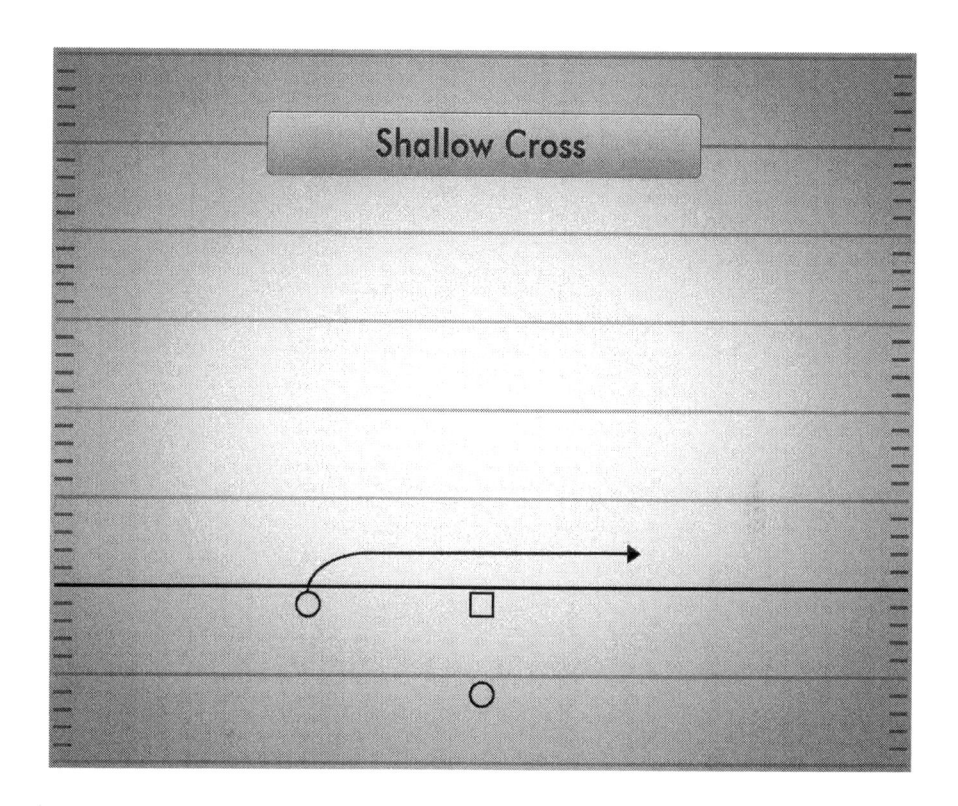

ROUTE DESCRIPTION

The Shallow Cross route is meant to come across the very bottom of the defensive formation as possible. It can be used as a distraction for the linebackers to keep them from dropping back too far, or if the linebackers are in the habit of dropping back immediately, then the Shallow Cross is a great route to expose the middle of the field.

*Plays containing the **Shallow Cross** Route:*

7, 8, 11, 15, 16, 18, 23, 24, 29, 30, 31, 36, 65, 66, 69, 73, 74, 81, 82, 89, 94, 123, 124, 127, 131, 132, 134, 139, 140, 145, 146, 147, 152, 181, 182, 185, 189, 190, 192, 197, 198, 203, 204, 205, 210, 239, 240, 243, 247, 248, 250, 255, 256, 261, 262, 263, 268

ROUTE DESCRIPTION

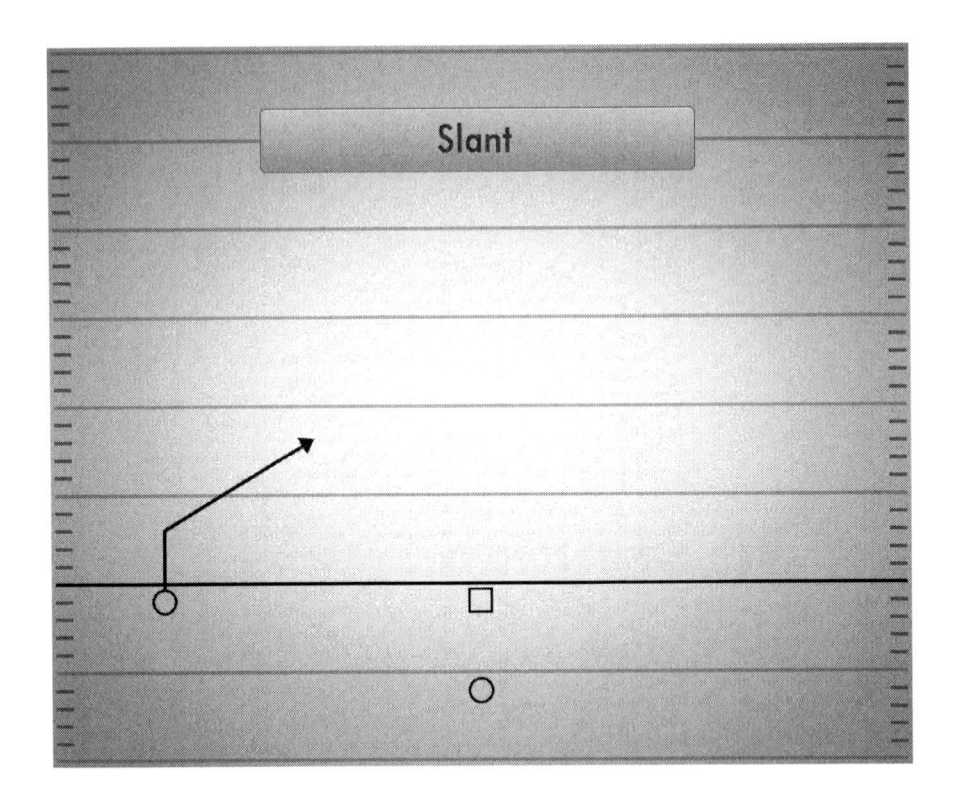

The Slant route is a quick route intended to pick up a small chunk of yards in critical situations. It is absolutely imperative that the route is run across the defenders face, meaning that the WR has to run inside the defender so that the WR is closer to the ball being thrown from the Quarterback. No more than two or three steps should be taken upfield before the shallow diagonal cut inside.

*Plays containing the **Slant** Route:*

29, 41, 42, 43, 44, 87, 99, 100, 101, 102, 145, 157, 158, 159, 160, 203, 215, 216, 217, 218, 261, 273, 274, 275, 276

ROUTE DESCRIPTION

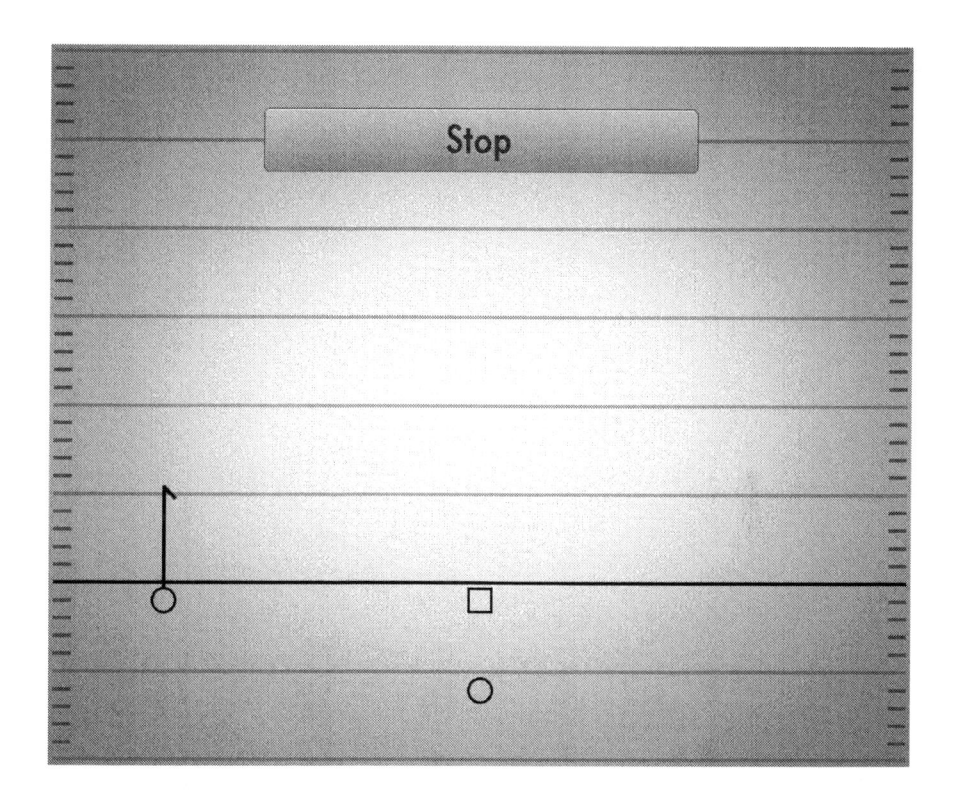

The Stop route is a short 5-yard route where you turn around towards the Quarterback immediately after reaching 5 yards downfield. You want to plant hard and avoid drifting backwards so the Quarterback has a steady target to aim for. This is an easy way to pick up a quick 5 yards if the defense is playing too far off. For a longer version of the Stop route, see the Curl route.

*Plays containing the **Stop** Route:*

6, 9, 10, 12, 14, 17, 28, 29, 37, 39, 45, 46, 52, 55, 64, 68, 70, 72, 75, 86, 87, 95, 97, 103, 104, 110, 113, 122, 125, 126, 128, 130, 133, 144, 145, 153, 155, 161, 162, 168, 171, 180, 183, 184, 186, 188, 191, 202, 203, 211, 213, 219, 220, 226, 229, 238, 241, 242, 244, 246, 249, 260, 261, 269, 271, 277, 278, 284, 287

Streak

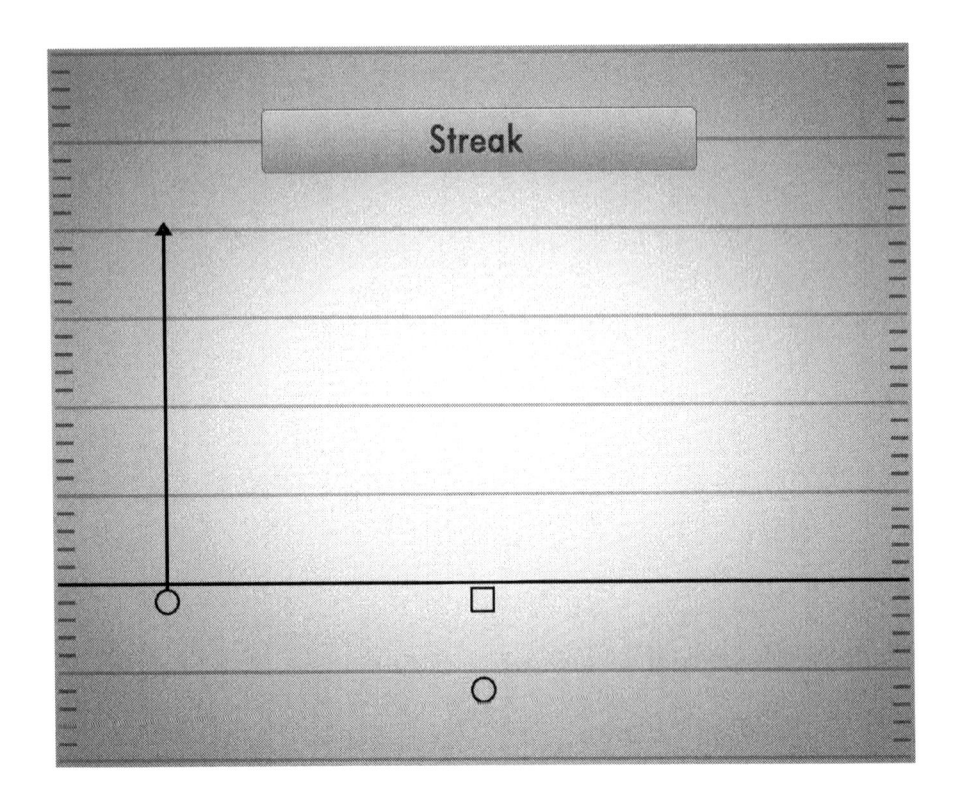

ROUTE DESCRIPTION

The Streak route is called in order to have the Wide Receiver get downfield as quickly as possible. Make a fast release off the line of scrimmage, and try to run past the entire defensive secondary for the deep ball downfield.

*Plays containing the **Streak** Route:*

7, 11, 16, 19, 20, 28, 58, 65, 69, 74, 78, 86, 116, 123, 127, 132, 135, 136, 144, 174, 181, 185, 190, 193, 194, 202, 232, 239, 243, 248, 251, 252, 260, 290

Wheel

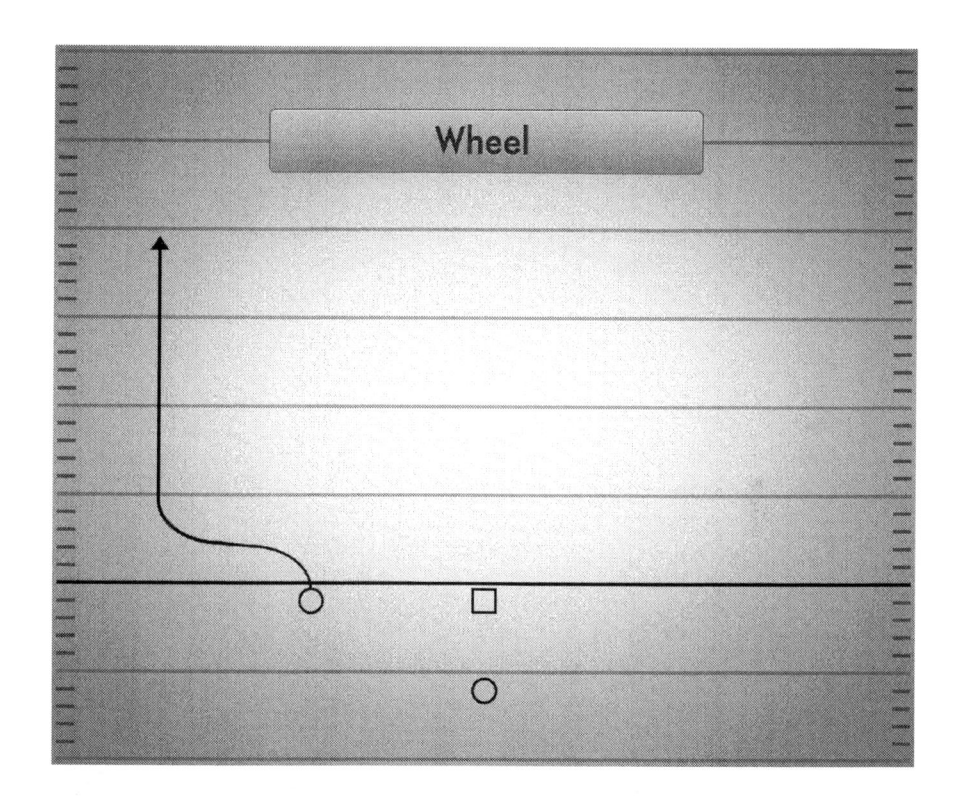

ROUTE DESCRIPTION

Think of the Wheel route as a quicker version of the out and up. The outside motion makes the defender hesitate and consider coming short to guard an Out route. However, the WR is planning to peel up outside and aims to run up the sideline as fast as possible. This route creates mismatches by allowing a faster Slot Receiver to outrun a slower inside defender.

*Plays containing the **Wheel** Route:*

22, 23, 30, 80, 81, 88, 138, 139, 146, 196, 197, 204, 254, 255, 262

ROUTE DESCRIPTION

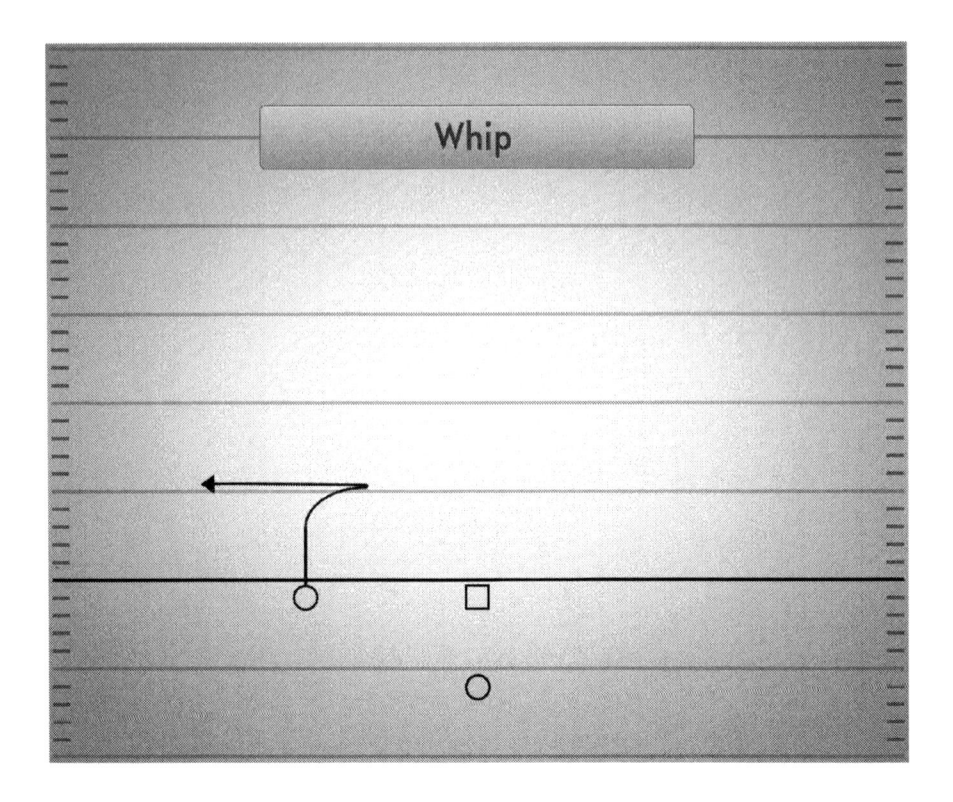

The Whip route is a simple double move that does not take as long as deeper double move routes. It is important to make the initial move inside look like you are running a Slant route of a quick in route. The hard move inside gets the defense flowing inside, but the quick pivot outside is even more important to get separation from the defender.

*Plays containing the **Whip** Route:*

9, 33, 67, 91, 125, 149, 183, 207, 241, 265

Index

Distance

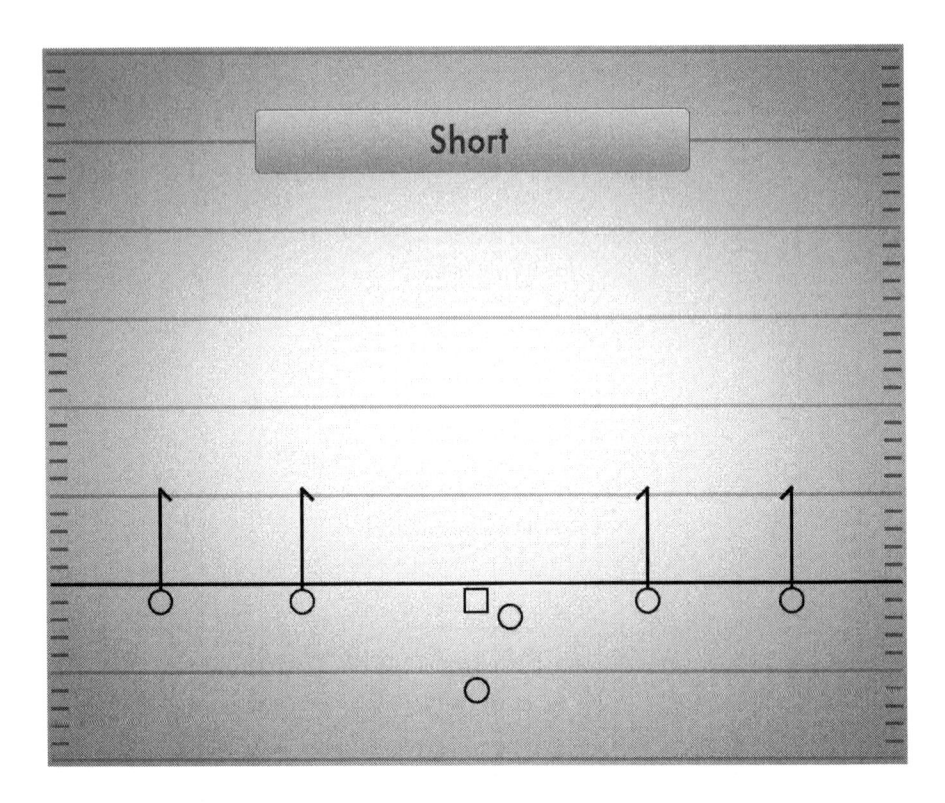

SHORT YARDAGE PLAYS

6, 7, 8, 9, 12, 16, 17, 23, 24, 25, 26, 28, 29, 30, 31, 34, 37, 39, 40, 41, 43, 46, 52, 53, 54, 55, 56, 57, 59, 60, 61, 64, 65, 66, 67, 70, 74, 75, 81, 82, 83, 84, 86, 87, 89, 92, 95, 97, 98, 99, 101, 104, 110, 111, 112, 113, 114, 115, 117, 118, 119, 122, 123, 124, 125, 128, 132, 133, 139, 140, 141, 142, 144, 145, 146, 147, 150, 153, 155, 156, 157, 159, 162, 168, 169, 170, 171, 172, 173, 175, 176, 177, 180, 181, 182, 183, 186, 190, 191, 197, 198, 199, 200, 202, 203, 204, 205, 208, 211, 213, 214, 215, 217, 220, 226, 227, 228, 229, 230, 231, 233, 234, 235, 238, 239, 240, 241, 244, 248, 249, 255, 256, 257, 258, 260, 261, 262, 263, 266, 269, 271, 272, 273, 275, 278, 284, 285, 286, 287, 288, 289, 291, 292, 293

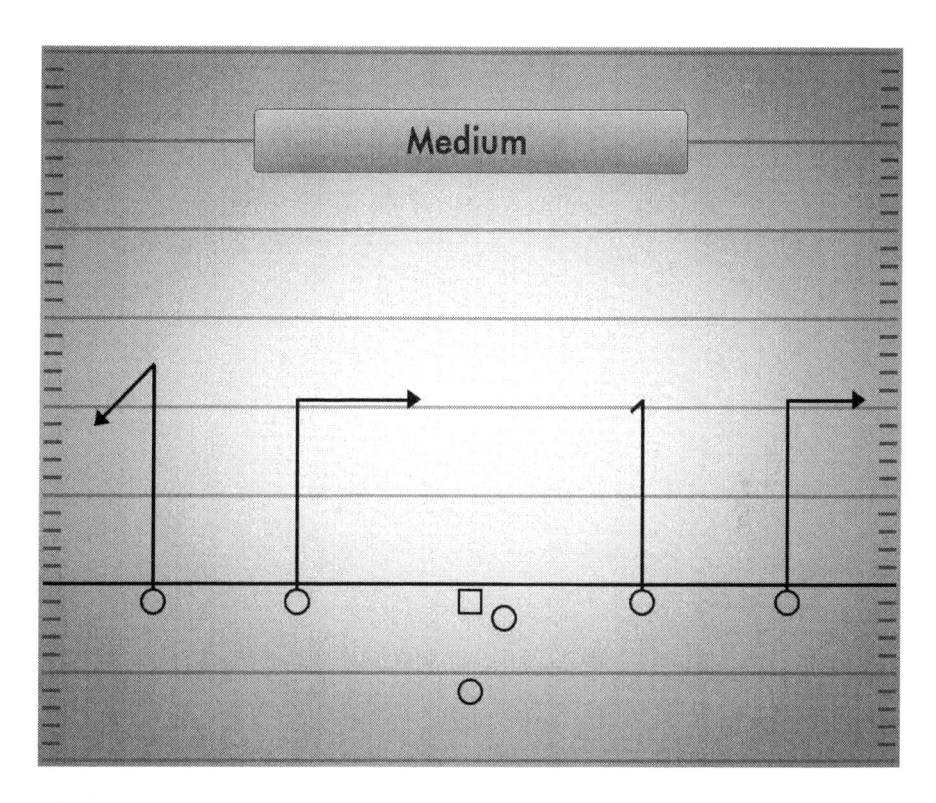

MEDIUM YARDAGE PLAYS

6, 7, 8, 9, 10, 18, 23, 24, 28, 29, 33, 38, 46, 47, 48, 53, 55, 56, 57, 59, 60, 61, 64, 65, 66, 67, 68, 76, 81, 82, 86, 87, 91, 96, 104, 105, 106, 111, 113, 114, 115, 117, 118, 119, 122, 123, 124, 125, 126, 134, 139, 140, 144, 145, 149, 154, 162, 163, 164, 169, 171, 172, 173, 175, 176, 177, 180, 181, 182, 183, 184, 192, 197, 198, 202, 203, 207, 212, 220, 221, 222, 227, 229, 230, 231, 233, 234, 235, 238, 239, 240, 241, 242, 250, 255, 256, 260, 261, 265, 270, 278, 279, 280, 285, 287, 288, 289, 291, 292, 293

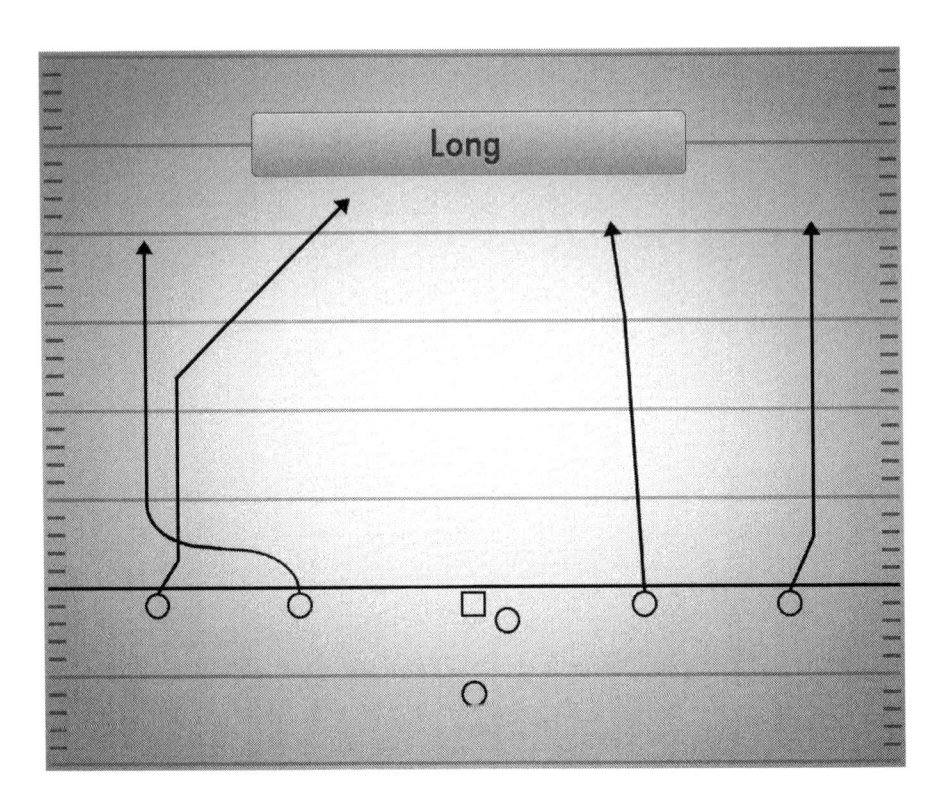

LONG YARDAGE PLAYS

7, 8, 10, 11, 13, 14, 15, 16, 17, 19, 20, 21, 22, 24, 27, 29, 30, 32, 33, 35, 36, 39, 42, 44, 45, 47, 49, 50, 51, 58, 65, 66, 68, 69, 71, 72, 73, 74, 75, 77, 78, 79, 80, 82, 85, 87, 88, 90, 91, 93, 94, 97, 100, 102, 103, 105, 107, 108, 109, 116, 123, 124, 126, 127, 129, 130, 131, 132, 133, 135, 136, 137, 138, 140, 143, 145, 146, 148, 149, 151, 152, 155, 158, 160, 161, 163, 165, 166, 167, 174, 181, 182, 184, 185, 187, 188, 189, 190, 191, 193, 194, 195, 196, 198, 201, 203, 204, 206, 207, 209, 210, 213, 216, 218, 219, 221, 223, 224, 225, 232, 239, 240, 242, 243, 245, 246, 247, 248, 249, 251, 252, 253, 254, 256, 259, 261, 262, 264, 265, 267, 268, 271, 274, 276, 277, 279, 281, 282, 283, 290

About the Author

DILLON HESS

Dillon Hess feels awkward writing this section about himself. He supposes that he should just write about football since that is what this book is all about.

Dillon was a two-time Texas All-State Quarterback at Colleyville Covenant Academy in Colleyville, Texas. He threw for over 5,000 yards passing and scored 70 total touchdowns during his high school football career. He played four seasons of college football at Beloit College where he was the captain his senior year.

If the Best Flag Football Plays book sells enough copies to make him a multi-billionaire, Dillon plans on buying an NFL football franchise and making himself the starting Quarterback.

Printed in Great Britain
by Amazon